KU-175-440

Mastering 3D Animation

Mastering 3D Animation

SECOND EDITION

TEXT AND ILLUSTRATION BY
Peter Ratner

ALLWORTH PRESS
NEW YORK

© 2004 Peter Ratner

All rights reserved. Copyright under Berne Copyright Convention, Universal Copyright Convention, and Pan-American Copyright Convention. No part of this book may be reproduced, stored in a retrieval system, or transmitted in any form, or by any means, electronic, mechanical, photocopying, recording, or otherwise, without prior permission of the publisher.

05 04 03 02 01 00   5 4 3 2 1

Published by Allworth Press
An imprint of Allworth Communications
10 East 23rd Street, New York, NY 10010

Cover design by Derek Bacchus
Interior design by Sharp Des!gns, Inc., Lansing, MI
Page composition/typography by Peter Ratner

ISBN: 1-58115-345-7

LIBRARY OF CONGRESS CATALOGING-IN-PUBLICATION DATA
Ratner, Peter.
  Mastering 3D animation / text and illustrations by Peter Ratner.-
2nd ed.
      p. cm.
  Includes index.
  ISBN 1-58115-345-7 (pbk.)
  1. Computer animation. 2. Three-dimensional display systems. I.
Title.

  TR897.7.R39 2004
  006.6'96-dc22

                              2004004429

Printed in Canada

Dedicated to Sharon,
Ori, and the ECK

Contents

PART III
PREPARING FOR 3D ANIMATION

CHAPTER 9: LIGHTING

CHAPTER 10: SURFACING TECHNIQUES

PART IV
CHARACTER ANIMATION FUNDAMENTALS

CHAPTER 11: EXPRESSING EMOTION WITH FACIAL ANIMATION

CHAPTER 12: PRINCIPLES OF ANIMATION: THE ELEMENTS OF ACTION

CHAPTER 13: MORE PRINCIPLES OF ANIMATION: MOVEMENTS OF THE FIGURE

CHAPTER 14: COMPOSITION AND CINEMATOGRAPHY

Foreword

Technology affects art. Three great changes have taken place in the history of Western art, and all of them are the result of scientific breakthroughs.

The first great transfiguration occurred during the Renaissance. Paintings no longer lacked perspective and looked flat or distorted. Renderings became accurate depictions of people and events. What could have brought about such a dramatic change from the flat and misshapen depictions of the medieval era? The answer is optics.

The earliest records describing the device that would come to be known as the camera obscura, date back to the fifth century B.C., by the Chinese philosopher Mo-Ti. His creation of an inverted image created by light rays passing through a pinhole in a dark room was later named by the German astronomer Johannes Kepler.

Leonardo da Vinci clearly described the camera obscura in his notebooks. In his book *Magiae Naturalis* (1558), Giovanni Battista della Porta recommended the use of this instrument as a resource for artists. With the addition of the convex lens, the image quality improved greatly. Later on, the camera obscura evolved into the photographic camera.

The second great change occurred in the latter half of the 1800s, with the advent of Impressionism. This movement was started by a handful of artists who set out to capture nature's fleeting moments. Their work reinvigorated painting. Using sketchy techniques, they applied colors directly on the canvas. Sometimes they mixed the colors on the painting itself, and other times they placed the colors next to each other so that the process of optical mixing would blend them in the viewer's eye.

This art movement owes its birth to a number of technological innovations. Photography helped the artists with composition and helped them see how a moment or a movement can be caught in time. Newly available tubes of paint allowed them to easily work outside. Artists used to grind and mix their own pigments with oil. These mixtures were then stored in pig bladder pouches. Metal tubes preserved the pigments longer and gave artists the opportunity to take extensive painting trips outdoors.

During the Industrial Revolution, scientific research into the physics of color and optics taught the Impressionists how to achieve a more exact representation of the effects of light in nature. It was a time of discovery. The steam engine gave the masses greater mobility. Ordinary people's lives changed with inventions such as the power loom, camera, streetlights, cast iron, and steel. Technological progress created a climate in which individuals felt they could do anything.

The third major turning point in art is taking place at this very moment. It has been termed the Information Age and has brought about an unprecedented number of inventions. For the first time in our recorded history, people around the world are linked electronically. The foremost invention that has brought about such a great change is the computer.

Advanced 3D software and the computers capable of handling it are changing the nature of art. This combination of painting, drawing, and sculpture is a new art form that challenges the intellect and the creative nature of the artist.

Today, in its infancy, 3D modeling and animation is one of the least-understood disciplines. Due to the complexity of the software, most people are not motivated to learn about computer animation. Aside from overcoming the technical difficulties, there are many other skills animators have to learn. Some of these are drawing, painting, modeling in three dimensions, lighting, texturing, cinematography, sound syncing, and animating. One would be hard-pressed to find any other artistic field that requires such a broad range of creativity, knowledge, and technical skills.

Most animation studios appreciate the overwhelming burden that one person would have to carry to know everything about 3D. This is one of the reasons why studios split the tasks up among lighting specialists, modelers, texture artists, render wranglers, animators, and so on. However, to reach that level, aspiring artists have to produce an animation tape, and this often requires the application of every 3D animation skill.

The purpose of this book is to provide readers with a set of learning tools to help them create a respectable animation. Many 3D modeling and animation essentials have been outlined in various formats. Some are presented in tutorial form, while others are merely explained. "Since most artists are visually oriented, numerous illustrations have been provided, along with models and sample animations on the CD-ROM. If you have a slow CD-ROM drive, then it is recommended that you copy the QuickTime animation movies to your hard drive so that they will play in real time.

As an animation professor at James Madison University, I have had the opportunity to try out and refine all of the written and illustrated material in my introductory, intermediate, and advanced classes. The results have been positive, and it has been gratifying to see so many of my students find work in large and small animation companies, gaming studios, and multimedia firms.

I hope that this book will prove to be a useful resource for most readers, no matter what platform or software they are using. Software changes often, and focusing too much attention on it detracts from the attention that should be paid to the key principles of 3D animation. Books that are overly dependent on specific software quickly become dated and sometimes have a very narrow focus.

Before using this book, you should know how to operate your particular 3D software package. Most have good manuals that make it possible to learn a great deal in a fairly short time. Although these software texts teach how to use animation tools, technical writers often lack the skills and fine arts knowledge needed by computer artists. Thus, they are unable to communicate how to use the tools to create art in an expressive style.

Space and time constraints prevent software writers from dwelling too long on these principles of modeling and animation.

Those of you in academia (professors and students), as well as those of you studying on your own, might find it helpful to use the semester schedules found in the back of the book. These calendars have a timetable with assignments that correspond to the various chapters of the book. Since these can also be found as Microsoft Word documents on the CD-ROM, you can alter them to fit your own schedule.

I would like to acknowledge Patrick Wilson, a former student who worked quite a few years as a 3D modeler and director of lighting at PIXAR. His expert advice helped me a great deal when writing about lighting.

Another invaluable contributor to the lighting chapter was Avi Das, a color and lighting artist at Digital Domain. Avi was full of ideas and interesting facts about lighting. I owe him a great debt.

This book would be incomplete without mentioning the efforts of some of my former students. Their animations and models can be found on the accompanying CD-ROM.

One of the most invaluable contributors to 3D modeling has been Peter Levius. His site can be found at:

www.3d.sk/

It is by far the best place to find template photos of humans. This is definitely the Internet's most important site for 3D modelers.

I would be remiss not to credit the contributions of my brilliant son, Ori. At the age of seventeen, he thought up the technique for creating a pinhead with displacement mapping.

A final thank-you goes to my wife, Sharon, who has been very patient and supportive during the time I have spent on this project.

I hope you enjoy the creative process and find satisfaction in making new discoveries. Feel free to e-mail me at *ratnerpj@jmu.edu* about your progress.

PETER RATNER
Professor of 3D Computer Animation
School of Art and Art History
James Madison University

About the CD-ROM

Thank you for purchasing this book. Although the CD-ROM does not contain any software programs, it does include models, animations, textures, and color images to help you work your way through the book. Hopefully, the CD-ROM will serve you even when you are not using the text, by providing you with some useful tools that you can apply to your own animation projects.

Technical Requirements

Mastering 3D Animation, 2nd Edition should work with most high-end software. These are:

- Maya (Alias/Wavefront)
- Lightwave (NewTek)
- 3D Studio Max (Discreet)
- Softimage (Avid)

Other software packages will work for some of the exercises but may lack the capabilities required for character modeling and animation such as subdivision/subpatch surfaces, and skeletal/shape shifting deformations.

All the movies on the CD-ROM are in QuickTime format. If you do not have the latest version of QuickTime on your computer, you can go to the Apple site to download it for free. *http://www.apple.com*

To play the movies in real time, you should copy them to your hard drive.

The images and textures on the CD-ROM have been saved as JPEGs (.jpg). Most image browsers should be able to open these. The Photoshop™ brush file (.abr) in the Chapter 10 folder can be utilized for creating grime textures. Perhaps they will serve as a starting point for your own unique brush styles.

Organization

The folders or directories are arranged by chapters. Each folder contains the materials for one chapter. The book will direct you to view specific animations that illustrate the technique or instructions put forth in that chapter.

If you need templates of generic 3D male and female models, you can find some that my students modeled in the folder labeled "Human Templates." These models are their self portraits and can be used as proportion guides. They are saved in Wavefront (.obj) format. The 2D Templates folder located inside the Human Templates folder contains some screen shots of details on models, some anatomy illustrations, and photos that can also be used as modeling templates. Hopefully, you will not utilize any of the student models for your own animations or commercial uses. The book will teach you to create and animate your own. Using someone else's models defeats the book's purpose.

Like all great art, skillfully executed models and animations have the false appearance of requiring little effort. Anyone who studies this book will realize that this ease is just an illusion. However, if you find 3D modeling and animation as fascinating as I do, you should discover that investing years of dedication to this discipline will be well worth the effort. Best Wishes on your endeavors.

Peter Ratner

QuickTime™ is a registered trademark of Apple Computers

Maya™ is a registered trademark of Alias/Wavefront

Lightwave™ is a registered trademark of NewTek, Inc.

3D Studio Max™ is a registered trademark of Discreet

Softimage™ is a registered trademark of Avid

Photoshop™ is a registered trademark of Adobe, Inc.

PART I

3D Modeling and Animation Fundamentals

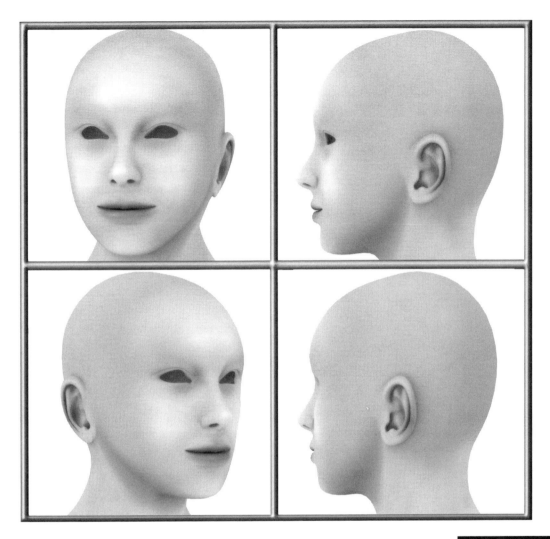

CHAPTER 1

The Fundamentals of 3D Modeling

Three-dimensional modeling can be compared to sculpting. Models are built by manipulating an object. Surfaces are pushed, pulled, subtracted from, and added to during the creation process. In order to judge the work, the artist has to view it from every angle.

Although contemporary sculpture can take almost any form, 3D modeling bears the most similarity to traditional clay or wax sculpting. The artist usually begins with two-dimensional sketches or photographs depicting the object from different angles. These are then used as templates for producing the three-dimensional work.

In the hands of an experienced artist, the selection of tools takes place mostly subconsciously. The professional sculptor and 3D computer modeler are so familiar with their respective instruments that they can focus most of their attention on the work itself. A subconscious use of one's equipment frees the conscious mind for the task at hand.

This does not mean that tools play a minor role in the creation process. Painting could not exist without brushes and paint, and the same holds true for any of the other arts. Instruments for expression have always been the forerunners of the various art fields.

Today, the computer and software are responsible for the creation of an entirely new subject area. By their very complex nature, they have brought about a branch of knowledge that, I would venture to say, is the most challenging of all art disciplines.

Traditional art is mostly an intuitive process of an emotional nature. The materials have a tactile quality, which directly affects the senses of touch, smell, and sight. Computer art differs from this because its complex nature requires a cerebral

approach. It is mostly done through sight, which is the vanguard of thought.

Fortunately, 3D modeling and animation is evolving to the point where it is also becoming an intuitive art form. New software developments and improved hardware are making it easier for artists to focus less on the tools and more on the creative process itself. This does not mean that one can just jump right in and create great works of art. Just like any other art field, it requires years of study and work. One has to master the tools before one can hope to achieve anything worthwhile.

Many parallels exist between traditional art making and 3D computer art. Both fields have been used for commercial purposes. Nevertheless, by their nature they should be perceived as fine arts disciplines. The similarities and differences between traditional sculpture and 3D modeling will become more apparent as you work through the various exercises.

Polygons vs. Splines and NURBS

3D modeling uses a variety of splines, NURBS, or polygons. Splines are flexible line segments defined by edit points called vertices. Non-Uniform, Rational B-Splines, affectionately known as NURBS, are flexible lines used to create smooth curves and surfaces. These are characterized by a set of control vertices (CVs) that influence the object or shape in their vicinity. The overall form of the object is determined by the location of the control points in space. Splines or NURBS are used to define the edges of objects. A series of splines or NURBS connect to make a wireframe mesh.

A polygon is a portion of a plane bounded by three or more lines or segments. A polygon can be planar, non-planar, convex, or concave. The lines connecting the vertices of a polygon are straight. When compared to the curved lines of splines or NURBS, the straight edges of polygons are initially at a disadvantage. A close-up view of a polygon-based object has a segmented look, while the spline and NURBS object appears smooth. The straight edges of a polygon used to mean that many had to be laid end-to-end to make an object appear curved.

Besides the fact that polygons can be rotated in any direction and joined in a variety of ways, they also have a few other distinguishing characteristics. They can be convex, concave, or have holes in them, and their vertices can even double back so that a surface intersects itself. The ability to easily join polygons at their vertices and to split them anywhere makes this a very flexible system of modeling. Polygon modeling is well suited to objects that have varying degrees of detail.

Adjoining groups of polygons form polyhedra. The first five regular uniform polyhedra are known as regular convex uniform polyhedra or Platonic solids. The remaining four regular uniform polyhedra are called regular non-convex uniform polyhedra or Kepler-Poinsot solids.

Polyhedra, which have a similar arrangement of polygons of two or more different types, are called semi-regular polyhedra or Archimedean solids. They are distinguished from prisms, antiprisms, and elongated square gyrobicupola by their spherical symmetry. There are thirteen semi-regular polyhedra.

Polygons can be arrayed into innumerable convex and non-convex polyhedral structures. Since polygon modeling usually involves starting with polyhedra, it becomes easier to visualize the build-ing of a three-dimensional object. Splines and NURBS often require outlining a shape first before making it into a three-dimensional form. Most of the time, creating 3D objects from 2D ones such as splines and NURBS is much more challenging than starting with a 3D polyhedra.

Subdivision Surface Modeling

In the past, when compared to splines and NURBS, polygons had many advantages, but their biggest drawback was that many of them were required to make objects appear smooth. More polygons demanded a greater amount of computer memory, which in turn slowed down the modeling and animation process.

All of this changed after software developers began to implement subdivision surface modeling. This method uses a low polygon control mesh that applies a smoothing algorithm to bend the edges of polygons, giving them a curved appearance. The overall polygon count remains low, while the subdivide command controls the degree of smoothness that is applied. Surface subdivision means that a given surface patch is subdivided into subpatches. Each subpatch has its own control vertices. Even though one can control the number of subpatches that are generated, the original set of control points or vertices remain the same. For example, when you have two adjoining polygons with six control points and a subpatch division of three (eighteen subpatches), it does not matter if you set the subpatch division to six (seventy-two subpatches), because you will still only have six control points regulating the extra subpatches. This is the reason one can keep the polygon count low and minimize the number of points on an object, making modeling a less confusing task.

By internally dividing polygons into smaller and greater numbers, higher subpatch divisions create smoother surfaces without the confusion of seeing a multitude of polygons. Most of the time, the graphics card, processor, and RAM capabilities determine the number of patch division that should be used. Patch value is also ascertained by how close or large the object will appear in an image or animation. If an object using a patch division of three looks smooth, then it is not necessary to use a higher value.

When investigating the merits of a 3D software package, be sure to examine its capabilities for subdivision or subpatch modeling. Aspiring 3D modelers should not even consider any software without robust subdivision modeling tools. Most of the high-end software packages that implement subdivision modeling have demo versions available for download. One of these even offers a free version for file transfer. The software is made by SGI/Wavefront and named Maya™. It is available with full functionality, except that its renderings have a watermark. The free version is meant as a learning tool and not to be used for commercial purposes. A number of download sites can be found by performing an Internet search for "Maya." Hopefully, other 3D software vendors will learn from SGI/Wavefront and also offer free educational versions of their software. Most educational institutions cannot afford to purchase expensive 3D software and their continual upgrades. Software companies will find that when students learn a particular software and later work for a company, they will influence that company to buy the software that they learned in school.

Due to the greater advantage provided by sub-division modeling, this book will concentrate solely on learning that system. If you also desire to learn spline and NURBS modeling methods, you can find them in my other book, *3-D Human and Modeling and Animation, 2nd edition*, ISBN 0-471-21548-1 (John Wiley and Sons).

Basic Subdivision Modeling

The first tutorial demonstrates how to model a simple cartoon character using subdivision modeling. As you work through the various subdivision modeling steps, it will become obvious that this process involves mostly pushing and pulling points. In this session, you will only have to use three tools:

1) A drag tool for moving individual points

2) A smooth shift tool that moves groups of polygons as one by first duplicating and then either reducing or expanding them as they are moved in an outward or inward direction. This is similar to an extrude or bevel tool, except that it affects groups of polygons as one rather than only one polygon at a time.

3) A spin quads tool that can be applied to adjacent four-point polygons (quadrangles, or quads) that share an edge. This tool merges the two polygons into one and then splits them using another group of opposing polygons. The two sets of polygons appear to spin each time the tool is applied. Rotating polygons in this manner helps fix unsightly seams in a subdivision mesh. Applying the tool three times spins the polygons back to their original position.

Besides these three tools, your software will also have to implement a symmetry function that mirror duplicates all modeling tasks across a center axis.

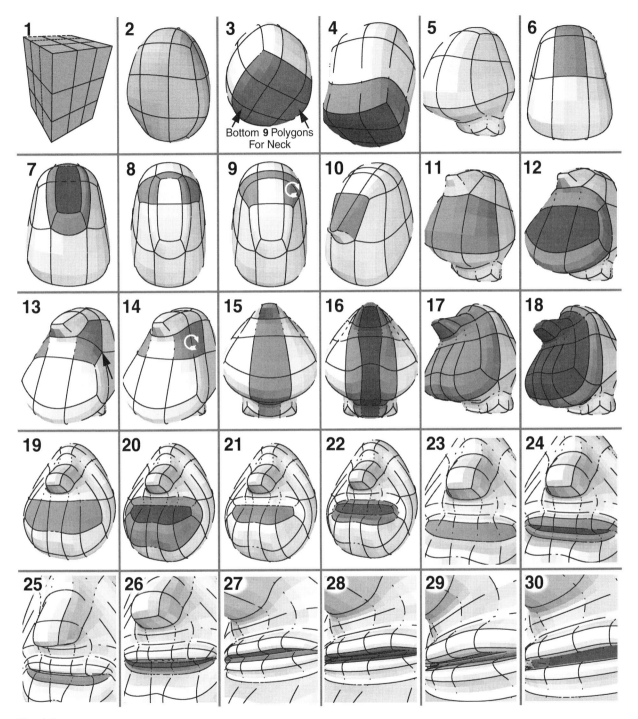

Fig. 1-1 Steps 1–30. Modeling the general shape of the head and the mouth.

If your software lacks these basic subdivision modeling tools, you can use the modeling tutorials found in chapters 2, 6, and 8. They show how to use subdividing, shaping, beveling, merging, mirroring, splitting, pulling points out and in, and attaching. These methods can be more time consuming, so be sure to ask your software company to implement the smooth shift and spin quads tools in their next upgrade.

Creating the Head and the Mouth (Figure 1-1)

The box is often the starting point in subdivision modeling. Moving points on it will make it into a sphere-like shape. Each person's cartoon character will vary in shape and size, so be sure to use the illustrations as a rough guide for your own creation.

Step 1. The front view, or z-axis, will serve as the front of the cartoon face. Make a box and go into its numerical settings. Next to segments, type in "3" for the x-, y-, and z-axes. For the center x-axis, type in "0." The box has to be on the 0 x-axis so that the symmetry function can work on both sides of the face equally. You can size the box according to the general proportion of your character's face.

Step 2. Turn on symmetry so that all your actions are duplicated across the x-axis. Execute the subdivision command. Begin moving points until your box starts to resemble the shape of your cartoon character's head. You can see in the second step of Figure 1 that this particular model will have a broad head.

Step 3. Select the nine polygons on the bottom of the neck. These will be smooth shifted in the next step to make the neck.

Step 4. Smooth shift the nine polygons on the bottom of the neck. In the numeric panel of your smooth shift tool, make sure that the smooth shift offset is set to 0 so that it does not foul up your symmetry operations. Move the smooth shifted polygons straight down in the side view.

Step 5. Move points to shape the chin and neck. Check the symmetry. Each time you do something to one side of the head, the action should duplicate itself on the other. If symmetry does not work, you will have to start again at step 1 and check that the box is exactly on the 0 x-axis.

Steps 6 and 7. Select the two middle polygons in the forehead and smooth shift them with an offset of 0.

Steps 8 and 9. Pick the five polygons in the forehead as indicated in the illustration, and initiate a spin quads command to rotate them one time.

Steps 10, 11, and 12. Begin to form the rough shape of the nose. Choose the three polygons around the mouth and smooth shift them (offset of 0).

Steps 13 and 14. After selecting the four polygons on the sides of the nose, spin quads two times.

Steps 15 and 16. Select the six middle polygons that begin at the bottom of the nose and extend to the lower part of the neck. Smooth shift the polygons.

Steps 17 and 18. The twenty-nine front polygons of the face should now be smooth shifted.

Steps 19 and 20. The five polygons of the mouth are smooth shifted.

Steps 21 and 22. The next five polygons of the mouth are smooth shifted.

Steps 23 and 24. After shaping the face, smooth shift the next five mouth polygons.

Steps 25 and 26. Work on forming the lips. Choose the five polygons of the lower lip and smooth shift them.

Steps 27 and 28. Drag points to continue forming the lips. Select the ten inner lip polygons and

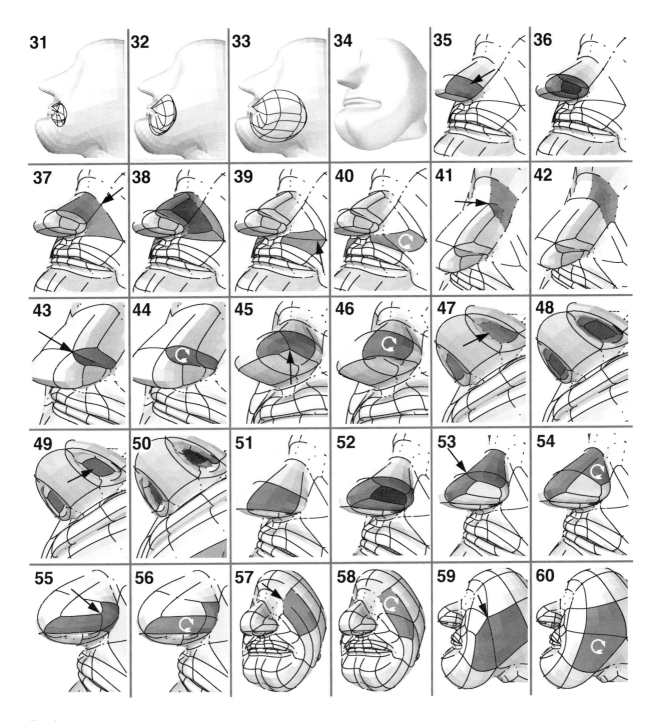

Fig. 1-2 Steps 31–60. Finishing the mouth and the nose.

smooth shift them.

Steps 29 and 30. Move the inner points of the mouth back a little. Select the ten inside mouth polygons and smooth shift them. Move the ten smooth shifted polygons further into the head and expand the polygons vertically to start the inside mouth shape.

Completing the Mouth and the Nose (Figure 1-2)

A few more steps will complete the mouth. A number of polygons will have to be rotated with the spin quads command in order to create the right shape for the nose.

Steps 31, 32, 33, and 34. Continue smooth shifting the back of the inside mouth polygons. Expand their shape so that later on you will have enough room to add teeth, gums, and a tongue. Continue refining the shape of the lips and the jaw.

Steps 35 and 36. Smooth shift the two polygons on the lower sides of the nose.

Steps 37 and 38. Smooth shift the four polygons on the sides of the nose.

Steps 39 and 40. Spin quads two times to the four polygons above the lips.

Steps 41 and 42. Spin quads one time to the four polygons on the upper sides of the nose.

Steps 43 and 44. Spin quads two times to the four polygons above the nose wings.

Steps 45 and 46. Spin quads one time to the four polygons above the nostrils.

Steps 47, 48, 49, and 50. Smooth shift the two nostril polygons. Move the smooth shifted polygons up a little. Smooth shift the two inside nostril polygons again and move them up into the nose more. Spin quads two times to the four polygons located at the beginnings of the nostrils, adjacent to the nose wings.

Steps 51 and 52. Smooth shift the two nose wing polygons.

Steps 53 and 54. Spin quads one time to rotate the six indicated polygons.

Steps 55 and 56. Spin quads two times to the six indicated polygons around the nose wings. Finish shaping the nose.

Steps 57 and 58. Spin quads one time to the four polygons near the eye area.

Steps 59 and 60. Spin quads one time to the four polygons along the jaw line, as depicted.

Completing the Eyes and Ears (Figure 1-3)

The following steps will complete the eye area and the ears. The ears are going to be modeled as very basic shapes. If you desire a more developed ear, then refer to steps 106 to 182 of the next tutorial on modeling a human head.

Steps 61 and 62. Spin quads one time to the four polygons above the corners of the mouth.

Steps 63 and 64. Smooth shift the eight polygons of the eye area.

Steps 65 and 66. Smooth shift the twenty-four polygons of the eye.

Steps 67 and 68. At the eye opening, near the nose and brows, spin quads one time to the four polygons.

Steps 69 and 70. Begin forming the eyebrows. Spin quads two times to the four eye corner polygons.

Steps 71 and 72. Select the four inside eye polygons and smooth shift them. Sculpt the shape of the eye sockets.

Step 73. Make a sphere for the eyeball. Its numerical settings should have ten sides and five segments, and should be facing forward on the z-axis. Move the front points of the second segment forward and closer together for the pupil. Name the ten front polygons "pupil" and assign a black shade to them. Inverse your selection and name

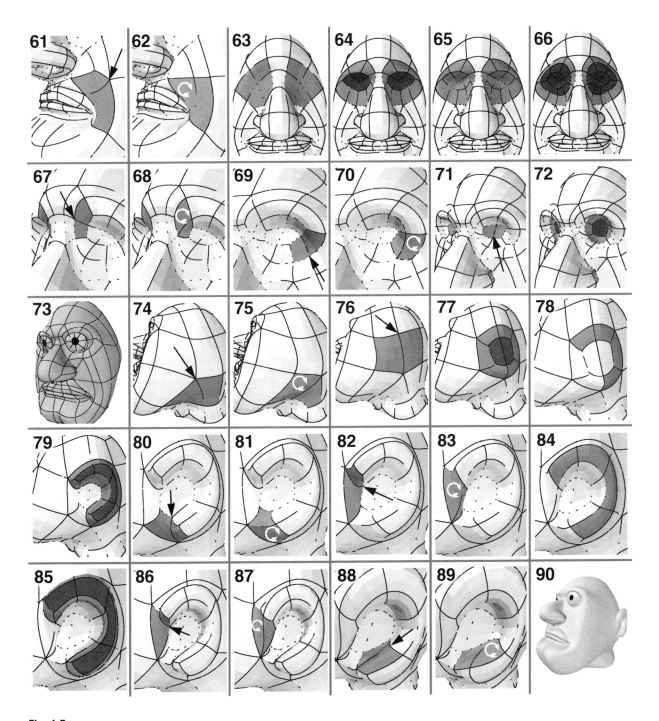

Fig. 1-3 Steps 61–90. Completing the face.

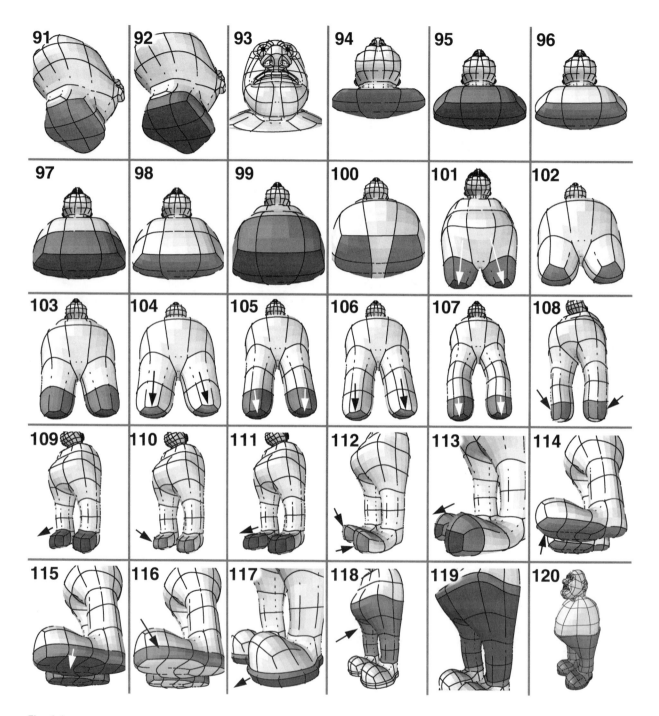

Fig. 1-4 Steps 91–120. Modeling the torso and the legs.

the rest of the polygons "eyeball" and give them a white shade. Scale the eyeball, rotate it outward a little, and place it in the head. You may have to move points around the eyeball so that it fits closely in the head.

Steps 74 and 75. Spin quads two times to the four polygons by the sides of the neck.

Steps 76 and 77. Start the ear by smooth shifting the four polygons in that location.

Steps 78 and 79. Select the eight polygons around the ear and smooth shift them. Move these new polygons out of the head a little.

Steps 80 and 81. Spin quads two times to the four polygons at the earlobe.

Steps 82 and 83. Spin quads one time to the four polygons near the beginning of the ear.

Steps 84 and 85. Smooth shift the eight polygons of the ear rim.

Steps 86 and 87. Move points to shape the rim of the ear. Spin quads two times to the polygons at the beginning of the ear rim.

Steps 88 and 89. Spin quads one time to the polygons located above the earlobe.

Step 90. Continue moving points until you are satisfied with the shape of the ears and the rest of the head.

Making the Torso, Legs, and Shoes (Figure 1-4)

The following instructions show how to make the body and legs by smooth shifting to create new polygons, moving them, and pushing/pulling points. For these steps, you will not have to spin quads.

Steps 91 and 92. Smooth shift the bottom nine polygons of the neck. Move them down a little in the side view and sculpt the neck and the beginning of the shoulders.

Steps 93 and 94. Select the bottom nine polygons, smooth shift, and move them down. Increase the width to start forming the upper torso.

Steps 95, 96, 97, 98, and 99. Continue smooth shifting and moving polygons down. After repeating these steps several times, you should have enough polygons to sculpt the shape of the torso.

Steps 100 and 101. After completing the shape of the torso, select the six polygons along its underside. Leave the bottom middle three alone. Smooth shift the six polygons and move the newly created polygons down to begin the legs. This is called branching.

Steps 102 and 103. Smooth shift the six polygons at the base of the legs and move them down. Begin to shape the legs.

Steps 104, 105, 106, and 107. Continue smooth shifting several more times and moving the bottom polygons down. Sculpt the shape of your character's legs.

Steps 108 and 109. Select the six polygons at the bottom and front of the legs that will be smooth shifted and moved forward to make the shoe (see illustration). Smooth shift them and move them forward a little.

Steps 110, 111, 112, and 113. Smooth shift several more times and move polygons forward according to the size of your character's shoes. Move points to shape the shoes.

Steps 114 and 115. Choose the twenty-four polygons at the bottom of the shoes, smooth shift them, and move them down a little.

Steps 116 and 117. Select the twenty-eight polygons around the soles of the shoes and smooth shift them. Move these new polygons outward a little. Continue shaping the shoes until you are satisfied with their appearance.

Steps 118, 119, and 120. Pick the sixty-three polygons of the pants and smooth shift them. Move points to tuck the bottom of the pants in and under so the hemlines appear to go over the

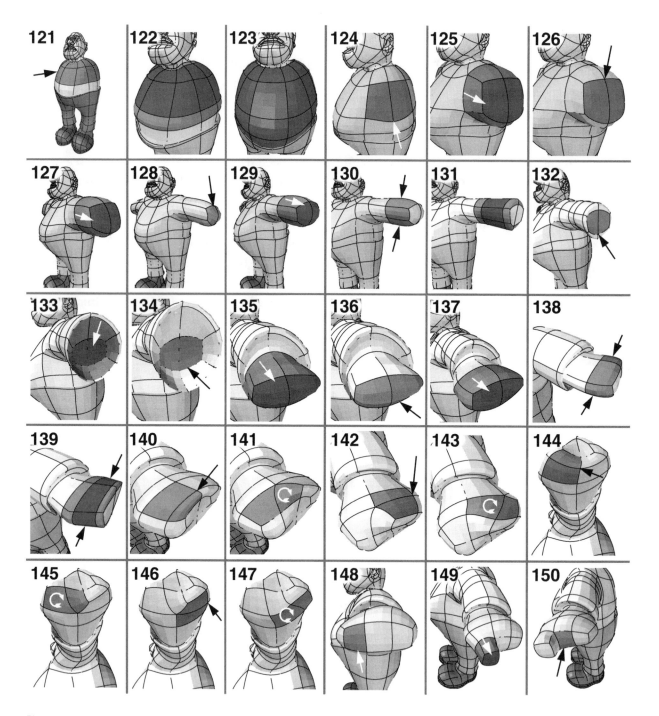

Fig. 1-5 Steps 121–150. Modeling the arms and hands.

tops of the shoes. Tuck the points of the waistline into the pants so the pants appear to cover the shirt. Continue refining the shapes of the pants, shoes, and shirt. You can also name and assign textures to these parts.

Completing the Shirt and Starting the Hands (Figure 1-5)

Continuing with the smooth shift method, the arms and hands will now be modeled. To prepare for smooth shifting of the fingers, some polygons will have to be rotated with spin quads.

Steps 121, 122, and 123. Select the twenty-four upper polygons of the shirt and smooth shift them. Move points to tuck the shirt into the pants and the neck into the shirt.

Steps 124 and 125. Start the arms by smooth shifting the four polygons on the sides of the torso. Move these polygons out from the body.

Steps 126, 127, 128, and 129. Smooth shift and move the arm polygons outward several more times until you have enough divisions to shape it.

Steps 130 and 131. Select the indicated twelve polygons around the end of the arms and smooth shift them.

Steps 132 and 133. Smooth shift and move the four polygons at the end of the arms into the sleeve.

Steps 134, 135, 136, and 137. Smooth shift the hand several times and move the polygons outward. Sculpt the hand without the fingers.

Steps 138 and 139. Select the twelve polygons around the end of the hand and smooth shift them. Improve the shape of the hand.

Steps 140 and 141. To make it easier to smooth shift out the fingers, some of the polygons on the hand will have to be rotated with a spin quads command. Referring to the illustration, select the four polygons of the hand and spin quads one

time.

Steps 142 and 143. Spin quads one time to the four polygons depicted in Figure 1-5.

Steps 144 and 145. On the underside of the hand, near the end, spin quads two times to the four polygons.

Steps 146 and 147. Continuing on the underside of the hand, spin quads two times to the four polygons. Refine the shape of the hand until you have three polygons facing outward. These will be smooth shifted to make the fingers. Since this is a cartoon character, we can take liberties and only give it three fingers.

Steps 148 and 149. Before selecting the first digit and smooth shifting it, check the hand for any additional polygons that might have to be rotated with the spin quads command. You might find some near and inside the sleeve that might improve the appearance of the hand if they are revolved. Select the first finger polygon at the end of the hand and smooth shift it. Move it outward a little.

Step 150. Select the next digit's polygon. The next step will have you smooth shift that one also.

Finishing the Cartoon Figure (Figure 1-6)

A few more steps will complete the hand and the cartoon character. You may decide to add other details such as buttocks, nails, a shirt collar, pockets, belt loops, and so on. You can do all of this with the smooth shift method.

Step 151. Smooth shift the second finger and move the polygons out a little.

Steps 152 and 153. Smooth shift the third finger and move it outward.

Steps 154, 155, 156, and 157. Select all three ends of the fingers and smooth shift them several times. Move points and polygons to shape the three fingers. Bend them into more natural,

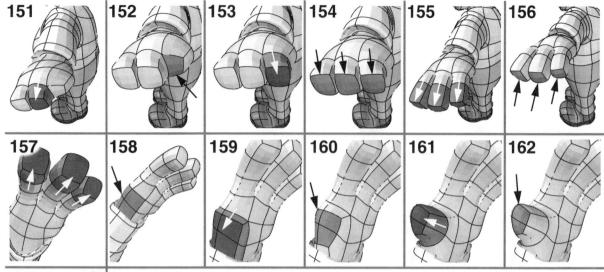

Fig. 1-6 Steps 151–163. Finishing the hands completes the cartoon figure.

Fig. 1-7 The final cartoon man.

relaxed positions.

Steps 158 and 159. Refer to the illustration to choose the eight polygons that will begin the thumb, and smooth shift them.

Steps 160 and 161. Select the eight new polygons and smooth shift these. Move them out to start the shape of the thumb.

Steps 162 and 163. Smooth shift the four polygons at the ends of the thumbs and move them outward. Continue refining your character and add other components that you think might improve its appearance. Figure 1-7 shows the cartoon man without any extra details.

Intermediate Subdivision Modeling

The following tutorial shows how simple it is to create a human head using the previously discussed modeling technique called subdivision modeling. Since this model will have more detail, the head just by itself will have more steps to follow than the entire cartoon character had.

Creating the Overall Shape of the Head and Making the Mouth (Figure 1-8)

This part of the exercise shows how to create the general form of a human head. As with most subdivision modeling, one usually starts with a cube. This is the reason that subdivision modeling is often referred to as box modeling. Now, some may wonder why we do not start with a sphere. A human head appears to resemble a sphere more than a cube, but when subdivision modeling, one finds it easier to split a cube into the various components of the head. A sphere is vague and difficult to measure, and lacks distinct areas of relation. The eye has a hard time focusing on any one part of a sphere. However, when you start with a cube,

any form can be built from it. A block is also easier to perceive in perspective, and appears to have the added dimension of weight.

Although the cube forms the basis of most subdivision modeling, it is important to shape and subdivide the object enough times so that the end result is not some blocky-looking model. A sculptor may start with a hexahedron of marble, but the subsequent sculpture of a human will not appear to have blocky dimensions. Usually it is laziness or insufficient time spent on the work that causes a subdivision model to seem blocky. Be sure to refer to the corresponding step numbers in the illustrations. Before starting this exercise, you should have read your software manual and have a basic understanding of the software's tools.

Step 1. Create a box that is divided into three segments on the x-, y-, and z-axes. Make sure that the box is located on the 0 x-axis so that you can model with symmetry on. This is very important, since you want all actions to be duplicated across the x-axis.

Step 2. Turn on symmetry mode. Execute the subdivision mode command to smooth out the box. Drag individual points to shape the object into a more spherical configuration. Try to mold it into the general contours of a head without the nose. Use a photo or sketch showing a front and side view of a human head as a modeling template. Shape the sphere according to the background templates.

Step 3. Select the bottom six polygons of the sphere, which will form the neck.

Step 4. Smooth shift the six polygons. Use an offset of 0 to maintain the functionality of the symmetry tool. Move the smooth shifted polygons down a little to start the neck.

Steps 5 and 6. Select the two polygons on the front of the head and smooth shift them.

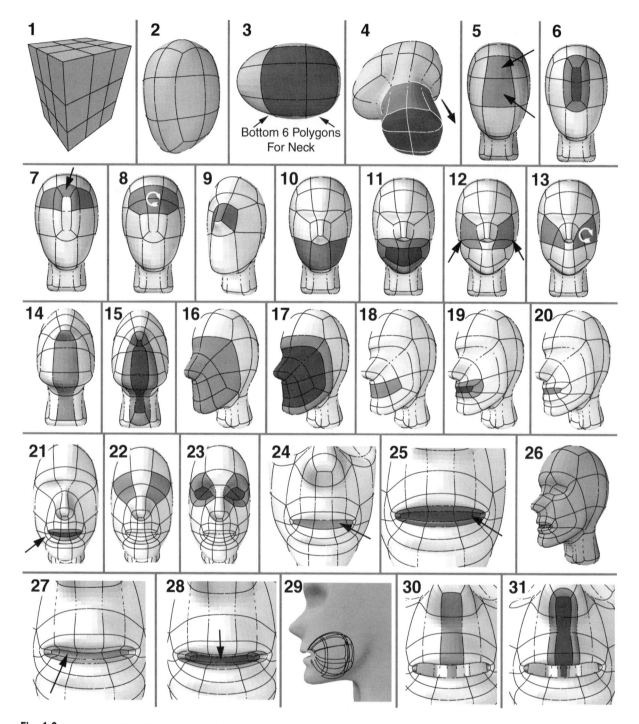

Fig. 1-8 Steps 1–31. Modeling the general shape of the head and the mouth.

Steps 7 and 8. Select the polygons indicated in dark gray in the illustration and spin their quads one time.

Step 9. Select the three indicated dark polygons and move their bottom points out a little to start the shape of the nose.

Steps 10 and 11. Select the three dark polygons depicted in the illustration and smooth shift them. Refine the shape of the jaw.

Steps 12 and 13. Select the two cheek polygons and spin their quads two times.

Steps 14 and 15. Select the six center polygons under the nose and extending to the bottom of the neck, and smooth shift them. Fine-tune this area by pulling and pushing points.

Steps 16 and 17. Choose the twenty-nine polygons on the front of the face and smooth shift them. Continue sculpting the head.

Steps 18 and 19. Pick the five polygons for the mouth and smooth shift these.

Steps 20 and 21. Select the five polygons inside the mouth and smooth shift these also. Define the form of the lips.

Steps 22 and 23. Select the four polygons around the eyes and smooth shift them. Shape the eye area.

Steps 24 and 25. Continue forming the mouth by choosing the five inside mouth polygons and smooth shifting them. Move these new polygons in a little toward the back of the head.

Step 26. Move points to improve the shape of the head.

Steps 27 and 28. Select the five inside mouth polygons and smooth shift them. Move them inside the head a little bit more.

Step 29. Continue smooth shifting and moving the inside mouth polygons. Move their points

until you have a spherical shape that will be large enough to contain the teeth, gums, and tongue. For future texturing, you can name this surface "inside mouth" and give it a dark red color.

Steps 30 and 31. Select the eight center polygons that start under the nose and continue along the inside of the mouth. Smooth shift them. Finish shaping the lips.

Starting the Nose (Figure 1-9)

The following steps show how to make the overall shape of the nose. Most of the time, you will be spinning quads and moving points.

Steps 32 and 33. Select the two polygons along the bottom sides of the nose and smooth shift them.

Steps 34 and 35. Pick the four large polygons along the sides of the nose and smooth shift them.

Steps 36 and 37. Choose the four polygons above the corners of the mouth and spin the quads two times.

Steps 38 and 39. Select the three middle polygons of the nose and spin their quads two times.

Steps 40 and 41. Spin quads for the two polygons in the middle and side of the nose one time.

Steps 42 and 43. Pick the two middle nose polygons and spin quads two times.

Steps 44 and 45. Choose the four polygons near the nostrils and spin quads one time.

Steps 46 and 47. Select the four polygons that run along the nostril area and spin quads two times.

Steps 48 and 49. Pick the six center polygons starting at the top of the nose and ending below it, and smooth shift them.

Steps 50 and 51. Choose the four polygons at the corners of the eyes and sides of the nose and

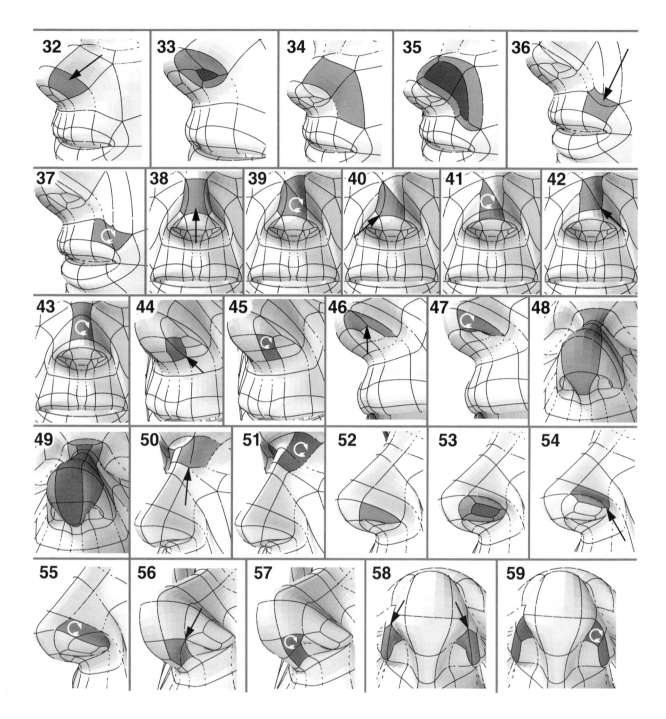

Fig. 1-9 Steps 32–59. Starting the nose.

spin quads one time.

Steps 52 and 53. Start the wings of the nose by selecting the two polygons above the nostrils, and smooth shift them.

Steps 54 and 55. Spin quads one time for the four polygons above the nose wings.

Steps 56 and 57. After selecting the four polygons below the nose, spin quads two times.

Steps 58 and 59. Spin quads two times for the four polygons below the nose wings.

Finishing the Nose and Starting the Eye (Figure 1-10)

Spinning a few more quads and smooth shifting the nostrils into the head will complete the nose. This set of steps will also begin the eye area.

Steps 60 and 61. At the corners of the nose wings, spin quads one time for the four polygons.

Steps 62 and 63. At the top of the nose wings, select the four polygons and spin quads two times.

Steps 64 and 65. Spin quads two times for the four polygons on the sides of the nose.

Steps 66 and 67. Choose the four polygons at the furrow of the cheeks and spin quads two times.

Steps 68 and 69. Smooth shift the two nostril polygons. Move the center nostril polygons slightly up into the nose.

Steps 70 and 71. Select the center nostril polygons and smooth shift them. Move them up into the nose.

Steps 72 and 73. Smooth shift the center nostril polygon and move it further up into the nose.

Steps 74 and 75. Spin quads one time for the four polygons at the corners of the nose wings.

Step 76. Refine the shape of the nose.

Steps 77 and 78. Select the eighteen polygons at the sides of the head, overlapping into the forehead and eye areas. Smooth shift them. Move points to improve the shape of the head.

Steps 79 and 80. Spin quads two times for the four polygons in the lower part of the eyes.

Steps 81 and 82. Pick the four polygons at the top portion of the back of the head and spin quads one time.

Steps 83 and 84. Choose the eight polygons inside the eye area and smooth shift them. Move them into the head a little.

Steps 85 and 86. Smooth shift the twenty-four polygons of the eye area and move them into the head some more.

Completing the Eye and Starting the Ear (Figure 1-11)

This next set of steps will illustrate the finalization of the eye area. It will also mark the beginning of the most complicated part, which is the ear.

Steps 87 and 88. Select the forty polygons of the eye area and smooth shift them.

Steps 89 and 90. Spend some time moving points in order to sculpt the eye area. Begin to form the eye sockets and the eyelids. To give yourself extra points for the corners of the eyes, select the four polygons located there and smooth shift them.

Steps 91 and 92. Pick the four polygons near the nose and spin quads two times to turn them in the right direction.

Steps 93 and 94. Choose the four polygons on the inside parts of the corners of the eyes and spin quads one time.

Steps 95 and 96. Spin quads one time for the four polygons on the upper side of the nose.

Steps 97 and 98. Select the six polygons that will form the upper eyelids and smooth shift them.

Steps 99 and 100. Spin quads two times for the four polygons at the outer corners of the eyelid area.

Steps 101 and 102. Pick the four polygons at

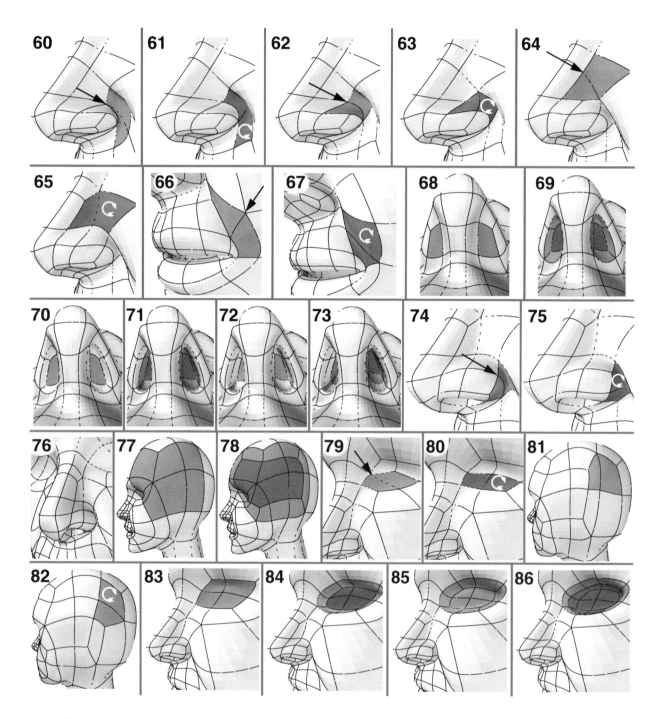

Fig. 1-10 Steps 60–86. Completing the nose and starting the eye.

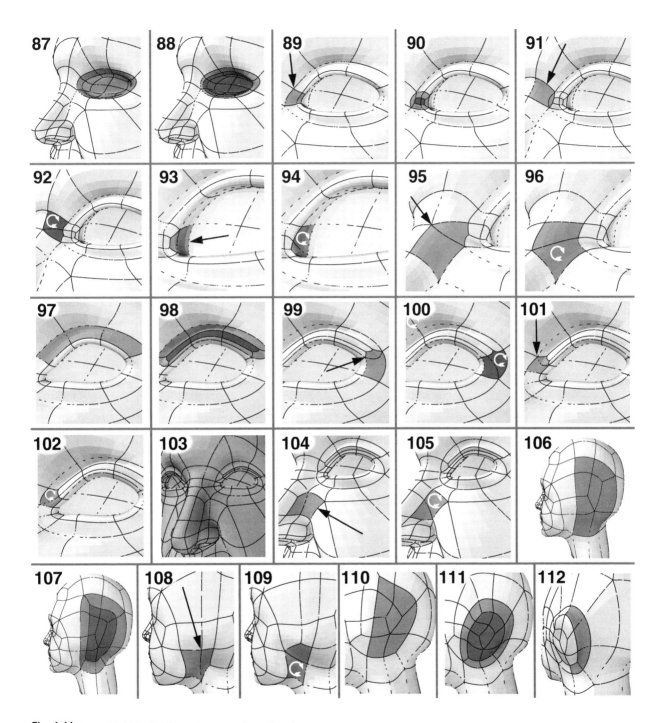

Fig. 1-11 Steps 87–112. Finishing the eye and starting the ear.

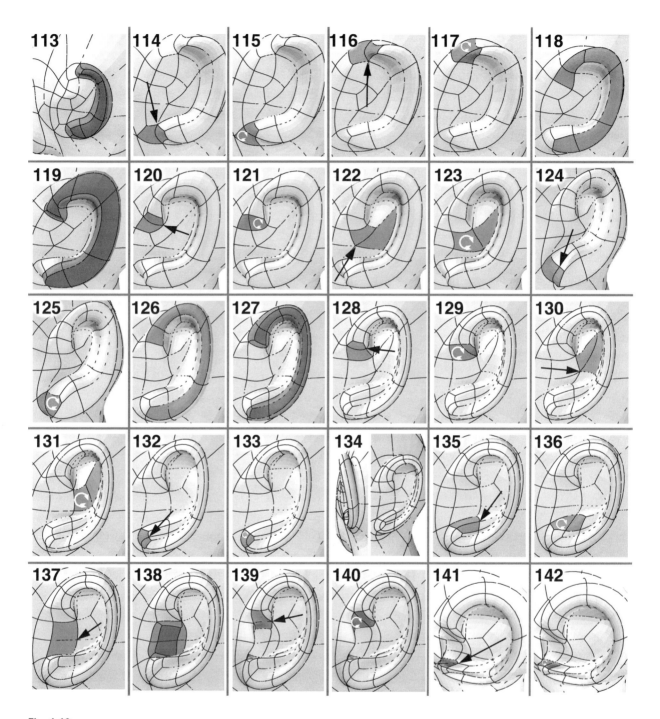

Fig. 1-12 Steps 113–142. Modeling the ear.

the inner corners of the eyelid area and spin quads one time.

Step 103. Move points to finish the eyes. You should have enough vertices to make the upper eyelid line. The middle points are moved back and up a little, while the ones right above are moved forward.

Steps 104 and 105. Locate the four polygons above the nose wings and spin quads one time.

Steps 106 and 107. Before starting the ear, you will need more points in that area. Therefore, select the sixteen polygons indicated in the illustration and smooth shift them.

Steps 108 and 109. At the top of the jaw line, spin quads one time for the four polygons.

Steps 110 and 111. Choose the sixteen polygons around the ear area and smooth shift them.

Step 112. Drag the ear polygons out a little from the head. Select the eights on the outer edge of the ear.

Continuing with the Ear (Figure 1-12)

Since the ear is one of the most complicated, if not the most complicated, parts of the human body to model, it will require more steps than the other areas covered so far.

Step 113. After selecting the eight polygons shown in step 112 (Figure 1-11), smooth shift them.

Steps 114 and 115. Move points to make a rough outline of the ear rim and outside bowl. Spin quads one time for the four polygons near the earlobe.

Steps 116 and 117. Spin quads two times at the beginning of the ear rim.

Steps 118 and 119. Smooth shift the twelve polygons of the ear rim.

Steps 120 and 121. Spin quads two times for polygons at the beginning of the ear rim.

Steps 122 and 123. Spin quads one time on the inside ear polygons.

Steps 124 and 125. Spin quads one time at the beginning of the earlobe.

Steps 126 and 127. Shape the earlobe and rim and smooth shift the twelve polygons of the ear rim.

Steps 128 and 129. Continue refining the shape of the ear and spin quads two times at the beginning of the ear rim.

Steps 130 and 131. Spin quads one time for the inside of the ear.

Steps 132 and 133. Spin quads one time at the beginning of the earlobe.

Step 134. Continue improving the shape of the ear.

Steps 135 and 136. Spin quads one time at the top of the earlobe.

Steps 137 and 138. The flap at the front that protects the ear canal will be modeled next. You will need more points, so select the polygons in that area and smooth shift them.

Steps 139 and 140. Move points to make the protective flap. Spin quads two times at the start of the ear rim.

Steps 141 and 142. Spin quads one time at the beginning inside portion of the earlobe. Your ear should now be almost complete, except for the inside bowl.

More Work on the Ear (Figure 1-13)

Due to its structural complexity, the ear should be broken down into separate parts. By modeling the outer shell or the rim first, one establishes the overall shape. The next steps will take you into the convoluted cartilage of the ear bowl. Besides spinning quads and performing a few smooth shifts to

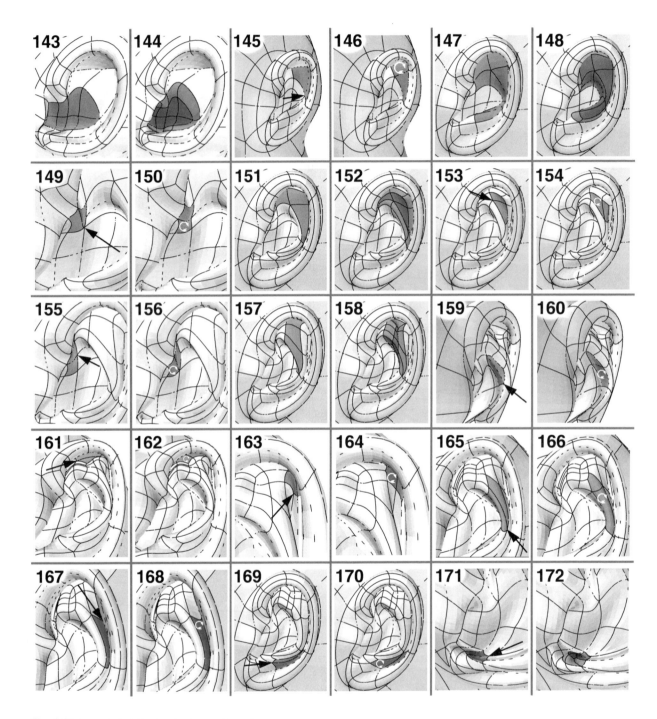

Fig. 1-13 Steps 143–172. Continuing work on the ear.

generate mores, you will mostly have to push and pull points. Some of you may now feel confident enough to work without following the steps exactly. As you set out on your own, be sure to refer to photos, sketches, or an actual model so that your depiction of the ear will be true to life. Keep in mind that from the side view, the angle of the ear is similar to the nose. From the back view, the rim forms a slight S-curve. Sometimes spinning quads, smooth shifting, and moving vertices can create overlapping points that occupy the same space. To remedy this, merge points and polygons every so often. You may even end up with three-sided polygons after merging.

Steps 143 and 144. Smooth shift the sixteen indicated polygons.

Steps 145 and 146. Use the extra points to model the protective flap of the ear. You can also move points inward for the ear canal. The extra polygons will help you shape the upper portion of the earlobe. Spin quads two times for the pictured polygons.

Steps 147 and 148. Smooth shift the depicted fourteen polygons.

Steps 149 and 150. Use the extra polygons to begin forming the inside of the ear and inner rim. Spin quads one time on the depicted polygons.

Steps 151 and 152. Smooth shift the six polygons shown in the illustration.

Steps 153 and 154. Spin quads one time on the indicated polygons and refine the ear bowl.

Steps 155 and 156. Refer to the illustration to spin quads two times. Pull and push points to improve the ear bowl.

Steps 157 and 158. Create more points by smooth shifting the portrayed eight polygons.

Steps 159 and 160. Move points to develop the inner cartilage of the ear. Spin quads one time for the depicted polygons.

Steps 161 and 162. Refer to the illustration and spin quads two times.

Steps 163 and 164. The illustration shows the next set of polygons for spinning quads two times.

Steps 165 and 166. Spin quads one time on the pictured polygons.

Steps 167 and 168. Spin quads two times on the polygons shown.

Steps 169 and 170. Near the earlobe, spin quads one time. Pull and push points until the ear looks almost complete.

Steps 171 and 172. To make the small bulging form above the earlobe, select the four polygons indicated and smooth shift them. Use the extra points to make the protruding shape.

Finishing the Ear and the Head (Figure 1-14)

Some more steps will finalize the ear. With a few more alterations, the head will be complete.

Steps 173 and 174. Spin quads two times for the polygons shown in the illustration.

Steps 175 and 176. Spin quads one time as shown in Figure 1-14.

Steps 177 and 178. Inside the ear bowl, spin quads two times.

Steps 179 and 180. Spin quads two times in the ear.

Steps 181 and 182. Move points to fine-tune and complete the ear.

Steps 183 and 184. Smooth shift the large single polygon in the middle of the forehead.

Steps 185 and 186. Spin quads one time on the polygons located on the sides of the forehead.

Steps 187 and 188. Spin quads one time near the top of the head.

Steps 189 and 190. On the upper sides of the head, spin quads one time.

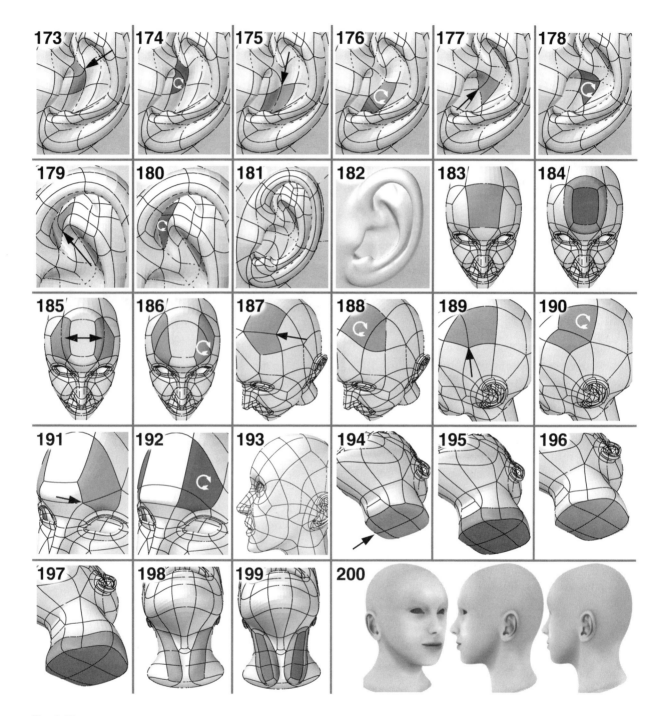

Fig. 1-14 Steps 173–200. Completing the head.

Steps 191 and 192. Spin quads two times above the eye opening.

Step 193. Push and pull points until the head looks the way you want. Besides smoothing out the forehead, you might want to bring out the cheekbones, improve the jaw line, shape the cheeks, alter the lower eyelids, and so on.

Steps 194 and 195. Select the six polygons located at the bottom of the neck and smooth shift them. Drag the new polygons down a little.

Steps 196 and 197. After selecting the new set of six polygons located at the bottom of the neck, smooth shift these also. Move points to extend the neck to the collarbone.

Steps 198 and 199. Smooth shift the six polygons that will form the sterno-mastoid muscles of the neck. Refine the shape of the neck.

Step 200. If necessary, continue making small improvements to the head.

Some Final Words

Modeling a head can be a challenge. The ear is perhaps the most demanding task for any 3D artist. At first glance, a 3D model may look fine, but if you take a closer look at the ear, you can quickly judge the artist's modeling abilities.

Since the polygon count on this head is quite low, you can reshape it into other heads with less trouble than it would take to start all over again with a simple box. You can continue using this method of subdivision modeling to complete the entire body. Chapters 2 and 6 show how to proceed. Instead of beveling, you will smooth shift. Rather than cutting and rearranging polygons, you can spin quads.

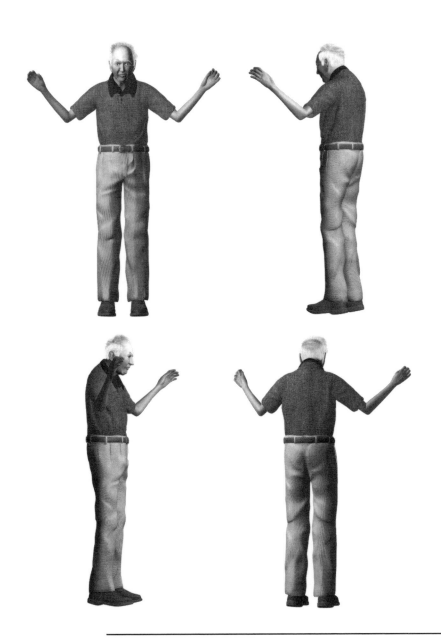

CHAPTER 2

Basic 3D Modeling

An introduction to 3D modeling usually means learning basic steps to creating simple objects. Students absorb more when they actually have to use specific modeling tools to create projects than they do from just reading about them. This chapter starts with an exercise that teaches basic 3D modeling with the goal of producing a simple cartoon character. The routines addressed here will be used later to make a more complex 3D model of a human.

Cartoon characters are usually very simple, with relatively few details. Some of their characteristics are extra-large heads, exaggerated facial features, three-fingered hands, and uncomplicated bodies. Hence, a cartoon character is a good subject for learning elementary 3D modeling techniques.

One should not mistake a cartoon character for a superhero type. Superheroes normally have extra-small heads compared to their overstated, muscular bodies. Their physiques have a great amount of detail, which requires a considerable understanding of anatomy. If you want to create a superhero, you should have more than a rudimentary knowledge of 3D modeling.

Those of you who are already familiar with basic subdivision modeling and have created cartoon characters using this method or the one in chapter 1 might want to skip ahead to the next part of this chapter. It teaches the steps to making the body for the more realistic character that was started in chapter 1 (Figures 1-8 through 1-14). Whether you make a cartoon character following the steps listed here or using your own method, you will need to create some type of two-legged being for use in chapter 3, Animating with Deformation Tools.

Modeling a Simple Cartoon Character

Before you start this process, it is recommended that you first make some sketches. At the minimum, you should have a front view and a side view of your individual (Figure 2-1, step 1). A viewpoint looking down can also be helpful. Be sure to make each sketch the same size and with the same proportions. Make all views into one document that can be imported into your modeling program. Set all views to show the one image with the various pose angles. This will save a lot of time because you will not have to line up and scale individual views to match each other.

The front view of the sketch template shows the arms extending outward in a straight line, away from the torso. It is much easier to model the arms this way rather than down by the sides. If you are not planning to use a top view, draw the hands facing toward you so that you can clearly see each finger. Spreading the fingers and thumbs apart also simplifies the work.

Rather than borrowing a well-known cartoon, try to create your own unique character. Even though yours may vary a great deal from the one used in this book, you should still be able to follow the same routines outlined in this tutorial.

Unlike the cartoon character of chapter 1, which was created in subdivision mode, this model is depicted in low-polygon count most of the time. Some people may find it easier to see the geometry in these low-poly illustrations of the cartoon.

Whereas the chapter 1 model used tools such as smooth shift and spin quads, this one can be built without the use of these. Bevel can be utilized in place of smooth shift and polygons can be cut, merged, and split. Points can be added to the polygons if your software is unable to rotate them with a spin quads command.

Modeling the Body and Part of the Face (Figure 2-1)

Step 1. In your modeling program, set up the front and side view windows to show the two templates. In the beginning, the work will proceed with subdivision surfaces turned off.

Step 2. As usual, begin by making a box. In your numeric settings, specify four segments on the x- and y-axes and three segments on the z-axis. Center the box at 0 on the x-, y-, and z-axes so that symmetry operations will be functional. Unlike the head in the first lesson in chapter 1, this head will be modeled later, after finishing the body. Since it is more difficult to model a head than it is to make the body, this will be saved for the final steps.

Step 3. After making sure the box is centered in your modeling universe, turn on symmetry. Select the two middle bottom polygons.

Step 4. Merge the two bottom polygons into one if you are bevel extruding. With smooth shift, you do not have to merge the polygons. Bevel or smooth shift the neck polygons. The offset should be at 0 to keep symmetry operations functional. Move the smooth shifted or beveled polygons down to make the neck. In this example, the character has a pencil neck. If you plan to make a thicker one and you are using a bevel tool, merge more polygons at the bottom of the head before you begin beveling.

Step 5. Once again, bevel or smooth shift the polygon down to start the torso.

Step 6. Bevel or smooth shift the polygon a few more times to finish the torso. Depending on the shape of your character's chest and abdomen, sometimes the beveled or smooth shifted polygon(s) increases in size, while other times, it will decrease.

Step 7. In this example, the shirt will cover the upper portion of the pants. If that is the case with your model, then follow this step to bevel or smooth shift the bottom polygon(s) up and into the abdomen.

Step 8. If you are beveling and you merged the bottom polygons into one, now split the bottom polygon in half. The resulting two polygons will be beveled or smooth shifted down to make the legs. When beveling the two polygons, you can do both at the same time. Smooth shifting requires that each is smooth shifted at separate times because smooth shift merges polygons before duplicating them. Smooth shifting requires that each polygon is replicated and moved at separate times because the smooth shift operation merges polygons before duplicating them.

Step 9. Select the two polygons at the bottom of the torso and bevel or smooth shift them down to make the legs. In this example, the legs are beveled or smooth shifted only to where the cuffs on the pants begin. You will have to decide whether to bevel or smooth shift the legs in sections—such as down to the knees, then again to the ankles—or just the entire length in one bevel or smooth shift. If you choose to bevel or smooth shift the entire length of the legs, split the leg polygons into sections with something like a knife or band saw tool. With symmetry active, work on only one side to shape each section of the legs according to your 2D template. Symmetry should automatically match each of your changes on the other leg.

Whenever you have a section that goes inside

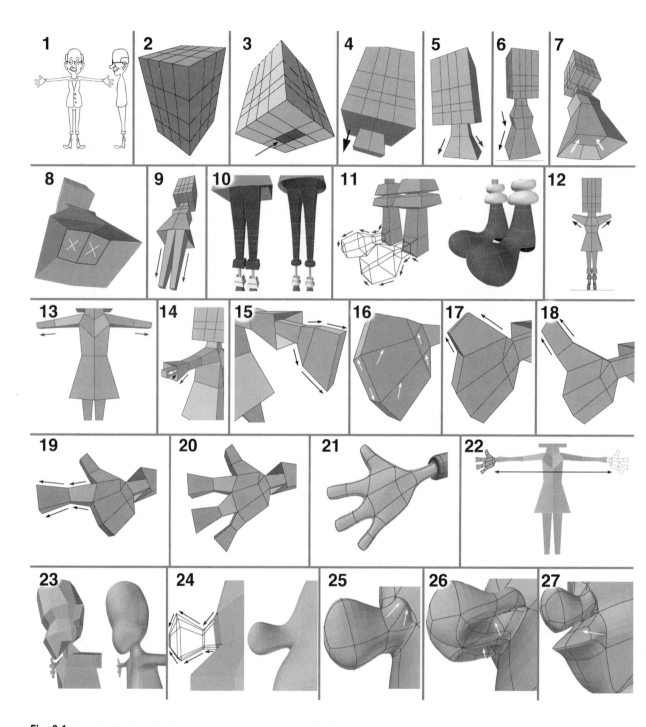

Fig. 2-1 Steps 1–27. Creating the cartoon body and starting the head.

another—such as legs under a skirt, a shirt worn on the outside, or feet inside shoes—split the polygons near the inside portion to keep the inward section from ballooning outward when in subdivision mode. A knife tool can be a tremendous help in cases like this.

Step 10. This example shows the shape of the legs in low-polygon and subdivision form. The pants have a cuff and are extra-short. The socks are gathered around the ankles. Beveling or smooth shifting the polygons to make them smaller and sometimes larger while moving them inside each other created this look. Experiment with different bevels or smooth shifts and move points in low and subdivision polygon mode until you get the results that you want. Be sure to split extra polygons at specific points by cutting across them with a knife or other means so that your model keeps the dimensions that you desire. Besides holding a model's form, these extra points will give you the extra control you need to shape it more precisely.

Step 11. To start the shoes, split the lower section of the legs. Select the two polygons at the bottom, facing toward the front. Bevel or smooth shift these out several times until you have the rough shape of a shoe. You can also split the bottom of these polygons for the soles and heels. With symmetry on, move points in low-polygon and subdivision mode until you are satisfied with the shape of the shoes.

Step 12. Now it is time to start the arms. Locate the polygons on the side of the torso near the neck. Bevel or smooth shift these out to the elbows.

Step 13. Bevel or smooth shift again to make the forearms. Adjust the shape of the arms.

Step 14. In this example, the figure has a sleeve. If this is what you want on your character, simply bevel or smooth shift outward making the polygon larger, bevel or smooth shift inward toward the

direction of the torso to pull in the size of the polygon, and finally bevel or smooth shift straight outward to make the wrist. As mentioned before, you may need to split the polygons near the inside of the sleeve to keep it from ballooning outward when in subdivision mode.

Step 15. Start the hand by beveling or smooth shifting outward twice. The second section stops just before the fingers begin to spread outward from it.

Step 16. In order to have the fingers separate from the hand, you will need to divide the hand polygon into three sections (three fingers). If your software only allows subdivision surfaces for three- and four-sided polygons, make sure you do not have any with more than four sides. If you are not using symmetry, then work on only one hand. Divide it into four- and three-sided polygons. When it is completed, this hand can be mirror duplicated for the other side.

Step 17. Select the polygon at the top of the hand and bevel or smooth shift it up to begin making the thumb. The beveled or smooth shifted polygon should decrease in size a little.

Step 18. Bevel or smooth shift the thumb polygon up again to make the tip.

Step 19. Bevel or smooth shift out twice to make the forefinger.

Step 20. Using the bevel or smooth shift tool, finish the rest of the fingers.

Step 21. Turn on subdivision surfaces and refine the shape of the hand. You could divide the polygons some more for extra detail, but in this case, since it is a simple cartoon character, it will most likely not be necessary. If the hand has too much of a boxy look, add extra points, split polygons, and move the additional vertices to fix the shape of the hand.

Step 22. If you have not been using symmetry,

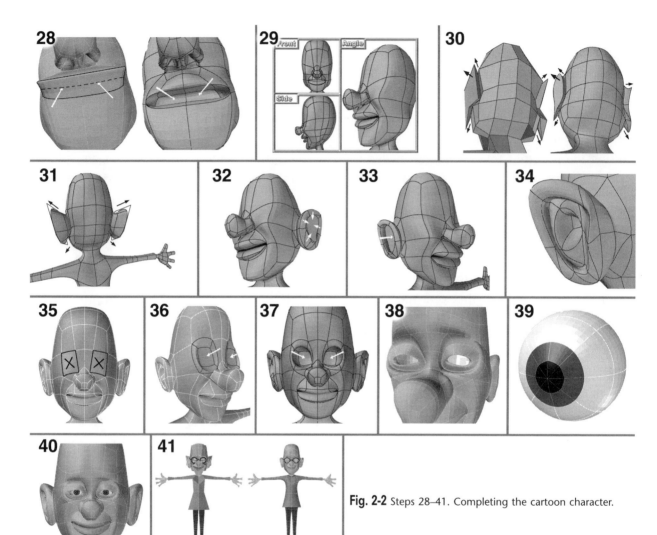

Fig. 2-2 Steps 28–41. Completing the cartoon character.

mirror duplicate the finished hand for the other side.

Step 23. You should now have a simple figure with a blockhead. Before proceeding to the head, use something like a knife tool to divide polygons at the elbows and knees. These are parts that will need the additional polygons to deform properly during animation. Start moving points on the head with subdivision surfaces turned on and off alternately.

Step 24. Find the two polygons from which you will now bevel or smooth shift out the nose. Smooth shift the nose polygons several times to get the general shape of the nose. If you are beveling, turn on low-polygon mode, merge the nose poly-gons, and bevel them several times in subdivision mode improve the nose's form.

Step 25. In low-polygon form, select the two polygons on each side of the nose and bevel or smooth shift them out and toward the face to make the nose wings. The beveled or smooth shift polygons should get smaller in size.

Step 26. After you improve the shape of the nose, you can turn off subdivision mode to start the nostrils. You will need to arrange the polygons at the bottom so that there are two that can be beveled straight up into the nose. This may mean having to split up some of them or rotating them with a spin quads command. Bevel or smooth shift the nostril polygons up several times and alter them in subdivision mode.

Step 27. Start the mouth by selecting the two polygons below the nose. Merge these into one and bevel or smooth shift both outward. Shape it to resemble your template. In this example, the character's upper lip will jut out a little.

Finishing the Cartoon Figure (Figure 2-2)

Step 28. In low-polygon mode, select the lower section of the mouth area. Merge the two poly-gons. Split them in a horizontal direction. Select the lower half of the two and bevel or smooth shift it inward several times to make the interior of the mouth. Rather than bevel or smooth shift, you may decide to just move the points back into the head and then split up the polygons of the interior mouth before finishing its form. In either case, split the two polygons that you initially divided horizontally. They should be separated vertically again so that you only have polygons with three or four sides. If you can spin quads, then you do not have to merge and split polygons again

because you simply rotate them to face the right direction.

Step 29. The lips can be modeled by either beveling or smooth shifting out the top and bot-tom mouth polygons, splitting them, or simply moving the existing points. Whichever method you use, be sure to work with subdivision surfaces on to complete the mouth.

Step 30. The illustration for this next step shows a low-polygon and subdivision surface version of the same head seen from the back. Polygons at both sides of the head are merged, arranged, and beveled or smooth shifted outward to start the ear.

Step 31. Bevel or smooth shift the ear polygons out one more time to make the outer rim of the ear.

Step 32. Once again, bevel or smooth shift the ear polygons, but move them into the ear and reduce their size.

Step 33. Bevel or smooth shift the ear polygons further into the ear.

Step 34. If you are splitting polygons instead of spinning quads, you will most likely have to work on only one ear. Symmetry operations will most likely not duplicate splitting and adding points across the x-axis. Select one of the interior ear poly-gons and split it up into three- and four-sided poly-gons. If you plan to make the ear more detailed than the one shown in this illustration, continue to split the polygons into even smaller ones. Delete the opposite inside ear polygon before mirror duplicating the inside ear sections. Turn on sym-metry and shape the inside of the ear by moving points. Remember, you are only making a cartoon character, so it is only an approximation of the ear. There is no need to strive for realism.

Step 35. To begin the eyes, set up the two eye polygons in a similar manner to the ones in the

Fig. 2-3 The final rendered cartoon character.

illustration.

Step 36. Select the eye polygons and begin beveling or smooth shifting them in a little.

Step 37. Finish the eye socket by beveling or smooth shifting the two polygons inward one more time.

Step 38. Hide everything except the eye sockets. Use a tool such as the knife to slice several times across the eye socket polygons near the opening, or use smooth shift and spin quads until you have enough points to model the eyelids. Show everything again and utilize the extra points derived from cutting across the sockets to shape the upper and lower eyelids.

Step 39. You can make a simple eyeball, iris, and pupil out of a sphere. Make it a low-polygon count one by setting the sides to eight and the segments to four. Subdivision mode will round it off sufficiently. Slice across the front of the eyeball several times, select each concentric circle, and name each surface as iris and pupil. Select the rest of the eyeball and name it "eyeball." For now, you

can just apply a color for the iris, white for the eyeball, and black for the pupil. In a later lesson, you will learn to make a more realistic eye with textures.

Step 40. Place both eyeballs in their respective eye sockets.

Step 41. You may also want to model some accessories, such as glasses, a hat, a scarf, a tie, and so on. If the character looks too boxy, split polygons and move the extra points to round the figure. Improve the appearance of the character by selecting different parts, naming, and then coloring each (Figure 2-3). If you know how to texture, then by all means, do so. The cartoon character that you modeled can be used in the next chapter to learn how a skeleton is set up and animated.

Modeling a More Complex Character

In the first chapter, you learned the principles of subdivision surface modeling. After completing the lesson, you had a finished head with facial features. Your first effort will most likely appear primitive, since the tools and the way to use them may have been unfamiliar to you.

Creating the cartoon character should have advanced your knowledge of subdivision surface modeling. Assuming that you are more comfortable with 3D modeling, it is time to create a more polished figure. The techniques that were discussed in previous lessons will still apply, but the increased level of detail will now require more effort on your part.

Since the first chapter outlined the manner in which to model a face, use it again to follow the steps and create an improved version. This time, employ either more intricate sketches or photos as your templates.

If you have access to a digital camera and can find someone to pose for you, then take front, side, back, and top photos. Be sure to get front, side, and back close-ups of the face, feet, and hands, since they are parts that require more detailed modeling. When you take photographs, position the model the same distance from you for all the views. To avoid distortion, use a long lens and place the camera's viewpoint midway to the model's body. Save yourself some aggravation by sizing the various views and placing them into one image file. Import that into your modeling program, and place the same image in the various view windows.

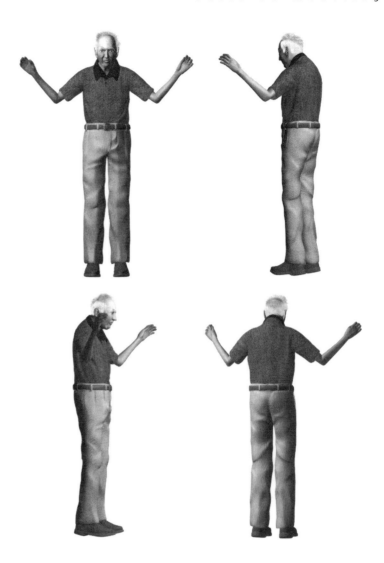

Fig. 2-5 The model that was created from the templates in Figure 2-4.

Figures 2-4 and 2-5 depict some templates and the resulting final model of an older gentleman. The chapter 2 folder on the CD-ROM includes Figure 2-5 in color (Chapter 2>Color Images>OldManViews).

Fig. 2-4 The templates used to make the model shown in Figure 2-5.

Fixing Unsightly Seams

Sometimes you may experience creasing, pinching, or ugly lines on the surface of your character's

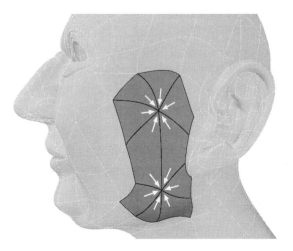

Fig. 2-6 Pinching and creasing due to more than four polygons converging at one point.

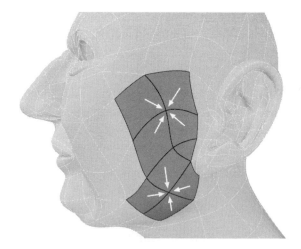

Fig. 2-7 Altering the polygon configuration so that only four converge at one point.

face. Often this is a result of too many polygons converging at a single point (Figure 2-6).

Some software programs have tools for spinning the orientation of polygons. A spin quad type of tool can be handy for taking adjacent four-point polygons that share edges, merging them, and splitting them using a different set of opposing polygons. This saves time by eliminating the manual labor of merging, adding points, and splitting polygons into different configurations.

Even with the best of tools, it sometimes becomes difficult to avoid getting triangles in your subdivision mesh. Triangles are like spearheads. When too many triangles point toward a vertex, it can create an indentation. Problem areas like this can often be fixed by merging neighboring triangles. You may also need to add extra points to certain polygons so that you can split them up in a way that creates four-sided polygons around specific points. Often four-sided polygons will solve these types of problems. Figure 2-7 shows the same area after triangles have been merged into quadrangles. Some polygons had extra points added to

them before they could be split and merged into four-sided ones. If you like solving puzzles, you should enjoy the challenge of altering polygons. The goal is to make mostly quadrangles and the smallest number of triangles possible.

Modeling the Torso (Figure 2-8)

Step 1. The main steps for modeling the head can be seen in the illustration. These steps are detailed in chapters 1 and 6; simply follow the previous instructions to create your own character's head.

Steps 2, 3, and 4. Select the bottom neck polygon and bevel or smooth shift it up slightly. Make that polygon a little larger. If you do not have a polygon at the bottom of the neck, simply select the points around the neck hole in a clockwise or counterclockwise manner, then make a polygon out of these. After beveling or smooth shifting the polygon up somewhat, bevel or smooth shift it down and out to make the shirt collar.

Step 5. The polygon located at the shoulders is beveled or smooth shifted down to make the

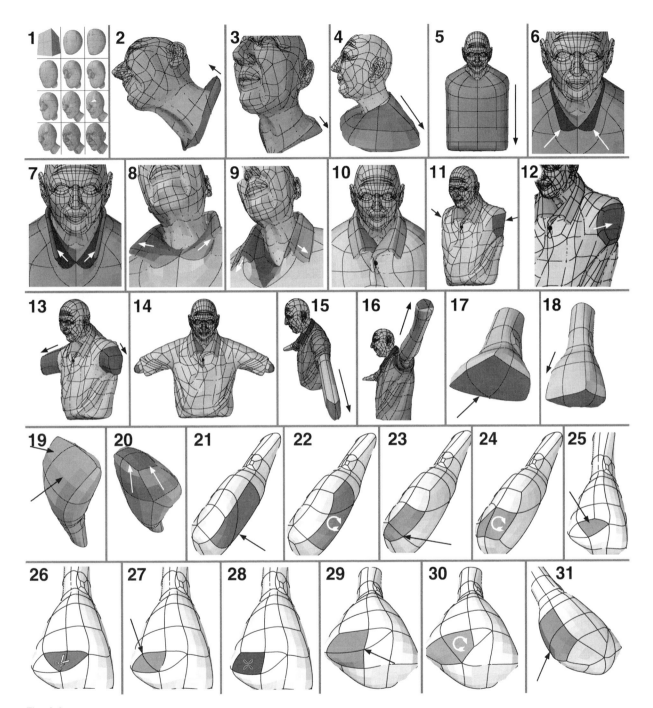

Fig. 2-8 Steps 1–31. Modeling the torso, arms, and hands.

shoulders. In subdivision mode, shape the shoulders according to your templates. Turn off subdivision mode and use a knife tool to slice across the torso horizontally until you have about five divisions. You can also smooth shift to make each division, but this will most likely take longer than slicing across the torso. After dividing the torso, turn on subdivision mode again.

Steps 6–10. This operation shows how to make a shirt collar. If this is too complicated or you are modeling a collarless shirt, skip to the next step. Select the polygons around the collar area and smooth shift them up, then outward, and finally down. If you are beveling, then turn on low polygon mode, select the polygons in the collar area, and split them into smaller, narrower ones. Select these polygons and merge them into one. Bevel it up and then bevel again outward. Bevel this long polygon one more time, but make the direction down. Split this large polygon into four-sided ones. Turn on subdivision mode and sculpt the collar. If you are smooth shifting and are trying to avoid having to split, add points, and merge points and polygons, you may have to spin quads to get polygons aligned in the right direction. Add buttonholes and some buttons.

Step 11. To prepare the sleeve, select the polygons where the sleeve will be beveled out and merge them into one. (Smooth shifting does not require merging polygons.) Before smooth shifting or beveling the arms out, spend some time on the shirt folds. Creases in the shirt consist of parallel lines. Usually, three lines running in the same direction will work. Sometimes it only takes two lines. One of these lines is pulled back or forward to make the crease or fold. Divide your polygons in such a way that you end up with lines running in the direction of the folds. You can have each

group of lines converge at beginning and end points. These start and end vertices will not be moved. If you are smooth shifting and spinning quads, keep the figure in subdivision mode. Those of you that are splitting, merging, and beveling polygons should work in low-polygon mode. After completing each set of lines, turn on subdivision mode. Pull points in and out until you see some folds develop. Viewing the shirt with smooth shade on will help you determine the right amount of creasing.

Steps 12 and 13. The arm sleeves will now be beveled or smooth shifted out. When beveling the arm, polygons will have to be merged first. Bevel or smooth shift the arms outward. If you are smooth shifting with symmetry on, you can select the polygons of the sleeves and smooth shift them in order to add more sections to the sleeves. If you are beveling with subdivision mode off, then divide the polygons with a knife tool. Rearrange the points on the sleeve so that you can make some folds on it. Work in subdivision mode to shape the sleeve and its creases.

Step 14. To make the beginning of the upper arm, or the wrist if you are modeling a long-sleeved shirt, bevel or smooth shift the end polygon(s) in a little and then back out. Beveling or smooth shifting in will give the shirtsleeve some thickness. Beveling or smooth shifting out will start forming the arm. For now, you only need to bevel or smooth shift the arm out a little past the sleeve. Some of you may have been working on only one arm without symmetry. If so, before mirror duplicating the sleeve and beginning the arm, delete the polygon on the opposite side that is situated at the sleeve opening. Mirror duplicate the finished arm sleeve and, if necessary, weld the points to the shoulder area. This completes the torso.

The Arms (Figure 2-8)

Steps 15 and 16. Select the polygon at the end of an arm. Bevel or smooth shift it out for the entire length, to the beginning of the hand. If you are smooth shifting with symmetry on, select the polygons in the middle of the arms and smooth shift again to give them more sections. Move points to shape the arm. When you need more sections, just select polygons around the arm and smooth shift again. If you are beveling without symmetry, you can just work on one arm. Turn off subdivision mode, and use a knife tool to split the arm vertically into sections. Later, after giving it the right shape, mirror duplicate the arm. Be sure to delete the end polygon near the sleeve before attaching the mirrored arm.

The Hands (Figures 2-8 and 2-9)

Step 17. Begin modeling the hand by selecting the end arm polygons and beveling or smooth shifting them outward a couple of times. Sculpt the wrist and the start of the hand by working in low-polygon or subdivision mode.

Steps 18–54. Create the rest of the hand (without the thumb and fingers) by beveling or smooth shifting several more times. Move points to give it a more accurate hand shape. If you are beveling, splitting polygons, adding points, and welding points, as well as merging polygons, then prepare the end polygons where the fingers will start so that they look like the four shaded ones in Step 45. If you are smooth shifting, then refer to steps 19–54 in Figures 2-8 and 2-9 to spin quads until you have the right configurations for making the thumbs and fingers. Step 19 shows how the two bottom hand polygons near the front are rotated and moved forward to make the front of the hand

at the start of the fingers. These two are then smooth shifted (Step 20). Spin quads is used on a few polygons so that they face in the right direction (Steps 21–24). The indicated polygon in Steps 25 and 26 is split in half. The polygon on the left and its neighboring triangle are merged into a quadrangle (Steps 27 and 28). Some more polygons are rotated with spin quads (Steps 29–38). Steps 38 and 39 show how the two polygons next to each other on the bottom of the hand, which look like triangles, are merged. In Steps 41 and 42, two polygons are rotated with spin quads. To prepare the four polygons for the knuckles, select the two polygons indicated in Step 43. Hide the rest of the polygons and turn off subdivision mode. Turn off symmetry. Insert a point and split the polygons so they look like the ones in Step 44. Merge the two bottom polygons. Weld the middle point of the three polygons to the bottom point of the triangle. Your hand should now look like the one in Step 45. You can repeat this process on the other hand or just delete the two polygons, mirror the new ones, and merge points so that both hands are the same. Turn on subdivision mode and symmetry again. Continue spinning quads (Steps 46–51). Merge the two neighboring polygons as depicted in Steps 52 and 53. Step 54 shows the polygons that are now going to be smooth shifted or beveled to make the thumb and fingers.

Steps 55–58. Select the thumb and four finger polygons and bevel or smooth shift them. Move them out a little. Smooth shift or bevel again until you have all the segments for the finger and thumb joints. Work on shaping the thumbs and fingers.

Step 59–63. Details on the hand can now be started. Begin by modeling the finger and thumbnails. Select one of the nail polygons and bevel or smooth shift it down and in a little (Steps 59 and

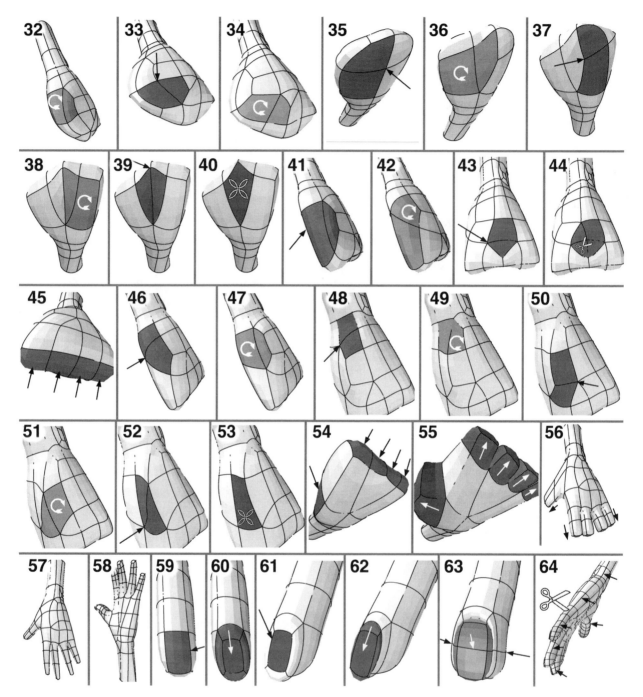

Fig. 2-9 Steps 32–64. Modeling the hand, thumb, and fingers.

60). Now bevel or smooth shift the same polygon a little above the finger and make its size somewhat larger (Steps 61 and 62). Use a knife tool to split the nail and the fingertip (Step 63). Move the middle points of the fingernail up slightly to curve the nail. In subdivision mode, shape the fingernail and tip of the finger. Follow the same steps to model the rest of the nails. When using the knife tool to split the fingernails (Step 63), you will most likely have to repeat this process on the other hand, or you can just finish splitting the nails and then mirror the hand to replace the one on the other side that does not have the nails split.

Step 64. Right now, each finger and thumb section only has four polygons. This makes the hand too boxy looking. If possible, in low-polygon mode, use a knife tool to split the hand, fingers, and thumb across their entire length. If the fingers are curved, you may need to manually split each polygon after adding points. Use the extra points to make the finger, thumb, and hand more round. Mirror duplicate the split hand to replace the older one on the other side.

Completing the Hands and Pants (Figures 2-10 and 2-11)

Steps 65, 66, and 67. Begin the knuckles by selecting the four polygons at the top of the hand close to where the fingers begin. Bevel or smooth shift them up and in a little. Split the knuckle polygons down the center. You will most likely have to add points and split the polygons after selecting the vertices in the right order. The lines on each knuckle will now look like a simple spider web. Be sure to shape the knuckles in subdivision mode by moving the middle points up slightly. Mirror the hand or repeat the steps for the other side.

Steps 68–72. Split or smooth shift and spin quads to make the furrows on the thumb and fin-

ger knuckles, and veins and creases on the hands. Sets of three lines running parallel to each other should be enough to make the creases and veins. This is the same method that was used to make wrinkles in the face and folds in the shirt. The middle line points are pulled down for creases and moved up to make the veins. These kind of modeled details often look better than applying a bump map to show creasing in those areas.

Steps 73–78. When modeling the pants, you should notice some parallels between the procedures outlined here and the previous ones for the shirt. Select the bottom shirt polygon and bevel or smooth shift it up and outward. This is similar to the first step that described beveling or smooth shifting the bottom neck polygon up and outward to start the shirt collar. Bevel or smooth shift the same polygon down to about the halfway point between the waist and the crotch area. Bevel or smooth shift once again so that the bottom polygons end where the legs will begin to fork into two separate parts.

Steps 79–83. Select the group of polygons for one of the legs and smooth shift it. Do the same for the other leg. If you are beveling in low polygon mode, merge the polygons of one leg first. After beveling it, do the same to the other leg's polygons. Move the smooth shifted or beveled polygons down a little. Bevel or smooth shift again and move the bottom polygons down to where the shoes will begin to show. You should now have the abdomen area and two legs.

Steps 84–88. Separate the two legs a little so that you can see a gap between them. Begin shaping the legs by first moving points to make them more round (Step 84). Split the pants polygons into cross sections (Step 85). Smooth shift or bevel the bottom polygons up into the pants several times (Steps 86–88). If you want to make cuffs,

Fig. 2-10 Steps 65–94. Completing the hand, thumb, fingers, pants, and belt.

then bevel or smooth shift the two bottom polygons up and out, down, and back up and into the pants legs.

Steps 89–94. Add belt loops by modeling a simple form that resembles a narrow box with two ends. Split the polygons at the waist and adhere duplicates of the belt loop to the pants. You might decide that you would rather smooth shift out the belt loops. Now it is time to start splitting up the polygons on the pants into parallel lines so that you can make the creases, pockets, and seams. After splitting up the polygons (or smooth shifting and spinning quads), move points just like you did

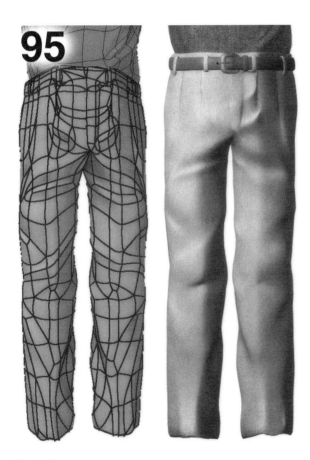

Fig. 2-11 Step 95. Completing the pants and belt.

with the shirt until you start seeing wrinkles in different places. When you have parallel lines running vertically at the zipper, you can tuck one set of points under the other. The same applies to pockets. You could save time by just making wrinkles on one pants leg and then mirror duplicating it to make the other. If you decide to do this, then be sure to alter the wrinkles on the second pants leg. If the pants have belt loops, then why not model a belt (Steps 92–94)? Often it is the details that make an image or images rich and full of variety.

Step 95 (Figure 2-11). Complete the pants by continuing to sculpt creases, pockets, and so on.

The Shoes (Figure 2-12)

Steps 96, 97, and 98. The final character modeling step is to create shoes. Since these vary a great deal, the example given here is of a generic type that should be fairly simple to model. You can follow these steps while creating your own brand of shoe. This modeling process can be applied to an assortment of shoe styles. Begin by creating a box that is approximately the same length and width of the shoe that you plan to model. Divide the polygons on the box and move points to make a simple shoe shape. Continue dividing polygons so that you have extra points that can be moved for a more detailed shoe. Split the shoe polygons up even more and sculpt the shoe and the shoe sole both in low-polygon and subdivision mode.

Steps 99–103. Select the polygons near the bottom that form the sides of the shoe sole. Smooth shift them outward. Use a stretch or scale tool to adjust the size of the shoe sole. If you are using a bevel tool, merge the polygons around the bottom of the shoe and bevel them outward a little. If you beveled the shoe sole outward, hide all the poly-

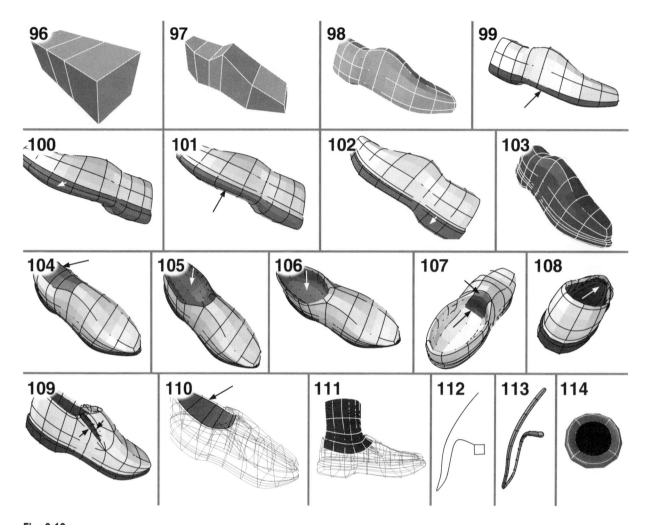

Fig. 2-12 Steps 95–114. Modeling the shoe.

gons except for the merged one that you beveled for the thickness of the sole. Split it into four-sided polygons. Turn on subdivision mode and continue refining the sole. If you see any pulling on some of the points, check to make sure you that you do not have any inside polygons. If you find any of these, delete them.

Steps 104–108. Make the shoe opening for the foot by smooth shifting the polygons down a few times in that area. For a bevel operation, merge the

polygons in that region. Bevel it down several times. Shape the shoe opening in subdivision mode. Select the polygons that will be beveled inward toward the toe area, and smooth shift them in that direction. If you are beveling, merge these polygons first. Bevel the merged polygon toward the front of the shoe.

Steps 109–114. Add details such as shoelaces or, as in the example (Step 109), an elastic band. To make the sock that goes into the shoe (Steps 110 and 111), select the points around the shoe opening and make a polygon out of them. Bevel or smooth shift the polygon upward several times and shape it in subdivision mode. If you model shoelaces, you can bevel or smooth shift a four-sided polygon a number of times, then shape it in subdivision mode. Another method is to create a spline that acts as a rail along which a four-sided polygon (Steps 112 and 113) can be rail extruded. Path extrude should also work well.

The shoelace holes and their outer rims can be made from a toroid that has four sections and four sides. This simple, boxlike toroid will bend into a more circular shape in subdivision mode (Step 114). The holes do not have to be drilled into the shoe, but can be mimicked by selecting the four inside center points of the toroid and making a polygon out of these. This inside polygon can then be assigned a black shade. Placing the toroid and its black center polygon partly inside the shoe surface should be sufficient to make the shoelace holes.

After scaling and moving the shoe and sock under one of the pants legs, mirror duplicate the shoe and sock to make a pair (Figure 2-13). The final rendered character can be seen in Figure 2-14.

If you want to continue working on your

Fig. 2-13 The final shoe and sock are mirror duplicated.

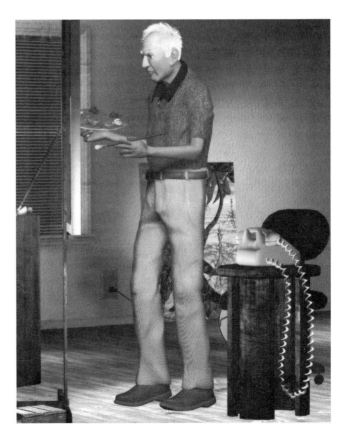

Fig. 2-14 The rendered old man character.

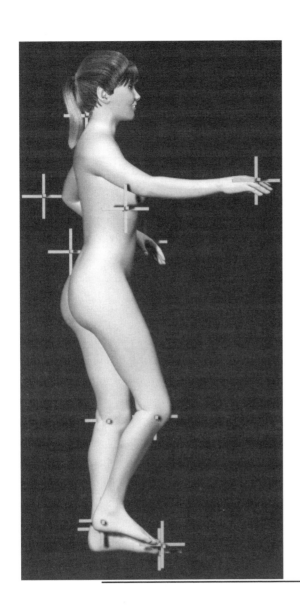

CHAPTER 3

Animating with Deformation Tools

Most 3D animation systems utilize skeletons, shape blending, sculpting, lattice, wire, and cluster deformers. These methods usually employ other objects that exert influence on the wireframe mesh. The most common technique uses skeletons. A skeleton is a structure for animating a character's articulated and hierarchical actions. It is similar to a real skeleton, except that the bones are not attached to muscles by tendons.

Human and animal anatomy has a much more complicated system of locomotion. Bones are moved by the contraction of muscles. One end of the muscle remains relatively fixed while the other end moves. As the muscle contracts, it draws one end toward the other and grows shorter and thicker. Muscles do not act alone. Whenever one or more muscles contract, other opposing muscles become active. These act as modifying or stabilizing factors to regulate the active muscle(s).

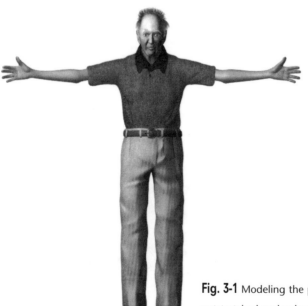

Fig. 3-1 Modeling the person with arms outstretched and palms forward.

Skeletal structures in animation are often used to simulate the actions of physical bodies. Unfortunately, since the computer models and the manner in which they are set up for animation lack the complicated systems found in nature, real-life movements are very difficult to achieve. Therefore, a number of different procedures have been developed to aid animators when they try to approximate the motions of true life-forms.

Preparing the Model for a Skeletal Structure

When bones are rotated inside a 3D model, they can often cause undesirable deformations on certain parts of the character. Crimping can occur at the elbow, knee, or shoulder joints, while other areas on the model may become malformed from the effects of bone influences. Until more sophisticated muscular-skeletal systems become available to most 3D users, artists will have to find other ways of posing their models with the least amount of distortion.

It is interesting to see the kind of "fixes" that 3D software developers provide until they can develop a more effective muscular-skeletal system. Some will offer the option of using lattice cages around the joints to make the bent object look more natural. Other deformers may include flexors to help create more natural dips and bulges. Splines may be utilized as wire deformers. Other choices may include the ability to set various percentages of joint compensation to a specific bone so that it does not cause the mesh to crimp like a

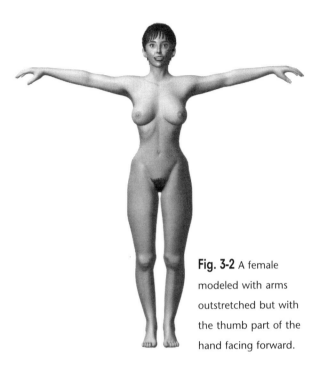

Fig. 3-2 A female modeled with arms outstretched but with the thumb part of the hand facing forward.

hand is visible in the front view and the back of the hand with the knuckles is visible in the back view, while the narrow hand sections can be seen in the top and bottom views.

The Figure 3-2 model was created with the broad part of the hand facing up and down. The palm can be seen in the bottom view and the top of the hand with the knuckles is visible in the top view.

Although modeling a character with the arms outstretched is often the easiest method, this method is not conducive to deforming the arms with bones. Since the most natural position for the arms is by the sides of the body, the bones that rotate the arms will have to be revolved quite a distance to get them there. This often creates

garden hose. They might also offer muscle flexing when a bone is rotated. Limited range might be another option to prevent a bone from exerting influence beyond its locality. There are many other alternatives that your software may offer. It is best to read the manual and perform your own experiments.

If you followed the instructions in the last chapter, you should have a model with its arms outstretched like the ones in Figure 3-1 or 3-2. The one in Figure 3-1 was posed so that the wide part of the hand faced forward in the front view. The open palm of the

Fig. 3-3 Bending the model in preparation for adding a skeleton.

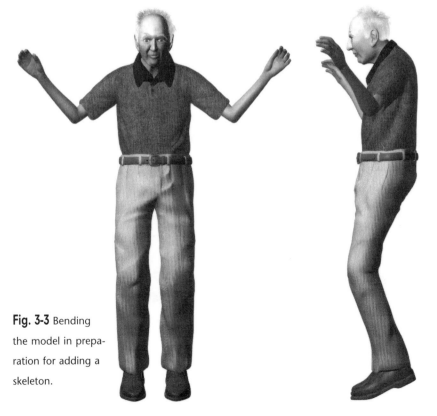

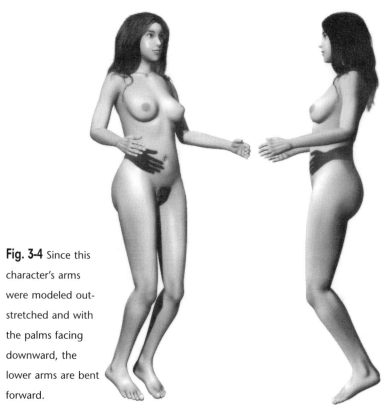

Fig. 3-4 Since this character's arms were modeled outstretched and with the palms facing downward, the lower arms are bent forward.

the problems of crimping and elbow distortion. It is easier to get fewer aberrations by straightening the arm with bones rather than trying to bend the lower arms forward with bones. Before adding bones, the legs are also bent forward while the lower legs are turned backwards.

Since the character from Figure 3-2 was modeled with the palms facing down, it appears a little different than the first model. Bending the lower arms at the elbow makes them come forward instead of up like the other figure's arms (Figure 3-4).

unwanted topographies in the armpit area. Bending the lower arm forward 45 degrees can also create undesirable distortions of the elbow, as well as crimping at the front of the elbow joint. Since the legs were modeled straight, bending the lower legs can cause the knees to stick out too much and also bring about pinching behind the knee joints.

In order to reduce many of these problems, you might want to pose your character in a manner that will create less distortion when the bones are activated. Figure 3-3 illustrates the first model from Figure 3-1. The arms are bent down halfway and the lower arms are turned forward. Since most arm movements do not go beyond the original modeled outstretched pose, it makes sense to place them halfway between there and the sides of the body. Bending the lower arms forward eliminates

Fig. 3-5 The skeleton inside the bent female model. The parent bone at the groin is the first bone created, followed by the hip bones, the upper leg bones, and so on.

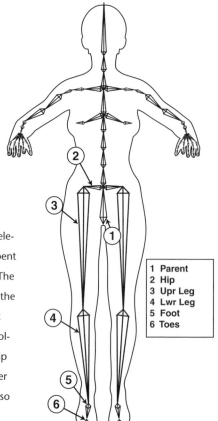

1 Parent
2 Hip
3 Upr Leg
4 Lwr Leg
5 Foot
6 Toes

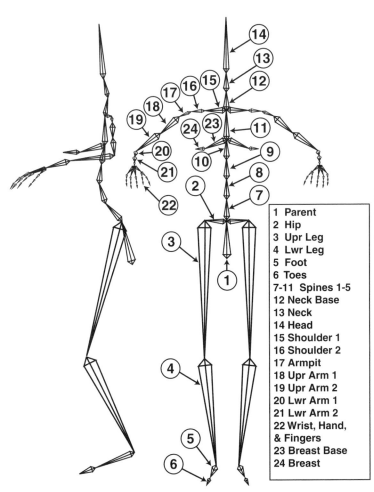

1	Parent
2	Hip
3	Upr Leg
4	Lwr Leg
5	Foot
6	Toes
7-11	Spines 1-5
12	Neck Base
13	Neck
14	Head
15	Shoulder 1
16	Shoulder 2
17	Armpit
18	Upr Arm 1
19	Upr Arm 2
20	Lwr Arm 1
21	Lwr Arm 2
22	Wrist, Hand, & Fingers
23	Breast Base
24	Breast

Fig. 3-6 Two views showing the order that all the bones were created in.

Fig. 3-7 A close-up view of the bones in the hand. The wrist bone is the parent of the hand, thumb, and finger bones.

Setting Up a Basic Skeletal Structure

There are many ways one can set up a skeleton. The method outlined here is one that works quite well. All animation software packages utilize different systems for creating skeletons. Rather than trying to write about every single one, the following instructions are in general terms that should work for most 3D animation software. You should be able to apply these directions by utilizing your own software's commands and procedures.

All the bones are child bones of a parent bone located at the groin area. This will be the bone that you draw first (Figure 3-5). If your software utilizes layers, create your bones in a separate layer from the model. Make the model visible underneath the layer with the bones. When you add the first bone, make the pointed end face up in the front view. Check the location of the bone in your various view windows.

The second bone is the child bone from the parent bone. The third bone is the upper leg bone, followed by the lower leg bone. Use Figure 3-5 as a guide for creating the first six bones. Rather than repeating the same procedure for the other leg, you can just mirror duplicate the bones, starting with the hip and ending with the toe bone. Use your hierarchical skeleton editor, such as a skeleton tree, to place the mirrored bones under the parent bone.

Figure 3-6 illustrates the rest of the bones located in the upper part of the body. The numbers correspond to the order that the bones are created. The breast bones (23 and 24) are only used in a

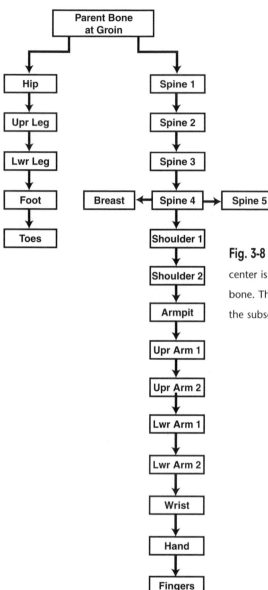

female character, for jiggling breasts. The arms and shoulders contain many bones since they help regulate the armpit and elbow areas. Users that work with software that does not utilize a muscle skeletal system often have problems getting the armpit section to look right during arm movements.

The bones in the hand can be seen in Figure 3-7. The hierarchy starts at the wrist bone. It controls the movement of the hand. There are five long

Fig. 3-8 A two-legged skeleton hierarchy. The center is located at the groin with the parent bone. The arrows point from the parent to all the subsequent child bones.

bones in the hand that lead to the beginning of the thumb and each finger. The thumb only needs two bones since the one in the hand leading to them controls the overall thumb movement. Each finger has three bones corresponding to its joints.

When you finish one arm and the hand, mirror duplicate it. In the hierarchical skeleton editor, place the mirrored arm and hand bones under the spine 5 bone.

In order to get a clearer idea of this skeletal system, refer to Figure 3-8. It illustrates how the parent bone sits on the top of the hierarchy. The spine and hip bones branch off from it in separate directions. The shoulder bones diverge from the spine to end at the fingers, while the neck and head bones separate toward a different destination.

Assigning Specific Vertices to Bones

Most 3D software that is meant for character animation has a method for assigning points on the model to specified bones. These vertices can

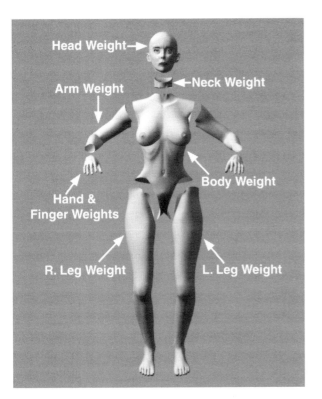

Head Weight →

Arm Weight

← Neck Weight

Body Weight

Hand &
Finger Weights

R. Leg Weight

L. Leg Weight

Fig. 3-9 Weight maps define the areas of the body that will be deformed by specific bones. Counting the finger, thumb, and hand bones, there are thirteen weight maps in total.

even be weighed so that one can assign a percentage weight to each point to indicate how much each section of the model should be affected by movement, rotation, or scaling. When the cluster of points is transformed, the mesh reacts according to the percentages specified. All of this depends on the amount of weight assigned to each. For example, a part of the model with points weighing zero will react slower to changes than other points with a weight value of one.

One simple technique for assigning weight maps that correspond to specific bones is to select different parts of the model by their numbers of polygons and naming each part's weight map. Figure 3-9 shows a body that is split into different

weight sections. Each piece is shown apart from the others so that the weight maps are easier to visualize. Start assigning a weight map to the right leg by selecting all its polygons. Once you have named the right leg weight, hide it. Select the left leg and assign a weight to it, then hide that leg as well. Picking each part and hiding it after assigning a weight makes it easier to select the next section.

Some segments of the body, such as the arms, are far enough away from each other that it is unnecessary to assign separate weight names to each. It is highly unlikely that the right arm bone will affect the left arm. In contrast, the legs are close enough to each other so that the left leg bone can pull on the right leg or vice versa. Therefore, each leg has its own weight map.

The fingers and thumb on one hand are close enough to cause unwanted pulling. Each digit should have its own weight name, but the fingers on both hands can share the same weight since they are far away from each other. For example, the index finger weight can be assigned to the index fingers of both hands. Figure 3-10 shows the weight names that were designated to the hands.

Later, after the bones are activated, be sure to check your weight maps by rotating the arms and legs. Chances are you will have to subtract weights from certain parts of the model. Using a brush type of tool you can weaken the influence of certain bones by subtracting weights from the mesh. For example, the arm bone may have too much influence on the torso, causing undesirable pulling around the armpit area. The brush tool can then be set to subtract or erase some of the extra weight that spills over into the torso.

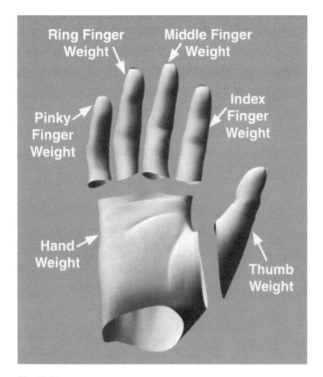

Fig. 3-10 The hand, finger, and thumb weight maps.

Controlling the Rotational Direction of Bones

Bones often do not act the way they should. When rotating them, it can sometimes be difficult to point them in the right direction. One may try to revolve a bone on its pitch (its tilt, or rotation around the x-axis) but, due to gimbal-lock or some other reason, it may go in a heading direction (its pan, or rotation around the y-axis).

Some of the more advanced 3D packages have methods of resolving these types of problems. They may utilize Quaternion Rotations rather than Euler angles that can cause gimbal-lock problems, or they may have a method for manually setting the ideal rotation of each bone. An example of this can be seen in Figure 3-11.

Editing the skeleton can bring up a visual representation of the bone direction. These are sometimes referred to as bone up-tags. In the example

of Figure 3-11, a smaller circle emanates from a larger one. It can be compared to the moon circling the earth. By moving the smaller circle, one can align the bone's rotational axis. Figure 3-11 shows the direction of each bone. You can use it as a guide when editing them.

Assembling an Inverse Kinematics Hierarchy

Kinematics is a branch of mechanics concerned with motion, without reference to force or mass. In 3D computer animation, kinematics usually deals with linked objects. After setting up a series of linked bones, parents that rotate or move in a chain subsequently affect the positions of their child bones. If the lowest part of a chain, like a hand, is rotated, it has no effect on any other items in the hierarchy.

Inverse kinematics (IK) is a system whereby a chain of bones or other linked objects can be moved or rotated by changing the position of the last object in a hierarchy (or the goal object connected to it). It is the reverse of forward kinematics (FK). With IK, moving the hand affects all the other parts joined to it.

Software companies implement skeletons and IK in a number of ways. The procedures for utilizing IK may differ, but the manner in which IK is used to accomplish certain objectives might be applicable to your software.

When applying IK, goal objects are often used to move the bones. Nulls, which do not render, are often used for goal objects. When a bone near the end of a hierarchy, such as the ankle bone, has a null as its goal object, moving that null propels the entire leg. The effects work themselves through the entire chain until a bone designated as unaffected by IK stops them. When you have goal objects, the bones will always try to point to them.

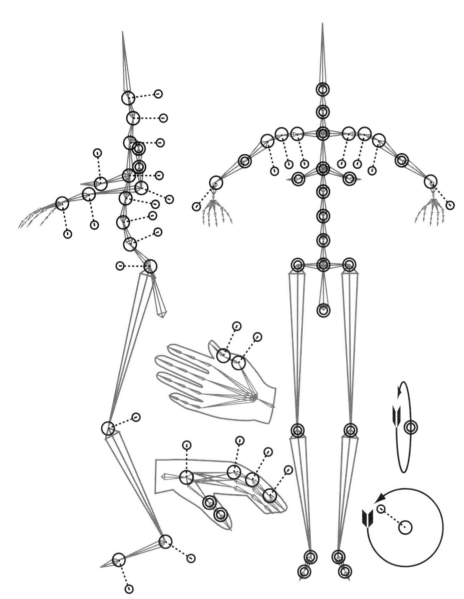

Fig. 3-11 Orienting the bones along the correct rotational axes. The bone up-tags indicate the direction of the bones' natural rotations. The smaller circle can be compared to a satellite circling a larger body (the larger circle). Some software packages allow one to manipulate the smaller circle toward the direction of the desired rotation.

An IK chain can have several goal objects. This is useful when you want to have more control over the object being deformed. One goal moves the bones, while the other is useful for making small adjustments. Usually, the second goal that adjusts the bones is parented to the first goal object. For example, the goal object at the elbow is parented to the goal object at the wrist, the goal object at

the neck is parented to the goal object at the spine, and the goal object at the ankle is parented to the goal object at the toe tip.

IK is not as precise as FK because all the movements on a chain of bones are compressed into a few goal objects. This means you could have two goal objects controlling six or more bones. Obviously, rotating each of those bones indivi-

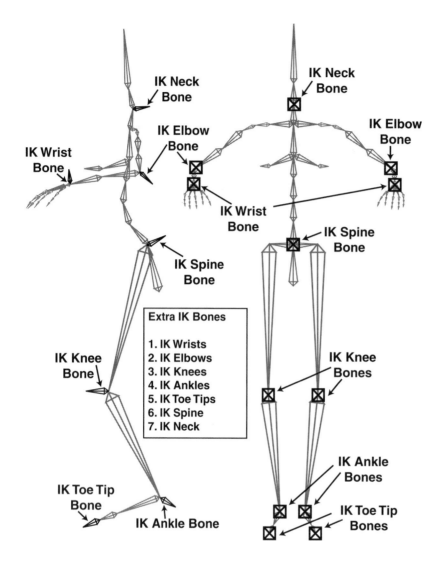

IK Neck Bone

IK Elbow Bone

IK Wrist Bone

IK Neck Bone

IK Elbow Bone

IK Wrist Bone

IK Spine Bone

IK Spine Bone

Extra IK Bones

1. IK Wrists
2. IK Elbows
3. IK Knees
4. IK Ankles
5. IK Toe Tips
6. IK Spine
7. IK Neck

IK Knee Bone

IK Knee Bones

IK Toe Tip Bone

IK Ankle Bone

IK Ankle Bones

IK Toe Tip Bones

Fig. 3-12 Step 1. Twelve extra IK bones that have no strength are created from their parent bones. These bones act as placeholders for the IK goal objects.

come the limitations of both IK and FK is to use a mixture of both. The skeleton could be set up to use mostly IK for the arm, spine, and leg movements, and FK for more precise head, hands, and feet motions.

The arm could have an IK chain that starts at the armpit and ends at the wrist. This will take care of all the arm motions. Rather than creating twenty goal objects for just the fingers and thumb, it is easier to rotate them with FK or morph targets. Subtle shoulder movements, such as shrugging or pivoting back and forth during a walk, can also be accomplished with FK. Making the shoulder 2 and the wrist bones unaffected by IK stops the IK chain at those precise areas so that FK can take over (Figure 3-8).

The leg is also moved with an IK chain, starting at the upper leg bone and ending at the toe tip bone. The entire leg can be moved easily with a goal object at the ankle and adjusted with goal objects at the toe tip and knee. The hip bones are unaffected by IK. The foot and toe bones are controlled with both IK and FK. By selecting the option of controlling them with keyframes, they can be turned to adjust the orientation of the foot. The upper and lower leg bones are manipulated

dually with FK will give one more control than trying to manipulate them with the two goal objects. Unfortunately, FK slows down the animation process too much, so the tradeoff is to sacrifice some control for speed. One way to over-

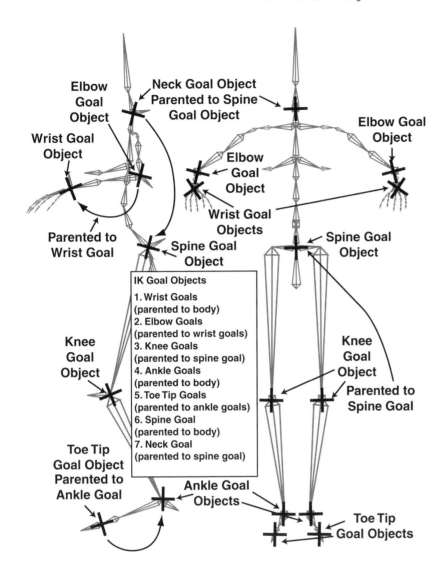

Elbow Goal Object

Neck Goal Object Parented to Spine Goal Object

Elbow Goal Object

Wrist Goal Object

Elbow Goal Object

Wrist Goal Objects

Parented to Wrist Goal

Spine Goal Object

Spine Goal Object

IK Goal Objects

1. Wrist Goals
(parented to body)
2. Elbow Goals
(parented to wrist goals)
3. Knee Goals
(parented to spine goal)
4. Ankle Goals
(parented to body)
5. Toe Tip Goals
(parented to ankle goals)
6. Spine Goal
(parented to body)
7. Neck Goal
(parented to spine goal)

Knee Goal Object

Knee Goal Object

Parented to Spine Goal

Toe Tip Goal Object Parented to Ankle Goal

Ankle Goal Objects

Toe Tip Goal Objects

Fig. 3-13 Step 2. IK goal objects are placed at the pivot points of the extra IK bones. The extra IK bones are set to have the handles as their goal objects. These IK goal objects, shown here as + signs, control the movements of any bones that have IK turned on.

advantage of rotating individual spine bones at sequential frame numbers. This gives the appearance of the spine bending like a whip, in which the motion works itself through the bones. All of this does take extra time and makes animating more complicated. With an IK-controlled spine that ends at the head bone, the more subtle head motions are manipulated with FK.

The parent is moved with FK so that the entire body can be moved up and down during motions such as walks and runs. While the parent bone goes up and down, the body is propelled forward.

The more advanced 3D software packages are quite flexible, allowing one to use any 3D object as a goal, as well as a mixture of IK and FK. If your software allows this, consider following these directions for a mixed IK and FK setup.

Step 1 (Figure 3-12). Create twelve extra IK

entirely with IK. Rotating the hips manually with FK prevents unwanted distortions in the groin area.

The entire spine, right above the parent bone at the pelvis and leading up to the head bone, can be controlled with two IK goal objects. Some may prefer to keep the entire spine unaffected by IK so that FK is used to rotate individual bones. Besides being more accurate, FK on the spine bones also has the

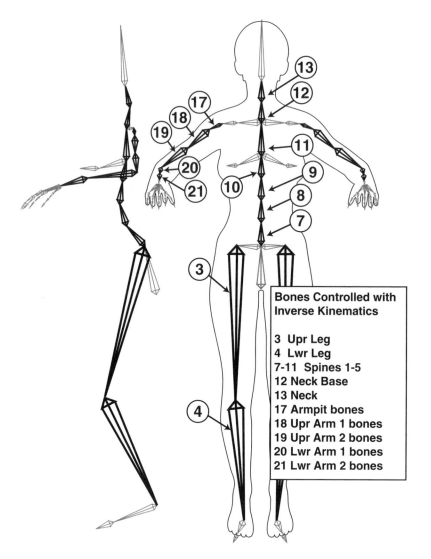

Arm 2 bones [Fig. 3-8])

Right and Left IK Elbow (children of the Upper Arm 2 bones [Fig. 3-8])

Right and Left IK Knees (children of the Upper Leg bones)

Right and Left IK Ankles (children of the Lower Leg bones)

Right and Left IK Toe Tips (children of the Toe bones)

A spine bone (child of the first spine, labeled #7 in Figure 3-14)

A neck bone (child of the neck base bone, labeled #12 in Figure 3-14)

Step 2 (Figure 3-13). Create twelve goal objects that will be used to move the skeleton. These goal objects could be nulls that do not render but are conspicuous during the animation process. You could also model them for easier visibility and then set them to be invisi-

Bones Controlled with Inverse Kinematics

3 Upr Leg
4 Lwr Leg
7-11 Spines 1-5
12 Neck Base
13 Neck
17 Armpit bones
18 Upr Arm 1 bones
19 Upr Arm 2 bones
20 Lwr Arm 1 bones
21 Lwr Arm 2 bones

Fig. 3-14 Step 4. The selected bones (darker and heavier lines) have inverse kinematics turned on. These are the bones that are manipulated with IK goal objects. The foot and toe bones can be controlled with both IK and FK.

bones that have no strength but will have specific goal objects assigned to them. These IK bones can have short rest lengths since they are only used as placeholders for the IK goal objects. The additional IK bones can be named:

Right and Left IK Wrists (children of the Lower

ble to the camera. Each goal object is moved to its corresponding extra IK bone. Place the goal objects so that their pivot points are in the same spot as the previously listed extra IK bones' pivot points.

Moving the body itself will not affect the feet if the goal objects at the toe tips are not parented to the body. The feet will remain anchored in the same spot while the motion of the body moves forward. This can be very useful when animating a walk. Since this is the most common movement, it helps tremendously to have the ability to anchor

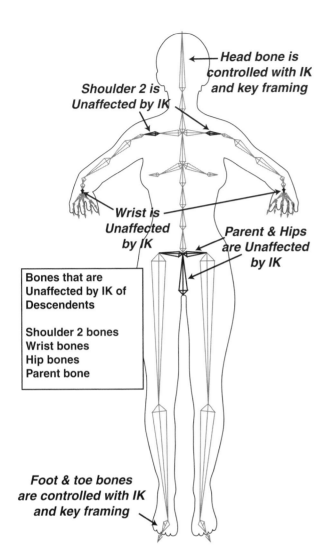

Head bone is controlled with IK and key framing

Shoulder 2 is Unaffected by IK

Wrist is Unaffected by IK

Parent & Hips are Unaffected by IK

Bones that are Unaffected by IK of Descendents

Shoulder 2 bones
Wrist bones
Hip bones
Parent bone

Foot & toe bones are controlled with IK and key framing

Fig. 3-15 Step 5. The bones that are set to be unaffected by IK. These bones and the head, feet, toe, and hand bones are manipulated with forward kinematics.

the feet to the ground. The goal objects at the ankles takes care of this. The rest of the goal objects are parented to something so that they move with the body. The goal objects and the manner in which they are parented are:

Right and Left Wrist Goal Objects (parented to the body).

Right and Left Elbow Goal Objects (parented to the Wrist Handles).

Right and Left Toe Tip Goal Objects (parented to the ankle goal objects).

Right and Left Ankle Goal Objects (not parented, so that the feet will stick to the ground or parented to the body to move with it).

Right and Left Knee Goal Objects (parented to the spine goal object).

Spine Goal Object (parented to the body).

Neck Goal Object (parented to the spine goal).

Step 3. Set the motion options for each of the twelve extra IK bones and turn on full-time IK for them. The twelve extra IK bones and their corresponding goal objects are:

Right and Left IK Wrists - goal objects - Right and Left Wrist Handles

Right and Left IK Elbows - goal objects - Right and Left Elbow Handles

Right and Left IK Toe Tips - goal objects - Right and Left Toe Tip Handles

Right and Left IK Ankles - goal objects - Right and Left Ankle Handles

Right and Left IK Knees - goal objects - Right and Left Knee Handles

Spine - goal object - Spine Handle

Neck - goal object - Neck Handle

Step 4. (Figure 3-14) In order for IK to work you will need to specify which bones are to be moved by the IK goal objects. Set the following bones to have inverse kinematics:

Right and Left Armpit bones

Right and Left Upper Arm 1 bones (Fig. 3-8)

Right and Left Upper Arm 2 bones (Fig. 3-8)

Right and Left Lower Arm 1 bones (Fig. 3-8)

Right and Left Lower Arm 2 bones (Fig. 3-8)

Right and Left Upper Leg bones

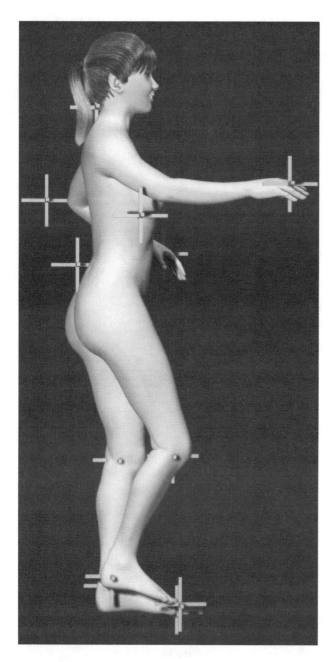

Fig. 3-16 A figure controlled with IK goal objects. Normally, the goals do not render. Mixing IK with FK makes it easy to move the figure fluidly with IK while still retaining the precision of FK. Animation with IK becomes similar to puppetry.

Right and Left Lower Leg bones

Spine bones 1–6 and the neck bone

Step 5. (Figure 3-15) The IK chains have to be limited to certain areas by making specific bones unaffected by the IK of descendants. It is at these points that IK ends and FK takes over. Set the following bones to be unaffected by the IK of descendants:

Right and Left Shoulder 2 bones

Right and Left Wrist bones

Right and Left Hip bones

Parent bone

The following bones are not set for IK. By leaving them controlled through key framing, you can rotate them individually for subtle adjustments.

Head bone

Parent bone

Hip bones

Feet bones

Toe bones

Shoulder bones

Wrist, Hand, Thumb, and Finger bones

Figure 3-16 depicts a female model with this type of IK setup. The goals are nulls that normally do not render with the model. In this case they were meant to be seen, but they could be set to be invisible to the camera.

If you decide to use this kind of IK setup, you should not see any distortion in your character's body. Some IK systems parent goal objects to bones. This kind of setup can cause severe distortion in the model. The arm could become stretched or squashed. This may be all right for cartoon characters that exhibit a lot of squash and stretch, but it may not work well for human models or any other ones displaying some semblance of realism.

Animating Without a Skeleton

Segmented character animation does not require a skeleton. When animating a puppet, mannequin, dummy, or robot, you can move and rotate the separate parts themselves. Unlike humans, animals, or creatures, the segmented model is not seamless at the joints, and therefore does not need a hidden skeleton to bend the sections (Figure 3-17).

Some software packages require that each segment be placed in its own separate layer. Other software has the user string together the parts in a visual hierarchy like that seen in Figure 3-18. Setting each segment's pivot point guarantees that the individual parts will rotate around their correct joint positions. The mannequin in Figure 3-17 can be used as a guide for

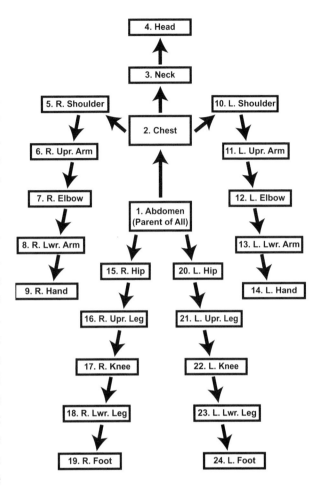

Fig. 3-18 The parenting order of each mannequin part. The abdomen is the parent of all. The chest is parented to the abdomen, the neck to the chest, the head to the neck, the shoulders to the chest, and so on.

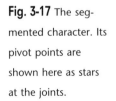

Fig. 3-17 The segmented character. Its pivot points are shown here as stars at the joints.

each point's placement. Every part must be hinged together in the right order. This is sometimes referred to as parenting: A child object is linked to a parent object.

Figure 3-18 shows the body's hierarchy, in which each segment of the mannequin is linked to

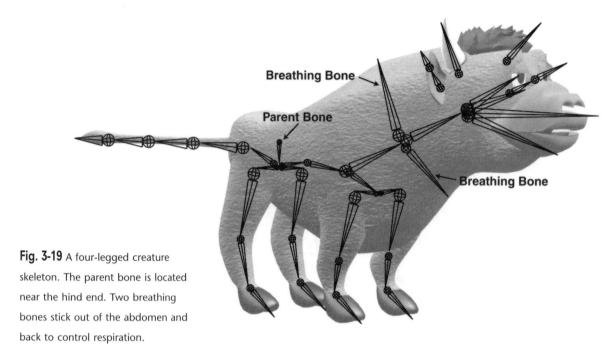

Fig. 3-19 A four-legged creature skeleton. The parent bone is located near the hind end. Two breathing bones stick out of the abdomen and back to control respiration.

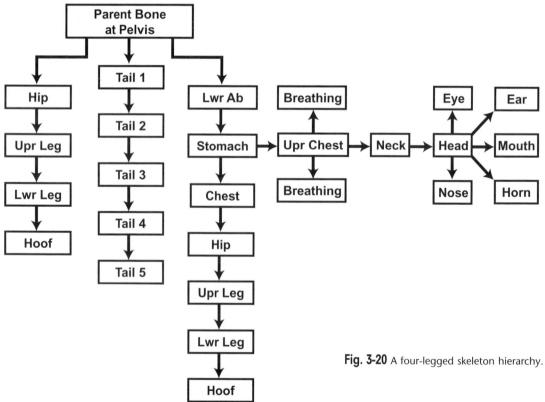

Fig. 3-20 A four-legged skeleton hierarchy.

another. The arrows point in the direction of the child objects. The numbers correspond to the order in which each section is linked. For example, the right hip is parented to the abdomen, then the right upper leg is parented to the hip, followed by the right knee, which is in turn parented to the right upper leg, and so on. Since the abdomen is the center of the body, it is designated as the parent to all. To translate all of the parts at the same time, you simply move the abdomen.

When a part is rotated, the linked sections will follow. Think of the segmented character as an exoskeleton. Its behavior is the same as the previously set up skeleton. The segments should rotate around their determined pivot points. Since the hierarchical setup is similar to a skeleton, one could use the same IK setup discussed earlier.

Creating a Skeleton for a Four-legged Character

Figure 3-19 shows the skeleton for a four-legged character. In some ways, it is similar to a two-legged character's skeleton, except that you now have a tail and another set of feet instead of hands. The parent bone is located near the rear and has tail, hip, and lower abdomen bones joined to it in a lower hierarchical order. Depending on how much you want to bend the tail, you can add more bones for extra flexibility.

The hierarchical arrangement of a four-legged skeleton can be seen in Figure 3-20. Each arrow points to a lower order of child bone. Special bones are shown in the face for software that does not allow the assigning of vertices to specific bones. Their function is to stabilize and keep other bones from distorting parts of the head. Most high-end 3D software implements weight maps, so it is not necessary to add these extra bones.

Once you have become familiar with the way your software creates skeletons, you can experiment with some of the techniques in this chapter. You can model your own human or two-legged character following the directions in chapters 1, 2, 6, and 7.

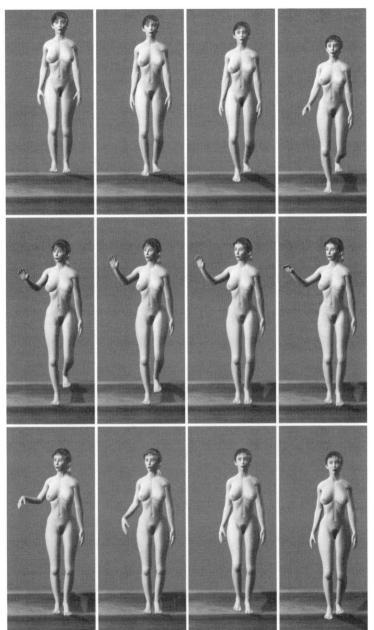

CHAPTER 4

Basic 3D Animation

Animation is a process in which the circumstances and aspects of a scene change over time. Events in 3D animation are created and controlled by key scenes. This is similar to traditional 2D cell animation, where the animator designs the important frames and a junior animator draws the intervening frames that act as transitions between the key frames. This process is referred to as keyframe animation.

Most animation software has a visible timeline along which special keyframes are set. If an object is placed in a special location at frame 0 and then moved at frame 10 to another location, the animation shows it moving from point A to point B within the ten frames. Objects or events that are acted upon at a certain frame usually have to be keyframed in order to register the change. For example, in Maya, one of the ways in which keyframes are set is by pressing "s" for "Set Key." You can also select "Set Key" from the Animate menu. In LightWave 3D, you set keyframes by pressing "Enter" on the keyboard or pressing the "Create Key" button and specifying the frame at which the motion key is set.

Not all events have to be keyframed to change. When painting weights on a surface of an object and then rotating the model, the difference in weights makes the object twist. Although the object's rotational values were keyframed, the twisting motion occurs automatically due to the dynamic nature of weights. There are many other dynamics, like wind, water, fire, gravity, smoke, and rain, that simulate real-world physics without having to be keyframed. An animator simply specifies the characteristics and actions of the object, and the software figures out how to animate it.

This chapter focuses on creating very simple keyframe animations. Before starting the anima-

tion process, you will need to set up the camera(s), lights, and the character with IK, then test the accuracy of the weight maps.

It is very difficult to discuss animation without referring to the principles of animation that were formulated by the Disney animators in the 1930s. This group of twelve principles forms the foundation of all animation. It makes no difference whether you are animating 2D or 3D characters. These principles are the underlying basis of all successful character animation. Chapter 12 describes these principles in detail. This chapter will mention a few of them as they relate to specific examples.

In addition to examining methods of animation, this chapter will also cover ways of editing animations. The companion CD-ROM contains example animations that serve as illustrations for the various ideas discussed throughout the chapter. These can be found in the chapter 4 folder.

Setting Up the Camera(s)

Normally, the first step to creating an animation is to set up the camera and its properties. After the view through the camera has been established, one can proceed to lighting and posing the figure.

Before you place the camera, set the zoom and lens focal length. This will establish the field of view. A wide-angle lens has a larger field of view, while a longer lens, such as a 70 mm, will have a narrower field of view but will not distort the character as much as a wide-angle lens. Higher zoom factors create longer lenses. Chapter 14 contains more detailed information about camera techniques and properties.

Utilizing a four-viewport layout is an excellent way of positioning the camera(s). With the four-

Fig. 4-1 These four views show the placement of the camera at frame 0.

viewport layout, one can look at the scene through the camera in one window while moving and rotating it around in the other three viewports (Figure 4-1). The top view allows one to place the camera either to the front, left, right, or back of the subject matter. The side views can then be used to place camera at eye level, or above or below the observed object. The camera can also be moved or rotated in the camera view. After establishing the camera viewpoint, keyframe it (create a motion key) at frame 0 or 1.

Placing the Lights

One of the more challenging endeavors involves setting up the lights. This is something many novice animators are unwilling to spend the time on, or else they lack the knowledge of how to do

it. They are usually quite surprised to see the improvement that the right kind of lighting can bring to a scene.

A character should have its own set of lights that do not affect anything else in a scene. An exception to this is when you designate a certain light(s) to cast shadows. These shadow lights have to act upon the environment, or your character would not be able to cast shadows on the floor, walls, and other objects.

Apart from the character's own lights, the surroundings have their lights too. It is not unusual to have thirty or more lights illuminating an interior. These lights are excluded from affecting the character(s).

Spotlights are the most flexible of all the lights and offer the greatest amount of control. Therefore, use them to illuminate your performers

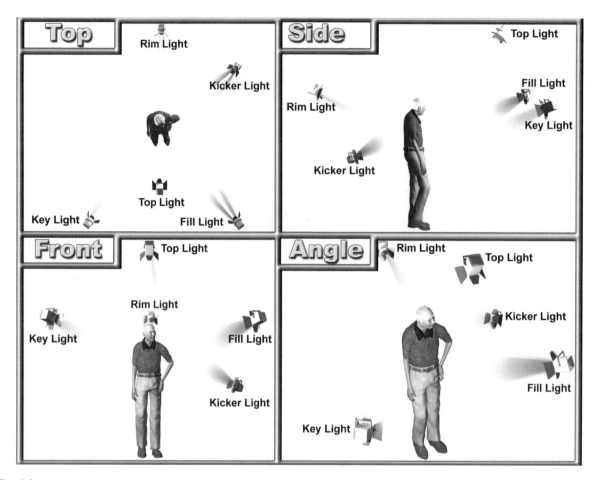

Fig. 4-2 Four views showing the position of the lights at frame 0.

and most of your scene. After you create the first light, parent it to a null object or to your character. Set its light property by giving it a color, a light intensity, and an intensity falloff. In the real world it is very difficult to find pure white light, so assign a color value to yours. You also need to establish its intensity or brightness. The intensity falloff mimics real-world lighting, which becomes weaker after a certain distance.

Rather than creating new lights and going through the process of parenting as well as setting their light properties, simply clone the original light. Place these duplicate lights around your sub-

ject and then adjust their individual light properties. Since these are all clones of the original light, they will automatically be parented to the same null or your character. Moving and rotating all the lights can be accomplished by manipulating the light null.

Figure 4-2 depicts a typical lighting setup. Using a four-viewport layout, one starts in the top view to move and rotate each light. By making one of the view windows the light view as seen through the light itself, one can see exactly what the selected light is pointing at. Even though chapter 9 discusses lighting in greater detail, a brief description of each light around the subject is listed here.

Key light: This is the main light and is usually the brightest. Its color is normally light yellow or one of the warmer colors from the color spectrum. This is the light that commonly casts a shadow. Place the key light in front of and to the side of the subject that you want illuminated the most.

Fill light: This is used to fill in the shadow side of the digital actor. It can be the complimentary color of the key light, or blue. A fill light should have a cool color assigned to it. Its light intensity is much less than that of the key light. Place the fill light to the opposite side of the key light.

Rim light: Sometimes artists prefer to have their characters stand out from the background. By placing a rim light behind and pointing at the back of the subject, you can make a kind of halo or outline of light show up along the object's edges. This makes the individual more distinct from the background. This light can be any color, but it is usually a warm one like the key light.

Kicker light: This light points at the key light to outline a part of the object. It is placed to the side and back of the person at a low level, pointing up. One can be quite creative when choosing a color for the kicker light.

Top light: Even though this light is placed above the subject, it helps to move it slightly forward in front of the subject, so that the face can be illuminated in a clear-cut manner. The top light is usually a warm color such as light yellow. Sometimes, the top light is also set to cast a shadow.

Contact lights: These are extra lights that can be placed above the feet to cast a shadow on the ground. They are composed of a positive and a negative light of equal but opposite intensity. By turning on cast shadows on the positive light

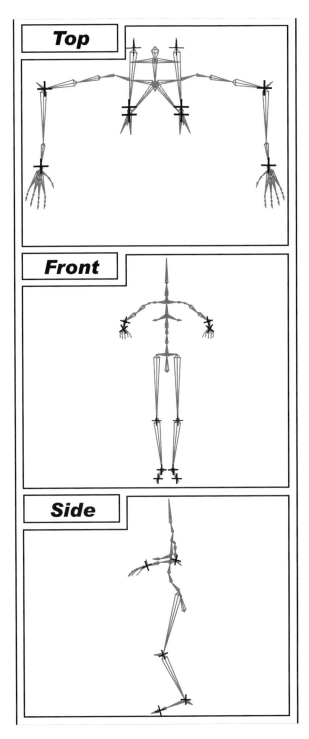

Fig. 4-3 Three views of the IK character. The legs and arms will have to be straightened.

and turning off cast shadows on the negative light, shadows are cast without adding any extra illumination.

After establishing your lights, you will need to make a number of renderings. Since you are only trying to see how the lights affect the person and the camera view, you do not need to make high-quality renderings with antialiasing on. Some software packages or plug-ins allow one to see real-time previews of the actual rendered scene. This kind of interactivity will speed up the lighting process tremendously.

Posing the Character

Once you have finished setting up the camera and lights, it is time to pose the subject. After activating its bones and rigging its inverse kinematics system (see chapter 3), move the goal objects to straighten the bent legs and arms (Figure 4-3).

An important step before animating the figure is the process of testing various deformations. Weight maps that control the manner in which bones deform the mesh may need to be adjusted.

Figure 4-4 shows the effect of a bad weight map around the armpit. Notice the way in which this area becomes misshapen from the faulty weight map's influences. By erasing the extraneous weight map impingement on the torso, you can raise the arm without pulling the torso mesh (Figure 4-5). Figure 4-6 illustrates the same model after correcting the weight map problem. The arm can be raised without deforming the torso.

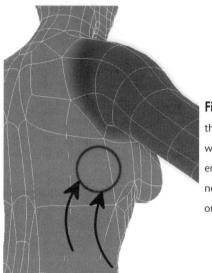

Fig. 4-5 Correcting the faulty weightmap by erasing the extraneous weightmap on the torso.

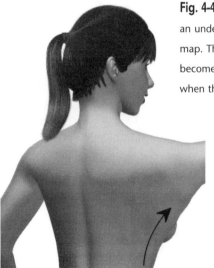

Fig. 4-4 The effects of an undesirable weight map. The armpit becomes distorted when the arm is lifted.

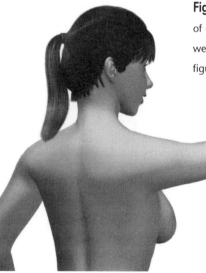

Fig. 4-6 The result of correcting the weightmap on the figure.

Sometimes a distorted mesh can be the result of neglecting to assign a bone weight map to the corresponding part of the object. If a bone does not have any weight map assigned to it, then problems will most like occur.

If you experience other problems that are not caused by weight maps, you will have to use your software's resources to correct them. Some software programs have the option of setting a bone's falloff, limiting its range, turning on joint compensation, adjusting its strength, and so on.

Consider turning off the strength of any extra bones, such as those used for IK goal objects. Some key areas to test and adjust are the joints located under the armpit, elbow, waist, and knee.

It is always a good idea to save the scene as a startup scene that can be used for other animations in the future. After it has been saved as a base scene, save it again under a different name containing the title of your animation.

One of the Twelve Animation Principles was called Solid Drawing. It meant that characters should have solid, three-dimensional drawing qualities. Disney's idea of a perfect animatable shape was one that had volume but still retained flexibility and strength without rigidity. This important principle is just as relevant today in 3D animation. A poorly modeled character will deform badly. No matter how great the animator's skills are, if the modeling is shoddy, it will ruin the animation.

Pose-to-Pose Animation

Disney's fourth principle of animation is called Straight-Ahead and Pose-to-Pose Action. The first means that the animator starts with one pose and then improvises the rest. Pose-to-Pose, on the other hand, does the opposite. Each pose is planned ahead of time. These prearranged poses can be in the form of either drawings or photos.

Beginning animators may want to use the pho-

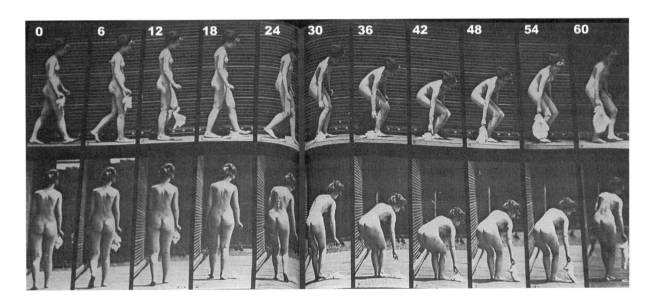

Fig. 4-7 A stop-motion sequence by Eadweard Muybridge. The numbers indicate the keyframes for each pose.

tographic references created by the great pioneering photographer Eadweard Muybridge (Figure 4-7). Some of these can be found in the chapter 4 folder of the CD-ROM.

A study of character animation would be painfully incomplete without considering the work of Muybridge. In his photographic volumes Human and Animal Locomotion (Dover Publications), he provided an invaluable resource for animators.

Muybridge introduced stop-motion sequences in the nineteenth century. He designed three batteries of cameras, with twelve lenses for each battery. The three batteries were placed at right angles to each other. All were focused on one subject. On each of the three twelve-lens cameras, every lens was exposed for a fraction of a second in succeeding order. When a model was photographed, thirty-six negatives were obtained. Each one contained a different stage of action from three different views.

During his many slide lectures, Muybridge demonstrated the fallacy of animal poses in ancient and modern art. He often shocked his audience by revealing their true movements in his stop-motion photographs. It was shown that even pigs showed grace and agility when they were galloping.

The photographs directly influenced famous artists like Eakins, Remington, Degas, and Duchamp. The impact of his work on artists, art students, animators, and illustrators can hardly be overstated. To this day, no body of work documenting human and animal movements equals that of Human and Animal Locomotion.

One other benefit found in the third volume of Human and Animal Locomotion is Muybridge's timing charts. These are the travel records of each photographed subject. You can match the time to the specific plate and know how fast the person or animal was moving. Once you have located the time, use the formula in Figure 4-8 to calculate the frame rate for each image.

Animating in Stages

One of the most puzzling aspects about animation is trying to figure out when to move each part of a body. Humanoid characters are made up of many components, each of which is moved at various times. Beginning animators often find it difficult to sort through the complexity of animating so many constituents.

The entire process can be simplified by animating in stages. Rather than trying to move every part at the same time, it is much easier to concentrate on only several sections. Once those components are animated, another segment of the figure is animated. After completing each part, the animator returns to the beginning frame to move another portion. These animation stages can be performed in this order and viewed as a movie in the chapter 4 folder of the CD-ROM (Chapter 4 > Animating In Stages Movies > Animating In Stages.mov).

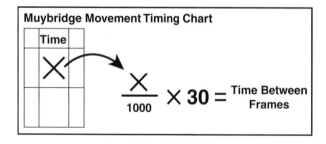

Fig. 4-8 Using Muybridge's timing charts, you can apply this formula to find out the frame rates for all his photographed movements. The x stands for the time that he recorded in his charts.

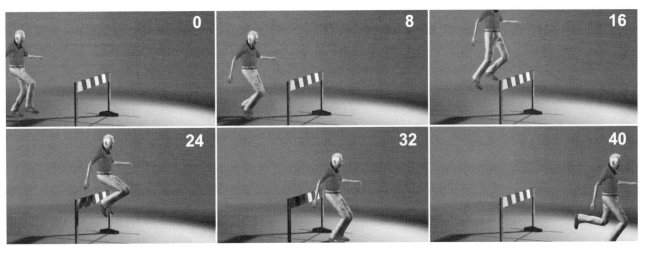

Fig. 4-9 Stage 1. Moving only the legs and the body.

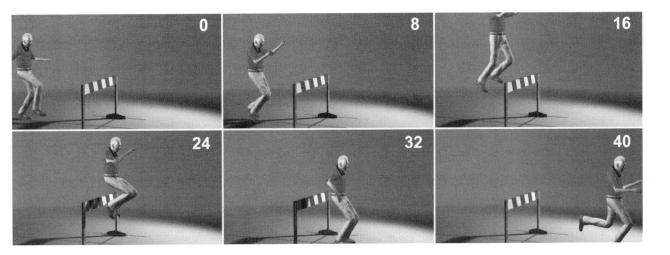

Fig. 4-10 Stage 2. Moving only the arms.

Move the legs and the body (Figure 4-9). This is usually the hardest part, but it establishes the pace of the animation. It is also the primary action of most animations.

Animate the arm movements (Figure 4-10). The activities of the arms are considered Secondary Actions, another one of the Twelve Principles of Animation. They support the main action and should be animated at different keyframes than the ones for the legs and body. If every movement

is keyframed at the same time, the actions will look too mechanical. This falls under the category of Follow-Through and Overlapping Action, one more of the Twelve Principles.

Rotate the spine, neck, and head (Figure 4-11). After completing the previous motions, start again at the first frame and animate the spine, neck, and head. If you use IK on the spine, you can simply move the goal object located at the base of the neck. If you use FK, individual bones are

77

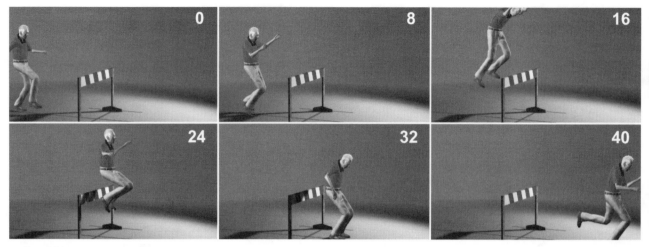

Fig. 4-11 Stage 3. Rotating the head, neck, and spine.

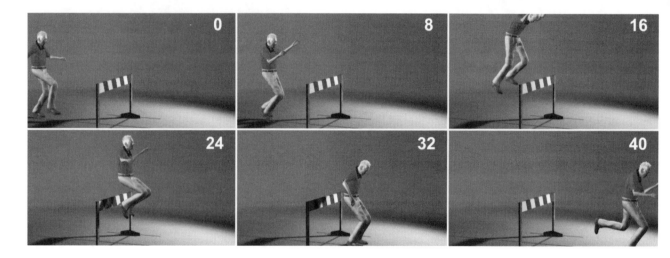

Fig. 4-12 Stage 4. Bending the fingers.

rotated. FK can be more precise and you can employ Follow-Through and Overlapping Action because each component—spine, neck, and head—rotates at different keyframes. One starts while another is already rotating. The section about shifting keys at the end of this chapter discusses an efficient method for speeding up this process. Rotating the spine will affect the arms. So, some may prefer to do the spine before the arms.

Bend the fingers (Figure 4-12). To some, moving the fingers may seem excessive, but the hands and fingers convey a great amount of information about a character's intentions. If the fingers are stiff throughout the action, the figure will appear unnatural. Fingers and thumbs can be rotated in a number of ways. One can put goal objects at the end of each finger and thumb. Using IK, the goal objects are moved to bend the fingers and thumbs.

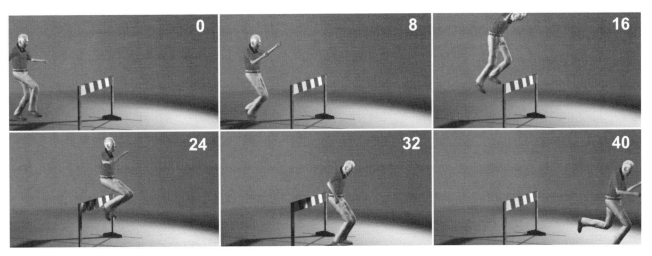

Fig. 4-13 Stage 5. Changing the facial expressions.

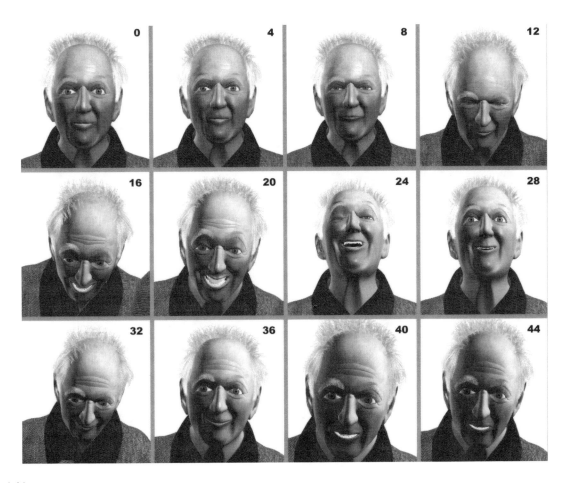

Fig. 4-14 Stage 5. A close-up view of the changing facial expressions.

If you are rotating bones with FK, bend the digits and save each motion file. In the future, whenever you need to bend a part of the hand, load the motion files for that particular finger or thumb. To straighten a finger(s), reset the bone(s) to the original extended positions. Morph targets for each finger can also be created. Each digit is bent in the modeling part of the program and saved as a separate morph target. During animation, one can use sliders to open and close the hand. Chapter 11 discusses morph targets in greater detail.

Change the facial expressions (Figure 4-13 and 4-14). The final pass is to go back and make facial expressions. The face exhibits more emotion than any other part of the body. One should always show facial expressions, even if it means just having the eyes blink and move.

Using a Graph Editor to Change an Animation

Most mid- to high-end programs have a graph editor. Its function is to estimate the values between keyframes as motion graphs or animation curves.

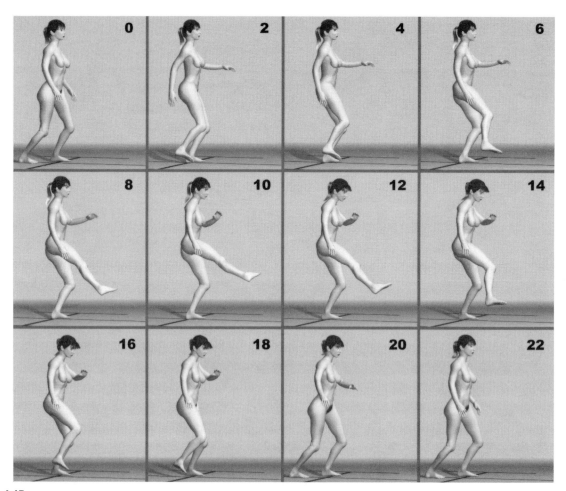

Fig. 4-15 Images from the low kick animation.

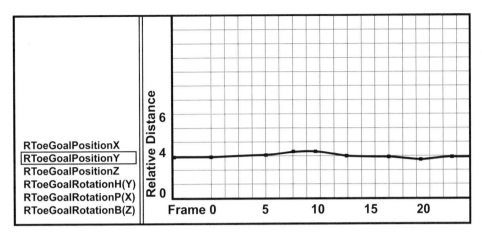

Fig. 4-16 The graph editor for the right toe goal object on the y-axis. The low kick has a small curve at frames 8 and 10.

They provide a visual representation of your object's activity. Editing animation curves can be a powerful tool for altering your animation's behavior.

The following section of this chapter discusses how to use the graph editor to exaggerate motions, repair flaws, and accentuate actions. Graph editors contain a set of robust tools that animators should not ignore.

Exaggerating Motions with the Graph Editor

In the chapter 4 folder of the CD-ROM, there is another folder named "Amplifying with Graph Editor Movies." The movie is named "Low&HighKick.mov," and it shows how altering the curve of a goal object can amplify the motion of the leg. Figure 4-15 depicts a female kicking low. The IK right toe goal object moves the leg up. Its position on the y-axis can be seen in the graph editor (Figure 4-16). Just before and at frame 10, the curve bulges up slightly, indicating the raising of the toe goal object.

Figure 4-17 depicts the same graph after altering it. The key positions of the goal object are raised in the graph editor at frames 8 and 10. This in turn affects the animation, as seen on the CD-

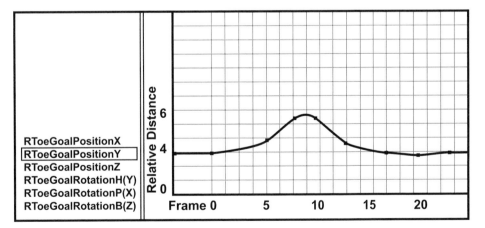

Fig. 4-17 Raising the right toe goal object's keyframes at 8 and 10 to increase its value on the y-axis. The higher curve results in a higher kick.

ROM and in Figure 4-18. It was not necessary to move the goal object itself. Rather, it was easier to go into the graph editor and move the points for that object up.

Expanding the curve of the graph editor made the animation more dynamic. This Principle of Animation is called Exaggeration. Without exaggeration, movements are often overlooked or appear unpersuasive.

Oftentimes, certain key motions are overlooked by viewers. Animators will then apply a motion hold. This means the movement is held for a number of frames before it is released. The graph in Figure 4-17 shows an example of a short motion hold. The goal object that raises the foot and leg is held in the same position at frames 8 and 10. When the goal object was keyframed at 8, it was also keyframed at 10. The identical keyframe at

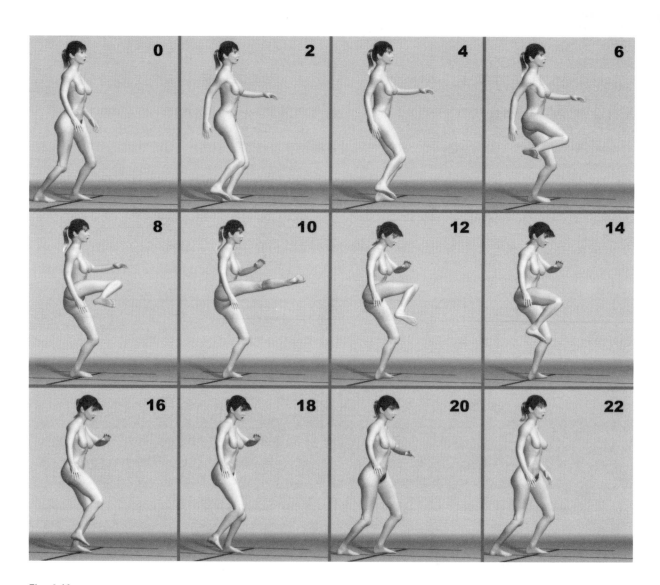

Fig. 4-18 Images from the high kick animation.

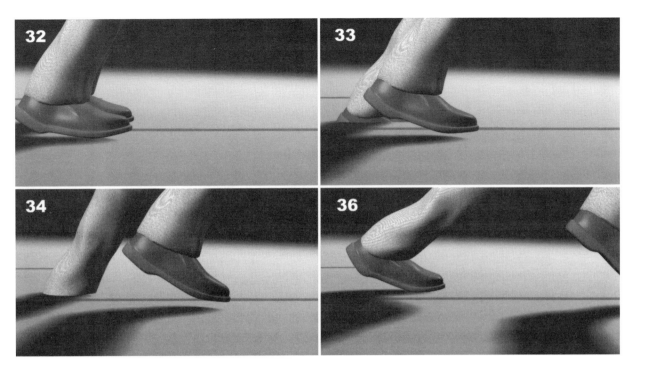

Fig. 4-19 The downward curve of two identical keyframes at frames 32 and 36 has the undesirable effect of a sinking foot.

10 held the leg in position for a fraction of a second longer than if it had been keyframed only once, at frame 8. A veteran animator knows when to apply a motion hold and when to let go of it. As you become more experienced, you will find yourself utilizing motion holds in practically every animation.

Correcting Flaws with the Graph Editor

The graph editor is sometimes the only tool that will work to correct certain imperfections in an animation. An example of this is when one is trying to keep a certain part, like a foot, in one spot. Figure 4-19 and the animations in the folder titled Straighten Curve Graph Editor Movies, located in the chapter 4 folder of the CD-ROM, show how a foot that is supposed to stay in place

slips below ground.

Even though the foot was keyframed twice in the same place at frames 32 and 36 (motion hold), it still slips down on the y-axis. The reason for this becomes evident when examining the graph editor

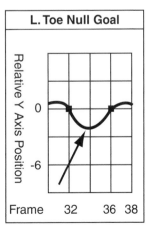

Fig. 4-20 The descending curve between frames 32 and 36 creates an unintended motion for the left foot.

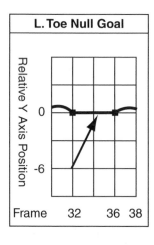

L. Toe Null Goal

Relative Y Axis Position

0

-6

Frame   32   36 38

Fig. 4-21 Setting the incoming curve at frame 36 to linear straighten it out.

cular system found in most mammals, motions normally occur in circular paths. While this is fine for most animations, it can pose a problem when one is trying to keep a certain portion of the figure from moving.

To correct this troublesome effect, one is forced to go into the graph editor to select the last frame at which the curve ends. This incoming curve is then set to linear, which in turn straightens the curve (Figure 4-21). Normally, the incoming curve has an arced spline. The effects of the straightened spline can be seen in Figure 4-22 and the animation on the CD-ROM. The foot no longer sinks into the ground.

Straightening a motion curve can also be applied to correcting facial animations. Figure 4-23 and the animation found in the folder titled Fixing Faces in Graph Editor Movies of the chapter 4 folder on the CD-ROM illustrate how a female

for the left toe goal object (Figure 4-20). Notice the downward curve between these two identical frames. This is because curves or arcs are built into animation programs to give a more natural look to most movements.

Arcs is another one of the Twelve Principles of Animation. It states that due to the skeletal/mus-

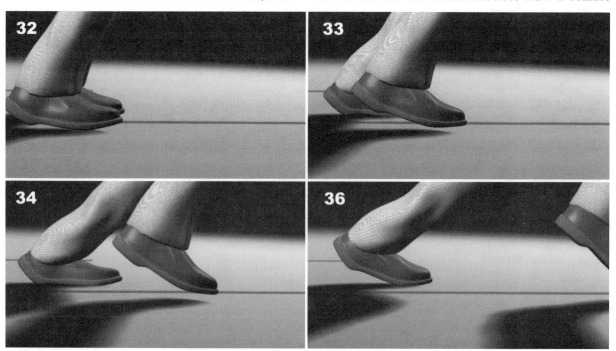

Fig. 4-22 After the curve is straightened, the foot stays in place.

Fig. 4-23 Images from the animation showing the open mouth smile beginning at frame 0.

modification starts at frame 0 and steadily grows to frame 10. Returning to the graph editor, an extra keyframe is added at frame 5 with a linear incoming curve (Figure 4-25). This has the effect of keeping the mouth from changing until frame 6. The motion hold for the mouth between frames 0 and 5 makes the facial expression more natural. The female turns her head slightly before breaking into a smile (Figure 4-26 and the movie on the CD-ROM).

Making Motions More Natural with the Graph Editor

The principle of animation named Follow-Through and Overlapping Action states that things do not come to a complete stop. If a character or one of its parts comes to a complete halt, it looks stiff and unnatural.

Figure 4-27 and the animation located in the

smile that occurs at frame 10 extends far too long from frame 0. When you are animating a change of facial expression which is to be completed by, for example, frame 10, the expression will automatically begin transforming at the previous keyframe, for example, frame 0. In this example, the face had not been animated before the smile, so the facial expression changes over the course of the entire animation. Of course, a smile normally does not last for a duration of 10 frames.

When examining the graph editor for the smile (Figure 4-24), it becomes apparent that the facial

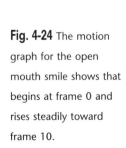

Fig. 4-24 The motion graph for the open mouth smile shows that begins at frame 0 and rises steadily toward frame 10.

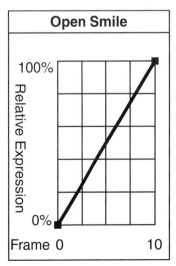

Open Smile

Relative Expression

100%

0%

Frame 0   10

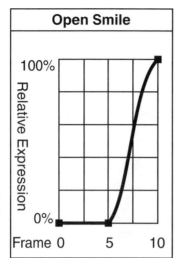

Open Smile

Fig. 4-25 Adding an extra keyframe at frame 5 and making the incoming curve linear. The open smile will now begin at frame 5 instead of at 0.

motion occurring at the end. This extra movement of the hand also works its way down the arm in a gradually decreasing gesture. This is also part of Follow-Through.

When you know that a gesture will stop, add an extra identical keyframe a few frames after. It will make the movement much more natural.

Editing the Timeline

Besides altering individual frames, most high-end 3D software allows one to change the entire timeline of a selected part or all items. Shifting keys

folder titled Adding Xtr Frame Movies found in the chapter 4 folder of the CD-ROM depict a female performing a knife-hand strike. The first part shows the hands coming to a dead stop. The second section of the animation illustrates the effect of adding the same keyframe for the hands (wrist goal objects and wrist bones) twice at the end. The graph editor (Figure 4-28) for the first animation shows how the motion curve stops at frame 15. The altered graph portrays an appended curve with an additional frame at 20. Frame 20 is identical to frame 15, and its incoming curve is bent down to give the hands and arms a little shaking motion.

You can test this subtle bounce by making a chopping motion in the air. Notice how your hand recoils a little. It is impossible to make this gesture without some

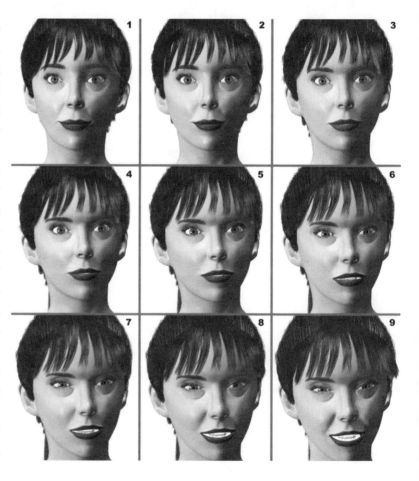

Fig. 4-26 Images from the corrected animation showing the open mouth smile beginning at frame 5.

86

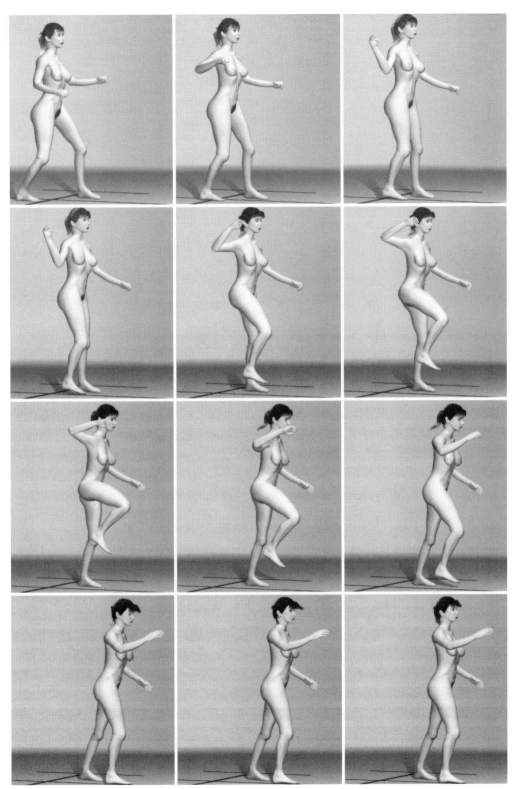

Fig. 4-27 The knife hand strike animation before editing it.

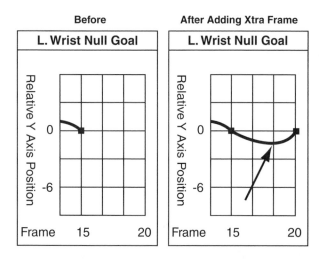

means that keyframes can be moved forward or backward along the time track. The range of values can be set with a property at the low frame and one at the high frame. Positive values move the action forward so the keyframes occur at a later time, while negative ones shift them backwards in time.

Scalng Keys entails extending or reducing either the length of all or just selected items. With low

Fig. 4-28 Before and after adding on a duplicate keyframe with a curve frame 20. This brings about a jiggle motion in the hand and arm.

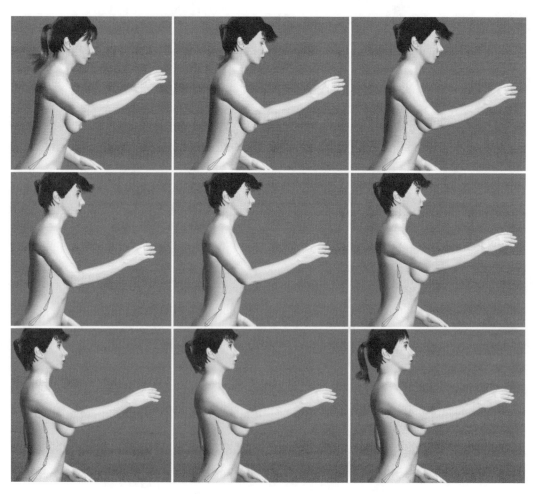

Fig. 4-29

Rotations of the spine bones. One follows another after shifting keys.

and high frame values, one can set the range of frames to be altered. Higher scale values broaden the timeline, thus slowing down the animation. To shorten the period of time and make events occur at a faster pace, scale percentages such as .5 will make a part or all of the animation twice as fast as before scaling keys.

Shifting Keys

Figure 4-29 and the animation movie in the shifting keys movies folder of the chapter 4 folder on the CD-ROM show how shifting keys can be applied to the spine. The curving action of the spine is an excellent example of Follow-Through and Overlapping Action. Rather than all the spine bones moving at once, they each follow one another. While one bone arrives at a stopping point, others are still in motion.

In order to get this whip-like effect on a forward kinematics spine, shift keys is applied after rotating each of the bones and keyframing them at the same frames. In the movie example found on the CD-ROM, all the spine bones began their default neutral positions at frame 10. Spine 2 was selected and in its shift keys box, the bone was shifted by one frame. Figure 4-30 shows this setting in the shift keys box. The effect of this was to move all the spine 2 bones one frame later along the time-line. Spine 1 began its rotation at frame 15. The

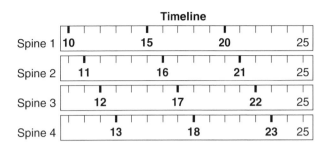

Fig. 4-31 The four spine bones and their individual timelines after shifting keys for spines 2, 3, and 4. The rotations are now successive.

spine 2 bone had it frames shifted to start its revolution at frame 16.

Figure 4-31 depicts the four spine bones and their corresponding timelines after each has had its keys shifted. Spine 3 had its keys shifted by 2 and spine 4 had a shift frames of 3. Shifting keys removed the tedium of trying to remember when to rotate one bone after another.

Scaling Keys

The animations in the folder titled Scaling Keys Movies found inside the chapter 4 folder of the CD-ROM and Figures 4-32 and 4-33 illustrate two views of an animation in which the motion of the female arm was altered by scaling its keys. The first part of the animation shows the arm making a waving motion at normal speed. For the second portion, the movements of the right wrist and the right elbow goal objects, as well as the right wrist bone, were scaled down by ½ (.5). This has the effect of making their motions twice as fast. In the third segment, the hand and arm motions were scaled by a factor of 2, making them move twice as slowly as the normal speed.

Figures 4-34 and 4-35 illustrate the effect that scaling has on a timeline. Figure 4-34 shows how

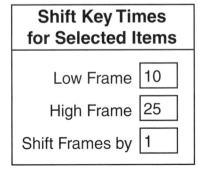

Shift Key Times for Selected Items	
Low Frame	10
High Frame	25
Shift Frames by	1

Fig. 4-30 Spine 2 is shifted one frame forward. Spine 3 is shifted two frames forward, and so on.

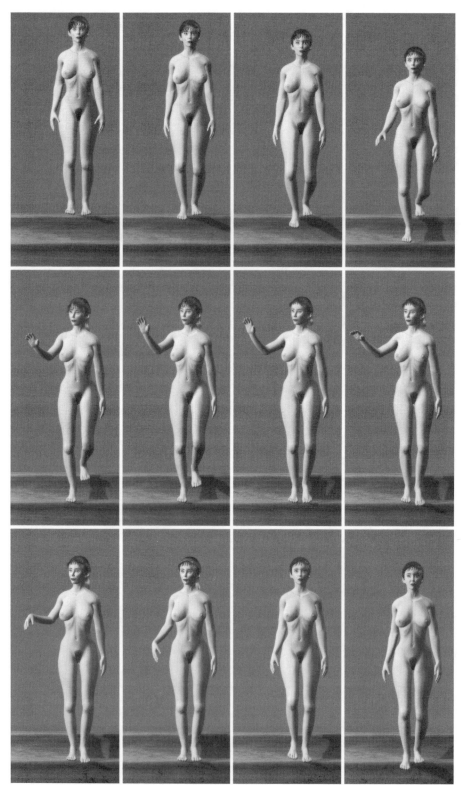

Fig. 4-32 Images from the animation showing the female waving her hand at a normal speed before Scaling Keys.

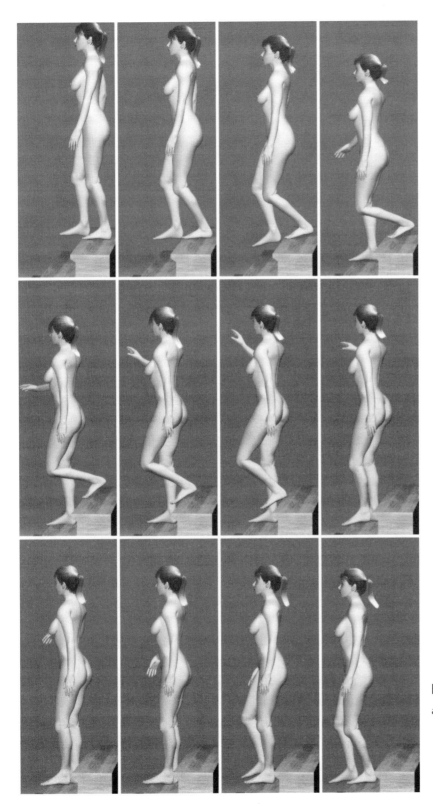

Fig. 4-33 A side view of the same animation.

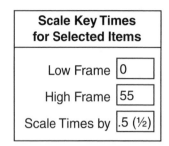

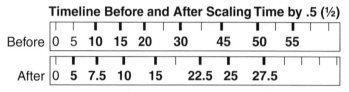

Fig. 4-34 Scaling key times by 1/2 makes the hand and arm movements twice as fast.

scaling times by ½ compresses the movement so that keyframe 10 becomes 5, 15 turns into 7.5, 20 changes to 10, and so on. Before scaling, the entire motion lasted 55 frames. After scaling, it is complete by frame 27.5.

The result of scaling keys up by two times can be seen in Figure 4-35. The keyframe at 10 changes to 20, 15 becomes 30, and so on. Before the change, the entire arm movement had a duration of 55 frames. After scaling it up, the length increased to 110, slowing down the gesture.

Scaling keys can be an excellent method for changing the timing of an animation. Timing is also one of the Twelve Principles of Animation. This is usually the first principle that novice animators have to contend with. To have the right sense of timing takes experience. At first, you may need to use a stopwatch or count the time it takes to perform an action. After a while, you will know instinctively when to hold,

how fast to move, and where to add accents to various motions.

Timing often governs how a movement will be interpreted. Whereas the hand motion appears to be a waving gesture to someone off screen, once the keys are scaled, the meaning of the flourish changes dramatically. When she waves quickly, it could be interpreted as her annoyance or dismissal of something or someone. The slow movement might mean that she is exhibiting a mannerism of affectation, or that she is reaching out to grab something.

You may also notice that in the animation, the female figure compresses when her foot touches down on the stair, and then expands again to its normal size. This bounce effect is another one of the Twelve Principles of Animation, called Squash and Stretch. It is employed to show weight, mass, and gravity. Without it, characters appear weightless and unreal. Depending on the size of your sub-

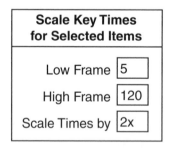

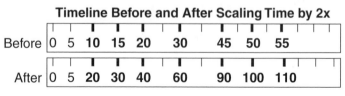

Fig. 4-35 Scaling key times by 200% makes the hand and arm movements twice as slow.

ject, Squash and Stretch is applied in different degrees. A heavy person would exhibit more Squash, while a lightweight only displays a little. When you compress a character, you can scale it down on the y-axis. To expand it, scale the character up on the y-axis.

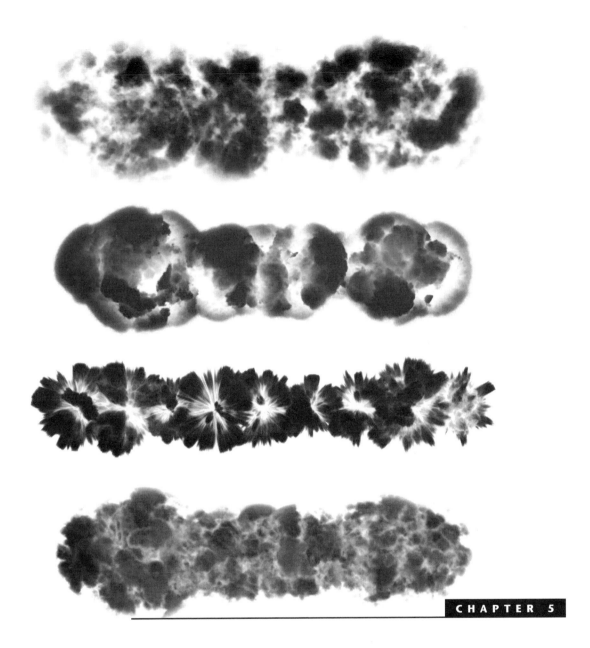

CHAPTER 5

Special Effects

Special effects often add a touch of brilliance and grandeur to an otherwise ordinary animation. This is a branch of computer graphics that is both enjoyable and full of meaning. There is no doubt that this multifaceted field could have an entire book devoted to it.

Many artists use visual effects to enhance their animations. These can range from corporate identity projects all the way to action sequences. Special effects may just involve the use of particles to simulate ordinary sparks from a grindstone, or they might be used to show a dazzling, cataclysmic explosion.

This chapter covers some of the more common effects used in animation, which include explosions, liquids, fire, electricity, and atmospherics such as steam, smoke, and clouds. In addition, real-life video effects mixed with 3D animation are examined.

Explosions

Some of the most frequently used visual effects are explosions. There is nothing like a violent burst of energy to get someone's attention. Unfortunately, due to their overuse, they have lost some of their excitement. There are many ways to create a computer-animated explosion, and artists are constantly trying out new methods for making more dazzling detonations.

The variety of explosions that you can create depends largely on your software's capabilities. Most mid- to high-end packages utilize particles in one form or another. Others use 3D volumes like voxels. A few have dynamics that simulate real-world physical forces.

The following examples range from simple explosions using just sprites and volumetrics

to a combination of fragments, particles, and volumetrics.

Making a Simple Explosion with Sprites

Sprites are two-dimensional slices of volumes. Voxels, on the other hand, are considered volumes because they have a three-dimensional quality. Unlike sprites, they appear to have thickness. Sprites have a gaseous look to them. Volumes take a much longer time to render than sprites. If rendering speed is a concern and you do not need to show a more solid 3D effect, consider using sprites.

Figure 5-1 shows a single 2560 x 1920 resolution image of a volume explosion using voxels. The rendering required three hours. The object was re-rendered with sprites mode on instead of volume (Figure 5-2). This time it rendered in only two minutes.

In this exercise, you can create a simple explosion with two nulls or objects that have sprites des-

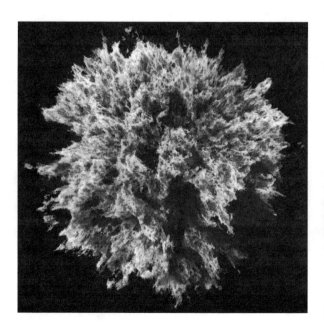

Fig. 5-1 A volume explosion.

ignated for their object types. If longer rendering times are not a problem, you can use volumes instead of sprites.

Create a null or object that you can apply the sprite onto. It will be used for the explosion part.

Select the null, and for shading, apply a gradient for its color. Make the gradient start with red and gradually turn into orange at the top. Set a luminosity gradient for the explosion sprite. Have it start black and end with white at the top. The luminosity value can be set to about 150 percent. Your software may also have the option of setting the thickness of the sprite by specifying the number of slices that will be used. Each slice takes a section of the volume. The more slices you use, the thicker the sprite appears to be, but more slices will slow down the rendering process.

Apply a procedural texture such as turbulence to it. Add a texture effect like billowing to make it move during the animation. Your software may also allow you to apply image clips to the sprite. A series of changing image clips can create some interesting effects.

After making a few test renderings and adjustments to your settings, clone the null, or the object that has the sprite or volume attached to it. The clone will be used to make the smoke part of the explosion. Change its color value from red and orange to dark and light gray. The rest of the settings can remain the same as the explosion sprite.

Animating the explosion involves correct pacing. At first there is the expanding explosion, followed by the billowing smoke. The explosion then contracts while the smoke continues to expand and dissipate. You can use the following instructions as a rough guide for the timing. Depending on the effect that you are trying to achieve, you may need to alter the rates of the explosion and

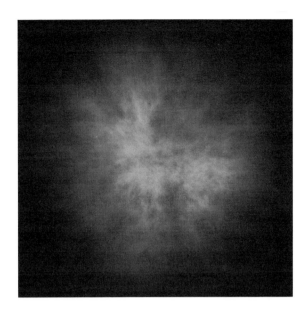

Fig. 5-2 A sprite explosion.

smoke dissipation.

Place both the explosion and smoke nulls together. You may decide to rotate one of them so that they appear a little different. To make it easier to move and rotate both at the same time, you may want to parent them to another null object.

Set up your camera and lighting. At frame 0, keyframe the null or both objects. Go to frame 10 and keyframe the null or both objects again. Move to frame 30 and rotate the null about 120 degrees clockwise in the top view and about 80 degrees clockwise in the front view. Keyframe the null at frame 30. If you did not parent the objects to a null, rotate and keyframe them according to the previously stated settings.

For particle size of your explosion and smoke sprites or volumes, set an envelope in your graph editor. Make the value for both 0 at frame 0. This means they will not be seen in the beginning.

Select the explosion sprite or volume, and for its particle size, scale it up to 100 percent at frame

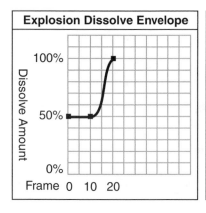

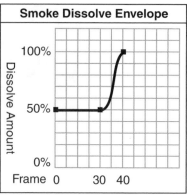

Fig. 5-3 A dissolve envelope is made for both the explosion object and the smoke object.

10. Make a new frame at 20 and size it down to 20 percent. Continuing in your graph editor, create another frame at 30 and scale it back down to 0 percent.

For the smoke particle size, go into the graph editor and make a frame at 20 and scale the size up to 100 percent. Create another frame at 30 and enlarge the particle size to 200 percent. The last step involves setting dissolve envelopes for both objects.

Figure 5-3 shows the dissolve envelopes for the explosion and smoke objects. The explosion object starts out at frame 0 with a 50 percent dissolve. This adds to the overall transparency of the object. Another 50 percent dissolve is set at frame 10, and a 100 percent dissolve is set at frame 20. This means the explosion disappears totally at frame 20.

The smoke object also starts with a 50 percent dissolve at frame 0. Another 50 percent dissolve is applied at frame 30. The smoke object disappears with a 100 percent dissolve at frame 40.

Create a 40-frame test animation of your explosion. The fiery explosion should quickly increase in size between frames 0 and 10. Its size decreases between frames 10 and 30. The dissolve envelope makes it disappear at frame 20. The smoke object increases in size between frames 0 and 30, and the dissolve envelope makes it disappear at frame 40. Both objects rotate during the animation, and the procedural texture moves throughout the sequence.

Figure 5-4 shows one frame from this kind of explosion. There are many ways to enhance this simple explosion. You can add particles, have objects break up, and introduce lens flares. These are discussed in the next part.

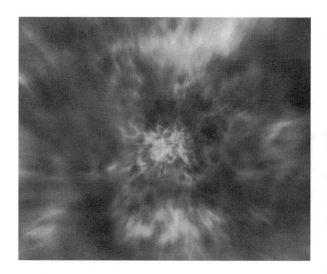

Fig. 5-4 A frame from the explosion.

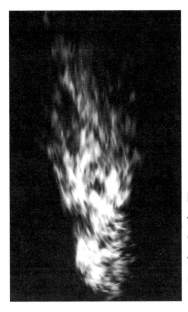

Fig. 5-5 A particle fire with a narrow emitter that is influenced by wind with a vortex mode.

Various Particle Effects

A particle is a point in 3D space that can be animated and assigned specified properties. Particles can have color gradients, velocity, collision detection, age, goal following, and so on. They can be influenced by dynamic forces such as gravity, wind, drag, and other particles and objects. All of this depends on the software that you are using.

Particles can be created by using a particle tool or by deleting surfaces from polygons, leaving only points to act as particles. Emitters are also used to generate particles. When you set up an emitter, you can usually specify the degree of the particle spread, the birth rate in particles per second, the speed at which they pour out, the size and shape of the emitter, and so on. The particles that are emitted can be influenced by other particles, collision objects, wind, gravity, and so on.

The following illustrations and text explain some of the many options that are available with particle effects. The manner in which particles are implemented varies greatly among all the 3D soft-

ware packages. Therefore, the description for each will have to be treated in general terms.

Figure 5-5 illustrates a fire that is made from particles. A wind item was added to the scene to agitate the particles. Some of the general settings used are:

Birth rate: 300 (This determines how many particles are born by seconds, frames, speed, collision events, wind, and so on.)

Generate by: Seconds (When speed is used, particles are emitted according to the movement of the emitter. This is similar to a salt and pepper shaker. Other options might include generate by wind, collision event, wind speed, and so on.)

Nozzle: Sphere (This determines the shape of the emitting source. The emitter can have a variety of shapes.)

Size effect: Size and density with a mass change (This means that when the emitter is scaled during the animation, size effect will determine the outcome scaling has on the particles.)

Generator size: X 300 mm
                    Y 1 m
                    Z 300 mm

(The generator size sets the size of the emitter.)

Particle limit: 10,000 (This determines how many particles are generated over the lifetime of the event. Higher numbers mean longer periods of particle emission.)

Usually a start and end frame can be set. The end frame might be classified as lifetime.

Motion settings define how particles are moved. Some of these could be:

Velocity: 100 percent (Higher values speed up the particles.)

Vector (miles per second)   X -700 mm
                              Y -350 mm
                              Z 0 m

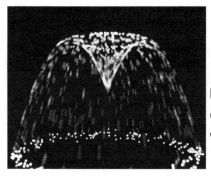

Fig. 5-6 Particles used to make a water fountain.

(Vector sets the initial direction of the particles. Other factors that will influence the direction of the particles are wind, gravity, a target item, and so on.)

Other settings, such as explosion and vibration, are implemented for effects that have different qualities than fire does.

Particles without sprites or volumes applied to them will only look like sparks. The fire is created by applying a sprite effect with a gradient shading of orange to yellow. A gray to white gradient is also applied for its luminosity. The density of the fire is controlled with another gradient that extends from black to white. A turbulence texture gives the particles an overall shape. For texture effect, velocity translate moves the texture in the direction of the particles.

Water effects can also be created from particles. Figure 5-6 shows one such application, which takes the form of a water fountain. Some of the settings that were used to make particles behave in this way are:

Birth rate: 30

Particle limit: 1,000

Motion vector: Y (the direction of the particles)

Gravity: y-axis -5

A water sprite was attached to the particles. The flat collision object on the bottom made the water droplets bounce.

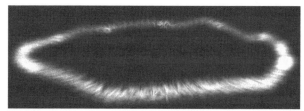

Fig. 5-7 An oval object was used to generate particles moving outward in a ring shape.

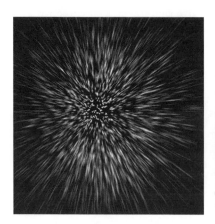

Fig. 5-8 A particle explosion with a gradient texture.

Fig. 5-9 An explosion composed of large particles with transparency maps.

Fig. 5-10 These particles have a displacement map to scatter them randomly. A glow effect was also applied.

An object can sometimes be used as a particle emitter. In Figure 5-7, an oval polygon emitted particles in a circular direction.

Gradients, image maps, and procedural textures can be applied to particles. Figure 5-8 shows an excerpt from an animation on the CD-ROM (Chapter 5 > Animation > Explosion > CD5-8 ParticleCloud.mov) of particles with a yellow to red gradient on them. Figure 5-9 shows larger particles with a color image map applied to them (Chapter 5 > Animation > Explosion > CD5-9 BlobbyParticles.mov). Figure 5-10 depicts particles that have been scattered with a displacement map (Chapter 5 > Animation > Explosion > CD5-10 DisplGlwParticles.mov). A procedural texture, image, movie, or gradient can be used to make a displacement map. Figure 5-11 (Chapter 5 > Animation > Explosion > CD5-11 Spiral Particles .mov) shows a particle explosion that follows a spiral path. A spiral-shaped object acted as the emitter. All four of these examples can be viewed as movies on the CD-ROM.

Dynamic forces can alter high-end particle effects. Since these vary a great deal among software packages, the following information describes how particles are produced with some of the more common dynamic forces.

When creating particles that stream out of emitters, it helps to position the camera at an angle or to the side of the emitter. This makes it easier to see the particles as they shoot out.

Figure 5-12 depicts particles streaming from an emitter. Particle collision was turned on so that particles colliding with a NURBS or polygon surface ricochet off. You may want to experiment with the emitter settings. Changing the spread, velocity, birth rate, and so on can yield some interesting results. A pipe, a gun, or a face with an open

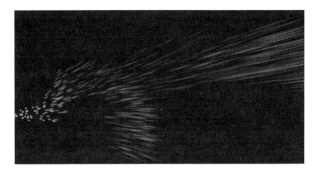

Fig. 5-11 Scaling the spiral particles during the animation produces another type of explosion.

mouth are a few of the objects in which the emitter can be placed. Bounciness or elasticity of the collision object can usually be adjusted. Friction or the roughness of the surface will also affect the manner in which particles bounce off the object. For example, a smoother surface will make the particles have more bounce. The CD-ROM contains an animation showing a particle collision (Chapter 5 > Animation > Explosion > CD5-12 Collision Particles.mov).

Gravity is another important dynamic quality

Fig. 5-12 Particles with collision detection bounce off a surface. A particle emitter creates the particles.

Fig. 5-13 Applying gravity to the particles enhances their physical presence.

that can usually be assigned to particles. It can be useful for water sprinklers, fountains, sparklers, and so on. Figure 5-13 shows the same emitter and collision objects as the ones in Figure 5-12, except that this time, gravity was applied to the particles. An animation showing how gravity affects the particles can be viewed on the CD-ROM (Chapter 5 > Animation > Explosion > CD5-13 Gravity Particles.mov).

Many other dynamic forces can be applied to particles. Some of these are force, drag, wind, and lifetime. Particles can even be set to follow or match goal objects. The CD-ROM contains an animation in which particles follow a null object as their goal (Chapter 5 > Animation > Explosion > CD5-13b Follow Goal Particles.mov).

Particles usually do not work that well on their own for explosions. Therefore, they are often used in conjunction with other forces to simulate detonations. One of the 3D effects that work very well with particles are voxels.

Using Voxels to Simulate Explosions

Voxels are 3D volumes that exist on the x-, y-, and z-axes. Imagine a series of cubes spaced on a 3D grid. Each cube can have several attributes. The most common ones are density, temperature, and velocity. Voxels are similar to pixels except for the fact that they are not limited to 2D space. Otherwise, a pixel and a voxel are identical because each represents a value at a position in space. Voxels have mostly been used in computational fluid dynamics and medical visualization. Now that animators have added them to their digital tools, we are starting to see some truly stunning effects.

Voxels are very useful for explosions. Since voxels are capable of showing much greater detail than polygons and can be blended into each other, they are perfect for billowing volumetric effects. Voxels can have envelopes to control their color gradient, size, luminosity, opacity, density, thickness, and so on. Different filters, textures, and blending modes can also be applied to voxels. Figure 5-14 illustrates various voxel-type explosions. A color image of the voxels can be viewed on the CD-ROM (Chapter 5 > Animation > Color Images > 5-14 Voxel Explosions.jpg). The voxels are attached to a row of nulls to give them their horizontal shape.

The most significant disadvantage of using voxels is the amount of memory required to store them. This problem should cease to be a concern as computers continue to become more powerful.

Figure 5-15 shows a frame from an explosion using voxels. One null was used as the goal object. The null was enlarged during the animation, thus creating the blast. The voxel fireball animation can be viewed on the CD-ROM (Chapter 5 > Animation

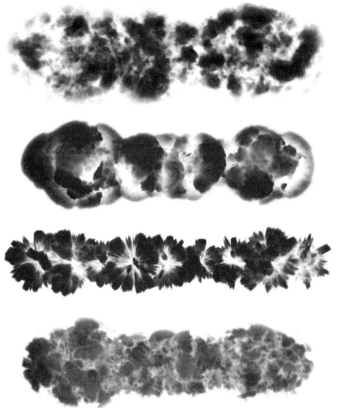

Fig. 5-14 Various voxel explosion clouds.

> Explosion > CD5-15 Voxel Fireball.mov). The CD also contains a voxel gradient explosion illustrating how voxels can have a gradient envelope applied to them that changes over time (Chapter 5 > Animation > Explosion > CD5-15b Voxel Grad Expl.mov).

Besides atmospheric effects, voxels can be used to render various surfaces. Some of these are liquids that will be discussed later. If your software implements voxels, you may be able to experiment by applying some of the previously discussed envelopes, filters, textures, and blending modes. If you attach voxels to objects, you can size, move, or rotate the object over time. Combining voxels with some of the previously discussed particle

effects can produce some dazzling animations. Figure 5-16 depicts a scene from a combination voxel/particle explosion. The particle and voxel explosions can be viewed on the CD-ROM (Chapter 5 > Animation > Explosion > CD5-16 Particle & Voxel.mov).

Polygon or NURBS Object Fragmentation

Although polygon or NURBS objects do not produce good explosions by themselves, they nevertheless form an important part of a total detonation. If you can show fragments of the damaged object(s) flying by the camera or through space, you will get a much more interesting explosion.

The following exercise uses a bottle, but any object can be broken into pieces. For example, you can show a spaceship breaking up. Figure 5-17 shows the bottle object after lathing a spline outline.

Place the finished bottle on the spot where it will blow up and save the model. Make a duplicate of the bottle and hide the original. Try not to move the duplicate. We want it to occupy the same space as the original bottle. Cut the duplicate up into fragments (Figure 5-18). A polygon object works better for this because you can use stenciling, slicing, and Boolean operations to cut across the polygons.

One method that works well for slicing objects apart is to make a 2D polygon shape with jagged edges in another layer. The shape can then be extruded to extend beyond the thickness of the bottle that you plan to cut up. A drilling operation

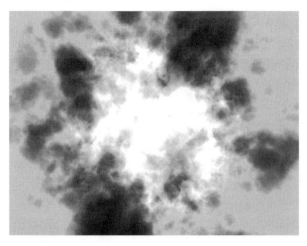

Fig. 5-15 A voxel-type explosion. In this case, the voxels were attached to one null that was enlarged during the animation.

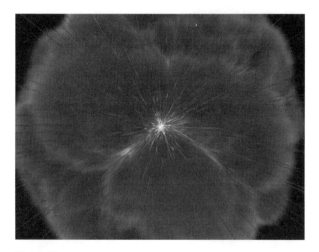

Fig. 5-16 Particles and voxels combined add to the fullness of an explosion.

is used to stencil the jagged object onto the bottle. If you named the stencil surface, it will be easier to select the fragment later. Continue creating jagged polygon pieces to stencil onto the rest of the bottle. Vary the size of the fragments. Approximately seven pieces should be enough. To give the pieces

some thickness, extrude each of them a little. Even though Figure 5-19 shows the separate pieces, you should keep them in their original location. During the animation, they will be moved apart.

The next step is to create a smoky and burnt-looking texture (Figure 5-20), which is then applied to the fragments' surfaces. The original bottle should have a clean look to it.

Some dissolve envelopes are now prepared for all of the fragments and the original whole bottle. In this particular animation, the bottle sits for thirty frames and then begins to break apart starting at frame 31. Figure 5-21 shows the dissolve envelope for the fragments. Between frames 0 and 30, the fragments remain invisible (100 percent dissolve). At frame 31, they suddenly show up (0 percent dissolve).

The undivided original bottle has the opposite dissolve envelope applied to it (Figure 5-21). It is visible for the first thirty frames (0 percent dissolve) and then disappears suddenly at frame 31 (100 percent dissolve). Frame 31 has the whole bottle disappear, while at the same time, the fragments appear and begin to move apart. One-thirtieth of a second is too fast for the human eye to notice the switch. It is another example of digital sleight-of-hand. This technique can be used for switching characters on the fly or for any other object that you wish to change.

Now it is time to create keyframes for the bottle and fragments. If you plan to apply this method to a moving object like a rocket, you should parent the fragments and the whole object to a null. You then move the null that, in turn, propels all the objects at once without having pieces come apart before their time.

Select one of the bottle pieces and keyframe it at frames 0 and 31. These two frames are identical,

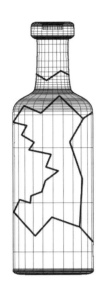

Fig. 5-17 (left) The bottle before slicing it up.

Fig. 5-18 (center)The jagged lines show where the bottle was cut apart.

Fig. 5-19 (right) A view of the separate bottle pieces.

so be sure to set the spline control to linear at frame 31. Do the exact same thing to the other fragments. Pick the first fragment again and advance to frame 41. Move and rotate the piece a little past the camera view so that it looks like it is hurtling away from the explosion. Once it is moved out of camera range, keyframe it at frame 41. Use your own judgment as to how fast you want the piece to fly. To make the fragment fly faster, place it further out of camera range or move it at an earlier frame than 41—perhaps at 36. Make

a preview to see how fast the piece flies.

Advance to frame 44 and select the next fragment to move and rotate out of camera range. Keyframe it at 44. You may decide to move it at an earlier or later frame depending on how fast you want it to travel. Continue moving and rotating the rest of the fragments out of camera range and keyframe them anywhere between frames 40 and 46. They should fly apart in different directions. Figure 5-22 shows some fragments at frame 37. Motion blur is turned on.

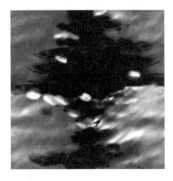

Fig. 5-20 The bottle fragments have a texture that makes them look burnt and smoky.

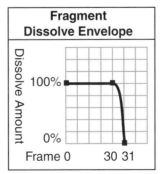
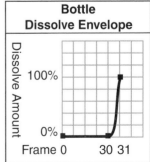

Fig. 5-21 A dissolve envelope makes the fragments invisible until frame 31. The bottle remains visible for the first thirty frames and dissolves completely at frame 31.

Adding Lens Flares

Lens flares bring a nice touch to explosions. They will look like bright lights that flare up quickly and die out. Aside from the lights that you are using to illuminate the scene, create three new lights for the lens flares. Make each of them a point light with an intensity of 50 percent. You may decide to give all of them a different color. Set your flares to have a central glow and a red outer glow. They can also have random streaks. A flare intensity envelope will have to be set for all three lens flares. Each one will vary by a few frames. Figure 5-23 shows the flare intensity envelope for the three lens flares. Lens flare number two had its frames shifted forward by two frames starting at 30. Number three lens flare had its frames shifted forward by four frames starting at 30. The first lens flare reaches its apex at frame 42 with an intensity of 150 percent, the second arrives at frame 44, and the third achieves its brightest point at frame 46. Figure 5-24 illustrates the lens flares combined with the flying fragments at frame 39. The CD-ROM contains a short animation showing only lens flares combined with particles (Chapter 5>Animation>Explosion>CD5-24 Particles & Lens Flares Only.mov).

Fig. 5-22 Bottle fragments flying away from the explosion at frame 37.

Combining Particles with the Fragments and Lens Flares

Particles form an important part of the explosion. Their fast movement and haphazard distribution in all directions contribute to the chaotic effect you are trying to achieve. As discussed previously, you can create particles with an emitter or from a point cloud. If you use an emitter, it should eject particles in all directions.

To make the particles appear more random, a displacement map is used. During the animation, the particle cloud will not only expand, but also scatter randomly in all directions as the displacement map affects its vibration, direction, and/or velocity. Figure 5-25 shows the particle cloud displacement envelope in which the displacement opacity turns to 100 percent after frame 30.

A gradient is applied to the particles. At frames 0 and 30, the original particle cloud is reduced in size to a value of 0 on the x-, y-, and z-axes. Frame 30 has a linear spline control to keep the zero size constant between frames 0 and 30. At frame 60, the particle cloud enlarges to 200 percent. This may vary according to the size of your object and the distance of your camera from the explosion. If you want the particle cloud to expand quickly and then slow down, you can insert an extra keyframe somewhere between frames 30 and 60. The in-between frame shows a higher percentage of growth than the ending one at 60 (Figure 5-26).

One final envelope needs to be set for the particle cloud. This is a dissolve envelope (Figure 5-27). Frames 0 and 42 have a 0 percent dissolve, which means that the particles remain opaque. Frame 42 has a linear spline control to keep the appearance of the particles constant up to that point. Between frames 42 and 60, the particles

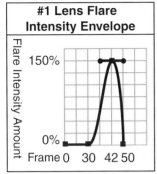

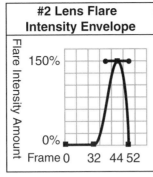

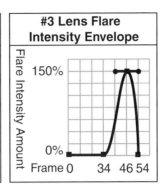

Fig. 5-23 The three lens-flare intensity envelopes.

become transparent and disappear.

Render a few test frames to see how the particle cloud works with the previously set objects and lens flares. Figure 5-28 depicts frame 38 from the particle, fragment, and lens flare parts of the explosion. The final step involves setting up a smoke and fire cloud.

Fig. 5-24 Three lens flares are combined with the fragments at frame 39.

Mixing in Fire and Smoke to Complete the Explosion

Two separate volumes or objects are added for the fire and smoke parts of the explosion. If your software implements volumes and sprites, you should be able to create very realistic fire and smoke. Particles can also serve as smoke and fire objects.

In the same scene that has the bottle, fragments, particles, and lens flares, create two nulls. Name one "Fire Null" and the other "Smoke Null." Assign your fire and smoke voxels to the appropriate nulls. Experiment with some of the volume or sprite settings until you are satisfied with the appearance of the fire and smoke. The two nulls that the volumes and sprites are attached to can be scaled over time or the volumes and sprites can have an envelope on their particle size. The fire will appear before the smoke, quickly grow, and then shrink to nothing. The smoke will show up

more gradually and retain its size, but will dissipate at the end.

Figure 5-29 shows the fire and smoke envelopes that control the scale of each over the course of 60 frames. The envelopes can be carried by the nulls, volumes, or sprites. The fire voxel, sprite, or null is

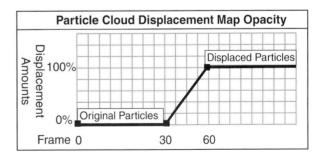

Fig. 5-25 A displacement map is added to the particles to randomize their movements. This envelope can be made to affect their vibration, direction, and/or velocity.

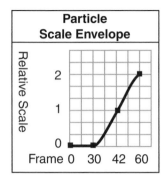

Fig. 5-26 The particle cloud is enlarged between frames 30 and 60.

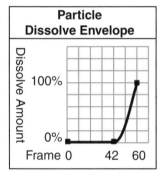

Fig. 5-27 A dissolve envelope is set to make the particles gradually disappear between frames 42 and 60.

scaled back to size 0 at frames 0 and 30. Frame 30 has a linear spline control to keep the size constant for the first thirty frames. At frame 40, the fire voxel, sprite, or null is enlarged four times. This may vary according to the location of your camera. Frame 50 shows the fire voxel, sprite, or null reduced dramatically to size 1; at frame 60, it is finally set to size 0. Placing the extra keyframe at frame 50 makes the reduction ease out. Instead of the fire gradually becoming smaller over twenty frames, it begins to shrink quickly for the first ten frames (40 to 50) and slows for the last ten frames (50 to 60).

The scale envelope for the smoke voxel, sprite, or null in Figure 5-29 depicts the same 0 setting for the first thirty frames, after which it enlarges dramatically until frame 60. As mentioned before, the size of your fire and smoke will vary according to

the placement of your camera.

Figure 5-30 illustrates the dissolve envelope for the fire voxel, sprite, or null. It is set to make the volume disappear between frames 40 and 50. This is usually adjusted in the voxel's settings. The smoke voxel's dissolve envelope, seen in Figure 5-31, controls the appearance and disappearance of the smoke. It is also important to set some kind of deformation to the fire and smoke voxels. This turbulence or billowing effect agitates the fire and smoke so that it does not just sit there, fixed in place. Test animations should determine the right effect speed.

Figure 5-32 shows a few frames from the final bottle explosion. The animation can be viewed on the CD-ROM (Chapter 5 > Animation > Explosion > CD5-32 Voxel Bottle Explosion.mov). Voxels were used for the fire and smoke parts of the explosion. Once you create an explosion of this type, it can be saved for future projects. The scene can have its keys shifted or scaled according to the animation in which you plan to use it. After adjusting the keys globally, you can import

Fig. 5-28 Particles are mixed in with the lens flares and fragments. This shot was taken at frame 38.

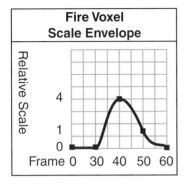

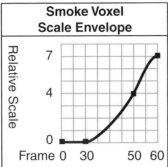

Fig. 5-29 After attaching the fire and smoke voxels, volumes, or sprites to two separate nulls, each null is enlarged at a different rate between frames 30 and 60. As an alternative to enlarging the nulls, the volume or sprite particles can be expanded.

it into your other animations.

Liquids

3D animation of fluids can mean any number of things: a water drop, waterfall, sludge, syrup, lava, and so on. Since there are so many variables when depicting liquids, it is necessary to limit the scope of this section to a few common ones like a water drop, running water, or thicker fluids like sludge or syrup.

Particle effects are used quite often when portraying running water. Combined with voxels, a realistic enactment of water becomes even more attainable. Emitters do not always have to be used with particle effects. A particle cloud can be created that morphs into another shape. Attaching voxels to the morphing particles produces some interesting effects. The first liquid, a water drop, makes use of this technique.

Animating a Water Drop

If your software allows you to create particle points from objects as well as to morph and attach voxels to them, you can try the following technique. If you do not have voxels or cannot make points out of objects, try this method with some creative texturing. Follow the steps, but use simple

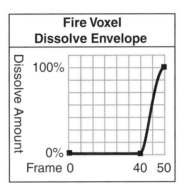

Fig. 5-30 To make the fire disappear between frames 40 and 50, a dissolve envelope is set for the voxels.

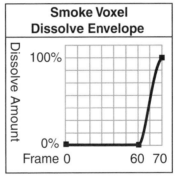

Fig. 5-31 The smoke voxels have a dissolve envelope. The smoke should clear between frames 60 and 70.

NURBS or polygon forms instead of particles. Shape-shift the objects into each other and texture them so that they will be similar to the surfaces described for the voxels.

Model a sphere with the poles pointing up and down on the y-axis. Use a taper tool in the top view to make the upper portion of the sphere narrow. It should resemble a teardrop. Delete the polygons and convert the remaining points to

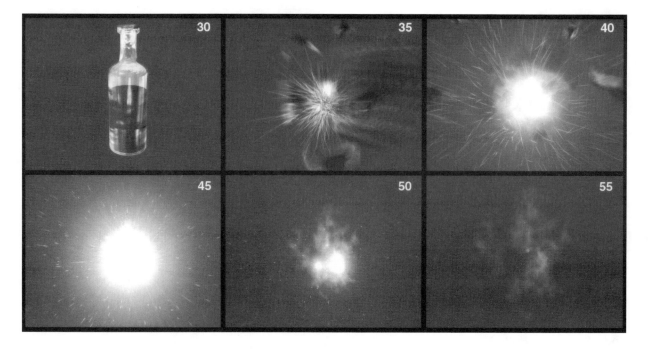

Fig. 5-32 Some shots from the final seventy-frame explosion. This one uses voxels for the fire and smoke objects.

polygons (Figure 5-33). Place the object in the center of the modeling universe. This is our primary particle cloud. Save it as "WaterDrop."

Figure 5-33 also shows the other particle cloud shapes that will now be modeled from the original. These will be the morph targets. For the first morph target, make the particle cloud long and narrow, make the second flat, and make the third with its points jittered. When the original drop begins to fall, it shape-shifts into a longer form, then flattens when it hits the bottom surface, and finally splashes (jittered points). Save each target with a separate name. Unless your software can handle morph targets or shape blends with different quantities of points, make sure each particle cluster has the same number of points.

Model a water faucet, pump, hose, or any kind of spout. Place the original particle cloud, named WaterDrop, in the tip of the spout. Keyframe it at

frame 0. Go to frame 7 and move the water drop down to where it would hit a surface before splashing, then keyframe it at 7. Advance to frame 10 and move the water drop particle cluster up a little to give the droplets some bounce.

Now it is time to set up the morph targets. Use the diagram in Figure 5-34 as a guide to arrange the three particle cloud targets. Each morph lasts about one frame. By the time you reach frame 7, the particles will have changed to the third target—jittered points. Be sure to indicate in your software that this is a multiple-target, single envelope.

The final step is to attach the voxels to the WaterDrop particles. The water surface for the voxels will most likely have a high transparency with medium refraction and specular setting. It should also have Fresnel effect turned on, which will make the surface appear more reflective when viewed edgewise and more transparent when seen straight on. A particle size envelope is set so that the particles appear to separate into drops after hitting the surface. The size is relative, but so that you can get an idea of the differences, the original size of the voxels is set at 3 between frames 0 and 8. At frame 11, the voxels are reduced to 0.5. As the particles change into smaller ones between frames 8 and 11, they separate into droplets. This occurs right after they hit the surface and bounce up.

Figure 5-35 shows a few frames from the water droplet animation that can be viewed on the CD-ROM (Chapter 5> Animation > Liquids > CD5-35 Water Drop.mov).

Running Water

Creating fairly realistic running water effects usually requires software with particles and particle emitters. The particles emanating from a source (emitter) form the foundation upon which voxels or other dynamic attributes are placed. This is a form of dynamic animation in which motions are calculated from one frame to the next. There is no keyframing involved. To make changes, you have to adjust dynamic forces like gravity, particle size, collision amount, and so on. The following instructions may serve as a guideline for creating running water. As usual, there will be some variables, depending on the software used and the effect that you are trying to achieve.

Create particles and an emitter. If you plan to apply volumes to the particles, use the smallest number of particles possible. It will cut down on the rendering time. About 200 particles should be enough. The emitter only needs to create about 100 particles per second. Of course, if you are not using volumes, you will want a higher number of particles per second.

The spread from the emitter should be fairly small, or about 15 degrees. This may vary according to the size of the spout from which the water pours. The speed of the particles should be fast. If the water runs from a faucet, rotate the emitter down 90 degrees on the z-axis, or pitch. Apply gravity to the particles.

Collision detection adds a nice touch to running water. The collision object should not have too much bounce. If you rotate the collision object down slightly, you can get an interesting water runoff after the water hits the surface. Figure 5-36 shows the particles as they stream down, collide, and run down the surface.

Once the flow of the particles has been set up, you can apply attributes and behaviors. This will vary a great deal according to the software. If you have volumes, apply them to the particle stream.

Some volume parameters for running water might be the metaball blending mode, a luminosity of 0 percent, diffuse level of 100 percent, specular level of 50 percent, low to medium glossiness, 100 percent transparency, low to medium refraction, Fresnel effect, and small reflectivity. Figure 5-37 shows a section of the water stream with volumes applied to the particles.

To make the animation more interesting, create some objects for the water to flow from and

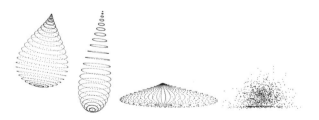

Fig. 5-33 A cluster of points in the shape of a water drop. The other three are the morph targets.

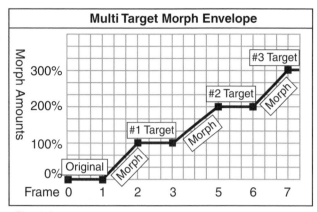

Fig. 5-34 There are three morph targets that the original water drop point cloud changes into. These occur very rapidly.

collide with.

Sludge

Thick, messy substances like sludge, syrup, slime, and muck can be made in a fashion similar to running water effects. It just takes a few extra ingredients, such as lumps, color, textures, and other surface effects, to turn them into sluggish masses.

The particles and emitter are made in a similar way to those for running water. Dynamic forces like gravity, collision, wind, and so on can be assembled according to the context of the animation. Since this will simulate physical forces, there is no need for keyframing.

Figure 5-38 shows how particles and an emitter are placed inside a pipe. Gravity and collision detection are turned on. The speed of the particles is set to fairly slow because the substance should appear to be sluggish. Figure 5-39 shows an image from the sludge animation, which can be viewed in several variations on the CD-ROM (Chapter 5 > Animation > Liquids > CD5-39 Sludge.mov). Voxels are applied to the particles. A metaball blending mode and texture are added to give the substance a lumpy look.

Atmospherics

Gases, steam, smoke, clouds, and other atmospheric conditions are usually created in a similar fashion to the previously discussed explosion, and

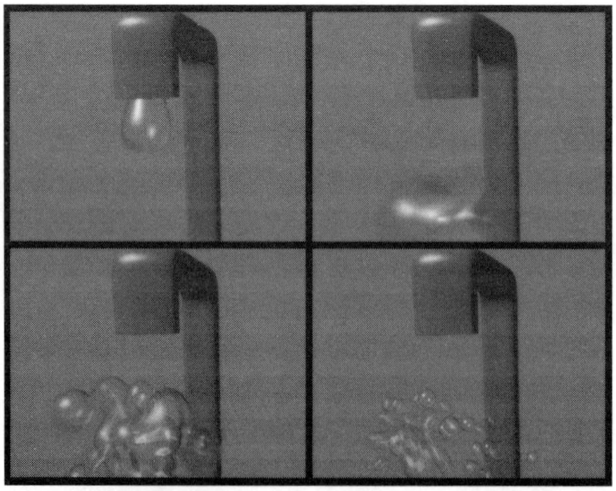

Fig. 5-35 Some rendered frames from the water drop animation.

Fig. 5-36 A stream of particles constitutes the groundwork for the running water animation.

Fig. 5-37 A close-up view of the water after applying voxels to the particles stream.

Fig. 5-38 The particles that will be used for the sludge.

Fig. 5-39 An image from the sludge animation. Voxels were applied to the particles.

Fig. 5-40 These particles will have the steam attributes placed on them.

fire clouds and particles often form their basis. Particles are set to have blobby surfaces like those found in metaball blending mode. The amount of mixture among blobs can be increased or decreased by the size of the particles or volumes. A steam or spray quality usually requires fast-moving particles pouring out of an emitter.

Steam

Figure 5-40 shows particles with about a 45 degree spread flowing out of a spray can nozzle. The number of particles used can be fairly low, with a medium to fast speed. In this case, the particles were parented to the nozzle and set to stream forth after depressing the nozzle button.

Adding a light to the particle stream often improves the look of steam. A light is placed behind the particles and points in the direction of their flow. Color also plays an important role in determining the outcome. This can be adjusted through the light's color or through the sprite surface. The particles should have a lifespan set so that the spray appears to dissipate after a certain distance. Transparency and glow settings should be adjusted for this type of effect. Figure 5-41 illustrates one frame from the steam animation found on the CD-ROM (Chapter 5 > Animation > Atmospherics > CD5-41 Can Of Steam.mov).

Clouds

Since smoke was described earlier under the explosion descriptions, the final atmospheric effect, clouds, is discussed briefly. A number of different software packages have the ability to render skies with clouds, either with plug-ins or with a built-in renderer. This does not mean that the clouds are actual volumes, but they appear to be so in the distance.

Fig. 5-41 One of the frames from the steam animation.

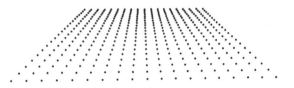

Fig. 5-42 A series of particles in a grid formation is created for the layer of clouds.

To make clouds appear volumetric, you will most likely have to use particles. Setting the blobbiness or metaball factor on them will determine the magnitude and thickness of the clouds. If you can use volumes or sprites, you should get an even higher degree of realism. The following instructions show how to make a layer of clouds from a series of particles in a rectangular pattern.

Depending on your software, you can make a 2D polygon rectangle with 20 segments on the x- and z-axes. The polygons are then deleted and the points converted to one-point polys. These points serve as the particles to which voxels are attached (Figure 5-42). Another approach is to use a particle tool and apply attributes to the particles to give them blobby surfaces with self-shadowing.

The context in which you want to show your clouds will vary greatly among users. In Figure 5-43, a mountain range was created and overlapped

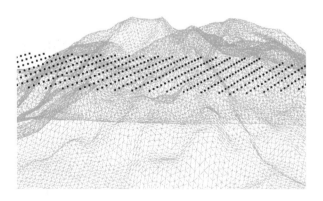

Fig. 5-43 The cloud particles extend through the mountain range.

Fig. 5-44 The final rendered cloud scene. Fog was turned on to make the clouds appear hazy in the distance.

with particles. This makes it look as if the clouds actually surround the mountains. You can add several sets of rectangular particle groups to show various strata of clouds. Some can be jittered or agitated to make the clouds appear more random. Be sure to turn on fog so that the clouds appear to be hazy in the distance.

The last step involves setting volumes or sprites to the particle points. Metaball blending mode is used with a light gray and white coloring. Luminosity is set at 40 percent, opacity at 10 percent, and density at 100 percent. A 100 percent size variation was chosen for the volumes or sprites. Figure 5-44 shows a scene from a short cloud animation that can be viewed on the CD-ROM (Chapter 5 > Animation > Atmospherics > CD5-44 Clouds.mov).

Fire

Fire is an effect that can be created in a number of different ways by using displacement mapping on objects, volumetric properties, particles, and dynamic forces like wind, drag, gravity, collision, and so on. Particles acting as sparks and smoke add another degree of realism to the animation. Particles can also be placed inside the fire and set to explode at different times. The resulting sparks bounce off the ground before disappearing. The following instructions show how you can use several different techniques to create a campfire, smoke, and sparks. Once you have your fire, you can take parts of it and alter them later for other effects such as a burning matchstick, torch, candle, and so on.

Modeling and Texturing Logs

You can model some logs out of cylinders.

Fig. 5-45 The log texture.

Fig. 5-46 The logs after stacking and surfacing them.

Jittering or displacing the points randomly should make them appear less perfect. A wood or bark texture applied as a planar image map on the z-axis works nicely (Figure 5-45). The finished pile of logs can be viewed in Figure 5-46.

Creating the Fire Objects

As usual, there are several methods you can use for making the fire. One of these is with volumetric or sprite effects such as voxels. Another approach is to use particles that have blobby surfaces similar to cloud or smoke objects, except that the texture is different and contains more velocity and turbulence. A fire can also be attained by using volumetric lights. Applying creative texturing to the lights transforms them into fairly good fire and smoke. The following directions explain how to make a volume or sprite fire and a volumetric light fire.

Using Volumes or Sprites to Make a Fire

The flames are sprites or volumes that have been attached to particles. The particle emitter is placed at the bottom of the logs. The following settings might help in approximating values for a fire.

Birth rate:	300
Generate by:	Seconds
Nozzle:	Sphere
Size effect: Size and density with a mass change	
Generator size:	X 1.5 m
	Y 50 mm
	Z 1.5 m
Particle limit:	10,000
Particle weight:	1
Particle resistance:	1
Velocity:	100 percent
Vector	X -700 mm
	Y -350 mm
	Z -350 mm
Gravity:	Y 1.5
Position blur:	100 percent
Parent motion:	100 percent

Settings for the volumes or sprites:

Object type:	Sprite
Particle size:	98 mm

Apply a white to black gradient for particle age

Size variation:	110 percent
Stretch direction:	Velocity
Stretch amount:	192 percent

Maintain volume	
Align to path	
Color: Orange to yellow gradient	
Luminosity: Medium gray to white gradient	
Density: Black to white gradient	
Number of slices:	1
HyperTexture: Turbulence	
Frequencies:	1
Small power:	.5
Texture amplitude:	377 percent
Texture effect:	Velocity translate
Effect speed:	100 percent
Scale:	X 2 m
	Y 2 m
	Z 4 m

The wind item is placed directly into the fire to fan the flames. It can have the following settings.

Wind mode:	vortex
Blend mode:	add
Size effect:	wind
Radius:	1 m
Power:	100 percent
Vector wind:	Y 380 mm
Turbulence size	X 1 m
	Y 1 m
	Z 1 m

It will take some experimenting with test animations to get the right settings for your specific project. Figure 5-47 shows rendered images from the particle/sprite fire (Chapter 5 > Animation > Fire > CD5-47 Particle Sprite Fire.mov).

Using Volumetric Lights to Make a Fire

Volumetric lights create the effect of visible light beams. With some creative texturing, they can make a decent low-tech fire. The main problem with volumetric lights is that their edges often

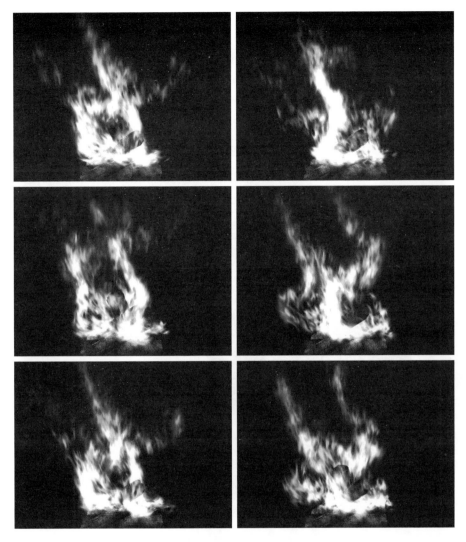

Fig. 5-47 Images from the final volume/sprite fire animation, composed of logs, sprite flames, and drifting particle sparks.

texture like turbulence and make the texture color yellow. Add a gradient texture on top of the yellow turbulence texture. Have it start with yellow on the bottom, then shift to orange, a transparent red, and finally an opaque white at the top.

In the graph editor, have the turbulence texture move up for the length of the animation. As mentioned before, the light itself should have a modifier on it so that it vibrates. After selecting the light, go into the graph editor and add a modifier such as oscillator. Apply it to all three axes for position, rotation, and scale. Experiment with the cycle time until you get a convincing fire light flickering effect. Set the duration for the entire length of the animation.

For the smoke, you can clone the volumetric light with all its settings. Place it a little above the fire light (Figure 5-48). The only thing you need to change on the smoke light is the color of the turbulence and gradient. Make these gray.

remain static, thus making the fire less convincing. One way to remedy this problem is to shake and rotate the lights during the animation, thus obscuring the static edges. This can be done through the graph editor by adding a modifier such as oscillator or noisy channel.

You can start by making a light and turning it 90 degrees so that it points up. In the light's item properties, turn on the volumetric lighting option. Enable the light to have a texture. Use a procedural

117

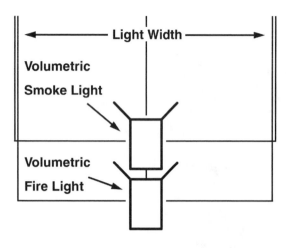

Fig. 5-48 Setting up the volumetric smoke and fire lights.

Once you are satisfied with the appearance of the fire and smoke, add particles for sparks, logs, a candle, a torch, and so on. A volumetric fire movie can be found on the CD-ROM (Chapter 5 > Animation > Fire > CD5-49 Volum Light Fire.mov).

Electrical Effects

Creating electrical effects, like lightning bolts or electrical arcs, is a much easier process than one would think. The electricity object requires minimal modeling skills, and the animation is simple and straightforward. Granted, there are plug-ins and other methods for creating electrical effects. The following directions should work for most software packages.

Modeling the Electric Object

Create a spline with 100 points. This line has to be surfaced and have the quality of showing up in a rendering. One way to achieve this is to make a single point, convert it to a polygon, and extrude it with a numerical setting of 100 segments. The result will be a line with 100 points on it (Figure 5-50).

Give the surface a name, such as "Bolt," and assign it a blue or yellow color. The next step is to animate the bolt.

Fig. 5-49 Images from the volumetric fire animation.

Using Displacement Mapping

Assign a displacement map to the 100-point line so that it deforms in a haphazard manner during the animation. For the displacement map, select a fractal bump texture. Set texture size to 10 mm on the x-, y-, and z-axes. The texture amplitude is .05 with three frequencies. A texture velocity of 1 millimeter on the x- and y-axes and 10 millimeters on the z-axis should also be set. Position your camera so that you can see the side of the electrical bolt. Scroll through the animation, and you should see the lightning bolt change its shape. It will most likely resemble a random jagged line like the one in Figure 5-51.

Surfacing the Lightning Bolt Object

The quality of the electrical object should be flat and glowing. Therefore, give it 100 percent luminosity. Diffuse, specular, reflectivity, and transparency levels should be 0 percent. Finally, apply a 100 percent glow to the bolt. Figure 5-52 shows a rendering of the surfaced electrical energy.

Adding a Skeleton

Aside from the displacement map, you can use bones to deform the bolt shape and bring about a higher degree of control during the animation. You can add as many bones as you want to the lightning object, but usually three is enough. Two placed at both ends and one in the middle should complete the skeleton. Rather than making child bones from one parent, make each bone independent from the others. After activating the skeleton, rotate and move the bones so that they resemble the ones in Figure 5-53.

Animating the Lightning

You can keyframe the bones in various posi-

Fig. 5-50 A lightning bolt is made from a single line with about 100 points on it.

Fig. 5-51 After applying a displacement map to the line, it starts to resemble the haphazard appearance of lightning.

Fig. 5-52 The lightning bolt after surfacing and applying glow. The image was rendered with motion blur on.

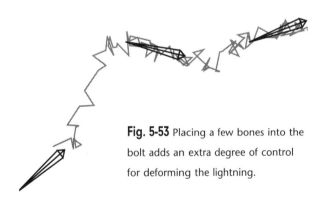

Fig. 5-53 Placing a few bones into the bolt adds an extra degree of control for deforming the lightning.

tions and gyrations to make an energetic effect. After setting a number of keyframes, you may decide to turn on repeat behavior for each bone. When you render the animation, be sure to turn on anti-aliasing, motion blur, and dithered motion blur. This will give the bolt a gauzy look (Figure 5-54).

To enhance the animation, you may want to try adding particles for sparks or creating some clouds,

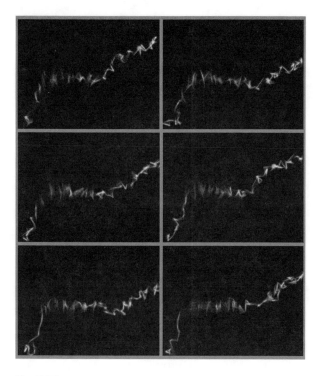

Fig. 5-54 Rendered frames from the final electricity animation.

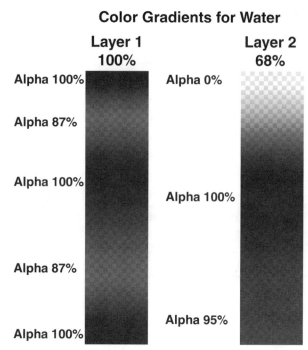

Fig. 5-55 The color gradients for the water. The alpha sections show the degree of transparency. Instead of black and gray, use a color such as aqua.

plasma bursts, and so on. Another option is to make a few other bolts and combine all of them in one animation. A few electrical animations can be viewed on the CD-ROM (Chapter 5 > Animation > Electrical > CD5-54a Electricity_w_Sparks.mov and CD5-54b Lightning Sparks & Smoke.mov).

A Body of Water

Making a body of water may not be part of special effects, but it is such a common occurrence when creating outdoor scenes that it deserves some discussion. Modeling the water object is a rudimentary task. The difficult part is texturing and displacing it correctly.

To make the body of water, create a single four-sided polygon that measures 2 km by 2 km. If you want a larger body of water, just increase the size. Turn on subdivision mode for the water object.

To make the surfaces for the water, go into its color properties. Apply two gradients to the water (Figure 5-55). Use blue, blue-green, or whatever color you think is appropriate to your project.

For the bump map, apply three procedural textures. The first one is a turbulence procedural texture with the following settings:

Layer opacity:	50 percent
Texture value:	80 percent
Frequencies:	3
Contrast:	0
Small power:	.5
Scale:	X 50 m
	Y 50 m
	Z 50 m

The next layer, which sits on top of the first one, is a smoky procedural texture that has these settings:

Layer opacity:	100 percent
Texture value:	60 percent
Frequencies:	3
Contrast:	0
Small power:	.5
Scale:	X 60 m
	Y 60 m
	Z 60 m

The final layer, which is on top of the other two, is a crumple procedural texture with these settings:

Layer opacity:	50 percent
Texture value:	90 percent
Frequencies:	2
Small power:	1
Scale:	X 2 km
	Y 1 m
	Z 2 km

The basic settings for the water surface are:

Luminosity:	0 percent
Diffuse:	80 percent
Specularity:	80 percent
Glossiness:	100 percent
Bump:	100 percent

Reflection, transparency, and refraction will be taken care of by adding real Fresnel and thin film shaders to the water surface.

The thin film shader changes the color spectrum according to the camera angle's relationship to the water surface. It creates an "oil film on water" effect. The base color is set to the primary wavelength. The angle variation is the angle at which the colors begin to shift. Color mixing with blend intermingles the pattern with the original surface attributes. The following are some setting used for the thin film shader to alter the look of the water. You may decide to try other settings.

Primary wavelength (nm):	aqua
Angle variation (nm):	5
Color mixing:	Blend at 5 percent

The way we perceive light reflecting off a surface and refracting through a surface varies according to the viewer's angle to the surface. Water appears to be clear when viewed at close range, but gradually becomes more reflective from further away. A real Fresnel shader is based on real physics. It calculates the falloff for the transparency value.

Specular polarization calculates how waves of light are restricted in their direction according to the surface's specularity. Reflective polarization calculates the behavior of light waves according to the reflective properties of a surface. The following settings can serve as a rough guide.

Specular polarization	100 percent
Reflective polarization	100 percent

After the water object has been surfaced, it is time to add a displacement to it. Displacing the surface will make waves on the water. Since this water object is only a single polygon with subdivision mode turned on, you will have to give it a very high subdivision level to see the numerous waves. Set the subdivision or subpatch level to the following settings.

Subpatch or subdivision level display: 150
Subpatch or subdivision level render: 300

Turn on bump displacement with about a 10 mm distribution. Turn on displacement map and assign a turbulence procedural texture to the water object. You can use the following settings as an approximation for the degree of displacement.

Layer opacity:	1 percent
Displacement axis:	Y
Texture value:	3155
Frequencies:	10

Fig. 5-56 An image from the body of water animation.

Contrast:	12 percent
Small power:	.4
Scale:	X 500 m
	Y 500 m
	Z 500 m

Apply a reference object such as a null that will not render to the displacement map. Move the reference object across the water surface to animate the waves. If you move the reference object null from one end to the other over the course of 120 frames, you should get the right amount of wave action. If the camera is facing the water on the –z-axis, move the null from the +z-axis toward the camera. To complete the water scene, add a sky and some land. Chapter 10 contains instructions for creating land and trees. Chapter 9 discusses ways to light an environment.

The land and sky should reflect in the water after you turn on ray trace reflection, ray trace refraction, and ray trace transparency. Be prepared

for long rendering times. The chapter 5 folder of the CD-ROM contains a short animation of a body of water. An image from the animation can be seen in Figure 5-56 (Chapter 5 > Animation > Body Of Water > CD5-56 Body of Water.mov).

PART II

Advanced 3D Modeling

CHAPTER 6

Modeling the Human Figure

There are many approaches to modeling the human figure. Most of these methods were designed to accomplish specific aims such as easier sculpting of facial features, better facial animation, easier texturing, and so on. Of all these techniques, subdivision, or subpatch modeling, has the scope to achieve all the necessary objectives for modeling a realistic human and achieving the subsequent goals of lifelike movements and facial expressions.

This chapter outlines a method for modeling a human female. If your desire is to model a male, then you can refer to my other book, *3-D Human Modeling and Animation*, 2nd Edition (John Wiley and Sons Publishers).

Although most facets of human modeling will be examined in this chapter, the following chapter will cover details such as hair, eyes, teeth, and so on. It is recommended that you work from photographs and photographic templates that show front, side, back, and perhaps top views of the figure.

In chapter 2 you learned how to model a figure with clothes. This time, the human will be undraped so as to make one more aware of human anatomy. During the greatest ages of art, the nude inspired the finest art works. Even when it no longer held sway over art movements, the nude still retained its importance in the academic training of artists.

The Greeks taught us in the fifth century that the nude is not just a subject to be studied and imitated, but an art form in itself. Their knowledge gave us an understanding of the actions and structural characteristics found in the nude. Artists who painted and sculpted the nude learned to convey weight, rhythm, mass, line, value, texture, and tension.

To be successful in depicting the human body, one needs to have an understanding of anatomy. Perceiving the nude means understanding it. Without any knowledge of anatomy, it is impossible to recognize the inherent form of the nude.

Anatomy for the artist does not imply a doctor's understanding of the body. Internal organs, blood vessels, muscles, and bones that are not visible at or below the skin surface are not a concern to the 3D modeler.

The 3D animator should have knowledge of the skeletal/muscular system and the manner in which it works as a mechanical device. Without this understanding, it is very difficult to portray the human character in its various attitudes and movements.

There are many excellent books on human anatomy for artists. This book does not pretend to be one of them. The study of anatomy requires an entire book devoted to the subject. Anyone who is serious about studying 3D human modeling and animation should have a collection of anatomy books.

The various steps in this chapter that describe the manner in which to model the figure also contain some illustrations of human anatomy. These pertain to the specific modeling task at hand. The anatomy illustrations are only meant as a visual guide to help you see what lies below the surface of the part that will be modeled. They do not identify the parts' individual anatomical details with medical names. If you wish to know the designations of different bones and muscles, they can be found in anatomy textbooks or online.

Even though males and females have their differences, they are structurally homological to each other. Fat deposits and variations in their skeletons account for the greatest deviations.

The greater quantity of fat in the female makes her appear smooth and flowing. Aside from sexual differences, she is normally smaller, except in the hips.

The difference in the skeletal structure makes the female slighter in proportion. Her head is smaller and positioned relatively higher than the male. The brow ridges, unlike the male's, are nearly absent, adding to the forehead's smoother and more rounded appearance. The width of the shoulders is less than that of the trunk. In fact, this is the opposite of the male, whose shoulders are wider than the hips. The thyroid cartilage (Adam's apple) is flat compared to the prominent one in the male.

The trunk of the female, in contrast to the male, has a shorter rib cage, with outwardly visible breasts. The female pelvis is shorter but wider and deeper, and leans forward. At the base of the spine, the sacrum is broader and inclines behind to form a full triangle. The two dimples of this triangle are clearly visible. Due to a wider pelvis and fat deposits, the female is broader at the hips. The side between the ribs and hipbone is longer owing to the female's shorter rib cage and pelvis. The buttocks extend to a lower level than the male. The female also has a smoother, more rounded abdomen, with a deeper navel.

The female upper arm is shorter, resulting in a higher location of the elbow. When the arms are resting at the sides of the body, the fingertips extend to a higher point at the thigh. The wrist and hand are smaller.

The wider hipbones separate the legs in their pelvic sockets to a greater degree. This makes the legs slant more toward the knees. The knees are fleshier, but the kneecaps and their ligaments are less obvious. The calves located below the knees are lower on the female. The feet are smaller.

Artists throughout the ages have tried to calculate the average size of a human. Despite all that, we still do not know the normal scale of the figure. Classic Greek and Renaissance bodies were eight heads tall. Mannerists such as El Greco and Pontormo painted long figures measuring nine heads or more.

The French anatomist Richer was the first to determine that the traditional measurement of the average human was about seven and one-half skull-lengths. Although in real life a figure of that height would seem well-proportioned, on a 2D surface the body appears much broader and stockier. To remedy this, artists have found that when portraying the nude as eight heads tall, the figure appears more slender and graceful.

One of the more difficult tasks for computer artists is to model objects in the right proportions. Therefore, in order to simplify your work and help you model more accurately, it is recommended that you take digital pictures of a nude figure. It is also advisable to take close-up views of the head, hands, and feet. Perhaps someone will create an online repository of assorted nude figures in their various poses. As more artists contribute to the site, these should serve as an invaluable aid to 3D modelers.

Modeling the Head

Before starting to model the face, it is recommended that you study the various muscles and their purpose. While reading about these muscles, you may want to use a hand-held mirror to observe their effects on various expressions.

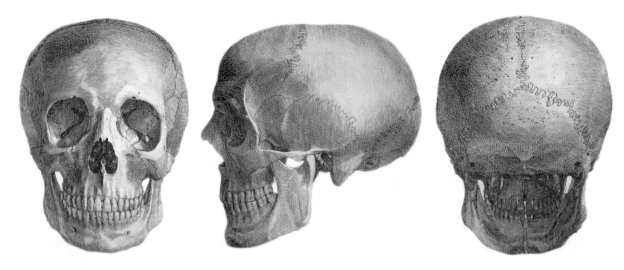

Fig. 6-1 Some of the more prominent features of the skull that affect the contours of the face are the forehead, eye sockets, nasal bone, cheekbones, the empty pockets between the jaw and cheekbones, and the chin.

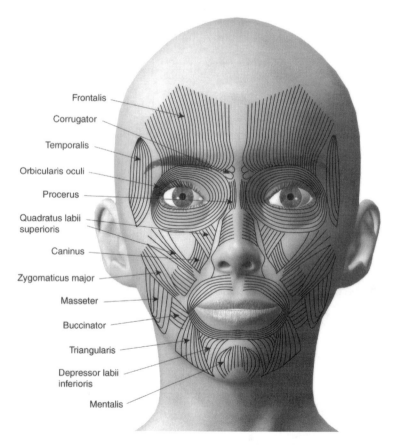

Frontalis
Corrugator
Temporalis
Orbicularis oculi
Procerus
Quadratus labii superioris
Caninus
Zygomaticus major
Masseter
Buccinator
Triangularis
Depressor labii inferioris
Mentalis

The Skull

Since the muscles of the head are thin and flat, it is the shape of the skull that dictates the overall form of the head. Figure 6-1 illustrates various views of the skull. Visualizing the skull beneath the head makes it easier to see the respective masses that shape the face.

The Muscles of the Head

It is important to note that no skeletal muscle acts on its own. When one muscle contracts or draws together its fibers, it activates other, opposing muscles, which in turn

Fig. 6-2 The muscles of the head are divided into three groups: scalp, face, and mastication.

modify the action of the original contracting muscle. Normally, the head is broken up into three sets of muscles. Most of these are small, thin, or deeply embedded in fatty tissue. A few of the muscles shown in Figure 6-2 warrant special attention. They play an important role in facial expressions and help define the contours of the face.

The *Masseter* and the *Temporalis* control movement of the jaw. These muscles are responsible for the closing and biting movements of the mandible. The muscles that open the jaw are deepseated inside the neck and are not readily visible.

The *Frontalis* is a broad, flat muscle located in the forehead. It wrinkles the brow horizontally and raises the eyebrows. It contributes to an angry or surprised look.

The *Corrugator* is a small muscle attached to the bridge of the nose. It dramatically affects the surface of the forehead when one frowns or expresses grief. By pulling the inner ends of the eyebrows together, it forces vertical wrinkles of the brow.

Circling the mouth is the *Orbicularis Oris*. This elliptical muscle has the unique characteristic of not being attached to any bones. Instead, it is connected to a number of small muscles pointing toward the mouth. It curls and tightens the lips. The creases that result from contracting this muscle radiate from the lips and can often be seen in the elderly.

The *Orbicularis Oculi* is another circular muscle circumscribing the eye. Its contractions create wrinkles at the corners of the eyes (crow's feet). Its primary function is to close the eyelids for expressions like squinting.

The *Zygomatic Major* angles from the side to the front of the face at the corners of the mouth. Its function is the energetic upward traction at the corners of the mouth. It takes fewer muscles to smile than it does to frown.

Located at the side of the nose are the three branches of the *Quadratus Labii Superioris*. Their function is to raise the upper lip for sneering.

The *Triangularis* and *Depressor Labii Inferioris* are responsible for the downward pull of the mouth and lips.

The *Mentalis* moves the skin of the chin and pushes up the lower lip.

Modeling the Head Steps

Step 1 (Figure 6-3). After loading your photo templates of the head, create a box that is similar in size to your background images.

Step 2 (Figure 6-3). Divide the cube into smaller

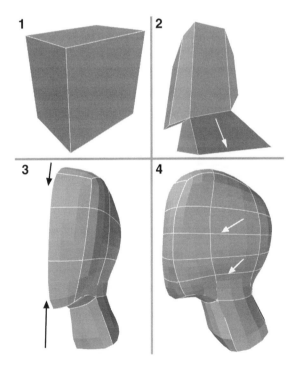

Fig. 6-3 Head Steps 1–4. 1) Making a box. 2) Dividing it and bevel extruding the neck down. 3) Dividing the head down the middle and shaping only half of it. 4) Adding extra lines for more detailed modeling.

sections and bevel extrude the neck part down.

Step 3 (Figure 6-3). At the 0 x-axis, split the head down the middle and delete one half of it. In subpatch or subdivision mode, refine the shape of the half-head.

Step 4 (Figure 6-3). Split the half-head into more sections and use the extra points to further refine the head.

Step 5 (Figure 6-4). The illustration indicates the region where the mouth will be modeled. This darker polygon is where the mouth will be split and beveled.

Step 6 (Figure 6-4). Split the polygons and move points so that the configuration looks similar to the darker polygons in the illustration.

Step 7 (Figure 6-4). Merge the two polygons of

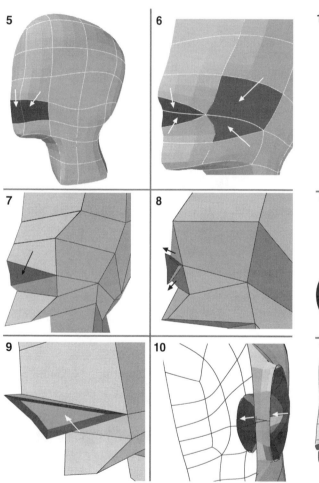

Fig. 6-4 Steps 5–10. 5) Preparing the mouth area (dark part). 6) The darker areas show where polygons are split and points moved. 7) Merging to upper and lower lips. 8) Beveling out the mouth. 9) Beveling in the mouth. 10) Beveling in to start the inside of the mouth.

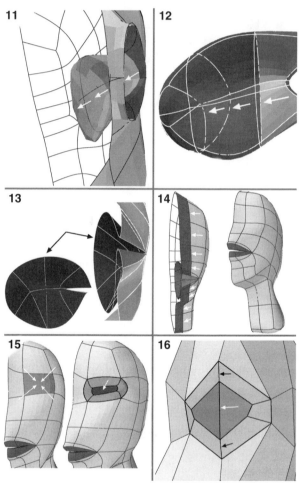

Fig. 6-5 Steps 11–16. 11) Beveling the inside of the mouth once again. 12) A few more bevels complete the inside of the mouth. 13) Shaping the inside of the mouth and splitting the back polygons. 14) Refining the half-lips. 15) Making the first bevel for the eyesocket. 16) Splitting the eye area in half.

the upper and lower lip so that the one polygon can be beveled in the next step.

Step 8 (Figure 6-4). Bevel out the mouth a little.

Step 9 (Figure 6-4). Bevel in the mouth to about the same plane as the polygons of the front face.

Step 10 (Figure 6-4). Bevel in the first part of the inside of the mouth.

Step 11 (Figure 6-5). Bevel in the second part of the inside mouth area.

Step 12 (Figure 6-5). Make several more bevels to complete the inside of the mouth.

Step 13 (Figure 6-5). Shape the inside mouth part so that it is rounder. If the back polygon has more than four sides, split it up into three- or four-sided polygons. Delete any inside mouth polygons that were created along the 0 x-axis from beveling. The half inside mouth should be an open form.

Step 14 (Figure 6-5). Fine-tune the shape of the lips. The half-mouth is now nearly complete.

Step 15 (Figure 6-5). Begin the eyesocket by selecting the polygon in that area and beveling it in once.

Step 16 (Figure 6-5). Divide the middle of the eyesocket and move points to give it a more almond-like shape.

Step 17 (Figure 6-6). Weld the two points at both corners of the eye opening. Merge the inside polygon (dark area in the illustration).

Step 18 (Figure 6-6). Bevel the inside polygon inward a little so that you have an extra line around the eye opening (dark part).

Step 19 (Figure 6-6). Bevel the eye opening polygon in once again.

Step 20 (Figure 6-6). Split the polygons around the eye opening and refine its shape.

Step 21 (Figure 6-6). The corner of the eye (dark part) should now be split and shaped. This is the area where the pink membrane will be seen.

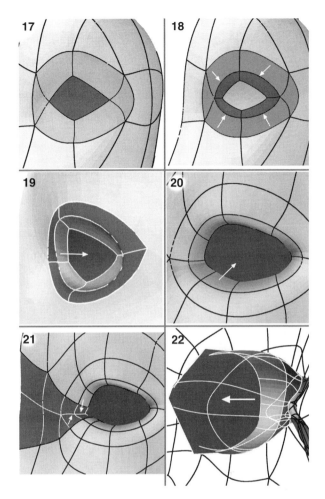

Fig. 6-6 Steps 17–22. 17) Welding points at both corners of the eyesocket and merging the two half-polygons (dark part). 18) Beveling in slightly to add a line around the opening. 19) Beveling in once more to begin the eye socket. 20) Pushing and pulling points and splitting polygons to improve the eye opening. 21) Dividing and moving points at the corner of the eye. 22) Beveling the eye socket in several more times.

Step 22 (Figure 6-6). Continue work on the eyesocket by beveling it in a couple more times.

Step 23 (Figure 6-7). Bevel the eyesocket in once

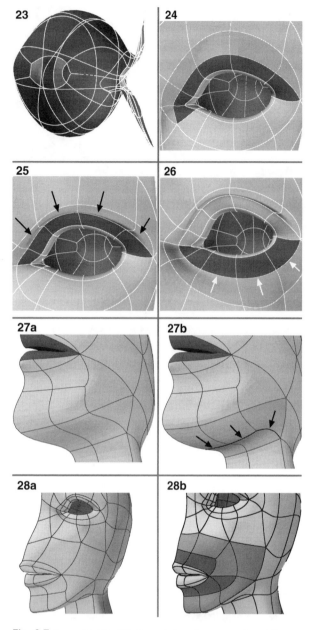

Fig. 6-7 Steps 23–28. 23) Completing the eye socket. 24) Dividing polygons above the eye opening. 25) Dragging points down to form the upper eyelid. 26) Splitting the polygons below the eye opening to make a crease. 27) Refining the jaw by splitting polygons. 28) Splitting polygons around the lips.

again. If necessary, split the back polygon into three- and four-sided polygons. Shape the eyesocket to make it round enough to accommodate the eyeball, which will be modeled in the next chapter.

Step 24 (Figure 6-7). Divide the polygons above the eye opening (dark area of the illustration). The resulting line will form the eyelid.

Step 25 (Figure 6-7). Drag the points above the dark part down and forward a little. Move the vertices of the top of the dark area back and up somewhat. This should form the upper eyelid.

Step 26 (Figure 6-7). Make the crease below the eye opening by splitting polygons. Move the points underneath the eye opening to create a line there. If your model has bags under the eyes, you can easily shape one with the two parallel lines.

Step 27 (Figure 6-7). The polygons below the chin should be split. Move the resulting points to improve the chin area.

Step 28 (Figure 6-7). Now it is time to begin polishing the shape of the head. This means that polygons in certain areas will have to be split into smaller ones, and some will have to be merged. Points will also be moved. If your software has the ability to spin quads, then use this option to find the best configuration for the different polygons. The dark parts in the illustrations indicate where you will have to split and merge polygons. Notice the change in polygons between Step 28a and Step 28b.

Step 29 (Figure 6-8). The polygons in the forehead region are too large, so they should now be divided into smaller ones.

Step 30 (Figure 6-8). The middle section on the side of the head running through the ear part is divided all the way down to the bottom of the neck.

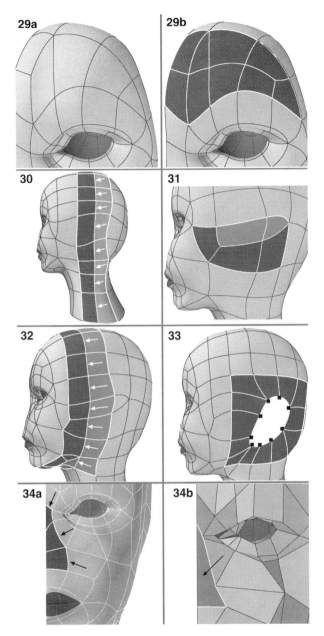

Fig. 6-8 Steps 29–34. 29) Dividing and shaping the forehead polygons. 30) Splitting the polygons in the center. 31) Dividing polygons by the ear. 32) Splitting polygons down from the top of the head to the chin. 33) Merging polygons into one for the ear location and arranging the nine points around it.

34) Beginning the nose by unifying polygons into one.

Step 31 (Figure 6-8). The polygons where the ear will be modeled are too large, so they should now be split into sections like those shown as darker values.

Step 32 (Figure 6-8). The illustration indicates the location where more polygons are split down and across the base of the chin.

Step 33 (Figure 6-8). Move points around the location for the ear so that you have a rough shape of its outline. You should have nine points outlining the ear. Merge the polygons where the ear will go. Continue moving points around this polygon until you have a shape similar to the white area of the illustration.

Step 34 (Figure 6-8). Split and move points on the polygons so they look similar to the dark area in the illustration where the nose will be modeled. Merge the three polygons into one.

Step 35 (Figure 6-9). Select the merged nose polygon and bevel it outward to make the general shape of the nose.

Step 36 (Figure 6-9). Divide the nose polygon into four-sided ones. Move points to shape the nose. A more detailed nose will be modeled after the next few steps, which involve refining parts of the face.

Step 37 (Figure 6-9). Use the dark areas of the illustration as a guide for splitting polygons underneath the nose.

Step 38 (Figure 6-9). Divide polygons on the cheek area.

Step 39 (Figure 6-9). Split more polygons next to the nose.

Step 40 (Figure 6-9). Divide polygons along the lower half of the nose and the cheek.

Step 41 (Figure 6-9). Make a line along the side of the nose next to the nose wing by dividing poly-

133

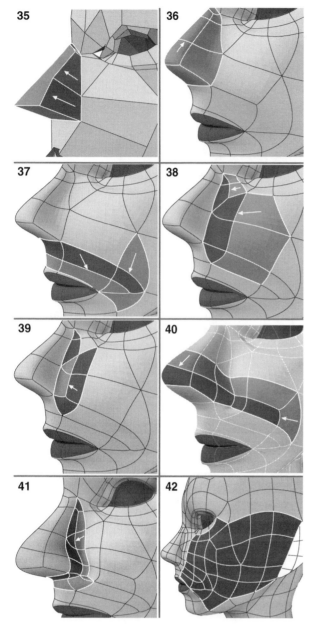

Fig. 6-9 Steps 35–42. 35) Beveling out the nose polygon. 36) Dividing the nose polygon so each section has four sides. 37) Splitting polygons and moving points below the nose (darker areas). 38) Dividing polygons next to the nose. 39) Refining the polygons next to the nose by splitting them some more. 40) Dividing some more polygons. 41) Making an extra line close to the nose wing. 42) Splitting polygons and moving points on the side of the face.

gons. Pull and push points to make the indentation that follows the edge of the nose wing.

Step 42 (Figure 6-9). Refine the side of the face (dark area) by further splitting polygons, rearranging them, and moving points.

Step 43 (Figure 6-10). Divide the polygons at the bottom of the nose so that you have one that can be beveled up to make the nostril (dark polygon in the illustration).

Step 44 (Figure 6-10). Bevel the nostril polygon inward a little to form the outer edge of the nostril.

Step 45 (Figure 6-10). Bevel the polygon up into the nose to make the first inside section of the nostril.

Step 46 (Figure 6-10). Bevel the nostril polygon up once more to complete the nostril. Move points to refine the nostril's shape. Notice the other inside views of the eyesocket and inner mouth forms.

Step 47 (Figure 6-10). Follow the illustration to make a line at the lower half of the nose. Pull and push points closer to each other to make the upper line of the nose wing more distinct.

Step 48 (Figure 6-10). Refine the shape of the nose at the top by splitting polygons and moving points. Notice the nose wing now has a distinct shape.

Step 49 (Figure 6-10). Use a set value to move all the points at the center seam to the 0 x-axis. This is important if you don't want to have holes and creases along the center of the face after mirror duplicating it. Check to make sure that there are no middle polygons for the inside mouth and eyesocket. When the face is mirrored, there should be a hollow for these without polygons dividing them in half. These kinds of polygons are an annoyance since they pull on the outer ones, creating unsightly creases. Check the nostril to make sure that you did not move any of its points to the

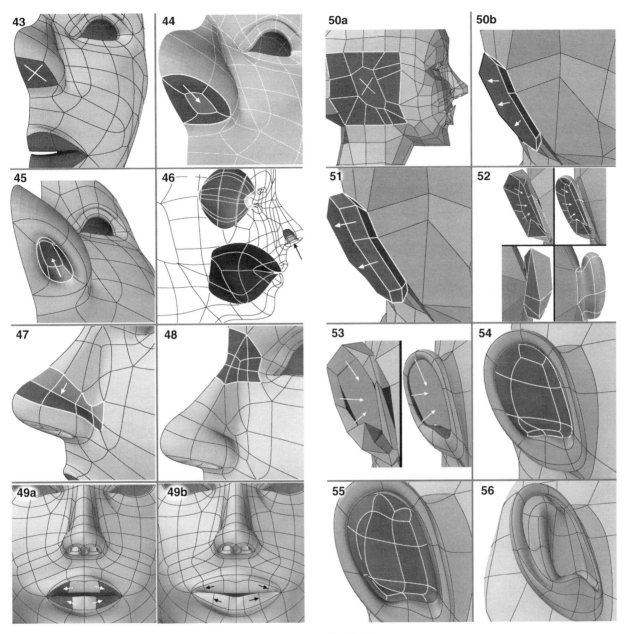

Fig. 6-10 Steps 43–49. 43) Starting the nostril by selecting the polygon to bevel up. 44) The first bevel of the nostril. 45) The second bevel of the nostril. 46) The final bevel of the nostril. 47) Creating the line for the upper portion of the nose wing. 48) Dividing polygons at the top of the nose. 49) Dividing polygons at the corners of the lips and refining their shape. Adjusting the width of the nose after mirror duplicating the half-face.

Fig. 6-11 Steps 50–56. 50) Selecting and beveling out the ear polygon. 51) Beveling out the ear polygon once again. 52) Beveling in and refining the rim of the ear. 53) Beveling in one last time for the bowl of the ear. 54) Dividing the inside ear polygon. 55) Dividing some more and moving points. 56) Shaping the inside of the ear.

0 x-axis.

Step 49 Continued. (Figure 6-10). Notice the dark areas at the corners of the lips. In order to make the lips look fuller, you should split their polygons once more in this area. Push and pull the extra points as well as the other ones to improve the shape of the lips. Mirror duplicate the half-face. Turn on symmetry and move the vertices around the nose to refine its form. Delete one half of the face so that you can concentrate on modeling one ear.

Step 50 (Figure 6-11). Select or create a polygon from the points around the ear opening. Bevel out the ear polygon so that it increases in size somewhat.

Step 51 (Figure 6-11). Bevel the ear polygon out once again so that it decreases in size a little.

Step 52 (Figure 6-11). Bevel in the outer ear polygon to begin the bowl of the ear. The polygon's size should decrease a little. Move points to improve the rim of the ear shape.

Step 53 (Figure 6-11). Bevel the ear polygon in a little more and make its size bigger. This will be the last ear bevel.

Step 54 (Figure 6-11). Split the beveled ear polygon up into three- and four-sided polygons.

Step 55 (Figure 6-11). Divide the polygons of the upper portion of the inside ear. Begin shaping the inside ear.

Step 56 (Figure 6-11). Move points inward to form the ear canal.

Step 57 (Figure 6-12). Model the small dimple at the top of the inside ear after splitting some of the polygons.

Step 58 (Figure 6-12). Sculpt the ear flap after dividing polygons. Make the transition between the ear and the side of the head smooth. It should appear seamless.

Step 59 (Figure 6-12). Continue modeling the ear flap by splitting polygons and moving points.

Step 60 (Figure 6-12). Continue dividing polygons on the inside part of the ear so that you can refine its shape by pulling and pushing points.

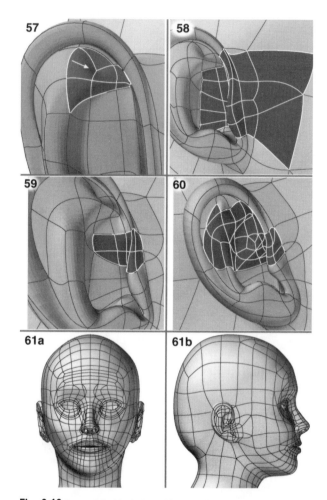

Fig. 6-12 Steps 57–61. 57) Dividing and moving points for the upper part of the ear bowl. 58) Splitting polygons and moving points to make the ear flap. Smoothing the section between the ear and the head. 59) Dividing and moving points to refine the shape of the ear flap. 60) Splitting and pushing/pulling points to complete the ear. 61) Mirror duplicating the half-head. If necessary, refining parts of the head with symmetry on.

Step 61 (Figure 6-12). Make sure all the points along the center seam of the head are at the 0 x-axis. Mirror duplicate the half-head and make sure the points are merged at the center seam. If needed, finish the head by moving points with symmetry on.

Modeling the Torso

The chest is built around the bony structure of the ribs, spine, shoulder blades, collarbone, and breast-bone (Figure 6-13). These bones support the muscles and protect the internal organs. In its most basic form, the chest is cone-shaped. Twelve ribs on each side form the walls of the upper torso.

Each rib fastens to the spine, and the top nine are also attached to the breastbone in front. The upper torso bones greatly influence the muscles. These bones will often show on the surface and affect the outside structure. Modeling the chest incorporates this bony framework. The collarbone and shoulder blades define the top shape of the chest and make it seem wider than it is. The movement of the shoulder bones is significantly noticeable under the skin. The spinal column is discernible in the center of the back. The breastbone forms a flat, downward wedge in the middle of the chest. The lower part of the ribs is often visible along the forward sides of the chest.

The pelvic area contains the hipbone, which

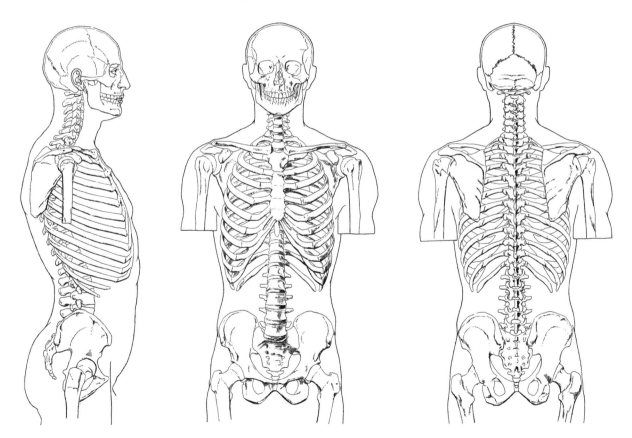

Fig. 6-13 The upper body skeleton.

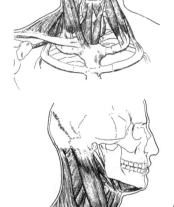

influences the pattern of the muscles, hence determining the shape of the lower abdomen. On the sides, you can usually feel and see the upper contour of the pelvis. All the actions that the human body is capable of originate in the back of the lower torso. From the hips and pelvis, these movements are transmitted up and down the entire body.

The Muscles of the Torso

The visible muscles of the front neck start behind the ears, angle toward the center of the breastbone, and attach to the collarbone (Figure 6-14). The back of the neck has a large triangle-shaped muscle named the *Trapezius*. It supports

Fig. 6-14 The muscles of the neck.

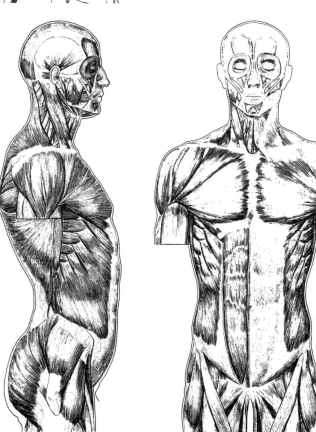

Fig. 6-15 The muscles of the upper body.

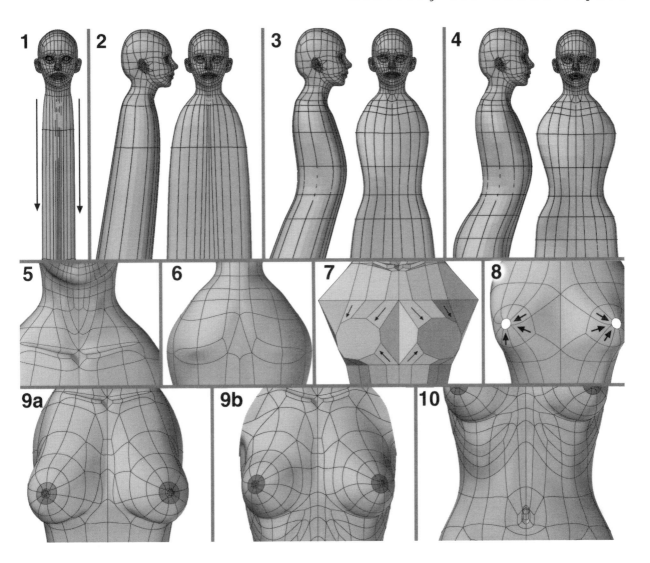

Fig. 6-16 Torso Steps 1–10. 1) Selecting or making a polygon at the bottom of the neck and beveling it down. 2) Starting the torso shape by making it broader. 3) Slicing across in several places and moving points in at the waist. 4) Dividing polygons some more for extra points that are moved to improve the torso. 5) Dividing polygons and pulling/pushing points to make the neck and collarbone. 6) Splitting polygons at the upper back to form the shoulder blades. 7) Merging polygons in the breast area and beveling outward. 8) Beveling the breasts again and forming the shape around the nipples. 9) Beveling several times to make the nipples. Dividing the breast polygons and moving points to improve its shape. 10) Splitting polygons and pushing/pulling points to form the lower ribs and navel.

the weight of the head in the back.

The chest muscles proceed outward toward the arms to form the front wall of the armpit (Figure 6-15). The trapezius muscle that originates at the base of the skull radiates across the back of the neck toward the shoulders and down, where it converges in the middle of the back.

It is interesting to note that muscles do not end at the joints. Rather, they cross over them to attach to bones on the other side. Mobility would be impossible if the muscles did not cross over joints. Since the muscles become thinner at the joints, beginners often think muscles end there. So the tendency is to draw, sculpt, or model the figure as if it was made up of separate sections. Sometimes this is called the "sausage-link syndrome."

A vertical central groove divides the front part of the torso. It originates at the pit of the neck and ends at the navel. To the artist, it is useful for placing the masses of the chest.

When the arms are raised, the abdominal (or thoracic) arch becomes a highly visible form below the rib cage. It almost acts as a line separating the

upper torso from the lower one. The upper part of the torso is more bony in appearance, while the lower torso has a fleshier look. The waist is high on the female, and the buttocks form a butterfly shape.

Modeling the Torso Steps

Step 1 (Figure 6-16). At the base of the neck, select the polygon or create one first from the points there. Bevel it down to the groin area.

Step 2 (Figure 6-16). With symmetry on, make the torso wider.

Step 3 (Figure 6-16). Slice across polygons to divide them. Move the extra points to create a rough shape of the torso.

Step 4 (Figure 6-16). Split polygons on the torso again and model the curves of the back and sides.

Step 5 (Figure 6-16). At this point, you can delete half the torso along the 0 x-axis. You should find it easier to just work on one half and later mirror duplicate it. The illustrations show both halves so they can be seen in relationship to each other. Divide polygons at the front of the neck and upper

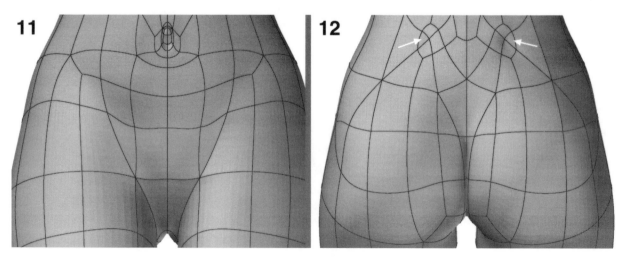

Fig. 6-17 Steps 11 and 12. 11) Dividing the polygons at the lower abdomen and pushing/pulling points below the navel. 12) Splitting polygons at the back of the pelvis. Points are moved to shape the buttocks, the hips, and the two dimples of the pelvic crest.

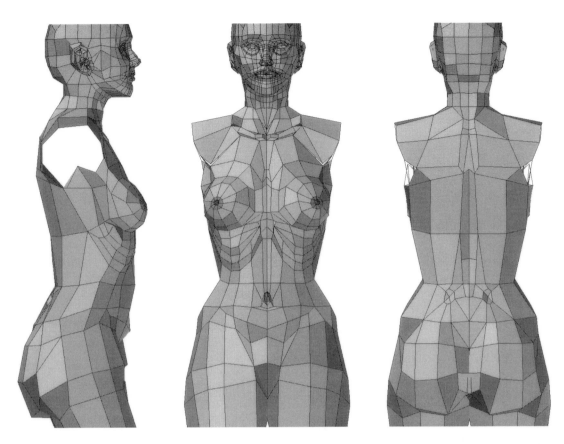

Fig. 6-18 The female torso in low polygon mode.

torso. Push/pull points to shape the neck and collarbone.

Step 6 (Figure 6-16). Model the shoulder blades after splitting polygons.

Step 7 (Figure 6-16). Merge the polygons at the breast and arrange the points to form a round shape. Bevel extrude this polygon.

Step 8 (Figure 6-16). Bevel out again so that the polygon becomes smaller where the nipple begins. Remember that the breasts point outward and the nipples up.

Step 9 (Figure 6-16). Bevel the nipple out and in about four times. Weld the points at the tip. Refine the shape of the breast. You may need to mirror the torso just to see the relative distance between the two breasts. Of course, their shape varies a

great deal and should be proportional to the size of your model.

Step 10 (Figure 6-16). Split and model the polygons of the lower ribs and navel.

Step 11 (Figure 6-17). The front of the lower section of the torso should now be split into smaller polygons. Push and pull points to make the shape of the hips, the plateau of the navel and abdomen (which are mostly covered with fat), the pubic arch, and the slight hollow where the upper legs join the torso.

Step 12 (Figure 6-17). Model the back of the lower torso. Divide polygons and move points to shape the buttock and the dimple at the pelvic crest. After making sure that the points at the seam are on the 0 x-axis, mirror duplicate the half-torso. The points along the 0 x-axis and base of the neck should merge. With symmetry on, con-

 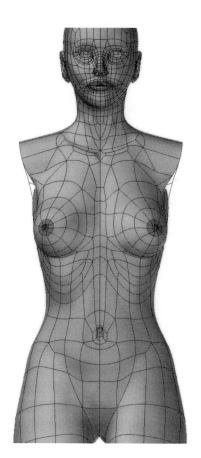 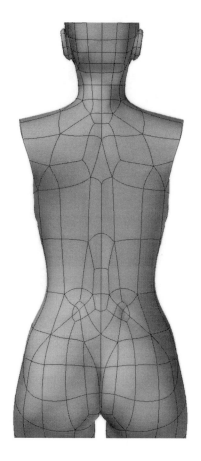

Fig. 6-19 The female torso in subdivision mode.

tinue shaping the buttocks. You need to have both halves of the torso visible in order to model this part correctly.

Figures 6-18 and 6-19 show the finished torso in low polygon and subdivision mode.

Modeling the Arms

The most maneuverable part of the body is the arm. The combined movements of the shoulder girdle, hand, and fingers create an almost unlimited mobility.

The Bones of the Arm

The arm has a similar combination of bones to the leg: one on top and two on the bottom (Figure 6-20). The most common places where the skeleton of the arm becomes visible on the skin surface are the top of the arm bone where it meets the collarbone, and at the elbow, wrist joint, and knuckles.

Unlike the legs, the arms are not built to support the body. Therefore, their bones are slender and their joints are capable of the widest range of motions possible. The ball-and-socket joint at the shoulder gives the arm the potential to rotate in any direction. The hinge joint at the elbow revolves the lower arm forward. Another hinge joint at the wrist rotates the hand in any direction.

One of the forearms can cross the other, allowing the hand even greater mobility.

The Muscles of the Arm

Four main groups form the arm muscles. Two of these are in the upper arm. They control the hinge joint of the elbow. When the arm hangs at the side, they can be seen at the front and back (Figure 6-21).

Two muscles of the top front group connect to the forearm and control its forward rotation. The back group of muscles appear as one when the arm is in a relaxed state.

The two groups of forearm muscles operate the wrist joint. Their actions are very intricate because they also twist the forearm and move the fingers.

The muscles in the hands do not influence the shape of the fingers and thumb as much as the

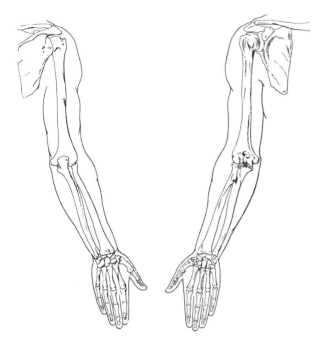

Fig. 6-20 Front and back views of the arm bones.

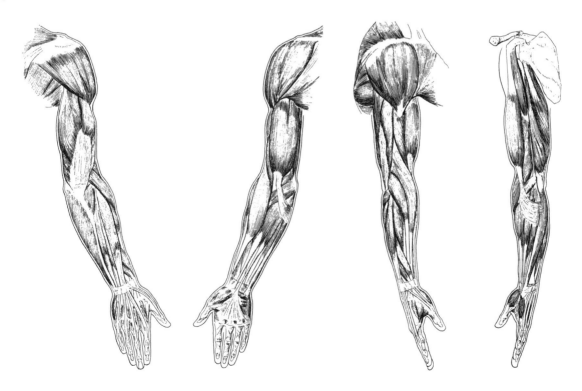

Fig. 6-21 Views of the arm muscles.

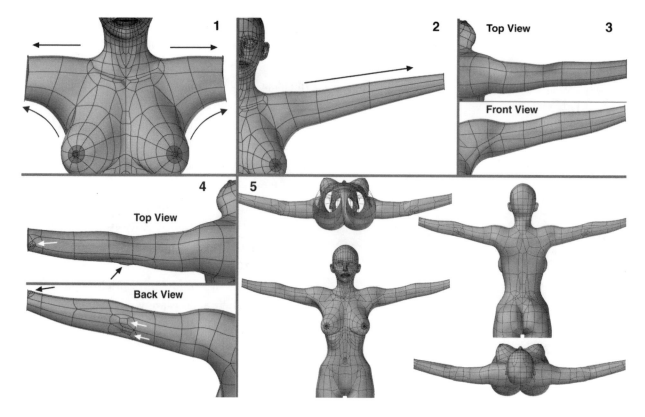

Fig. 6-22 Arm Steps 1–5. 1) Merging polygons between the shoulder and armpit, and beveling it out. 2) Beveling the entire length of the arm. 3) Slicing across vertically to create more polygons. Moving points to give the arm a rough shape. 4) Adding details, such as the surface characteristics of the elbow and wrist bones. 5) Mirror duplicating the finished arm.

skeleton does. Therefore, when modeling the hand, it is important to pay attention to its skeletal form.

Modeling the Arm Steps

Step 1 (Figure 6-22). It will be easier if you concentrate on modeling only one arm and then later mirror duplicate it to attach to the opposite side of the body. Find the group of polygons on the side of the torso from which the arm will be bevel extruded. Merge these into one and make the first bevel that forms the shoulder.

Step 2 (Figure 6-22). Bevel the arm polygon all the way to the wrist.

Step 3 (Figure 6-22). Slice in a vertical direction to split the arm up into smaller sections of polygons. Be sure to split the polygons across the elbow joint and once above and below it. Begin to shape the arm by pushing and pulling points.

Step 4 (Figure 6-22). Refine the arm by continuing to move points and splitting polygons where necessary. Add details, such as the prominent bones at the elbow and wrist. Make the armpit and shoulder muscle more defined.

Step 5 (Figure 6-22). Mirror duplicate the finished arm and attach it to the other side of the figure.

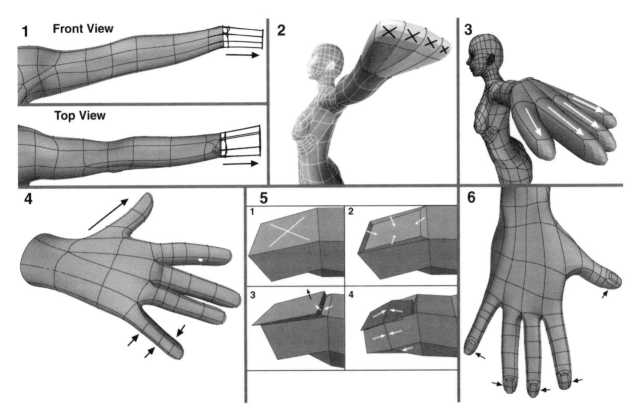

Fig. 6-23 Hand Steps 1–6. 1) Beveling out the polygon for the hand. 2) Dividing the hand polygon so that four polygons can be beveled out for the fingers. 3) Beveling out the fingers. 4) Beveling out the thumb and dividing it and the fingers into sections. 5) Beveling the fingernail polygon down and up and then splitting it in half. 6) Creating the rest of the fingernails.

Modeling the Hand Steps

Step 1 (Figure 6-23). As with the arm, you can concentrate on modeling only one hand and then mirroring it so that it can be attached to the other arm. Select the polygon at the wrist and bevel it out for the length of the hand, but not the fingers.

Step 2 (Figure 6-23). Divide the end of the hand polygon into four. Split across the hand so that you do not have any polygons with more than four sides.

Step 3 (Figure 6-23). Select the four polygons at the end of the hand and bevel them out for the length of the fingers.

Step 4 (Figure 6-23). Bevel out the thumb.

Divide the fingers and thumb polygons by slicing across their joints. Be sure to also slice polygons where the fingernails begin.

Step 5 (Figure 6-23). Follow the steps in the illustration to model a fingernail. The top polygon is beveled down and made slightly smaller. It is then beveled up and increased in size. Slice across the middle of the nail polygon and fingertip. This will keep the nail from ballooning out in subdivision mode. Improve the shape of the nail.

Step 6 (Figure 6-23). Continue modeling the rest of the nails or attach copies of the first one to the other fingers and thumb. Vary the nail according to the size and shape of the other digits.

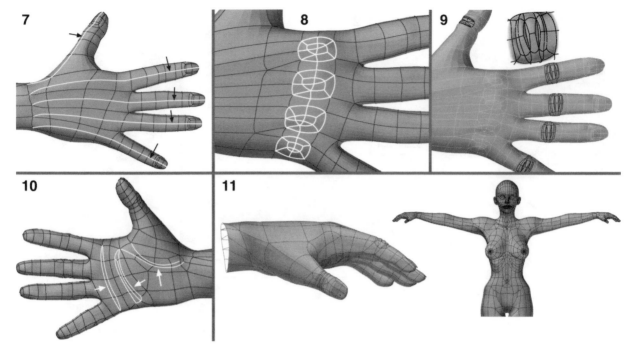

Fig. 6-24 Steps 7–11. 7) Splitting the fingers and thumb across the top and pulling those points up to make the thumb and fingers more round. 8) Dividing polygons at the knuckles and pulling/pushing points. 9) Modeling the crease marks of the finger and thumb joints. 10) Splitting polygons and moving points to make the major lines of the palm. 11) Bending the fingers into their more relaxed state. Mirror duplicating the hand and attaching it to the other arm.

Step 7 (Figure 6-24). The fingers and thumb are still somewhat boxy because they are composed of only four polygons each. Divide the fingers, thumb, and hand across the tops of their lengths. The white lines in the illustration indicates the location of these. The points on these new lines are then moved up slightly.

Step 8 (Figure 6-24). The white lines on the illustration shows where you should now split polygons to make the knuckles. Move the center point of each up a little.

Step 9 (Figure 6-24). The dark lines in the illustration display the location of the crease lines on the fingers and thumb. After splitting polygons in parallel lines like these, move the points of every other one down a little to form slight depressions.

Step 10 (Figure 6-24). Model the major creases on the palm by creating parallel lines (white lines in the illustration). Pull and push points until you get the slight concavities.

Step 11 (Figure 6-24). Bend the fingers and thumb into their more natural relaxed poses. Mirror duplicate the hand and attach it to the other arm.

Modeling the Legs

Three basic parts make up the leg. These are the thigh (upper leg), lower leg, and foot. Even though the bones of the pelvic girdle are considered part of the torso, the muscles of the hip are usually described along with those of the leg.

The Bones of the Leg

Artists should be aware of the key areas where the bones of the leg are visible (Figure 6-25). These are the kneecap, shinbone, the upper part of the calf bone (next to the knee), the lower part of the calf bone (outer ankle), and the lower part of the shinbone (inner ankle).

The leg bones are somewhat similar to the arm bones in that both have one on top and two at the bottom, as well as similar joints. By contrast, the leg bones are heavier and stronger. This is due to their weight-bearing function and design for mobility. The leg joints are not as versatile as those of the arm.

The Muscles of the Leg

The leg muscles are not as well-defined as those in the arms, but they give the leg its total shape (Figure 6-26). The longest muscle in the body starts at the side of the hip and runs in a sweeping arc to the inner knee. One can see this curve in the developed legs of athletes.

In the side view, the thigh is rounded in front and back. The calf of the lower leg is also round, but the front shinbone, which is mostly exposed, makes the lower front part of the leg somewhat flat.

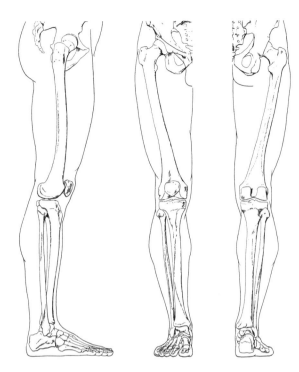

Fig. 6-25 The bones of the leg and feet.

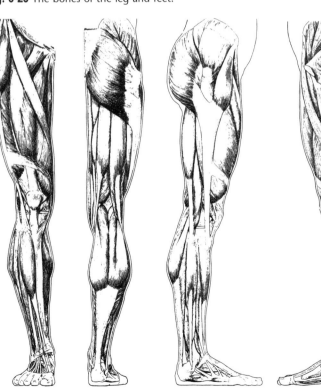

Fig. 6-26 The muscles of the leg.

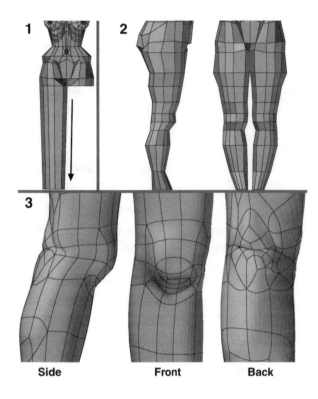

Side   **Front**   **Back**

Fig. 6-27 Leg Steps 1–3. 1) Beveling down the leg polygon. 2) Slicing across the leg and shaping it. 3) Dividing the polygons and moving points at and behind the knee.

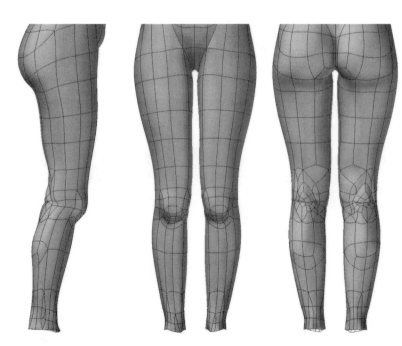

Modeling the Leg Steps

Step 1 (Figure 6-27). Similarly to the arm, there is no need to model both legs at the same time. If you have not done so already, split the polygon at the base of the groin in half. Select one of these two polygons and bevel it all the way down to the bottom of the foot.

Step 2 (Figure 6-27). Cut across the polygons of the leg in a horizontal direction. It is important to slice through the middle of the knee as well as above and below it. Give the leg its overall shape by pushing and pulling points.

Step 3 (Figure 6-27). Model the knee and the back of that joint. Spend some more time refining the shape of the leg.

Step 4 (Figure 6-28). Mirror duplicate the leg and weld or merge points to attach it to the other side of the body.

Modeling the Foot Steps

When you model the foot, it is important to pay attention to its skeletal structure (Figure 6-29). Most of the muscles in the foot are either between or underneath the bones. Therefore, their influence on the shape of the foot is not as great as that of the bones.

Step 1 (Figure 6-30). Select the polygons at the front of the foot and merge them into one.

Step 2 (Figure 6-30). Bevel the front foot polygon forward to where the toes will begin. Give it a rough shape.

Step 3 (Figure 6-30). Split the

Fig. 6-28 Step 4. The legs after mirror duplicating.

front foot polygon into five sections for the toes.

Step 4 (Figure 6-30). Bevel out the toes.

Step 5 (Figure 6-30). Slice across the toes to split them into sections at the joints and the beginning of the toenail. Pull and push points to refine the

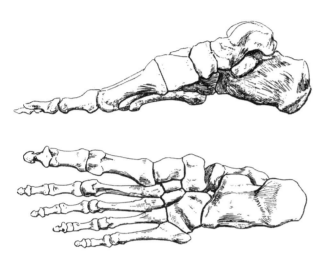

Fig. 6-29 The foot bones.

shape of the toes.

Step 6 (Figure 6-30). Begin the toenail by selecting the top front polygon of the large toe.

Step 7 (Figure 6-30). Bevel the toenail polygon down and make it somewhat smaller.

Step 8 (Figure 6-30). Bevel the toenail polygon up and scale it larger.

Step 9 (Figure 6-30). Slice across the middle of the toenail and through the toe itself. Move points to finish the toe. Follow the same steps to make toenails for the other four toes. It is important to slice across the top of the toes the same way as the fingers and thumb. The extra lines are then used to pull points up in order to make the toes more round.

Step 10 (Figure 6-31). Finish the work on the foot by improving its shape. You will most likely have to split some of the larger polygons.

Step 11 (Figure 6-32). Mirror duplicate the completed foot and attach it to the other leg. Bend the

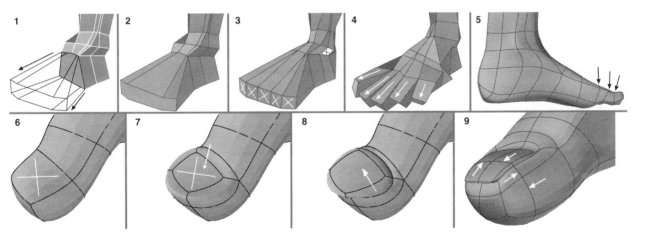

Fig. 6-30 Foot Steps 1–9. 1) Merging the front foot polygon so it can be beveled out. 2) Beveling the front foot polygon forward. 3) Dividing the front polygon into five sections for the toes. 4) Beveling out the toes. 5) Slicing across the toes to make more points that can be moved. Shaping the toes. 6) Starting the toenail by selecting the top polygon at the toe tip. 7) Beveling the toe polygon down and scaling it smaller. 8) Beveling the toe polygon up and enlarging it. 9) Slicing across the middle of the toenail and toe tip. Dividing the toes across the top to make them more rounded.

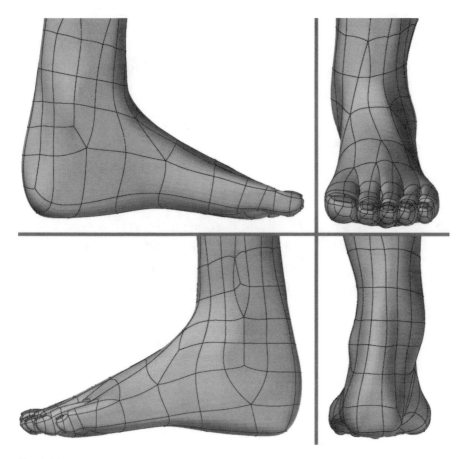

Fig. 6-31 Step 10. Finalizing the foot and toes in the various view windows.

arms and legs so they will deform better during animation.

Except for some details, this completes the nude figure. In the future, rather than starting from a box again, you may decide to just use this model as a base. You should find it easier to reshape a completed model into other ones with different proportions. Be sure to make the facial morph targets (chapter 11) before you do this. It will save a lot of time because you will not have to model new ones for the next figure. Of course, if the face has a radical makeover, you will have to adjust some of the morphs.

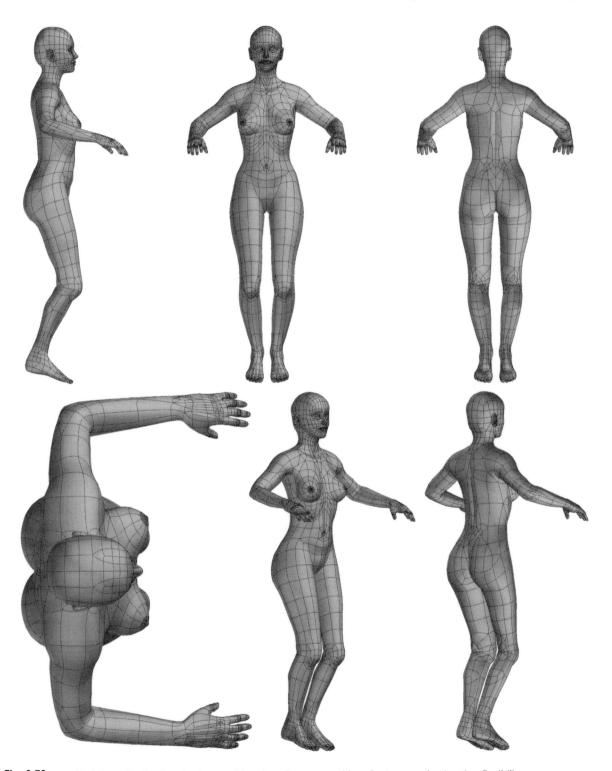

Fig. 6-32 Step 11. Mirror duplicating the foot and bending the arms and legs for improved animation flexibility.

CHAPTER 7

Completing the Figure

In the previous chapter, the female was modeled except for a few important details. This chapter shows how to finish the nude by modeling teeth, gums, a tongue, an eye, eyelashes, eyebrows, and hair. If you have been following the previous chapters to model several different characters, it should be fairly easy to complete the model. Although 3D modeling will continue to be a time-consuming task, you should find that it is not as challenging as it was in the past.

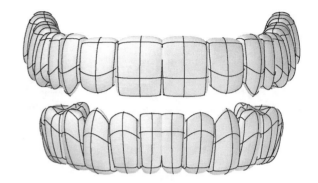

Fig. 7-1 The teeth are made up of simple split boxes that have been shaped into a few different configurations. They are shown here in subdivision mode.

Modeling the Mouth Parts

The mouth consists of the teeth, gums, and tongue. The modeling steps for each part are explained separately. You can use the 2D templates in the chapter 7 folder of the CD-ROM (Chapter7 > Mouth & Eye Templates) or refer to a medical textbook.

Modeling the Teeth Steps

Step 1 (Figures 7-1, 7-2, 7-3, and 7-4). You only need to model half the teeth. Later, these can be mirror duplicated for the half on the opposite side. Start with a simple box and model the front upper tooth by pulling and pushing points. You will most likely have to divide the box at least once.

Step 2 (Figures 7-1, 7-2, 7-3, and 7-4). Duplicate and reshape the first tooth into the second one next to it. Continue modeling the rest of the teeth. The molars are more complicated and thus will need more divisions.

Step 3 (Figures 7-1, 7-2, 7-3, and 7-4). When you finish modeling the upper teeth, make sure they are arranged in a horseshoe shape. Mirror duplicate them to complete the upper teeth.

Step 4 (Figures 7-1, 7-2, 7-3, and 7-4). You can

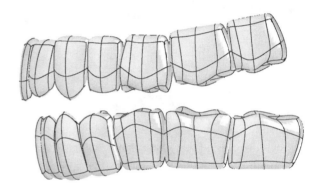

Fig. 7-2 A side view of the teeth.

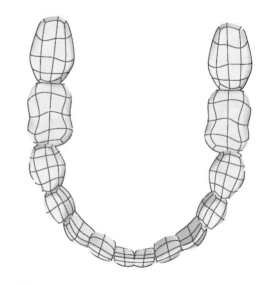

Fig. 7-3 A top view of the bottom teeth.

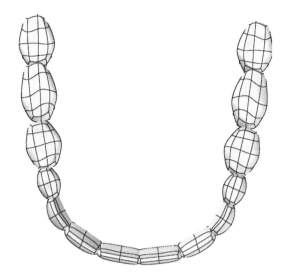

Fig. 7-5 Gums Step 1. Making a flat box.

Fig. 7-4 A bottom view of the upper teeth.

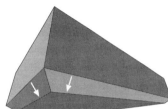

Fig. 7-6 Step 2. Beveling down and in a little.

now either mirror duplicate the upper teeth on the vertical axis and reshape them into the lower teeth, or start the lower teeth from the beginning with a box.

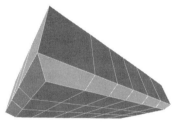

Fig. 7-7 Step 3. Dividing the box into smaller sections.

Modeling the Gums Steps

Step 1 (Figure 7-5). In the usual manner, start with a box. Make it fairly flat. Only half the upper gum will be modeled, and later it will be mirror duplicated.

Step 2 (Figure 7-6). Select the gum polygon located on the underside of the box and bevel it down a little. It should also be scaled down.

Step 3 (Figure 7-7). Split the gum polygon into smaller sections for sculpting.

Step 4 (Figure 7-8). Refer to the different views in the illustration and shape the half-gum. Place it over the upper teeth and scale it to fit over half the dentures. Pull/push points on the bottom so the gum fits between the teeth.

Step 5 (Figure 7-9). Adjust the final half-gum shape in subdivision mode.

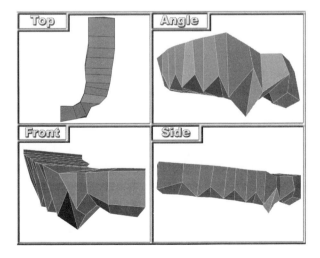

Fig. 7-8 Step 4. Several views showing the half-gum in low-poly mode after pulling and pushing the bottom points.

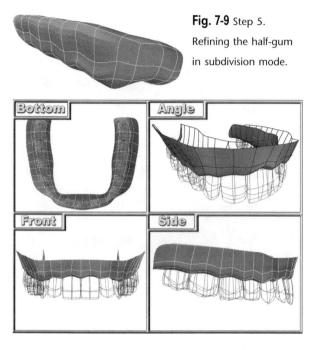

Fig. 7-9 Step 5. Refining the half-gum in subdivision mode.

Fig. 7-10 Step 6. Mirror duplicating the half-gum after deleting the middle polygons at the 0 x-axis.

Step 6 (Figure 7-10). Select the middle polygons at the 0 x-axis and delete them. Mirror duplicating would cause them to become inside polygons that pull on the outside ones. Use a set value to move the middle seam points to the 0 x-axis. Mirror the half-gum and merge points in the center. You can use the completed upper gum to model the lower one, or start from the beginning with a flat box and repeat the previous steps.

Modeling the Tongue Steps

Step 1 (Figure 7-11). The half-tongue will be modeled and later mirrored. Make a box.

Step 2 (Figure 7-11). Bevel one side back at an angle and make it smaller.

Step 3 (Figure 7-11). Bevel the side back again.

Step 4 (Figure 7-11). Merge the three polygons at the rear and bevel them toward the back.

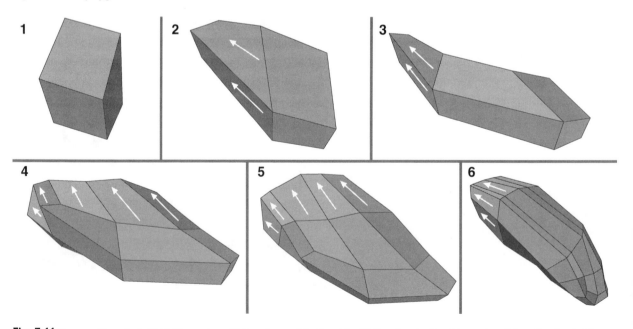

Fig. 7-11 Tongue Steps 1–6. 1) Making a box. 2) Beveling out to the side. 3) Beveling to the side again. 4) Beveling back. 5) Beveling back again. 6). Beveling once more.

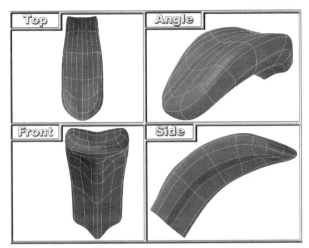

Fig. 7-12 Step 7. Beveling back and down and mirroring the tongue.

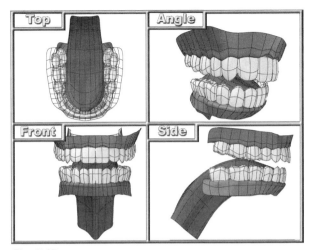

Fig. 7-13 Step 8. Putting all the mouth parts together.

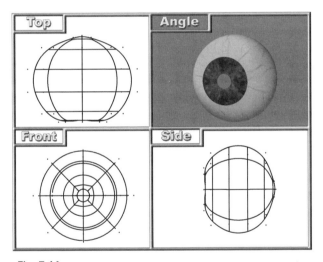

Fig. 7-14 Eye Step 1. The eyeball and iris are one connected object.

Step 5 (Figure 7-11). Bevel the rear polygon back once again.

Step 6 (Figure 7-11). Bevel back once more.

Step 7 (Figure 7-12). Bevel the back of the half-tongue again. Shape the tongue so that it curves back and down. Delete the middle polygons along the 0 x-axis seam. Use a set value to move the middle seam points to the 0 x-axis. Mirror the half-tongue and merge the duplicate points along the center seam.

Step 8 (Figure 7-13). Place the teeth, gums, and tongue together. Put them in a layer with the figure in a background layer. Scale the parts to fit the inside of the mouth. You may have to switch layers and adjust the figure's mouth cavity. Cut and paste the mouth components into the same layer as the figure. Later, when you make morph targets (chapter 11), the teeth and tongue will be moved according to the various mouth poses.

Modeling the Eye Parts

The eye parts are fairly simple objects made from spheres. They resemble the components of a human eye which can be viewed in most medical textbooks. The chapter 7 folder of the CD-ROM contains 2D templates in a folder titled "Mouth&EyeTemplates" that you might find useful.

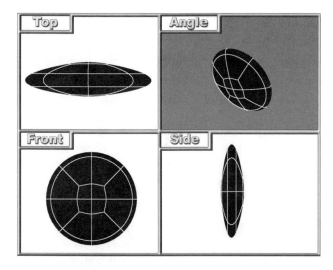

Fig. 7-15 Step 2. The lens, or pupil, is a saucer-like disk that sits behind the iris.

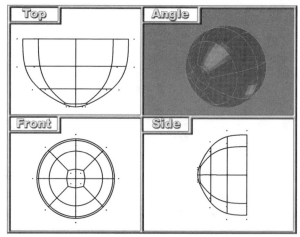

Fig. 7-16 Step 3. The cornea covers the front of the eyeball and iris. It can be formed from a half-sphere.

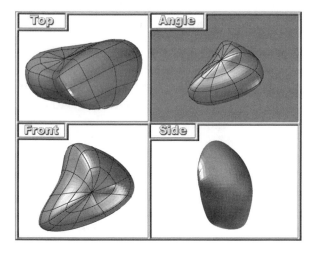

Fig. 7-17 Step 4. The Caruncula Lacrymalis, or pink membrane in the corner of the eye. It is modeled from a primitive.

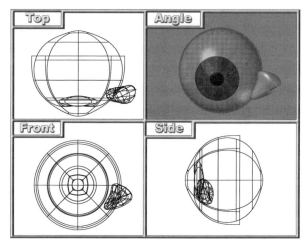

Fig. 7-18 Step 5. All the eye components are put together.

Modeling the Eyeball Steps

Step 1 (Figure 7-14). Create a sphere on the z-axis that has ten sides and five segments. This is a low-polygon ball that will become smooth with subdivision surfaces. Slice across the front polygons to create the section that will form the iris. Slice at the end of the iris and delete those poly-gons so that you have a small hole in the center of the iris. The lens or pupil will be placed behind this hole. Push the points around the hole back a little. Select the iris polygons and name them "iris." Inverse the selection and name the polygon surfaces "eyeball."

Step 2 (Figure 7-15). Create another simple sphere and flatten it so it looks like a flying saucer.

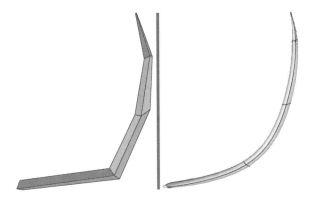

Fig. 7-19 Eyelashes Step 1. A single eyelash is made from a long-divided three-sided pyramid and then bent. It is shown here in both low-polygon and subdivision modes.

Fig. 7-20 Step 2. Placing eyelashes one at a time. Mirror duplicating the upper and lower eyelashes.

Scale it down to fit behind the lens opening of the iris. Name its surfaces "lens" or "pupil." Its color should be black.

Step 3 (Figure 7-16). Create a half-sphere that is slightly larger than the eyeball and protrudes in front of the iris. This is the transparent cornea, which has a very high gloss.

Step 4 (Figure 7-17). Create the small pink membrane for the inner angle of the eye. It can be made by reshaping a sphere or a divided cube.

Step 5 (Figure 7-18). Place all the eye components together and scale them to the eyesocket. Surfaces for the eye and mouth parts will be

assigned in a later part of the chapter. After that, the eye parts will be rotated in the top view so they tilt a little to the side. It is easier to apply textures when the eye is facing forward rather than angled.

Modeling the Eyelashes and Eyebrows

The eyelashes and eyebrows are easy to model but take a very long time to place correctly. In essence, each hair is placed in the eyelids and eyebrow. If you have the patience, then it is recommended that you model these. One could use a hair generator for the eyelashes and an image map for the

eyebrows, but these are usually inferior to making actual hair models.

Modeling the Eyelashes Steps

Step 1 (Figure 7-19). Create a long, three-sided box with the points on one end welded together. Bend the object so that the tip is on top. Duplicate the eyelash several times and shape duplicates into a variety of sizes.

Step 2 (Figure 7-20). Refer to close-up photos of people's eyes as you place each eyelash into the upper and lower eyelids. Although this process may seem tedious and too time-consuming, if it is done right, it will be worth it. Rotate the eyelashes so that you have variety. Some will bunch up and

159

Fig. 7-21 The eyebrows after placing individual strands. Only the ends of the hairs should penetrate the head.

overlap, while others at the corners are more sparse. When you finish the upper and lower eyelashes, mirror duplicate them for the other side of the face.

Modeling the Eyebrows

Figure 7-21 illustrates a pair of eyebrows modeled from individual strands. You can use the eyelash objects to make the eyebrows. Make these longer, straighten them a little, and then bend them sideways slightly. Refer to close-up photos of eyebrows as you place each hair on the brows.

Placing single hairs like this could take several hours or more, so have patience.

Texturing the Human

Texturing or surfacing techniques will be covered in more detail in chapter 10. Since we are in the process of finalizing the human, it is more appropriate to discuss texturing the model in this chapter. Figure 7-22 depicts two views of the same female, one without and one with textures.

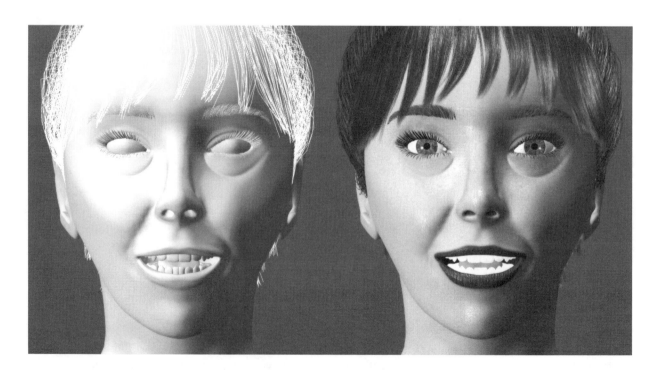

Fig. 7-22 The face, before and after adding textures.

UV Mapping the Face

Imagine an object with grid lines running horizontally and vertically. When one line intersects another, there is a point. Let us say that you have a texture that you want to apply to this object. The most accurate way to put on this texture is to draw the same number of grid lines over it, then place it point by point on the object. The location of the points on the texture correspond to the same ones on the object. This, in effect, is what UV mapping does. It is the most accurate method for surfacing an object.

Projection techniques for surfacing are limited to the x, y, and z planes. Therefore, they do not work very well for organic-type objects, which often have a mesh running at angles to these three axes. Since UVs are in effect pinned to the mesh, they conform to the various directions that it takes.

When you create a UV map, it flattens a rounded or angled surface (Figure 7-23). A picture of this flattened mesh is brought into an image editor. A texture can then be applied accurately to the image of the UV mesh.

A 3D paint program can also be used to make UV maps. The model is painted and the software remembers which pixels were applied to which points on the mesh.

The following instructions show how you can make a UV map for the face. UVs will also be used to texture the iris and eyeball.

Step 1. Assuming that the face of your human is looking toward you in the front view, select all the polygons on the forepart of the face. This would mean everything from the forehead and a little below the chin and in front of the ears. It should resemble the shape of a mask. Name these polygons "UV Face." If you prefer to texture the entire head at once, select the entire head surface and name it "UV Face."

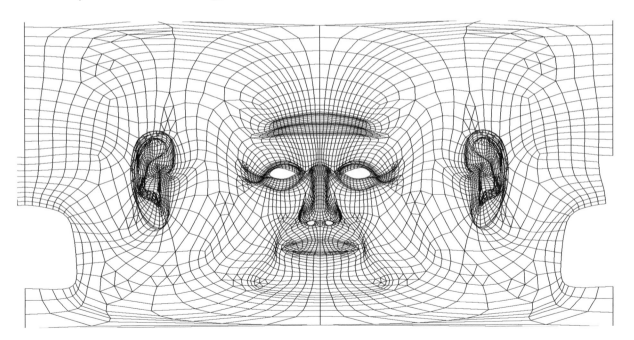

Fig. 7-23 A human head, unrolled and with a UV spherical map on the y-axis. Textures are painted on top of this.

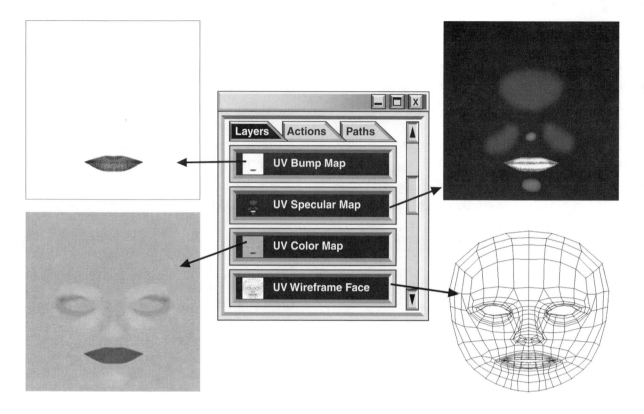

Fig. 7-24 The UV maps seen as layers in an image editing program.

Step 2. Hide everything else except for the UV Face polygons. Create a new UV texture that is spherical on the y-axis. If you are UV mapping only the front of the face, create a new UV texture that is planar on the z-axis. In your UV window, you should see the mesh flattened (Figure 7-23).

Step 3. Make the UV view window as large as possible and perform an image capture or a print screen of the flattened UV map.

Step 4. Paste the captured image of the UV mesh into an image editing program and crop around it. If you need to make the image more visible, turn up the contrast and then invert it.

Step 5 (Figure 7-24). Add a transparent layer on top of the captured UV mesh image. You can now paint the different textures of the face over the UV mesh picture, or sample from a photograph.

Step 6. Create an overall seamless skin texture. You can do this by sampling an even surface from the color image of the face. Copy the selection and paste it into its own document. Make the image seamless by using a filter such as offset. Define a pattern with this seamless picture. Make a new layer on top of the color image map of the face. Fill this layer with the skin pattern. You can use this skin surface on the rest of the nude model.

Step 7. In the second layer, paint your textures for the entire head. If you are just painting the front of the face, select the outer edge of the color face that is in your second layer. Feather the selec-

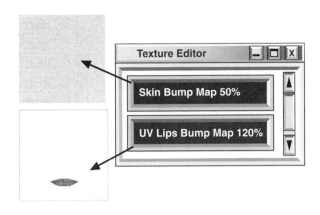

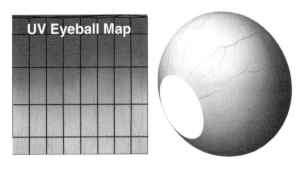

Fig. 7-26 UV mapping the eyeball.

Fig. 7-25 A texture editor in a 3D program with several bump map layers.

tion and delete the color image at the edges. Place the overall skin texture that is in the third layer underneath the second one. You should now see the overall skin blending into the color face at the edges. Blend the skin color into the color face by cloning from it, so that the transition between the seamless skin texture to the face is smooth and even.

Step 8. Merge the second and third layers (overall skin and face color).

Step 9. (Figure 7-24). Create a third layer on top of the layer with the UV color map. Fill it with black and lighten parts of the face that will look more shiny. This layer is your UV specular map. Lessen the opacity of this layer so that you can see the UV wireframe layer underneath. You will also have to hide the layer containing the UV color map. Now that you can see the parts of the face in the wireframe face layer, start lightening sections such as the forehead, lips, tip of the nose, and front of the chin.

Step 10. Copy the lips from the UV color map layer and paste them into a new layer on top of the UV specular map layer. This will be the UV bump map. Increase the contrast on the lips and make them grayscale. Bump and specular maps do not register as color maps. Increase the visibility of the lip texture so that the bump map has more distinct lines in it. If you want to make other creases on the face, paint other lines in the UV bump map layer.

Step 11 (Figure 7-25). You should now have a UV bump map, UV specular map, and UV color map for the face. Copy and paste each of these into their own document and save them. Create another document that is the same size as the other face maps and fill it with the overall skin pattern. Save the seamless skin pattern.

Step 12. In your 3D program, apply the various maps to the UV face. For color, assign the UV color map. For specularity, designate the UV specular

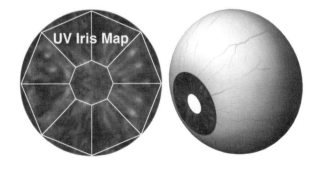

Fig. 7-27 UV mapping the iris.

map, and for bump, specify the UV bump map.

Step 13. The UV bump map can also have another overall skin bump applied to it. The illustration shows how a texture editor could have two layers of bump maps. The lip bump is underneath the seamless skin bump. The higher value of the lip bump will make it visible along with the overall bump map. In the chapter 7 folder, there is another folder, titled "Human Textures," which contains a seamless skin bump texture, as well as other ones that you can use.

Step 14. Apply the seamless skin texture to the rest of the model, except for parts like the fingernails. Try cubic mapping and let the texture repeat. Since the edges of the UV face map were blended into the overall seamless skin texture, you should not see any lines where the UV map meets the cubic mapped skin texture.

Step 15. Take the overall bump texture and put it on the model using cubic image mapping. It should have the same value and size as the bump map that was placed on the UV face.

You can use UV mapping to paint textures on the entire body. This is preferable to overall seamless textures if your goal is to create a very realistic looking person.

UV Mapping the Eyeball

Step 1 (Figure 7-26). Select the eyeball polygons and specify a UV map for them. Spherical or cylindrical on the z-axis should work fine.

Step 2. Place the eyeball texture as a background image behind the UV view window. Adjust the mesh to the eyeball texture in the UV view window.

Step 3. Assign the eyeball texture to the eyeball in your texture editor.

UV Mapping the Iris

Step 1 (Figure 7-27). Select the iris polygons. These should already be named "iris." Create a UV map for it that is planar on the z-axis.

Step 2. Place the iris texture as a background image behind the UV view window. Adjust the mesh to the iris texture in the UV view window.

Step 3. Assign the iris texture to the iris in your texture editor.

Surface Values for the Human

The following lists some surface values that you might find useful when texturing your human. Of course, it is understood that values vary according to software and individual taste.

Teeth

Color: White
Luminosity: 60 percent
Diffuse: 30 percent
Specularity: 80 percent
Glossiness: 30 percent
Reflection: 0 percent
Transparency: 0 percent*
Translucency: 50 percent
Bump: 100 percent**
*A slight edge transparency can be applied.
**The bump can be a fractal noise procedural texture that is twice as long as it is wide.

Gums

Color: Pink
Luminosity: 0 percent
Diffuse: 100 percent
Specularity: 100 percent*
Glossiness: 40 percent
Reflection: 0 percent
Transparency: 0 percent

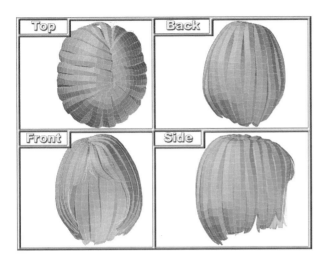

Fig. 7-28 Object Hair Step 1. Creating the hair model from long, flattened cylindrical shapes.

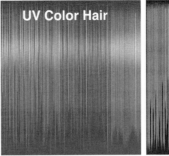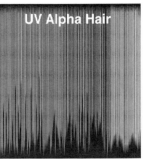

Fig. 7-29 Step 2. Painting a UV color hair map and an alpha map for transparency mapping.

Bump: 100 percent**

*A small fractal noise procedural texture can be implemented for specularity.

**The same fractal noise can be used for the bump map.

Tongue

Color: Pink

Luminosity: 0 percent

Diffuse: 100 percent*

Specularity: 100 percent

Glossiness: 40 percent

Reflection: 0 percent

Transparency: 0 percent

Bump: 100 percent**

*Adding a tiny crust procedural texture to the diffuse properly makes the tongue appear somewhat rough.

**The same crust procedural texture is also applied as a bump map.

Cornea

Color: N/A

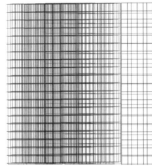

Fig. 7-30 Step 3. Specifying the UV map for the hair object.

Luminosity: 0 percent

Diffuse: 50 percent

Specularity: 400 percent*

Glossiness: 80 percent

Reflection: 5 percent

Transparency: 100 percent

Bump: N/A

Creating Hair

There are many approaches to modeling hair. In fact, it becomes even more confusing when one considers all the different hairstyles that people wear.

Normally, your choices are dictated by the type of software that you are using. If it implements pixel shaders that render fur and hair, you can make a more realistic hairdo. Pixel shaders are pro-

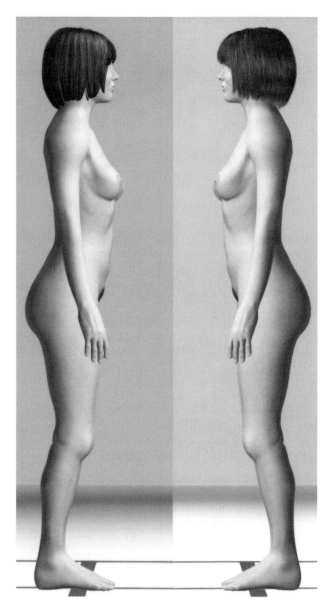

Fig. 7-31 Two different methods for creating hair. The female on the left has hair made from an object that is transparency mapped, while the one on the right is wearing a wig made with a hair generator.

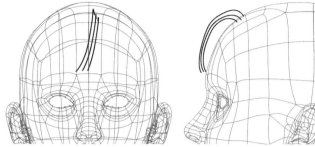

Fig. 7-32 Pixel Shader Hair Step 1. Making the first three strands for the bangs.

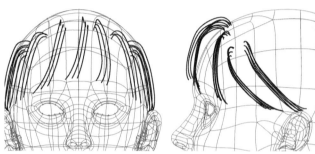

Fig. 7-33 Step 2. Duplicating and distributing the hair groups across the forehead.

grams that process pixels. These generators can be used to perform mathematical operations that render fur and hair.

If your software does not have this ability, you will most likely have to do some creative texturing and/or model a hair object(s). Transparency mapping makes the hair object appear as if it is made up of many hair strands. The first set of instructions explains how to make hair from objects rather than with a hair generator.

Hair Object(s) Steps

Step 1 (Figure 7-28). Make long, flattened, cylindrical objects and place them on the head as if they were really fat hair strands. Be sure to overlap

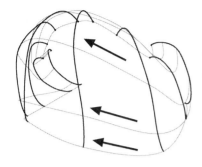

Fig. 7-34 Step 3. Connecting the corresponding hair splines.

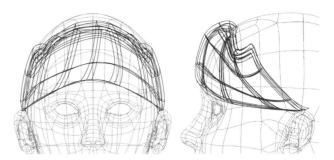

Fig. 7-35 Step 4. The three groups of hair meshes after connecting each set of splines.

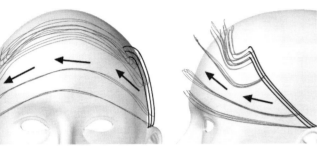

Fig. 7-36 Step 5. Deleting the vertical splines, except for those at the beginning of the forehead. These are rail cloned across the horizontal splines.

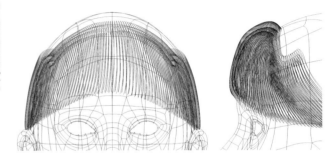

Fig. 7-37 Step 6. Rail cloned guides for the bangs.

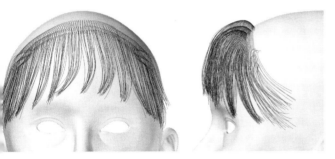

Fig. 7-38 Step 7. The guides are jittered and brought together at the ends.

them. Give the object one texture name.

Step 2 (Figure 7-29). Create a color image map that has thin vertical lines. Make another transparency map image from the original that is white where the color strands are and black in the spaces between them.

Step 3 (Figure 7-30). Make a UV map of the hair object and apply both the transparency and the color map as the UV hair texture.

Figure 7-31 shows a rendering of the same female wearing a hair object with transparency mapping and hair made from a pixel shader.

Hair Generator Guide Steps

If your software has a hair generator or plug-ins available, you can use the following instructions to make long hair guides. Your hair generator can then use these guides to create more hairs. Even though this tutorial shows how to make a ponytail hairstyle, you might still be able to utilize the information to create whatever hairdo you want.

Step 1 (Figure 7-32). Create a spline that sticks into the scalp a little bit and whose end sticks out

167

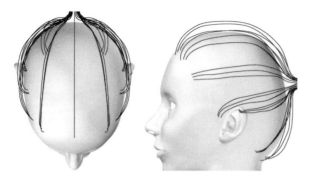

Fig. 7-39 Step 8. New sets, each consisting of three hair guides, are created across the scalp. These lead toward the ponytail.

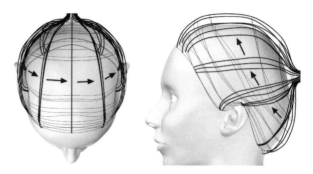

Fig. 7-40 Step 9. All the splines are connected to make the rails.

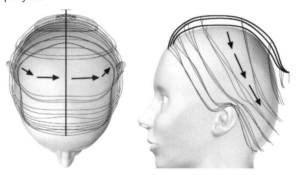

Fig. 7-41 Step 10. After deleting all the original splines except for the top middle ones, the three are rail cloned around the head.

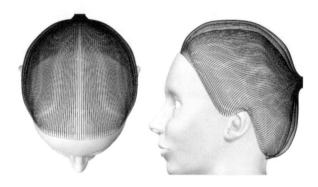

Fig. 7-42 Step 11. The rail cloned splines of the scalp.

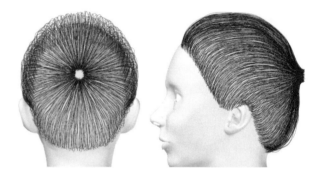

Fig. 7-43 Step 12. Jittering the rail cloned hair.

and hangs down over the forehead. This short strand of hair has approximately seven vertices. Make two duplicates of the hair strand and arrange them similarly to the illustration.

Step 2 (Figure 7-33). Duplicate the three hair splines and place them next to the first set. Continue copying, pasting, and placing the set of three hairs until they are arranged around the forehead. It is important to always have the first point of each spline inside the scalp.

Step 3 (Figure 7-34). Hide all the hair splines, except for the top ones that run across the forehead. Start on one end, select each corresponding

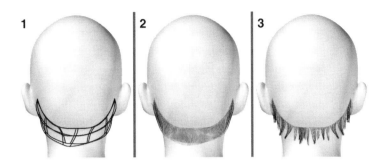

Fig. 7-44 Step 13. Making the hair strands at the bottom of the scalp.

point, and create a spline that connects across these vertices. Do the same for all the other points until you have a mesh of vertical and horizontal splines.

Step 4 (Figure 7-35). Hide this mesh and connect the middle, vertical splines. Finally, connect the splines that are closest to the head. You should now have three sets of connected splines.

Step 5 (Figure 7-36). The horizontal splines that were the result of connecting the vertical ones will now be used as the rails when performing a rail clone. A rail clone is an operation that duplicates splines and polygons across a given path such as a spline(s). Delete all the original vertical splines, except for the ones at the side and the beginning of the forehead. Place the horizontal splines (the rails) in a background layer.

Step 6 (Figure 7-37). Rail clone the three vertical splines. For segments, pick length, make the clone uniform, type "80" for the number of strands, and turn off oriented and scaling. If 80 yields too many hair strands, you can always cut back on the amount.

Step 7 (Figure 7-38). Right now, the hair strands are too even, so they need to be jittered a little bit. Bring the ends of the hair together so that groups

appear to bunch up.

Step 8 (Figure 7-39). Now it is time to make the hair that runs across the scalp toward the back. The beginning overlaps into the bangs and ends where the ponytail will begin. Create three sets of splines that run the length of the head. The third spline is the one that is furthest from the scalp. Duplicate the set of three splines and distribute each group around the head. Make sure the beginning of each spline is inside the scalp.

Step 9 (Figure 7-40). Create rails for rail cloning by connecting all the splines. Since the splines circle the head, the connecting ones will be closed splines that form an oval shape.

Step 10 (Figure 7-41). Except for the middle and top three splines, delete all remaining original ones that lead to the ponytail. Place the oval connecting splines (the rails) in a background layer.

Step 11 (Figure 7-42). Rail clone the three

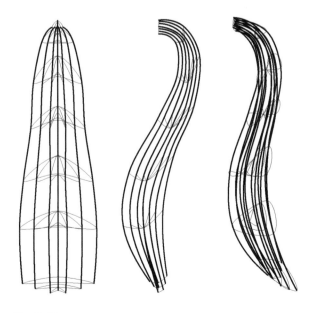

Fig. 7-45 Step 14. Connecting the ponytail splines.

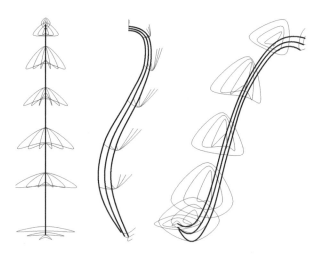

Fig. 7-46 Step 15. After connecting the vertical splines, all are deleted except for the middle group of three.

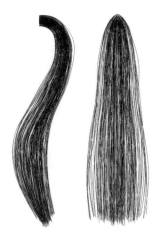

Fig. 7-47 Step 16. The rail cloned pony tail. The splines are also jittered.

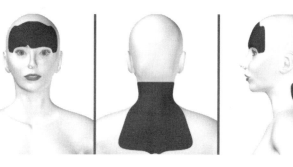

Fig. 7-49 Step 18. Modeling collision objects so that the hair that is affected by soft body dynamics does not penetrate the skin.

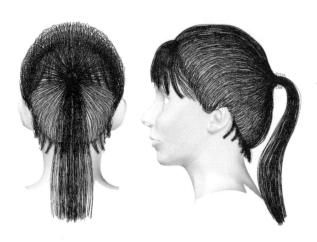

Fig. 7-48 Step 17. All the hair guide sections combined. A ponytail holder is also modeled.

splines using the same settings as before, except this time, make the number of splines greater, perhaps 200.

Step 12 (Figure 7-43). Jitter the rail-cloned hair a little to make it more irregular.

Step 13 (Figure 7-44). Make the short hairs at the base of the scalp. Use the same method as the one for the bangs. Since the hair is thinner there, you can use sets of two strands instead of three.

Step 14 (Figure 7-45). Start the ponytail by making long hair splines. Create a set of six on the z-axis and another six overlapping ones on the x-axis. Be sure to start at the top, near the ends of the scalp strands. Connect across each strand, making closed, oval-like splines. Start by connecting the outside splines and gradually work your way in.

Step 15 (Figure 7-46). Delete all the original vertical splines except for the three middle ones near the head and neck.

Step 16 (Figure 7-47). Rail clone the three ponytail splines. Make about 80 strands. Jitter the ponytail hairs a little.

Step 17 (Figure 7-48). Model a ponytail holder. This completes the steps for making long hair guides.

Step 18 (Figure 7-49). In most cases, soft body dynamics are applied to the hair. This utilizes a physics emulation software engine that can estimate the effects of movement, wind, and gravity. The objects that are affected by these forces

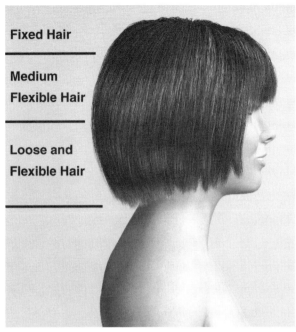

Fig. 7-50 Sections of the hair that are affected and unaffected by soft body dynamics.

become flexible soft bodies. Collision objects can be set up so that the soft body—in this case, the hair—does not penetrate the skin. Since the only flexible parts of the hair are the bangs and ponytail, it is not necessary to use up extra memory creating a large collision object. The illustration shows the areas that have a collision object. These are made from parts of the model so that they fit closely against the skin.

Parts of the hair should have their surfaces named according to the amount of influence soft body dynamics will have on them. Figure 7-50 shows how three separate surfaces define the flexibility of the hair. Figure 7-51 depicts the completed female.

Fig. 7-51 The finished female model.

CHAPTER 8

Modeling a Background

It is important to know how to model the inanimate, 3D items that make up our surroundings. While human figures are the most difficult objects to make, in many cases you will find that the creation of an environment will challenge your modeling abilities. In this chapter, you will see a variety of objects to model. Sometimes the approach to making them is similar to previous modeling exercises. At other times, you will learn that new methods of modeling will have to be employed.

This chapter will take you through the various steps to creating a living room (Figure 8-1). A variety of familiar objects will be modeled. Depending on your abilities, you may decide to make different objects or change the look of some of the ones found here. The idea is not to impose specific techniques, but rather expose you to different styles of modeling.

When you make inanimate 3D objects, it is important to consider the manner in which they will be textured. Many times, an object can be made very simply, with the textures adding the detail. Even though chapters 9 and 10 discuss lighting and surfacing, this chapter will also refer to certain ways of texturing and lighting an object(s). A digital camera can be an essential tool when texturing these objects.

Fig. 8-1 Figures in a living room environment.

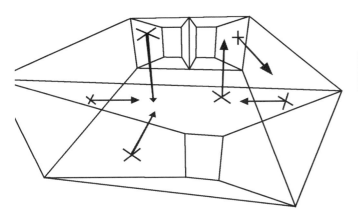

Fig. 8-2 Building the four walls, floor, and ceiling. The surface normals face inward.

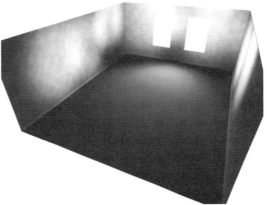

Fig. 8-3 The rendered room. Since the surface normals are facing inward, the camera can be placed outside the room.

Modeling Walls, a Ceiling, and the Floor

One of the simplest tasks is to make the enclosed space that will be filled with an assortment of objects. After determining the layout of your interior, make adjoining walls that are connected to each other, the floor, and the ceiling. Each of these can be a four-sided polygon. Using a Boolean or solid drill operation, you can make openings for windows.

If you make the polygons face inward, the camera can be placed outside of the room (Figure 8-2). Since the surface normals are facing in, the outside surfaces will be invisible. Your camera placement will no longer be hampered by the interior space, and you can use long lenses for less distortion.

The baseboard covering the joint formed by a wall and the floor should also be modeled. Create a polygon that shows a profile of the baseboard and then extrude it for the length of one wall. Duplicate it for the rest of the walls.

Add textures on the walls, floor, and ceiling. Set up your lights so that parts of the room, such as the corners, have shadowed areas. Spotlights usu-ally work best, since they can be controlled in many ways. Place rows of these lights around the room. You may need about sixteen lights to illuminate the ceiling, floor, and walls. Later, when you add objects to the room, exclude these lights from them. Any objects that hang on the walls, such as pictures and windows, should not be excluded from the room lights. Rugs should not be excluded either. The rest of the furniture and other room contents will have their own lights. You can see that after a while, your room will have quite a few lights in it. It is not unusual to have 30 to 50 lights in a room. For easier identification, be sure to name your room lights.

Windows

The window that will be modeled in the next several steps is made up of a number of components (Figure 8-4). First, there is the molding around the glass. Then there is the window blind, and finally, the valance, a decorative framework to conceal cur-

Fig. 8-4 A rendered window.

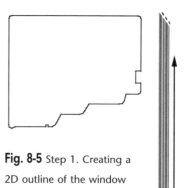

Fig. 8-5 Step 1. Creating a 2D outline of the window molding.

Fig. 8-6 Step 2. Extruding the 2D window molding outline.

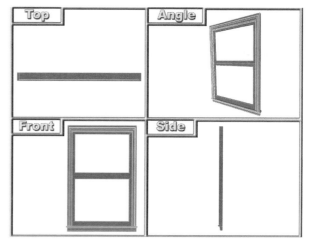

Fig. 8-7 Step 3. Different views showing the finished window frame. Each section was extruded and placed against its neighboring one.

tain fixtures at the top of the window casing. In addition to this, you may decide to include curtains or other drapery. As you work through this exercise, sit by a window or use photos as reference. The modeled window will face toward you on the z-axis.

Step 1 (Figure 8-5). Create one polygon in the top view. Add points to it and shape it like the one in the illustration.

Step 2 (Figure 8-6). Extrude the polygon along the y-axis. Slice the ends of the molding at 45-degree angles so that you can place duplicate ones right up against it.

Step 3 (Figure 8-7). Place duplicate moldings against each other to make a rectangle shape around the window glass. Shape the bottom shelf of the window frame. Add extra molding on the inside of the window frame.

Step 4 (Figure 8-8). Create a polygon for the

Fig. 8-8 Step 4. After drawing the outline of one window blind, it is extruded.

Fig. 8-9 Step 5. Two holes for the strings are drilled into the single window blind section.

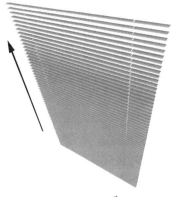

Fig. 8-10 Step 6. The single window blind is cloned sixty times with an offset of 1 inch on the y-axis.

Fig. 8-12 Step 8. The drapery that forms the valance is made from a rectangle split into about 300 polygons. An image or texture of the drapery is UV mapped onto the wire mesh.

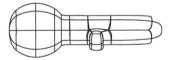

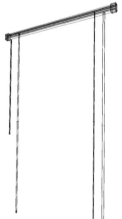

Fig. 8-11 Step 7. A box is made for the top of the blinds. Cords and a pole with a hook are also added to the blinds.

Fig. 8-13 Step 9. Points are moved on all three axes to get the billowing look of the valance.

Fig. 8-14 Step 10. The rod that holds up the valance is made from a sphere with one side that has been beveled out.

outline of one of the window blinds in the side view. Extrude this 2D polygon along the x-axis.

Step 5 (Figure 8-9). Cut two holes into the single window blind, through which the cord will be

threaded.

Step 6 (Figure 8-10). Clone the single window blind sixty times on the y-axis with an offset of 1 inch. If you want your blinds to be tilted up or down, rotate the single blind before cloning it.

Step 7 (Figure 8-11). Model the casing for the top of the blinds out of a box. Add cords, a pole, and a hook to the blinds.

Step 8 (Figure 8-12). For the drapery, create a rectangle that is divided into approximately 300 polygons. UV map an image of a valance or a cloth with vertical folds onto this flat polygon.

Step 9 (Figure 8-13). Shape the valance by moving points forward and backward, as well as up and down and sideways. Try to get the wavy look of the drapery. Follow the curves of the UV-mapped image.

Step 10 (Figure 8-14). Make the rod that holds up the valance out of a sphere. Select the polygons on one side of the sphere and bevel, smooth shift, or extrude them out on the x-axis. After placing it behind the valance, you can mirror duplicate it for

Fig. 8-15 The rendered TV stand.

the other side. Both ends should stick out a little on either side of the valance.

A TV Stand or Cabinet

The first object that will go into the living room is a cabinet which will hold up a television (Figure 8-15). It is a fairly simple component that only requires rudimentary modeling skills.

Step 1 (Figure 8-16). Create an oblong box.

Step 2 (Figure 8-16). Bevel the front inward to make the polygon smaller, but do not bevel it back. It should be on the same plane as the original front polygon.

Step 3 (Figure 8-16). Bevel the same polygon back, almost to the rear polygon of the box.

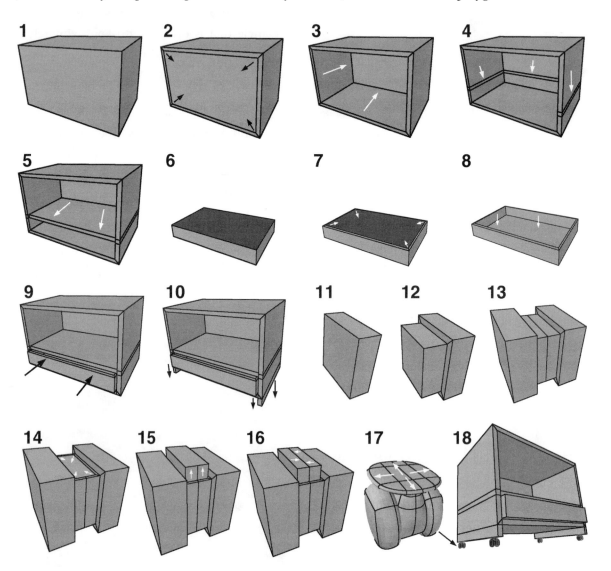

Fig. 8-16 Steps 1–18. Modeling the TV stand.

Step 4 (Figure 8-16). Make two parallel slices across the box. The two slices are going to make a shelf.

Step 5 (Figure 8-16). Select the polygon at the back of the inside section of the cabinet, between the two slices. Bevel it forward to make a shelf.

Step 6 (Figure 8-16). Make a low-set box that fits snugly in the opening underneath the shelf. This will be the cabinet drawer.

Step 7 (Figure 8-16). Select the top polygon of the box that will be the drawer and bevel it in a little, but not down.

Step 8 (Figure 8-16). Bevel the polygon down so it makes the hollow of the drawer.

Step 9 (Figure 8-16). Slide the drawer into the cabinet.

Step 10 (Figure 8-16). Make the two sides that will hold the wheels by beveling the polygons down.

Step 11 (Figure 8-16). The next set of steps will show how to model the wheels. Start with a narrow box.

Step 12 (Figure 8-16). Bevel one side in to make the polygon smaller, but do not move it out yet. Bevel the same polygon again, but this time straight out.

Step 13 (Figure 8-16). Mirror duplicate the object so that the points in the middle seam are merged.

Step 14 (Figure 8-16). Merge the top two middle polygons. Bevel the merged polygon in a little to make a smaller one. It should be on the same plane as the original merged polygon.

Step 15 (Figure 8-16). Bevel the polygon straight up.

Step 16 (Figure 8-16). Split the polygon that you just beveled up into two.

Step 17 (Figure 8-16). Slice across the middle section that was beveled up. Smooth shift this new top section outward. Move polygons until it looks like the one in the illustration. Turn on subdivision mode for the wheel. Refine its shape. Apply an appropriate surface to the wheel object.

Step 18 (Figure 8-16). Clone the wheel and place each copy at the bottom of the cabinet. You might want to rotate some of them so they appear more random rather than all facing the same direction.

A Television

A TV is another fairly simple object to model (Figure 8-17). It is basically a box that is beveled several times.

Step 1 (Figure 8-18). Make a fairly flat box.

Step 2 (Figure 8-18). Bevel the back polygon toward the rear and in a little.

Step 3 (Figure 8-18). Bevel the polygon in a little, but keep it on the same plane as the last one that was beveled.

Step 4 (Figure 8-18). Bevel the polygon back and

Fig. 8-17 The rendered TV.

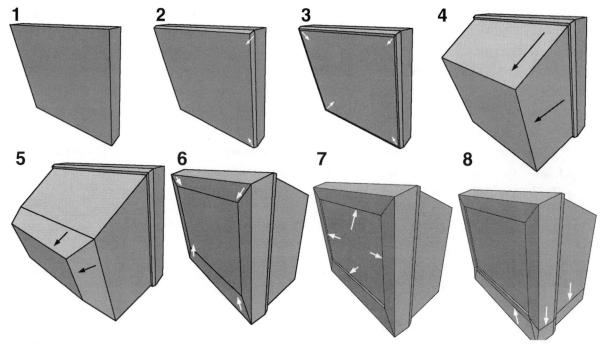

Fig. 8-18 Steps 1–8. Modeling the television.

in. Move the bottom points so they are all lying on the same plane. Even though the top of the TV angles down, the bottom of it is flat so it can rest securely on the stand.

Step 5 (Figure 8-18). Bevel the rear polygon one last time to the back and in. The bottom of this last section does not sit flat on the stand, but angles up.

Step 6 (Figure 8-18). Select the front polygon and bevel it in to make it smaller while keeping it on the same plane.

Step 7 (Figure 8-18). Bevel the polygon straight back slightly. This will be the glass portion of the TV.

Step 8 (Figure 8-18). Slice across the bottom of the TV and move points to angle it forward a little. You can continue to slice parts of the television and bevel sections for other details, such as speakers or control buttons.

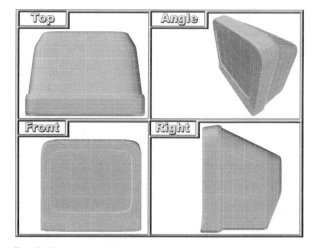

Fig. 8-19 The TV in subdivision mode.

Figure 8-19 illustrates the completed TV in subdivision mode. The television can now be placed on top of the TV stand.

Fig. 8-20 A rendered sofa.

A Sofa

One of the most common pieces of furniture is the sofa (Figure 8-20). Modeling the couch can be fairly simple, especially if you devote more time to surfacing it. There is no need to sculpt every crevice and detail when you can take digital photos of one and UV map these onto your model.

Step 1 (Figure 8-21). Create a polygon that forms a simple profile of the sofa.

Step 2 (Figure 8-21). Bevel or extrude it for the width of one and a half seats, not the entire length of the sofa.

Step 3 (Figure 8-21). Split the original polygon into two four-sided ones.

Step 4 (Figure 8-21). Split the polygons vertically across the front of the couch.

Step 5 (Figure 8-21). Select the polygon that will form the armrest and bevel it up and in a little.

Step 6 (Figure 8-21). Bevel the armrest polygon up and outward a little.

Step 7 (Figure 8-21). Bevel the armrest up.

Step 8 (Figure 8-21). Bevel the armrest in and up a little.

Step 9 (Figure 8-21). Slice across the backrest polygons.

Step 10 (Figure 8-21). Select the headrest polygon and bevel it forward and in somewhat.

Step 11 (Figure 8-21). Select the polygons next to the headrest. Merge them and bevel them out a little to make a cushion. Split these polygons up again into four-sided ones. As an alternative, you can smooth shift the polygons and thus avoid the

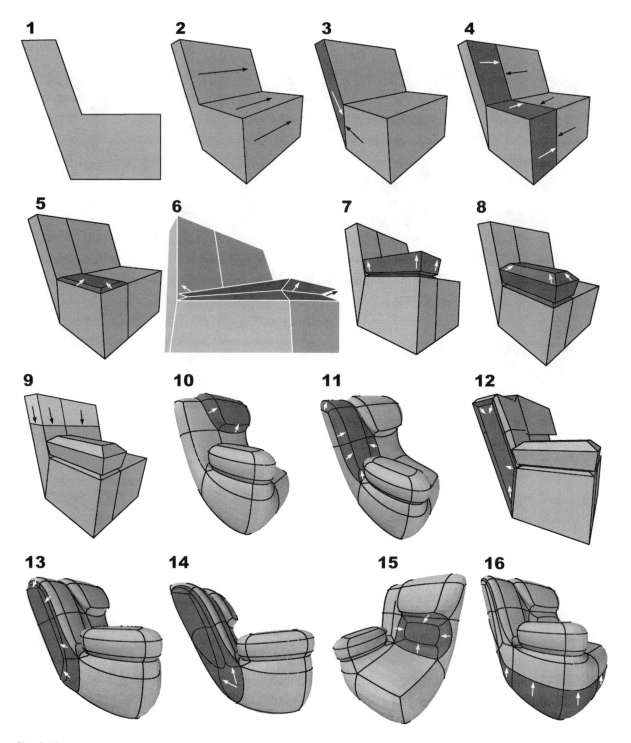

Fig. 8-21 Steps 1–16 for modeling a sofa.

extra effort of merging and again splitting polygons.

Step 12 (Figure 8-21). Merge the polygons on the side of the sofa backrest and bevel the polygon in to make a slightly smaller one.

Step 13 (Figure 8-21). Bevel the polygon out and in a little to make the side more rounded.

Step 14 (Figure 8-21). Rearrange the side polygons so they look more like the ones in the illustration.

Step 15 (Figure 8-21). Select the polygon below the headrest cushion and bevel it out to make the backrest cushion.

Step 16 (Figure 8-21). Slice across the bottom of the sofa.

Step 17 (Figure 8-22). Merge and split polygons on the side of the couch until the configuration is similar to the one in the illustration.

Step 18 (Figure 8-22). Select the two front polygons and bevel them forward.

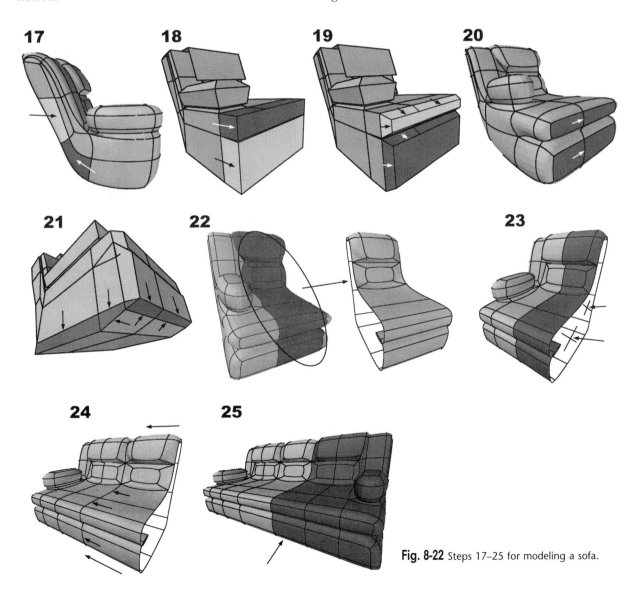

Fig. 8-22 Steps 17–25 for modeling a sofa.

Fig. 8-23 The rendered love seat.

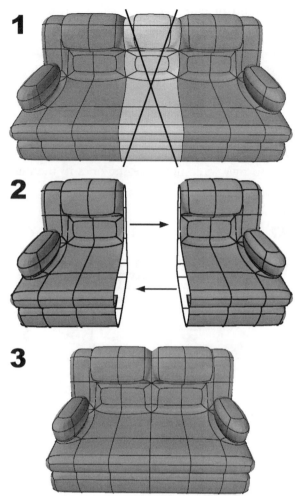

Fig. 8-24 Steps 1–3 for making the love seat from the sofa.

Step 19 (Figure 8-22). Bevel the two front polygons in and forward a little more.

Step 20 (Figure 8-22). Split the front polygons into four-sided ones.

Step 21 (Figure 8-22). Slice across the bottom of the sofa and arrange the polygons similarly to the illustration.

Step 22 (Figure 8-22). Select and copy the polygons of the seat and backrest of the sofa. They are shown in the illustration as darker polygons with an oval around them. Paste them into a second layer.

Step 23 (Figure 8-22). Delete the polygons on the side next to the seat and backrest. The reason for doing this is that when the duplicate seat and backrest are placed against them and their adjoining points are merged, these polygons would fall inside the ones that pull on the outer ones. The result is some unsightly pinching in places.

Step 24 (Figure 8-22). The duplicate seat and backrest that was pasted into another layer also has a side with polygons that should now be deleted. Line up the duplicate seat and backrest so the points butt up against the sofa in the first layer. If the sofa is facing toward you in the front view, the points in both layers should be lined up along the same value on the x-axis.

Step 25 (Figure 8-22). Copy the sofa from the first layer and paste it into a third layer. Mirror it to make the other end of the sofa. Line it up with the one in the second layer so that the end points share the same value as the ones in the second layer. You should now have the sofa's right side in layer 1, its middle in layer 2, and its left side in layer 3. Bring all three sections into one layer and merge their points along their adjoining seams.

A Love Seat

Here is one of the easiest modeling tasks found in this book. The love seat can be made by simply altering the sofa (Figure 8-23).

Step 1 (Figure 8-24). Select the middle seating section of the sofa and delete all those polygons.

Step 2 (Figure 8-24). Move the two end sections together and merge their end points.

Step 3 (Figure 8-24). If you already UV mapped the sofa, it will not be necessary to texture the love seat. The original UV maps should still work.

A Coffee Table

Unlike many other objects, a coffee table does not require deforming a wiremesh (Figure 8-25). It is constructed by putting together a number of different pieces. The process is similar to fabricating a real table, except that it does not require a hammer, nails, or pegs.

Step 1 (Figure 8-26). A flattened box with rounded corners will be used to make most of the table sections. Start by making a box with the following settings:

> Width: .3"
> Height:1' 2"
> Depth: 3"
> Axis: Y
> Radius: 3'
> Radius segments: 4
> Segments X: 1

Fig. 8-25 The rendered coffee table.

> Segments Y: 1
> Segments Z: 1

Step 2 (Figure 8-26). Select half of the polygons on the x-axis and delete them.

Step 3 (Figure 8-26). Copy and paste the object into another layer and rotate it in the top view -90 degrees. Line it up with the object in the first layer and delete the end polygons.

Step 4 (Figure 8-26). Place the two pieces together and merge their adjoining points.

Step 5 (Figure 8-26). Select points on the inside section of the merged pieces and make polygons out of these. You should now have one foot for the coffee table.

Step 6 (Figure 8-26). Mirror duplicate the feet, and place them for the width and length of the table.

Step 7 (Figure 8-26). Select one of the feet sections. Cut off the 45-degree section and delete it. Take the remaining part, rotate it, and stretch it to make one of the connecting pieces between two of the legs. Duplicate clone this part and place the sections around and against the legs to make a frame of the table.

Step 8 (Figure 8-26). Make a flattened box with

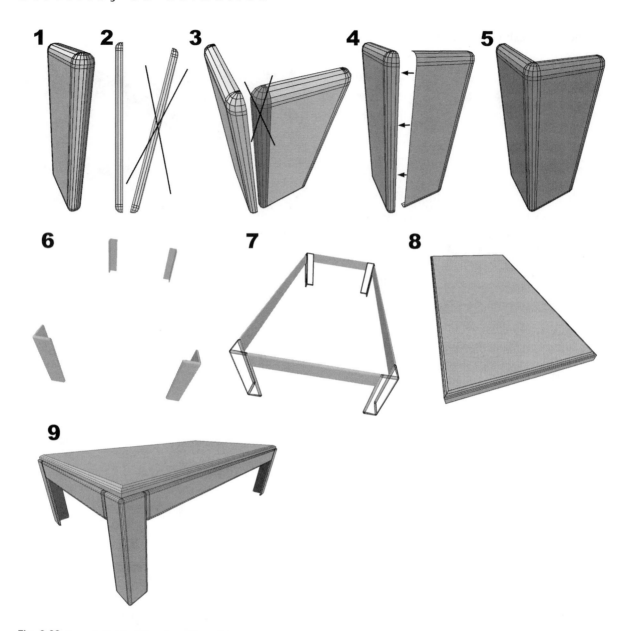

Fig. 8-26 Steps 1–9. Modeling the coffee table.

rounded corners or reshape a previous section for the table top.

Step 9 (Figure 8-26). Scale the table top piece so that it fits between the legs and frame. It should be set right up against the inside surfaces of the legs and frame, and stick up above them. Select all the polygons of the completed table that face up or down on the y-axis. UV map a wood texture on this axis. UV map on the z-axis the same wood texture on all the polygons that are facing the z-axis. UV map the wood texture on all the polygons facing the x-axis.

Fig. 8-27 The rendered bookshelf.

making the top polygon slightly larger on the z- and x-axes. Bevel the same polygon straight up without changing its size. The third bevel moves the polygon in a little on the sides and the front, but straight up in the back. The final bevel for the top of the bookshelf moves the polygon up and in on the front, sides, and back.

Step 5 (Figure 8-28). Make the sections for the shelves by slicing across the entire width of the bookshelf. Create four cuts for two shelves.

Step 6 (Figure 8-28). Select the two polygons at the back of the bookshelf that are the result of slicing. Bevel them forward. UV maps can be made the same way as those for the coffee table. The polygons for each individual axis are selected and UV mapped accordingly.

A Hardback Book

Once you finish the bookshelf, it is time to fill it with books. While it does not require too many steps, a few of the routines require some modeling skills.

Step 1 (Figure 8-29). Create a narrow box.

Step 2 (Figure 8-29). Duplicate the box and paste it in another layer. Place the second box so that it intersects into the first box (black outlines).

Step 3 (Figure 8-29). Use a Boolean operation to subtract from the first box. This will create a book jacket that has some thickness.

Step 4 (Figure 8-29). In order to make the jacket more round at the ends, smooth shift the polygons out a few time and scale them down a little. Create a box for the inside pages. It should fit closely against the inside jacket polygons.

Step 5 (Figure 8-29). The vertical indentation that runs down near the book spine can be made by slicing straight through on the y-axis.

A Bookshelf

This is a piece of furniture that can be completed fairly quickly. It is basically a box that is beveled several times (Figure 8-27).

Step 1 (Figure 8-28). Create a box with a narrow depth (z-axis).

Step 2 (Figure 8-28). Bevel the front in to make a smaller polygon, but keep it on the same z-axis as the original one.

Step 3 (Figure 8-28). Bevel the polygon straight back without changing its size. Move it back so that the rear of the bookshelf has the same thickness as the sides.

Step 4 (Figure 8-28). Create the top of the bookshelf by first beveling straight out and to the sides,

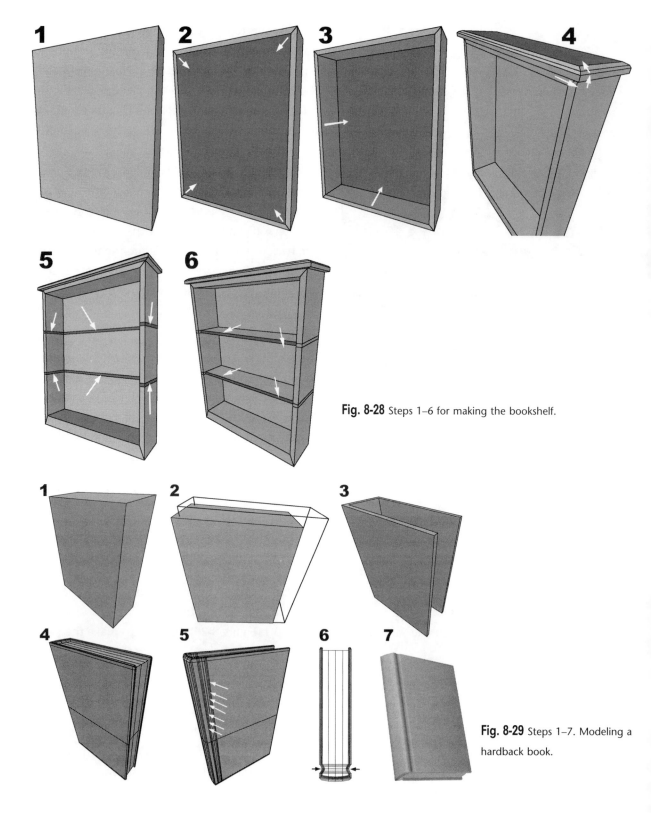

Fig. 8-28 Steps 1–6 for making the bookshelf.

Fig. 8-29 Steps 1–7. Modeling a hardback book.

Fig. 8-30 The rendered lamp table.

Step 6 (Figure 8-29). After making several of these vertical parallel slices, move points in to make the crevice.

Step 7 (Figure 8-29). Closely spaced lines are bump mapped onto the page portion of the book. The hardback portion can be UV mapped with a title, or wrapped in a thin sleeve with an illustration.

A Lamp Table

These types of end tables have a variety of shapes. The one used in this exercise is a little offbeat (Figure 8-30).

Step 1 (Figure 8-31). Create a polygon that has

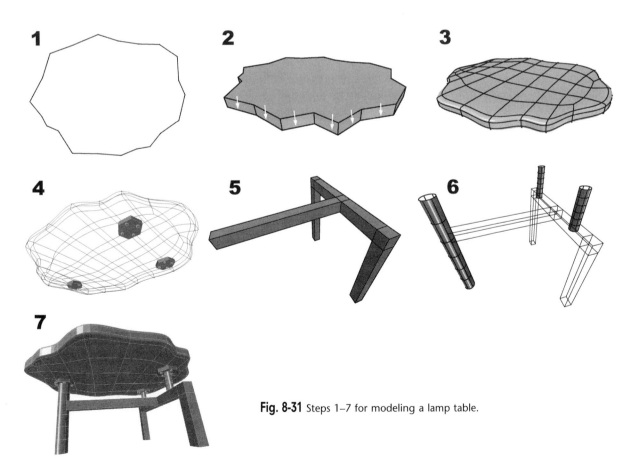

Fig. 8-31 Steps 1–7 for modeling a lamp table.

an amorphous shape.

Step 2 (Figure 8-31). Extrude or bevel the polygon down.

Step 3 (Figure 8-31). Split the top and bottom up into smaller polygons and turn on subdivision mode.

Step 4 (Figure 8-31). Make some hexagons for the fasteners under the table top.

Step 5 (Figure 8-31). Bevel a cube up and out in several directions to make the framework and two of the legs.

Step 6 (Figure 8-31). Add some cylinders for the supports and one of the legs.

Step 7 (Figure 8-31). Put all the pieces together. Apply a metal surface to the legs and frame. The table top can have a marble type of surface. All the textures on the lamp table can be procedurals.

A Lamp

Since most lamps are symmetrical, a lathing operation will be utilized here. Extruding parts of it should make it more interesting (Figure 8-32).

Step 1 (Figure 8-33). In the front view window, draw one side of the outline of your lamp without the shade. Select the points in order and make a polygon out of them. The middle set of points should be on the 0 x-axis.

Step 2 (Figure 8-33). Lathe the half lamp outline on the y-axis with six sides. There is no need to use more sides, since the lamp will be rendered with subdivision surfaces.

Steps 3, 4 and 5 (Figure 8-33). Select the polygon faces on each of the six sides and bevel or smooth shift them out. These will have a glass surface applied to them, while the polygons between them will be metal.

Steps 6 and 7 (Figure 8-33). Make the lamp

Fig. 8-32 The rendered lamp.

shade by lathing an angled, long rectangular polygon.

Steps 8 and 9. Add other details such as a light bulb, switch, stem, and so on. Most of the time these are not necessary, since the lamp shade covers them.

A Hanging Plant

An interior scene can look austere without the presence of some living organisms. Plants will always make an environment appear to be more

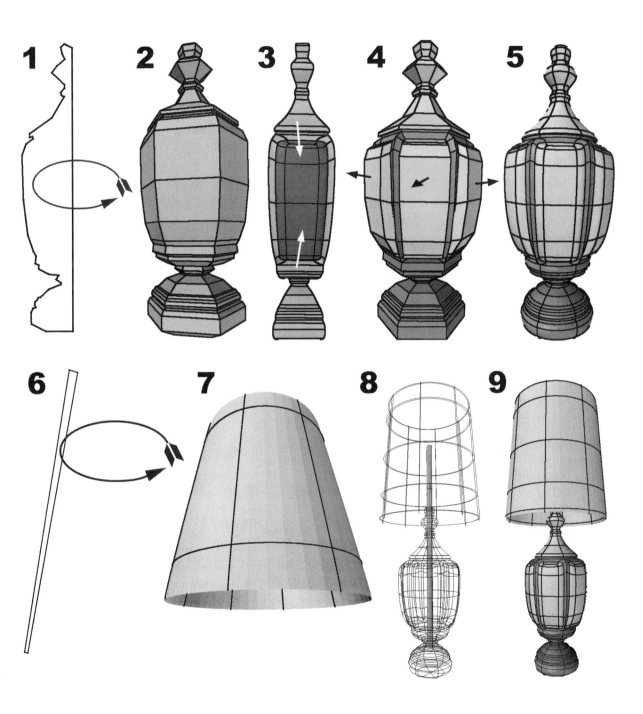

Fig. 8-33 Steps 1–9. Modeling a lamp.

suitable to live in (Figure 8-34). A tree generator works well for quickly creating plants. The leaves are usually the problem because such a great quantity is needed, memory requirements increase greatly. One way to remedy this is to just make branches and then use a fur/hair generator for the leaves. The following instructions demonstrate how a plant can be made by modeling leaves and stems.

Step 1 (Figure 8-35). In your top view window, make a polygon that has a leaf shape. Split it up into sections.

Step 2 (Figure 8-35). UV map an image of a leaf

Fig. 8-34 A rendered hanging plant.

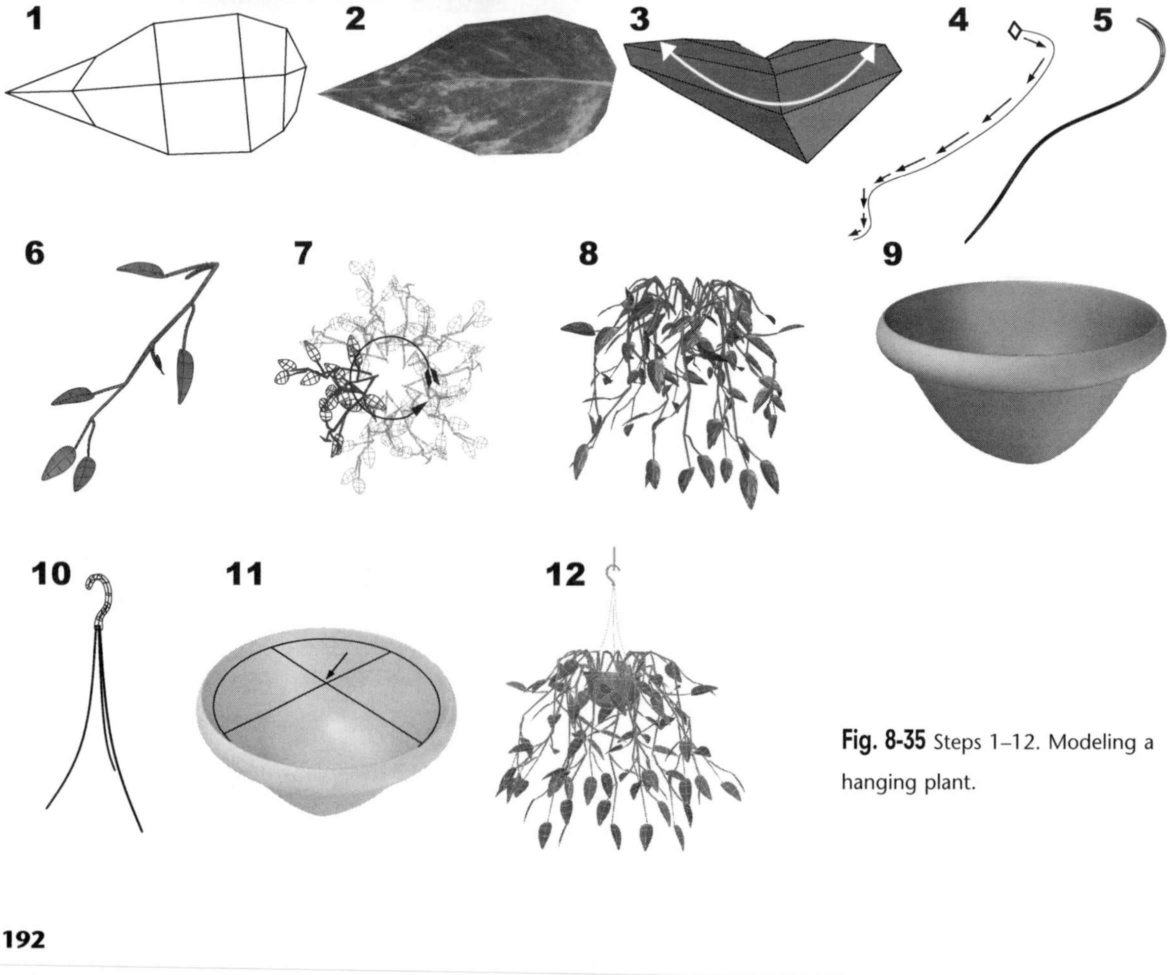

Fig. 8-35 Steps 1–12. Modeling a hanging plant.

on the y-axis onto the leaf model.

Step 3 (Figure 8-35). Select the points along the leaf's middle seam and move them down to bend it a little.

Step 4 (Figure 8-35). Create a spline that curves down in the direction of a stem.

Step 5 (Figure 8-35). Make a four-sided polygon and rail extrude it along the length of the spline.

Step 6 (Figure 8-35). Select points at different sections of the stem. Make polygons out of these and bevel extrude them to make offshoots from the main plant stem. Clone the leaf and place the copies at the ends of the branches. Rotate the leaves in various directions.

Step 7 (Figure 8-35). Use a radial array to clone the stem and all its leaves around the y-axis.

Step 8 (Figure 8-35). Move some of the stems and leaves to give them a more haphazard appearance.

Step 9 (Figure 8-35). Make a pot for the plant by lathing a polygon that has been shaped into its profile.

Step 10 (Figure 8-35). Create a hook and hanging wires to attach to the plant pot. You can use rail extrude to make these.

Step 11 (Figure 8-35). Make a polygon around the inner perimeter of the plant pot. Apply a texture that looks like dirt to it.

Step 12 (Figure 8-35). Create a ceiling hook and attach the hanging pot to it. Apply textures to the pot, hook, and hanging wires.

TV Trays and Stand

The goal of this exercise is to end up with four TV trays hanging from a TV tray stand (Figure 8-36). All the components are put together from simple objects, such as boxes with rounded corners. There

Fig. 8-36 The rendered TV trays and stand.

are no beveling or extrusion methods employed.

Step 1 (Figure 8-37). Create a flat box with rounded corners in the front view. This will be the top of the TV tray. Apply a UV surface to it.

Step 2 (Figure 8-37). Make another long box with rounded corners for a support underneath the tray top. UV map the same wood texture onto it. Stick some button-shaped fasteners into it.

Step 3 (Figure 8-37). Copy and paste the support from step 2 into another layer. Extend its length. This will be one of the legs.

Step 4 (Figure 8-37). Make a copy of the leg from step 3 and move it next to leg number one.

Step 5 (Figure 8-37). Use the support from step 2 to make two more supports. Rotate these 90 degrees and make them smaller. Place them at opposite ends in the middle on the underside of

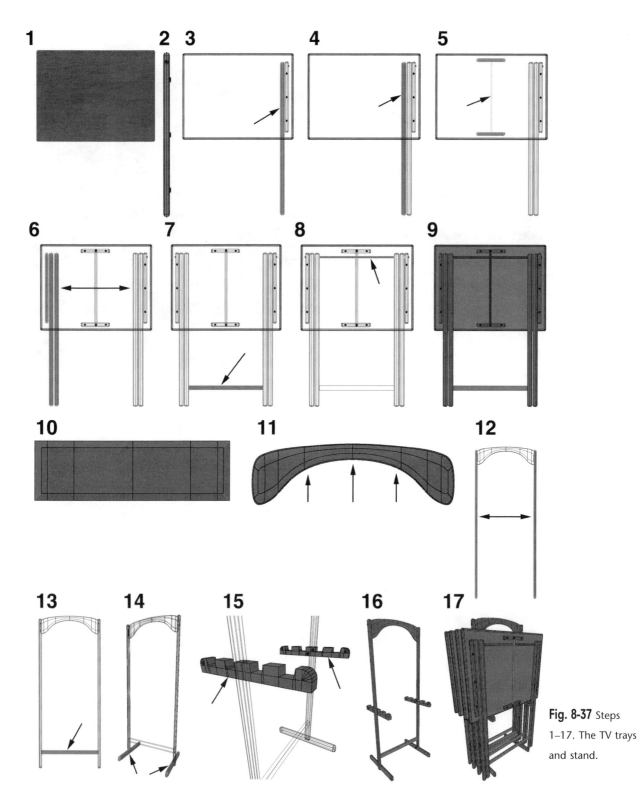

Fig. 8-37 Steps 1–17. The TV trays and stand.

the tray top. Create a flat box with rounded corners that spans the length of the two small supports. Apply a metal texture to it. Add some fasteners to the two small supports.

Step 6 (Figure 8-37). Mirror duplicate the first support and the two legs along the x-axis.

Step 7 (Figure 8-37). Create a flat box that spans the length between the two inner legs. Place it near the bottom of the legs.

Step 8 (Figure 8-37). Add a cylindrical object that extends between the two inner legs.

Step 9 (Figure 8-37). Make three copies of the original TV tray and stack them together. The next series of steps will have you model a stand to hang these on.

Step 10 (Figure 8-37). Create a flat box with beveled edges. Divide it up vertically.

Step 11 (Figure 8-37). Turn on subdivision mode and move points up to give it an arch. Make the top curve down at the ends. This will be the upper section of the TV tray stand.

Step 12 (Figure 8-37). Copy one of the legs from the TV tray and extend its length. Place it at one end of the upper section. Mirror duplicate it for the other side. Add some fasteners.

Step 13 (Figure 8-37). Make a long box that extends from one leg to the other, near the bottom.

Step 14 (Figure 8-37). Construct two feet for the legs. These should have rounded edges. Place them on the inside of the legs and add fasteners.

Step 15 (Figure 8-37). Make a piece of wood with notches in it that will hold up the TV trays. You can make the notches with a Boolean subtract operation or by moving points. Duplicate it and place the two pieces below the middle section on the inside of the legs. Add fasteners.

Step 16 (Figure 8-37). If you have not done so

Fig. 8-38 The rendered electric plug and outlet.

already, apply the wood texture to the completed TV tray stand.

Step 17 (Figure 8-37). Place all four TV trays on the stand. You may have to adjust the placement of the notches on the pieces that hold up the TV trays. Two trays are placed on either side of the stand.

Electric Cord and Wall Socket

One of the most common objects found in all living spaces is the electric outlet and cord (Figure 8-38). The most complicated part is the electric plug that is inserted in a socket to make an electrical connection. Beveling a number of times creates

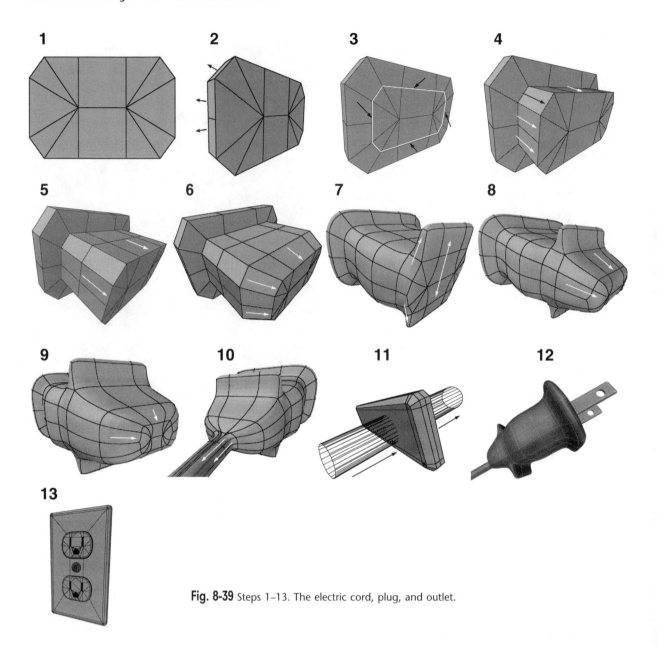

Fig. 8-39 Steps 1–13. The electric cord, plug, and outlet.

most of this object.

Step 1 (Figure 8-39). Make an octagon that is split into three- and four-sided polygons.

Step 2 (Figure 8-39). Bevel, smooth shift, or extrude it to give it a little thickness.

Step 3 (Figure 8-39). Split the front polygons so that you have a smaller octagon shape (white lines in the illustration).

Step 4 (Figure 8-39). Bevel, smooth shift, or extrude the smaller octagon in the front.

Step 5 (Figure 8-39). Extrude it out again.

Step 6 (Figure 8-39). Extrude it once more, but give it an inset to make it smaller.

Step 7 (Figure 8-39). Slice across the last extruded section and bevel, smooth shift, or extrude both ends up and down.

Step 8 (Figure 8-39). Select the polygons at the end and extrude them out and in a little.

Step 9 (Figure 8-39). Extrude the end part of the plug and make it the height and width of the cord.

Step 10 (Figure 8-39). Extrude the cord from the last section of the plug. Make it long enough to extend to the nearest appliance, such as the TV. Slice through the cord a number of times so that you can bend it into a more natural shape.

Step 11 (Figure 8-39). Make the two pins that are inserted into the electric plug. A flat, beveled box that has a hole cut into it works fine. Use a Boolean subtract operation to make the holes.

Step 12 (Figure 8-39). Insert the two metal pins into the end of the plug. Apply textures to the electric cord and plug.

Step 13 (Figure 8-39). The wall socket can be made from a beveled box. The sockets are cut into it and beveled in, beveled again to make them smaller, and finally, beveled out a little. The receptacle holes can be Boolean subtracted from the two sockets. Add the head of a screw to the wall socket, and you are done.

Paintings, Photos, and Frames

Our living room would not be complete without some paintings and photos on the walls (Figure 8-40). Good art never fails to transform rooms from sterile, philistine environments to sophisticated surroundings.

Step 1 (Figure 8-41). Make a four-sided polygon, which is going to be proportional to your painting.

Step 2 (Figure 8-41). Bevel or extrude it back to give it a little thickness, like that of a canvas on a stretcher. Make the back polygon bigger. You should now have the outer part of the frame.

Step 3 (Figure 8-41). Select the front polygon and bevel it in a little to make it smaller, but keep

Fig. 8-40 The rendered painting and frame.

it on the same plane as the original.

Step 4 (Figure 8-41). Bevel the polygon back a little and in so that it is slightly smaller.

Step 5 (Figure 8-41). Bevel the polygon in a little to make it smaller, but keep it on the same plane as the original.

Step 6 (Figure 8-41). Bevel the polygon forward so that it is almost even with the edges of the frame.

Step 7 (Figure 8-41). Map a picture of a painting onto the last beveled polygon. Apply surfaces to the frame and sides of the canvas. Duplicate the painting, scale the copies, and hang them with different paintings mapped onto them on various walls. Photos with frames can be made in a similar fashion. An extra polygon is placed in front with a glass surface.

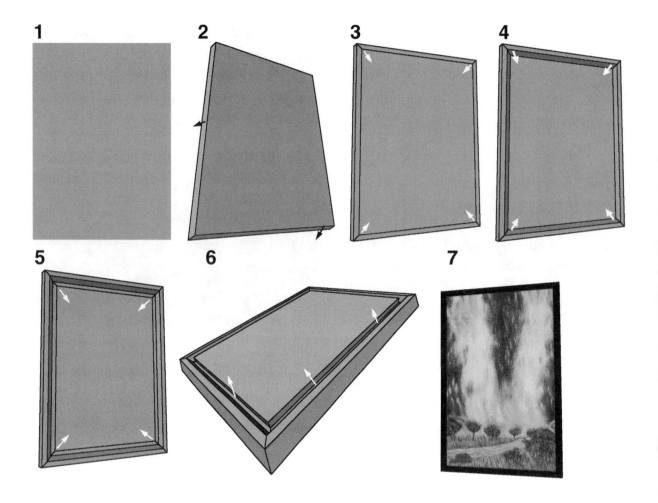

Fig. 8-41 Steps 1–7. Modeling the canvas and frame.

PART III

Preparing for 3D Animation

CHAPTER 9

Lighting

Light and color are synonymous terms. When writing about one, it is difficult to ignore the other. Painting with color in 3D means painting with light. Light and color are the most relevant mediums in computer art. Light varies not only according to the amount present in a setting, but also in relationship to neighboring light sources. Since this book has only black-and-white illustrations, it is difficult to show the effects of color and light. Therefore, a number of 24-bit color illustrations have been placed on the CD-ROM.

An expert use of light means controlling it not only by selecting the correct light type and modifying it by degree of falloff, intensity, and color, but also by moderating its influence through the skillful placement of other lights in a scene. These change a scene's character. One example can be seen in Figure 9-1. A strong light source next to an object causes it to lose saturation, making it look too light and washed out. If you were to turn down the light's intensity, other areas would become too dark. One solution to this problem is to place a negative light source next to the washed-out part of the object, thus cutting down the strength of the first light. The negative light absorbs extra light in a specific part of the scene, making it a great tool for localized control. Negative lights have a number of other useful functions that will be discussed in a later section.

Light Types

Some of the most common light types can be viewed in Figure 9-2. Most 3D software packages utilize these in one form or another. Some, like spotlights, are used quite commonly, while others, like ambient light, are utilized sparingly. Many times, a light type is chosen for the quality of its

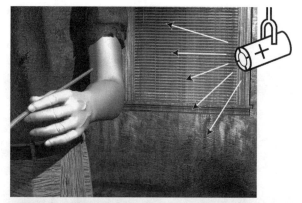

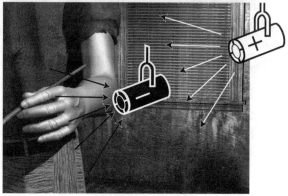

Fig. 9-1 In the upper portion, a spotlight's brightness washes out the fingers and hand. When a negative light is added in the lower half, the extra light intensity is absorbed.

shadows. For example, distant, point, and spotlights produce hard-edged, ray-traced shadows, while linear and area lights create soft-edged, ray-traced shadows.

Ambient light creates a uniform and directionless light source. Since it penetrates every part of a scene, it is often used as a fill light. Most professionals try to keep ambient light to a minimum because of its tendency to make scenes look flat and washed out. Figure 9-3 shows the effect of ambient light. Notice how the scene lacks contrast due to the lack of diversity in the lighting setup. It is usually recommended that ambient light be turned down to about 5 percent to 10 percent.

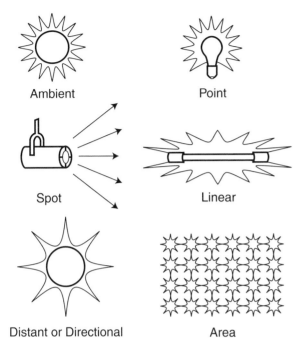

Ambient   Point

Spot   Linear

Distant or Directional   Area

Fig. 9-2 Some common light types. Ambient lights illuminate uniformly in all directions. Point lights are similar to light bulbs. Spotlights cast light in one direction. Linear lights are like a line of point lights. Distant or directional lights are like the sun. Area lights are like a group of point lights illuminating in all directions.

Spotlights are some of the most commonly used light types. This is partly due to the fact that their flexibility gives the user a great amount of control. You can set the spotlight angle to shine on a larger or smaller part of the scene. The direction of the light is easy to handle. In addition, some software packages only let the user create shadow maps or depth-map shadows with spotlights. Unlike most ray-traced shadows, shadow maps are soft-edged. They also render faster. Shadow maps are usually calculated by what areas are hidden when viewed from the light's view. Normally, you would not assign shadow maps to more than one or two lights. Figure 9-4 illustrates the use of spotlights and shadow maps. The scene appears similar to stage lighting.

Area lights are like a rectangular array of lights (Figure 9-5). They send light out in all directions. Due to their ability to create soft-edged, ray-traced shadows, they can produce some of the highest-quality renderings. Unfortunately, this comes at a steep price. A scene that would normally render in one minute could take forty minutes with area

Fig. 9-3 Too much ambient light weakens any contrast in the image. Notice how much detail is missing.

Fig. 9-4 Spotlights are used to make this scene look more dramatic.

Fig. 9-5 Area lights create pleasing, soft, ray-traced shadows, but the rendering time can be forty times longer than normal.

Fig. 9-6 Linear lights yield results similar to area lights—except that the shadows are not as soft—but rendering takes only half the time.

lights. Another aspect of these lights is that they can usually be scaled in size.

Linear lights (Figure 9-6) are similar to area lights in that they also produce soft-edged, ray-traced shadows. These lights also have longer rendering times, although not quite as protracted as

area lights. Linear lights are like a row of lights. Normally, these lights can be scaled.

Distant or directional lights are meant to simulate the effects of sunlight (Figure 9-7). Like the sun, their light rays travel parallel to one another in the direction the light is pointing. The light usu-

Fig. 9-7 Distant or directional lights act similarly to the sun by illuminating everything equally. Shadows are hard-edged and difficult to control.

Fig. 9-8 Point lights placed around a scene give soft illumination to objects, although the ray-traced shadows have hard edges.

ally travels through objects. For example, if you place a box in a scene, the distant light would illuminate the interior as well as the exterior. Distant or directional lights have no obvious source and do not decay with distance. Therefore, it does not matter where you place these lights, because far-off objects receive the same illumination as closer ones. Since distant lights illuminate everything equally, a total reliance on them produces a monotonous lighting scheme.

Point lights illuminate equally in all directions from a central source (Figure 9-8). They can be compared to bare incandescent light bulbs. Careful consideration should be given to the placement of point lights. Used in conjunction with spotlights, point lights can be useful for filling out areas of low illumination as well as reducing light by setting them with a negative intensity.

Lighting Arrangements

Although there is no set formula for placing lights in a scene, basic, classic configurations are used extensively in the real world as well as in computer graphics. The following common lighting arrangements should serve as a starting point to much more interesting and creative approaches. Even though these configurations rely on only four lights, it is recommended that many more lights be added to simulate radiosity, create extra shadows, and enhance the mood through color.

Each object could easily require six lights. Some of these might include a top light, key (main light), a fill light (fills out the shadow side), a rim light (points from the back toward the camera to outline the figure), a kicker (points in the opposite direction of the key light to outline part of the figure from one side), and an eye light (highlights the eyes). Other colored lights could be added to make the object look more interesting. The fill light might be colored blue or purple, while the key light could have a warm color such as light yellow.

Figure 9-9 shows a basic light setup in which the color values and emotional impact are weak. Due to the key (main) and fill (softens shadows) lights having similar settings, the objects lack

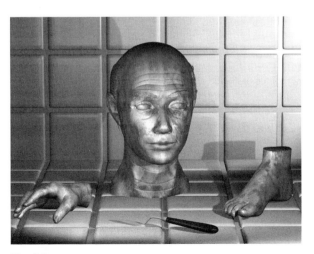 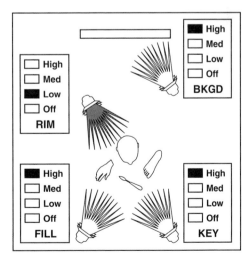

Fig. 9-9 A basic lighting setup. The image lacks contrast due to both the key and fill lights having the same high settings. Increasing the rim light's intensity separates the objects from the background. A lower fill light setting increases contrast.

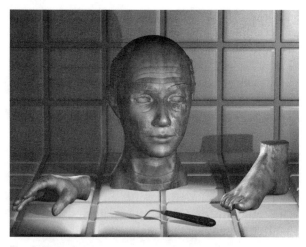
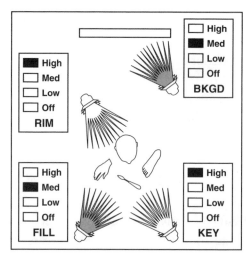

Fig. 9-10 A more dramatic lighting arrangement. The high rim light illuminates the edges of objects, and the lower fill light setting adds deeper shadows.

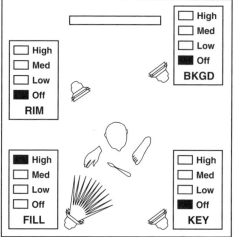

Fig. 9-11 A very contrasty lighting setup. Since the fill light is the only source of illumination, the resulting deep shadows hide much of the detail.

contrast and are washed out in areas. A lower fill light setting and stronger rim light (back light) can make this scene more dramatic.

A better lighting arrangement can be seen in Figure 9-10. Having the fill light at a lower setting and the rim light higher helps to define the features of all the objects.

A very simplified lighting setup can be viewed in Figure 9-11. Only one light is used, and it is not even the key light. The dimmer fill light creates deep shadows that obscure most of the detail.

Turning off all the front lights and only using the back lights make objects appear as silhouettes (Figure 9-12). This is a useful device that is used in broadcasting when someone is being interviewed anonymously.

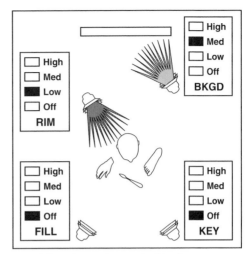

Fig. 9-12 A silhouette lighting scheme. The lack of illumination in front of the subject obscures its identity.

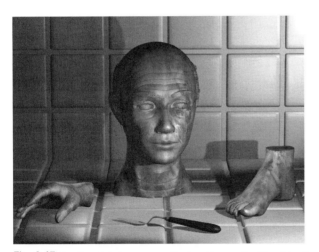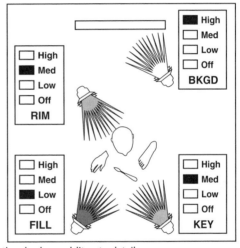

Fig. 9-13 A softer lighting setup. Contrast is good without having the shadows obliterate detail.

A more subdued arrangement can be found in Figure 9-13. The front lights have a lower setting, while the strongest light is the bounce light in the back. This lighting arrangement can serve as a good starting point for the placement of other lights.

A darker and more mysterious mood can be set up with the fill and rim lights set high (Figure 9-

14). A few other well-placed, low-level lights can enrich this scene.

Moving the lights to a lower level and projecting their beams up at the subject can make things look strange (Figure 9-15). It is reminiscent of a child shining a flashlight upward from below the chin.

Nighttime illumination can be created with

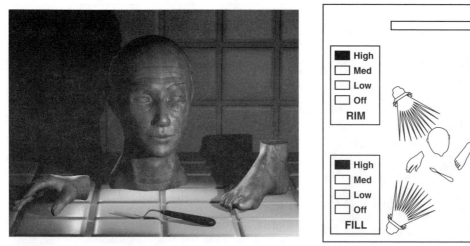

Fig. 9-14 A contrasty lighting arrangement due to the lack of a key light. It can be used to convey a mood of mystery.

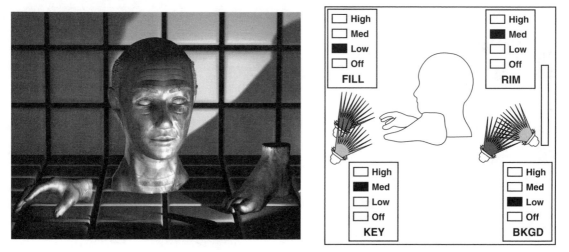

Fig. 9-15 Lighting from below can make objects look eerie. The effect is a favorite with producers of mystery and horror films.

lights shining down on the subject (Figure 9-16). To enhance this scene, you should place more lights around the objects but with lower settings. Negative lights can also be combined with the others to soften the bright spots. The standard four-light setup can be enhanced with the addition of one top light.

Lighting Hints

Animation companies, just like movie studios,

often use specialists to set up the correct lighting for their scenes. The following section was compiled from interviews with one of my former students—Patrick Wilson, who worked as a lighting specialist at PIXAR—and Avi Das, a color and lighting artist at Digital Domain. Both of them shed light (pardon the pun) on the inner workings of lighting for animation.

Use Negative Lights

Shadows under the feet are often hard to con-

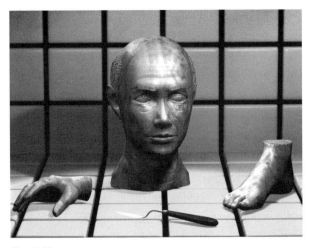

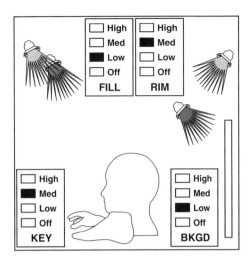

Fig. 9-16 Lighting from the top can simulate indoor nighttime illumination.

trol. If your software allows you to parent lights to the feet or the bones/joints of the feet, you can create your own shadows without too much trouble. Figure 9-17 shows two pairs of lights. One pair is negative and the other duplicate pair is positive. The positive lights cast shadow maps or depth map shadows, while the negative lights do not project shadows. In other words, shadow type or project shadows is turned on for the positive lights, while it is turned off for the negative lights.

Figure 9-17 shows the four lights separately for the sake of clarity, but in reality, each set of positive and negative lights occupies the same space above each foot. All the lights have the same intensity, but you can control the value of the shadows by setting different intensities to the negative lights. If both the positive and negative lights have the same intensity settings, they will cancel each other out. The overall illumination stays the same, while shadows are cast under the feet. These are sometimes referred to as contact shadows.

Negative lights can also be used to make parts of a scene darker. A good application of this is to place them in corners of rooms or in other spots where you do not want illumination. Figure 9-18

Fig. 9-17 Two pairs of spotlights are parented to the feet. One set has a positive intensity, while the other has a negative intensity. Each negative and positive pair has the same settings and, unlike the illustration, occupies the same space. This results in shadows under the feet (arrows) without any extra illumination.

shows the effect of negative lights along the bases of walls and corners of a room. It is as if you were using a sponge to soak up light.

As shown in Figure 9-1, negative lights can be used to cut back intense illumination in a scene. They can keep objects from losing their contrast

Fig. 9-18 To darken corners of rooms or other areas, place negative lights to create shadows.

Fig. 9-19 The top image is rendered with hard-edged, ray-traced shadows while the bottom one has soft-edged shadow maps.

and help regulate the values in a scene. Another advantage to negative lights is that they do not increase rendering time. They eliminate all lighting calculations in the influenced area.

Rely Mostly on Shadow Maps or Depth Map Shadows Rather Than Ray-traced Ones

Rendering shadows using ray tracing produces sharp shadows that take a relatively long time to render. Many artists consider scenes with ray-traced shadows cold. You can render shadows much faster while obtaining smooth, soft-edged shadows of equivalent quality (Figure 9-19).

To get a basic understanding of how shadow maps are generated, a few terms need to be clarified. Z depth describes how far away objects are in a scene. Normally, Z depth information is calculated by how far objects are from the camera. With depth map shadows (shadow maps), the shadows are calculated by how far they are from the light sources that are casting them. The renderer uses this information and the position of the light sources to determine which items produce shadows. It stores all this information in the Z-buffer. This extra memory usage means that you often have to limit the number of lights casting shadow maps. Usually, only one or two lights are set to produce shadow maps. Using Z depth information makes it hard to get a perfect depth placement of objects. The result is that aliasing problems can appear. This can usually be remedied by allocating more memory to the renderer and setting a higher shadow map size.

Simulate Radiosity with Colored Bounce Lights

Ray tracing creates a ray for each pixel in a scene and traces its path, one at a time, all the way back to the light source. A value for each ray is calculated as it travels through and bounces off various surfaces. To minimize rendering time, many renderers trace rays of light backwards from the camera to the light source. This eliminates the extra calculations needed to trace light rays that never reach the camera itself. Ray tracing does not calculate the effects of light as it bounces off one surface and illuminates another.

Radiosity rendering calculates the amount of light that is transmitted from one surface to another. This process continues to follow the light until it is fully absorbed by all the surfaces or dissipates in space. Radiosity calculations require a great amount of memory and raw computing power. Renderings are usually very time-intensive.

To simulate radiosity, place colored bounce lights in your scene. These can be pointed at surfaces that would show light from nearby objects. Figure 9-20 shows the location of several colored bounce lights. These point to the ground surface next to objects that reflect colored light onto it. The spotlights make it look as if various paint tubes are spilling their colored lights onto the tiled floor. A color image of this scene can be viewed on the CD-ROM as CD9-20. (It's called 9-20 Fake Radiosity.jpg).

It may take a little extra time to place bounce lights in your scene, but the rendering time will be much quicker than a true radiosity rendering. Placing similar colored lights next to surfaces will greatly improve the quality of your renderings.

Ask Yourself: What is the Emotional Goal of the Scene?

Before lighting a scene, think back to situations you have been in. If the scene is going to be romantic, then you might use diffused light with warm shadows. Color sketches can be a great aid

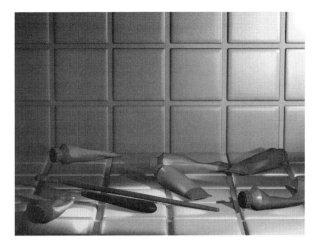

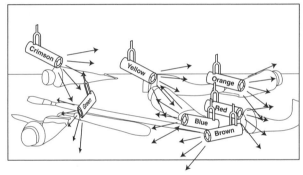

Fig. 9-20 Colored bounce lights simulate radiosity by making surfaces look as if they are receiving light from other objects.

in planning the lighting setup (Figure 9-21). They will save you time because you will not have to do as many test renderings before deciding on the final appearance of your environment. If you are averse to leaving your computer, sketch the scene in an image manipulation program before starting to light it in 3D.

Use Falloff or Decay and Link Lights to Specific Characters

Limiting the effect of each light gives you greater control over the scene's lighting arrange-

211

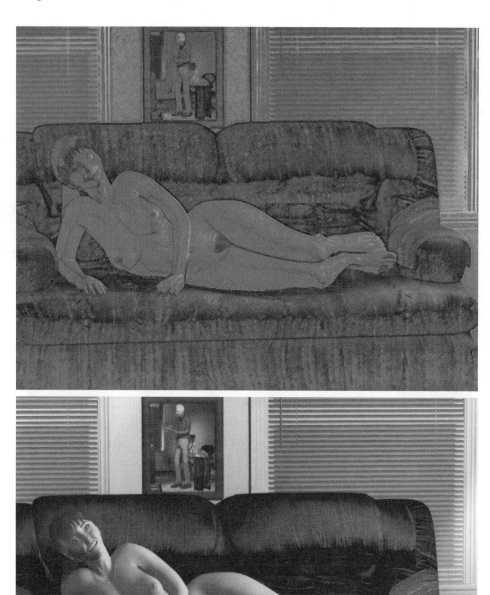

Fig. 9-21 Sketching first, on or off the computer, can speed up the process of lighting a scene.

ment. When lights are set to have falloff or decay, they will simulate light in the physical world, which becomes weaker with distance (Figure 9-22). Some software programs allow you to link lights to specific objects so that they affect only these and not adjacent ones. This is very useful for lighting characters. When the character approaches other objects or characters, its lights will not affect them. This is where computer graphics lighting reigns over set lighting. In a set, a light illuminates everything in its path unless stopped by a flag.

Use about six lights per character. Some of the lights that shine on the shadowed parts of a character can be colored blue or purple for a richer look. All lights should have a hint of color because pure white light rarely exists in our world.

Fig. 9-22 Lights with falloff or decay imitate real-world properties. They also make it easier to control a scene's illumination.

Illuminate Scenes with a Variety of Lights

Try not to skimp on the number of lights in a scene. When you consider all of the various types of lights, like bounce, fill, rim, kickers, negative, key, background, and so on, you could easily end up with 50 to 100 lights in a large scene. Localized lights with falloff or decay and lights

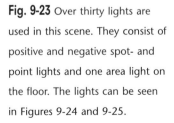

Fig. 9-23 Over thirty lights are used in this scene. They consist of positive and negative spot- and point lights and one area light on the floor. The lights can be seen in Figures 9-24 and 9-25.

Fig. 9-24 The lights used in Fig. 9-23 as viewed through the camera. A number of lights are behind objects, and other lights and are out of camera view and cannot be seen.

Fig. 9-25 An overview of all the lights used in the Fig. 9-23 scene. Positive and negative lights often occupy the same space. The lights appear to be stacked on top of each other, when in reality they are spaced along the z-axis.

assigned specifically to individual objects may add up, but they allow a greater degree of control. Typically, a scene might have no fewer than 30 lights (Figures 9-23, 9-24, and 9-25). Each light has a reason for its existence; otherwise, it is a waste of rendering time. One light can be set to cast the main shadows, and a negative light with the same settings (except for its negative value) will cancel out the luminosity of the light. The result is that the positive light only casts shadows, but does not add to the brightness of the scene. Other negative lights provide a few areas of shadow, while contact shadows (Figure 9-17) contribute a few more. A color image showing an example of indoor lighting with over 30 lights can be viewed in the chapter 9 folder of the CD-ROM. It is titled, "9 - 23 Many Lights In Scene.jpg."

When starting to light an interior, use a very low-intensity overall light to establish the basic ambience. This ambient light can vary among slight purple, blue, or even green. Fluorescent lights radiate a greenish hue. Then begin to add brighter lights with local influence only. Each object has its own set exclusive lights that do not influence any other objects in the scene. Vary the cone angles and penumbras (soft edges of lights). These lights should dissipate after a specified distance, as in real life. One example is a bar scene in which many lights with differing falloffs allow shadows to occur between lights. If there is a row of lights along a corridor, the intensity and the falloff or decay can vary as well. This prevents the lighting from looking flat and produces a visually interesting setting. In the physical world, light bulbs vary in age, with some more intense than others. The older ones have a slightly cooler temperature. These have more decay (lower falloff setting) and warmer colors. To break up a uniform look, project a slight noise pattern through some of the lights. This technique is discussed in the next section on light gels.

Outdoor scene lighting can sometimes be

Fig. 9-26 Outdoor lighting can be accomplished with a key light acting as the sun, a rim light, and localized lights for objects and characters.

accomplished with far fewer lights. The first step involves setting up the ambient light. It should be at a very low setting and its color should be context-specific. A bright daylight exterior has an unsaturated blue ambience. This kind of light scatters as it penetrates the atmosphere. The key light, which in this case simulates sunlight, is set up next. A yellow/orange distant light works unless you want it to cast shadow maps. Your software may limit you to using a spotlight. The key lighting colors are generally warmer and less intense for sunrise and sunset scenes. Once this is established, point a complementary colored light (blue to purple) from the opposite direction toward the key light. The intensity should be about 30 percent to 40 percent and fill in the shadow side. Once this basic lighting has been established, look for areas where local lighting effects should happen. For example, Figure 9-26 depicts an outdoor scene with two characters with their own set of lights, which include the key, fill, and kicker lights. Extra

lights are placed around the scene to bring out specific details like trees, grass, and so on. Negative lights are placed in parts of the scene to soak up extra light or to create more shady areas.

Another application of local lighting can be found in city scenes. Two white buildings next to each other at 45-degree angles to the sun's rays have one of their sides in the shadows. One building can reflect a pale yellow light onto the other building's shadow side creating a slight radiosity effect. This can be achieved by placing a light inside the building that is reflecting luminosity and pointing it at the one receiving the light. If the building that is reflecting is of a different color, the bounce light projects the wall's hue onto the other building.

Midday scenes are generally accomplished in a similar manner, except for the change in color and intensity of the key and fill lights. Unlike early morning or late afternoon, when the key light reflects the sky with warm colors, midday light has

Fig. 9-27 Light gels can be placed in the path of a spotlight or mapped to the light itself. The light becomes a slide projector.

Fig. 9-28 The use of light gels in an underwater scene. The animated gel texture is placed on the top light to create patterns on the swimmer and on the bottom surface.

a light blue color. For a very bright day, you can increase the luminance of your objects. This brings down the shadow densities. The effect is similar to days when you have to squint your eyes. To make it appear as if sunrays bounce off the ground and illuminate the undersides of objects, place a low-intensity fill light under the ground. Point it up and turn off its shadows and set a falloff. The color of the light could be pale brown. Sometimes it only takes three or four lights to illuminate an outdoor scene.

Try Using Light Gels

For more realistic lighting, try incorporating light gels in your scenes. Gels are patterns, images, textures, gradations, and so on that are placed in front of lights. For example, in computer graphics, a fractal noise shader or texture can be projected from a spotlight. The light acts similar to a slide projector. The fractal noise breaks up the light, simulating real-world spotty, inconsistent lighting

(Figure 9-27).

In cinema, lighting gels are sometimes referred to as gobos or kukalories. Any cutout or semi-transparent image can be placed in front of a light source. A good use of gels is found in underwater scenes. Figure 9-28 shows the effects of a gel placed on a top light. The mapped image has a slow texture velocity, which makes the underwater patterns move. An animation of this underwater effect can be viewed in the chapter 10 folder of the CD-ROM as "10-23UnderwtrTrnprncMap.mov," and as an image file in the chapter 9 folder called "9-28LightGelsUnderwtr.jpg." Another important element of underwater scenes is the use of blue fog to make objects fade quickly in the distance.

Animation companies like PIXAR create animated shaders for light gels. For example, a shader consisting of a tree with branches and moving leaves is projected on the ground, producing an active shadow.

Use Volumetric or Fog Lights for Dramatic Effects

Volumetric or fog lights can be seen as they move through space. In the physical world, tiny airborne particles reflect light in the air. Light streaming through the window of a dusty room, or a lighthouse illuminating a hazy night, are just

Fig. 9-29 Volumetric lighting can enhance the mood of a scene, but it does increase rendering time greatly.

two examples of volumetric lighting. If you are looking for a way to make lighting more dramatic, you might try volumetric lighting, but be prepared for very long rendering times (Figure 9-29). A color image of volumetric lighting can be viewed on the CD-ROM (9-29Volumetriclighting.jpg).

Since volumetric lighting can greatly increase rendering time, you may decide to try this technique for faking volumetrics. Using an object for the light and applying some creative texturing, you can cut back rendering time to a fraction of what it takes to render real volumetric lighting.

Fake volumetric lighting can be accomplished by modeling the shape of the light beam (Figure 9-30). A transparency map is created for the object. It consists of a light to dark gradient, as seen in Figure 9-30. This map is used to soften the edges of the object. The lightest areas show the object most clearly, while the darker ones obscure it. A fractal noise pattern of white and gray is applied to the object. The transparency is set to 60 percent and

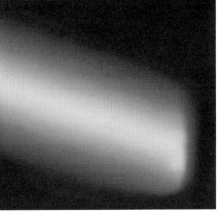

Fig. 9-30 Fake volumetric lighting can speed up the rendering process dramatically. The volumetric light object on the left has the transparency map (shown on the right) applied to it. Its surface has transparency with fractal noise, edge transparency, and glow. Fig. 9-31 shows the result.

Fig. 9-31 The fake volumetric effect after surfacing. Rendering time was minimal compared to real volumetric light rendering.

the transparency map is placed on it as a negative image. Edge transparency and glow are also applied to the object. The result can be viewed in Figure 9-31 and seen in color on the CD-ROM as "9-31FakeVlumetricLight.jpg."

Mood Lighting

Lighting and color play an important role in establishing the mood or emotional quality of a scene. Before setting up lights, visualize the type of illumination you desire. Use reference materials if you need to. Studying the works of artists like Rembrandt, Monet, Caravaggio, Vermeer, Parrish, and many others will prove to be an invaluable resource to draw from. The following suggestions for lighting may serve as a starting point, or at least show some ways to light a specific scene.

Romantic Scenes

Warm colors like red, orange, and yellow are usually associated with feelings of affection and passion. Soft, warm lights and shadows with low contrast can give the scene a glowing quality. The key light is placed high above, while the fill light is set lower to soften the density of shadows.

Crime Scenes

Cool colors play a primary role here. Blue can make the scene look cold. An almost white, harsh key light conveys an uneasy feeling. Design your lights in a way that will produce deep pockets of shadows. Lighting for a scene like this can be a mix of the naturalistic and pictorial. Naturalistic lighting uses logical sources of lights, while pictorial lighting is for aesthetics. Backgrounds should be out of focus to convey a sense of insecurity and danger. A wash of green light on background walls and objects can make the scene look unhealthy. Dark shadows and strong contrast play an important role in scenes like these. Avoid using warm-colored lights.

Fantasy Scenes

Fantasy scenes can be designed in a great variety of ways. The lighting design is mostly pictorial. The entire lighting setup should be directed toward an aesthetically pleasing environment. Pastel colored lights can be used. All lights and shadows should be soft. Extreme light and dark values should be avoided. Of course, all of this depends on the mood that you are trying to establish.

Corporate Scenes

Office space should feel emotionless and sterile. Since most office spaces use fluorescent lights, a pale green key light from above can simulate this. The scene should have very little contrast, which can be accomplished by increasing ambient lights or fill lights. A scene like this can have an enormous amount of light; therefore, shadows should be soft and almost nonexistent, especially for thinner objects.

Horror Scenes

Lighting for horror scenes can be similar to crime scene lighting. There should be high contrast with many shadows. The difference between the two is that in horror scenes, warm luminosity can be emitted from key and fill lights. Light gels are very useful here to project extra objects into the scene. This makes the environment appear to contain more than is actually modeled. For example, a dead tree with branches stretching out ominously and a noose swaying in the breeze can be projected onto a dimly lit, blood-red wall. Volumetric lights coming through a window can also give the scene an appearance of mystery and drama. All of this makes the scene appear disturbing or chilling.

Hostage Scenes

Try to imagine a scene where a hostage is bound to a chair and is being interrogated by terrorists. You can place a key spotlight inside a modeled light bulb hanging right above his head. It would cast a very harsh light, creating deep shadows under his eye sockets and chin. The light can be parented to the modeled light bulb, which, in turn, might slowly swing back and forth, creating a disturbing play of light and shadow on the man's face and body.

The light should have a narrow cone angle and soft penumbra (edge angle) so that it does not influence much beyond the prisoner himself. The falloff should be enough so that the far reaches of the room are dark. The walls can be seen through the use of soft blue fill lights. A window with bars can let some light into the room. A kicker light, consisting of harsh white or blue light and placed about three-quarters behind the prisoner, can be used to separate the prisoner from the background. It adds a sense of isolation to the prisoner.

Other characters can be seen as silhouettes against dimly lit, blue walls. They would look mysterious, unknown, and dangerous. A very faint light, of about 20 percent of the key light's intensity, can be placed under the floor, directly beneath the key light. It bounces up light from the floor and creates underlighting on the character for close-ups.

CHAPTER 10

Surfacing Techniques

3D animation involves building virtual environments. This means a lot of modeling followed by texturing. Knowing how to apply surfaces in a creative way will make your work look better and can save rendering as well as modeling time. Texture mapping can be the simple application of a color or image to an object. It can also be a very complicated process when trying to simulate special effects like those discussed in chapter 5. Surfacing often takes the place of complex modeling. Bump mapping is used to make fine details like wrinkles or hard-to-model crevices. Transparency mapping acts as a substitute for building complicated models like trees covered with leaves.

Texture Types

Surfacing normally means utilizing image maps or procedural textures. Image maps are digitized real-world images of brick, wood, fabric, and so on. They can make objects look photorealistic. The disadvantage to using them is that when seen in close-ups, they can show up as irregular surfaces due to the appearance of their individual pixels. To avoid this problem, high-resolution images can be utilized, but they require greater memory usage. Making the textures seamless so that they can be tiled is another solution, but the drawback is that a discernable pattern often arises on the surface of objects, which can make them look artificial.

Procedural textures, which are sometimes referred to as shaders, are images generated by mathematical formulas. They can take the form of two-dimensional or three-dimensional surfaces. Two-dimensional procedurals can be generated in an image editing program and then saved as image maps. Three-dimensional procedural texture maps

are defined in terms of points in three-dimensional space. Sometimes these are referred to as solid textures. They exist on the surface of the object as well as on the inside. Unlike 2D procedural textures, which are projected only on the outside surface of an object, 3D procedural textures are distributed throughout the object. If the object were sliced in half, you would find the texture inside of it. A procedural texture can be given parameters to vary its appearance in ways that are difficult to achieve with an image map. For example, an animated fire texture can look like it has flickering flames, or a water texture can be made to generate pond ripples. Unlike repeating image maps, procedural textures usually contain a random noise function, which makes them appear to lack any visible order. The disadvantage to procedural textures is that they are not very useful when trying to simulate realistic physical objects.

Rather than choosing either image maps or procedural textures, why not combine the two? Applying both to a surface can result in an interesting texture. The two can be used in any combination. For instance, you could use the procedural texture as a bump map and the image as a surface map. Figure 10-1 shows the image and procedural surfaces, and a mixture of the two. One is an image of wood, while the other approximates the look of wood grain through a random noise pattern.

Surface Appearance

Without using any textures or shaders, surfaces can be set to have different appearances. Luminosity, diffuseness, specular, reflectivity, transparency, environment and bump mapping, and more can modify the quality of objects.

Luminosity or incandescence denotes how

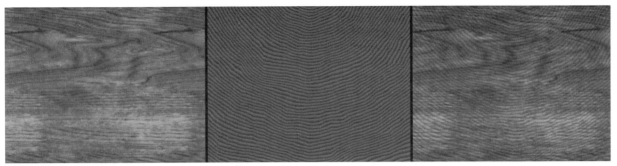

Fig. 10-1 Two types of textures and the combination of both. The wood grain on the left is an actual image of wood. The middle one is a procedural texture that approximates the look of wood grain. The image on the right is a union of both.

much a surface appears to be illuminated of its own accord. Objects seem to have an internal light. Figure 10-2 illustrates a sphere with various degrees of brightness. Luminosity scatters light evenly across a surface and makes the object appear flat like a disk. This can be useful when you need to project an image on a surface and you do not want the object to appear shaded.

Diffuseness reacts to light in different ways, depending on the position and orientation of the light source. The ability to scatter light across a surface is a characteristic of diffuseness. Figure 10-2 shows how various percentages of diffuseness affect the appearance of a sphere. The angle and position of the light source also plays an important factor here. Mapping an image on the diffuse level allows you to keep the original color of the object. The texture appears as a grayscale image, while the object retains its assigned color. Hard-looking metallic or reflective surfaces are made with lower diffuse levels.

Specular levels control the appearance of highlights on a surface. They determine how shiny an object appears. Figure 10-2 depicts the specular degrees on a sphere. The higher settings make the ball appear shinier. Rather than scattering light

evenly across a surface, specularity concentrates and focuses it on specific areas according to the light source. A specular map can be applied to a surface to control which areas should be glossy and which should be matte. For example, you can make a specular map for a face in which the parts that stand out more, like the nose, lips, forehead, and so on, can be painted lighter, and in turn, make those parts of the skin look glossier. Coloring the specular highlights with the same hue as the object makes it seem more metallic.

Reflectivity controls the mirror-like appearance of a surface. This can come about in several ways. The first method uses ray-traced reflections in which each pixel on the screen has a ray whose path is traced back to the light source. The characteristics of surfaces are calculated as the ray bounces off or travels through various objects. Ray tracing can yield very accurate reflections and refractions, but it does require longer rendering times. One way to speed up ray-traced reflection renderings is to turn down the recursion depth or ray recursion limit. This relates to the number of times that a ray is allowed to reflect off a surface. Usually a setting of 2 is enough for most circumstances. Reflection maps offer an

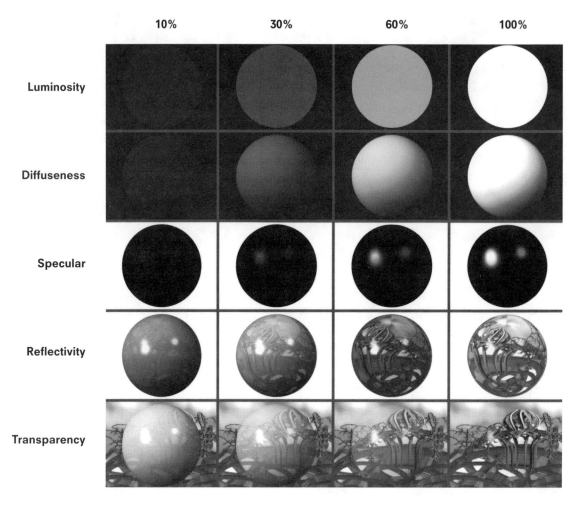

Fig. 10-2 A sphere showing various percentages of luminosity (or glow), diffuseness (or the way in which a surface scatters light), specular (or shininess), reflectivity, and transparency.

appealing alternative to ray tracing reflections. You can reduce rendering times greatly by applying an image map of a background or a simple noise pattern to your software's reflectivity options. Figure 10-2 shows a reflection map applied to a sphere in various degrees. The image is applied onto the ball with reflective surfaces, as if the environment is being reflected. Few surfaces have mirror-like qualities. Therefore, if you

want more realistic reflections, blur the reflection image map and turn reflectivity down to a lower percentage.

Transparency determines how much light is allowed to pass through an object. Figure 10-2 illustrates various degrees of transparency. The lowest setting makes the sphere appear more opaque. Except for the specular highlight, the highest transparency setting renders the ball invisible. Objects with transparency often "refract" light, which is the bending of light as it passes through objects. A judicious use of refraction keeps rendering times from becoming too lengthy. Transparency maps, which will be discussed later, are indispensable tools for artists who are trying to work under limited memory conditions.

Mapping Methods

Most software programs use a similar paradigm for mapping textures. The most common are planar, cylindrical, spherical, cubic, and front projection

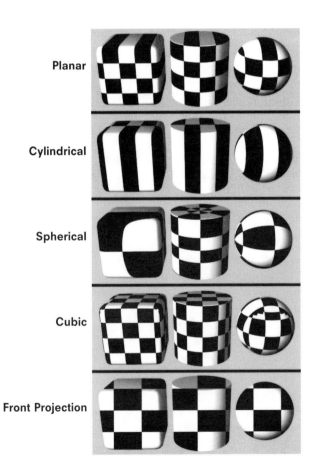

Planar

Cylindrical

Spherical

Cubic

Front Projection

Fig. 10-3 Five types of texture mapping.

(Figure 10-3). UV coordinate mapping is another method that will be discussed later. Since most objects are not simple primitives, it may take some experimenting with different image map types before deciding which system works best.

Planar image mapping (Figure 10-4) projects an image onto a surface similar to a slide projector. Normally, the texture can be applied on the x-, y-, or z-axis. If you modeled a car and it was facing forward on the z-axis, you could apply a decal to its hood using the y-axis. The doors could have decals applied to them on the x-axis and the front and back of the car could have maps applied using the z-axis.

Cylindrical image mapping (Figure 10-5) wraps a texture around an object similar to toilet paper around a roll. The map connects the two edges at the opposite end. Cylindrical image mapping is not used that often because it does not work too well with most complicated models. Using the previous car analogy, you would wrap the tailpipe on the z-axis. A can sitting on the dashboard could have its map applied on the y-axis. The tires could have a texture mapped on the x-axis.

Spherical image mapping (Figure 10-6) is similar to wrapping cloth around a ball. The texture at the specified axes is pinched. This compression at the poles distorts the mapped image. Usually the y-axis is used to map a texture on a spherical object, like the surface of a planet.

Cubic image mapping (Figure 10-7) projects an image onto all three axes at the same time. Along with planar mapping, cubic mapping is one of the more useful techniques for applying textures. It works well for applying maps onto complex objects because it does not distort the image. The one drawback is that it can show seams where the separate maps meet. When all else fails, try cubic

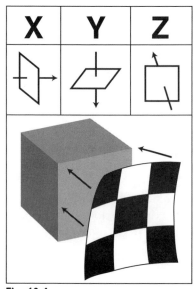

Fig. 10-4 Planar image mapping.

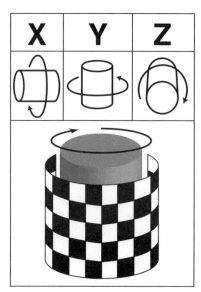

Fig. 10-5 Cylindrical image mapping.

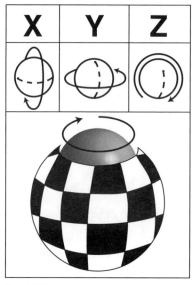

Fig. 10-6 Spherical image mapping.

mapping.

Front projection mapping (bottom image, Figure 10-3) is like taking a background image and projecting it directly onto an object. The texture does not distort and matches precisely the same surface used as a background image. The size of the texture remains the same as the background image. An example of utilizing front projection mapping occurs when you have a background image of trees and a dog is supposed to run out from behind them. Create a plane and place it in front of the background and somewhat to the side. Then use front projection mapping to map the same texture on this foreground plane. The trees match both the background and the plane, and you can now have the dog run out from behind the trees imaged on the foreground plane.

UV coordinate mapping (Figure 10-8) is very useful for precise mapping on curved surfaces. Unlike the other mapping features, which treat all objects as if they were simple shapes, UV coordi-nate mapping allows you to match a texture to the structure of the geometry. The space of a surface is defined by a U-horizontal value. It usually stretches from 0 on the left to 1 on the right. The V-coordinate space normally defines the vertical value and stretches from 0 at the top to 1 at the bottom. When a model is deformed during an ani-mation, the UV coordinate–mapped texture stretches and bends right along with it. Another way to identify U- and V-axes is to think of the U-axis as longitude and the V-axis as latitude. UV coordinate mapping is so precise that it allows

Fig. 10-7 Cubic image mapping.

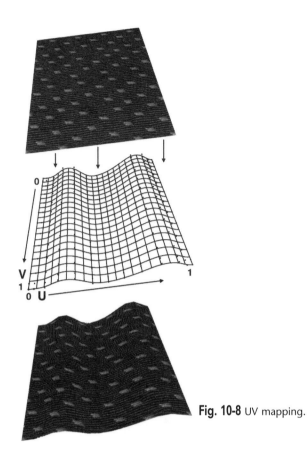

Fig. 10-8 UV mapping.

tions while darker areas appear as depressions, although this can easily be reversed by typing in a negative value for the texture amplitude. In reality, the surface remains flat and the elevated areas cannot project shadows. An easy way to spot bump mapping is to look along the edge of an object. The surface appears flat, while other areas that face toward the camera look bumpy. Bump maps should not be confused with displacement mapping. A displacement map actually alters the geometry of an object by moving its points in three-dimensional space.

Bump maps increase rendering times. Figure 10-9 shows a few simple objects without any surfacing on them. Figure 10-10 illustrates the same objects with only bump mapping applied to them. The second image took six times longer to render than the first. To save rendering time, you can fake bump maps by using photos that appear bumpy or altering even-looking ones. Most image editing programs have emboss or other filters to make surfaces appear bumpy.

pixel-to-vertex matching. The textures behave like elastic surfaces similar to rubber gloves on a surgeon's hands.

Bump Maps

Bump maps offer an appealing alternative when trying to model every single detail on an object. Simple models can look very complicated with bump maps. The position that surface normals face is changed during the rendering process so that light reflects in several directions from the surface. This simulates the way in which light reflects from rough objects. Lighter areas are rendered as eleva-

Fig. 10-9 The image without any maps.

Fig. 10-10 The same objects after applying only the bump maps shown in the bottom row.

Specular Maps and Diffuse Maps

Whenever you apply a bump map to an object, try to add a specular map along with it. The specular map causes highlights to appear in the lighter areas of the texture. It does not map a color to the surface, but makes parts of the model appear shiny. The type of light source and surface present also govern specularity. Therefore, highlights only occur near hotspots and not evenly across the entire surface.

Diffuse maps are very useful for aging a surface or making it appear grimy because they darken the colors of a surface. A diffuse map does not apply a color to a surface; instead, it causes variations in the object's color. Figure 10-11 illustrates the same objects that previously had bump maps

Fig. 10-11 The final image after applying specular and diffuse grime maps.

applied to them. With the addition of specular and diffuse dirt maps, the scene appears to have more individuality.

Creative surfacing requires more than just applying digitized photos or using built-in shaders (procedural textures). People once were fascinated with images of shiny spheres reflecting the surrounding environment. Earlier computer images were too flawless and did not relate to the imperfect world. It takes artistry to make a model look old, worn, dirty, and weathered. Many artists strive to create images that do not look as if they were computer-generated. They try to make animations or images that are super-realistic or computer art that has a personal style. In either case, they try to avoid making images that appear artificial and imitative.

One of the first steps for making worn-out, dingy, dusty, and weather-beaten surfaces is to create brushes in your favorite image-editing program. You can start by selecting parts of rusty, peeling, dirty, moldy, or any bumpy surfaces. Use a soft-edged feathered selection and copy it to a new file with a transparent background. You then define a new brush from the pasted texture. Another option is to use filters on it to make it a noisier texture or to roughen it up some more. Using a feathered selection will keep the edges soft so that one brush stroke can blend into another. Painting selections with a quick mask option allows you to create crosshatch and streak-effect brushes. To get you started, there are some predefined brushes on the CD-ROM, which can be used in Adobe Photoshop. They can also be viewed in Figure 10-12.

When you paint a surface with grime brushes, be sure to set the brush to fade after a certain number of pixels. It also helps to have a digitizing tablet

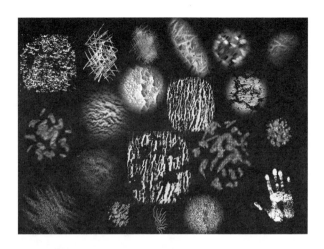

Fig. 10-12 Some grime brushes for creating worn surfaces.

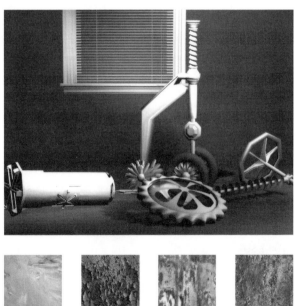

Fig. 10-13 The objects unsurfaced. The textures at the bottom will be applied to them.

Fig. 10-14 The same objects after adding the floor and grime textures.

and pen to vary the size of the brush stroke by pressure. Another technique you can use is to paint decay textures with black grime brushes first, then follow with white dirt brushes. This erases parts of the surface and makes it look more uneven.

Besides having a collection of grime brushes, you should also have a library of textures that show wear and tear on various surfaces. Photos of brush strokes, rust, dirt, peeling paint, dust, corrosion, and so on are invaluable materials. These images can be switched with one another so that they can be used as bump maps or as specular, diffuse, and image maps. Figure 10-13 shows a pile of junk in a room before the surfaces at the bottom are applied to everything. Figure 10-14 illustrates the same room and junk after applying only the surfaces shown in the previous illustration. A color image of this picture can be found on the CD-ROM (Chapter 10>ColorImages>10-14RustyJunk.jpg).

The same maps are used on different objects but applied in various ways. For example, if one texture is used as a diffuse map on an object, it might be applied as a specular map on another. Objects often have multiple texture maps applied to them. Several bump maps, as well as other types, are applied to the same object. By making some less opaque, the ones underneath show through in places.

Characters look more interesting when you apply grime, paint, and other textures to them and to their clothes. Figure 10-15 depicts an artist before and after applying various surfaces (the textured version of the artist is also available in color on the CD-ROM at Chapter 10>ColorImages >10-15ArtistTextured.jpg). Some were created using grime brushes, while others were developed from photographs and painted textures.

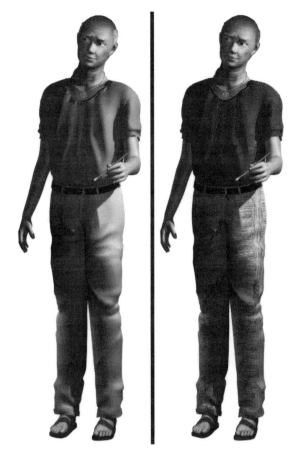

Fig. 10-15 The artist character before and after applying textures.

Transparency Maps

When it no longer matters how many polygons are in a scene because computers can render and display everything in real time, transparency maps will become obsolete. In the meantime, they are an important part of complex scene building. This is especially true when it comes to outdoor scenes with trees and plants. Anyone who has ever modeled a tree or used a tree generator knows that once the leaves are added, the polygon count can easily exceed 35,000. Moreover, this is only for one tree. Imagine a scene filled with dozens of trees and plants. Most desktop computers and even some workstations are not equipped to handle this many polygons.

Transparency maps are composed of two images. One image contains the actual rendered object, while the other is a negative image that blocks out everything except for the rendered object. Figure 10-16 shows tree renderings and their matching negative images. The negative images are identical to the corresponding tree pictures, except that they are white. They act like a cutout because everything within the white area displays the rendered tree image and everything that is black is transparent. When the positive and negative images are mapped onto an object, only the areas that fall within the white parts will be visible, while the black areas are rendered invisible. Other objects can be seen behind the black portions. The positive image is applied as a planar map to a flat polygon. The negative picture is added as a transparency texture with the exact same settings as the positive version, except that it is specified as a negative image.

To create a transparency map, you can render a 3D object like a tree. (Some can be found on the CD-ROM in the chapter 10 folder under "TreeTransprncyMaps," or you can use photos and illustrations.) Once you have your positive image, select it. For example, if it is a tree, you can usually render the original with an alpha channel. This makes it easier to select only the tree and its leaves. If you are using a photo or illustration, select only the tree and its parts. Fill the selected area with white, inverse your selection, and fill the background with black. Save this as your negative image.

The object used for mapping can vary in shape. Figure 10-17 depicts some commonly used forms for transparency mapping. A simple rectangle works fine in most circumstances. You can use the

231

Fig. 10-16 Complicated objects like trees can be made using transparency maps. The image of the tree and its alpha channel are mapped onto flat polygons. The only part of the image that is visible is the tree showing through the black part of the alpha map.

dimensions of your image maps to determine the height-to-width ratio of your rectangle. The direction that your plane faces determines which way you should map the image and its transparency map. For example, if the plane faces toward the front, use planar mapping on the z-axis. Two rectangles that intersect each other like those in Figure 10-17 can be used if the camera moves in your scene. The object will always appear three-dimensional because the image is mapped on both the x- and z-axes. The plane that faces to the right has the image and its corresponding transparency mapped on the x-axis, while the plane that faces forward has the exact same images mapped on the z-axis. Another option for scenes in which the camera moves is setting the flat planes to always face toward the camera. Depending on your software, this might require a plug-in or a script that tells the object to use the camera as its target. The half-cylinder shape shown in Figure 10-17 works fairly well in scenes with some camera movement. The only disadvantage to this form is that

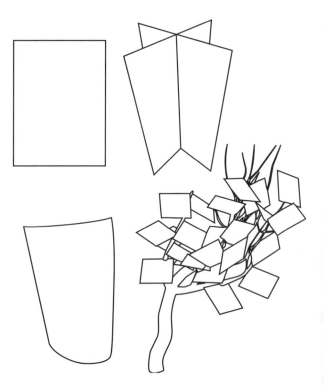

Fig. 10-17 Commonly used objects for applying transparency maps. The tree trunk and branches are part of a 3D model.

Fig. 10-18 The tree on the left illustrates the effect of transparency maps, while the one on the right shows the texture without the negative alpha channel.

it distorts the object somewhat, and the camera can only be moved halfway around it.

The fourth form in Figure 10-17 is a combination of 3D and 2D. A tree trunk and its branches are modeled, and flat planes are placed facing in different directions. Since all the planes are turned in various directions, the camera is free to move anywhere. Figure 10-18 shows the tree rendered without its transparency maps. Memory usage is fairly low and the leaves have a great amount of detail on them. If you plan to use this type of approach, make one plane (a rectangle or square) facing up in the top view. With UV mapping, apply the image and its transparency on the y-axis. Move the pivot point of the rectangle to the end, where the image is supposed to come from a tree branch. Clone the rectangle and place all the copies around the tree, with the pivot point touching the tree branch. Now rotate all the copies in different directions. Since the pivot point is against the tree branch, each plane can be revolved without separating from the tree. If you tried to map onto

planes facing various directions, the images would distort. Since the rectangle was facing up on the y-axis originally, the image mapped correctly and remained constant no matter which direction it was revolved toward.

Fig. 10-19 Transparency maps are very difficult to distinguish from 3D objects. Which of the two trees is the transparency map and which is a 3D model?

233

Fig. 10-20 The answer to the question asked in Fig. 10-19.

Fig. 10-21 The same scene from Fig. 10-22 and what it looks like before rendering.

Fig. 10-22 A scene filled with transparency maps. Some can be viewed in Fig. 10-21.

Fig. 10-23 An underwater scene with transparency-mapped objects.

Fig. 10-24 The transparency-mapped planes and the two 3D objects near the camera. Skeletons were placed inside the 2D objects as well as the 3D objects.

If you use high-quality renderings for your image maps, it is very difficult to tell whether transparency maps or 3D models are utilized in a scene. Figure 10-19 can be used as a test to see which of the two trees was rendered from a 3D tree. One of them is a rendering of a flat plane, while the other is the actual tree. The answer can be found in Figure 10-20.

Figure 10-22 illustrates a rendering of a complicated scene with many transparency maps. The color image can be seen on the CD-ROM (Chapter 10 > Color Images > 10-22 Rendered Scene With Trnprncy Map.jpg). To view some of the actual objects in the scene, refer to Figure 10-21. By keeping the environment memory usage low through transparency maps, you can utilize more characters with greater detail.

Objects that appear closer to the camera can be left as 3D models, while those that are further away can be simple planes with transparency maps. Figure 10-23 shows a complicated underwater scene with many plants, most of which are flat planes, as seen in Figure 10-24. Only the two plants

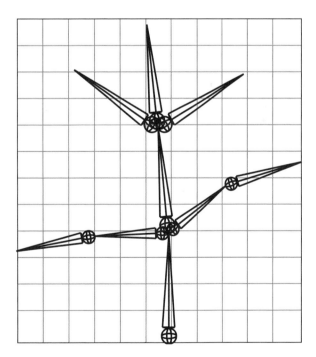

Fig. 10-25 The skeleton inside the flat, subdivided plane moves the transparency-mapped object.

Fig. 10-26 Displacement maps can be used to deform the actual geometry of objects. In this example, each of the grayscale gradient textures is used to make a different landmass.

closest to the camera are left as three-dimensional objects. To have the plants move slowly with the underwater currents, skeletons were placed in the subdivided planes (Figure 10-25). The chapter about lighting referred to this animation and can be found in the chapter 9 folder.

Displacement Maps

Displacement mapping deforms geometry based upon an image or a procedural texture. Unlike bump mapping, the silhouette of the object is consistent with the rest of the surface. Displacement mapping is very useful for creating terrains, billowing cloth, water ripples, flickering flames, and many other effects. The surface of an object is displaced according to the intensity of the pixels in the texture map. The lighter parts of the image cause greater displacements. Figure 10-26 displays a few textures used as displacement maps, along

with the terrains that were derived from them. Notice that the lighter parts of the images create greater elevations in the terrain.

If you plan to create a terrain using displacement mapping, be sure to experiment with various amounts of texture amplitude. A negative value works well for reversing the elevations. To get enough detail, use a high-resolution plane that has been subdivided many times. For example, a NURBS plane can have a setting of 22 for its U and V directions if the texture's measurement is 512 x 512 pixels. If you are working with polygons, triple the plane before displacing its surface. Once you are satisfied with the appearance of the displaced geometry, you can usually save the transformed object. The terrain model can then have additional alterations applied to it, like smoothing.

The following tutorial shows how displacement mapping can be used for many special effects. Perhaps you have seen it utilized in a movie when

Fig. 10-27 A pin device for making impressions.

Fig. 10-28 The needle object.

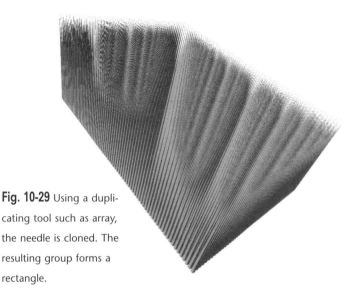

Fig. 10-29 Using a duplicating tool such as array, the needle is cloned. The resulting group forms a rectangle.

a character was trying to push through a solid object, like a wall. The wall appeared to bulge and take on the character's shape. A variation of this effect might be cloth deforming from a person pushing against it. Although the method outlined here has you displace a faceted object with a face, it can easily be adapted to recreating the previously described effects.

This tutorial has you create a gizmo composed of hundreds of tiny pins. When you push against the mesh of flat pins, it deforms outward on the opposite side, making an impression of the shape of your hand or whatever might be pressing against it (Figure 10-27). For those who are too lazy or do not have the time to make everything from scratch, you will find all the objects and textures on the CD-ROM in the chapter 10 folder within the folder "DisplacmentStuff."

The first step is to create the gizmo that will be deformed. Later, you can substitute this with anything—perhaps a wall or cloth. Make a flat pentagon on the y-axis. Its size can have radii of 2.7 mm

on the x- and z-axes and 0 mm on the y-axis. Extrude the pentagon up 13.5 cm on the y-axis. Select the points at the top of the extruded object and either weld them together or scale them down to 0. The object now has five sides at the bottom and comes to a point at the top (Figure 10-28).

This needle object will have to be cloned many times. If your software has an array option, set it to duplicate the needle 50 times on the x-axis and 70 times on the y-axis. The subsequent cube-like form is made up of these needles (Figure 10-29).

Fig. 10-30 A grayscale gradient is mapped to the face on the x-axis.

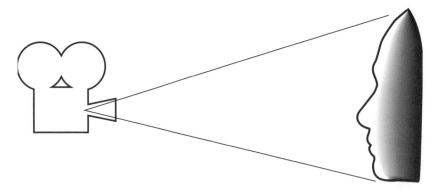

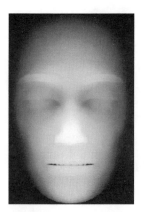

Fig. 10-31 A grayscale gradient is mapped to the face on the x-axis. The side view should show the closest portion to the camera as the lightest part, and the farthest as the darkest.

Fig. 10-32 The face is rendered with only a 95 percent ambient light.

In an image-editing program, create a grayscale gradient that starts with white on the left and becomes black on the right (Figure 10-30). Cut off the front part of a head so that you only have the face, which looks like a mask. You can use any object, but this tutorial refers to it as a face. Position the face to look straight at you in the front view (z-axis). Apply the gradient texture on the x-axis and set it to size automatically to the full scale of the face (Figure 10-31). Position the camera to look directly at the face and set its focal length to about 75 mm to avoid distorting the face.

Turn off all the lights except for ambient lighting, which is set at 95 percent. This creates an even dispersal of light with no shadows. Render the face with a black background. Notice that this type of lighting, combined with the gradient, produces an interesting effect. It makes objects appear smooth, with an inner light. This technique is useful for showing x-rays, smooth stone, ghosts, and so on.

The rendered image is now used as a displacement map. Turn the needle object so that the sharp points are facing down on the y-axis. The top view should have the dull ends facing toward you. Now

comes the fun part. Apply the displacement map (the rendered face) to the needle object on the y-axis. The texture amplitude should be about 100 percent, but you may have to try different settings. You should see the face pushing up through the needles. If you want the needles to appear metallic, apply a reflectivity map to their surfaces and

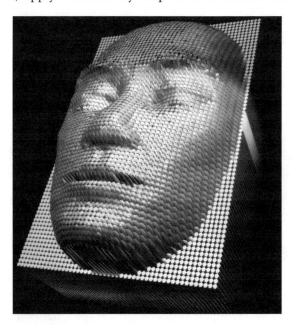

Fig. 10-33 The face pushing up against the pins.

set it to ray trace the backdrop. The reflection map looks like fractal noise that has been filtered to look like bumpy glass. This can be made by creating a cloud texture and applying an ocean ripple filter to it. Reflectivity may have to be turned down to about 80 percent. To speed up rendering time, turn down the ray-trace recursion limit to 1 or 2. The rendering can be sped up even more by turning off trace reflection. Figure 10-33 shows the final image.

The next step is animating the displacement

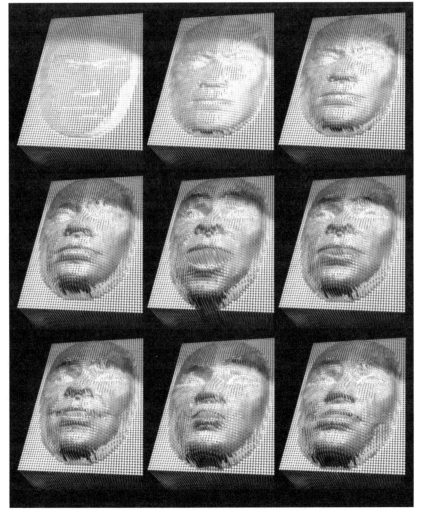

map. To have the face appear to push through the needles, set an envelope on the texture amplitude. For a thirty-frame animation, you can have the amplitude set at 0 at frame 1 and 100 percent, or whatever is desirable, at frame 30.

The animation can be made even more interesting by having the face change expressions after it is pushed up. Create an animation of facial expressions using the previous 95 percent ambient light setup. For the first thirty frames, the face should be still, because that is the part where it pushes up against the needles. Import a movie or image sequence and apply it as a displacement map. Use the same envelope that has the face push through over thirty frames. When you render the animation, it will apply all of the facial expressions as displacement maps throughout the sequence. An animation of this effect can be found on the CD-ROM in the chapter 10 folder, in Movies>10-33Displacement.mov. Images from it can be seen in Figure 10-34.

Fig. 10-34 Images from the pin-face displacement animation.

PART IV

Character Animation Fundamentals

CHAPTER 11

Expressing Emotion with Facial Animation

When you are animating emotion, facial animation has little substance if it is not combined with a relevant body posture. The attitude of the body should support the expression on the face (Figures 11-1 and 11-2).

Normally, the facial expression will show up first and will be followed by the movement of the body. The two occurrences are only fractions of a second apart. For example, if a person perceives something, the eyes are the first to move, followed by a turn of the head, then the shoulders, and finally the rest of the body.

Although the posture of the body reflects the mood on the face, this discussion will focus solely on the drama of facial expressions. The muscles of the face are close to the skin and reciprocally connected. To see this, close one eye and you can observe the upward movement in the corner of the mouth. One of the most important aspects of facial animation is that the combinations of various head muscles convey emotion. Even though you have to model the various expressions as single occurrences, it is the assemblage of these during the animation process that yields the appropriate

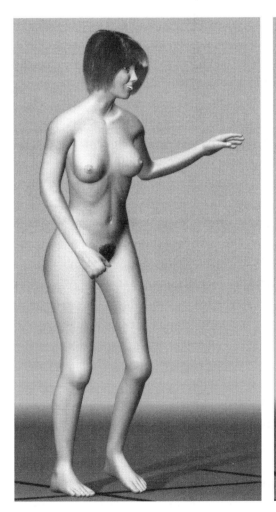

Fig. 11-1 (left) Happiness is expressed through a combination of bright eyes, upturned corners of the mouth, raised eyebrows, a lively stride, and raised shoulders and arms.

Fig. 11-2 (right) A coy demeanor can be displayed by biting down on the lower lip, casting eyes downward, bending the neck, and keeping the limbs close to the body.

 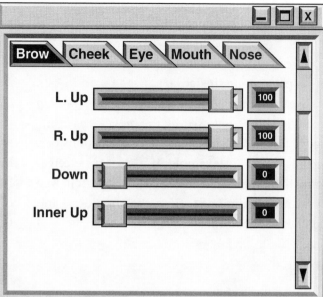

Fig. 11-3 Modeling the various expressions individually allows you the flexibility to combine them in numerous ways. Many programs, such as this one, use sliding buttons to blend the various expressions.

emotional state. Animated singly, the individual expressions by themselves create only mild drama.

So far, the discussion for manipulating geometry has centered on using images, procedural textures (displacement maps), and skeletons. Another method involves moving the actual points on an object to create variations of the original geometry. These, in turn, become morphing targets that allow you to shape-shift one object into another. The process is called metamorphosing or, more commonly, morphing. It provides greater control for changing the appearance of a model than displacement maps or skeletons. The reason is that the animator can use all the modeling tools available to change any point on an object. The transformed models are poses or different states into which the original object morphs.

For example, you start with a base model in which the face is neutral and all the muscles are

relaxed. Using the various modeling methods, such as a magnet tool, you can pull and push points around the mouth to model the same face smiling. This new facial pose is saved as a morph target. Returning to the neutral face, you can move the points on the eyelids to close the eyes. The new morph target is saved as one of the eye expressions. Continuing this process and always starting with the base neutral face, you can shape a number of expressions and save each one separately. The software allows you to blend the various expressions using percentages of each. Therefore, the face can be animated with a range of different emotions over a specific time period.

Most mid- to high-end software packages offer some kind of shape-shifting tool (Figure 11-3). These often use sliding buttons, which can generate various percentages for each facial movement. If eye, mouth, nose, eyebrows, cheeks, and other movements are modeled separately, you can achieve a diversity of expressions and phonetic shapes for speech. Because the muscles on the left and right sides of the face vary in strength, some features are modeled as separate left and right shapes. When modeling the following expressions, a hand-held mirror becomes an indispensable tool.

One way to illustrate the entire morphing process is through explaining how it is implemented in a specific software package. One of the better-known methods is found in LightWave 3D. It uses an operation called endomorphs. After modeling the various expressions or morph targets, all the information is saved in a single object file called an endomorph. Because all the information for the various states is stored within one base object, the original model can be changed without adversely affecting the morph targets. If you decide to add detail to the base model, the change works its way through all the various poses and modifies their point counts accordingly. Unlike some other software packages, you do not have to worry about keeping the same exact number of points on each separate morph target. Facial animation can take place directly in the scene with a floating palette of morph expressions.

Since there is no need to worry about point counts, you can start with a simple model, sculpt the various expressions, and then subdivide the base model later for a more detailed character and its various morph targets. A word of caution: The simple base model should have enough lines on it to shape creases in the forehead and make wrinkles on other parts of the face when the mouth, nose, and eyes change their appearance (Figure 11-4). Changes to the point counts should be made only on the base object and not on any of the morph targets.

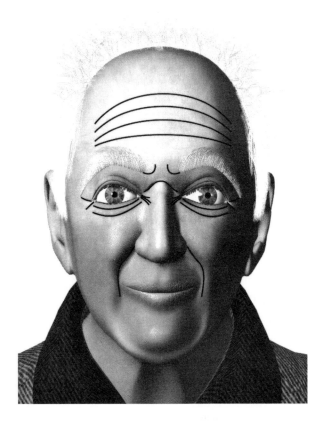

Fig. 11-4 Each black line on the face represents a set of three or four parallel lines. The middle line(s) of each set is moved to make wrinkles and creases.

The Basic Shapes

Despite the fact that the human face is capable of hundreds of expressions, you can model approximately forty-three basic features to achieve most countenances. Each of these has been divided into the following separate group: brows, eyes, nose, mouth, and cheeks.

Some skeptics may say that forty-three morph targets are not enough for dialogue and facial expressions. The fact that you can blend among each of them gives you a great variety of visages. For example, the mouth has twenty-three separate morphs. Blending different percentages between each of these can yield many shapes. The mouth is the most flexible part of the face and therefore has the most morph targets.

Before you begin to model the various expressions from the original face, be sure to add enough points and curves in specific areas that will be used for wrinkles and creases later. Some parts of the face that should have extra splines are the forehead for wrinkles, the base of the cheeks near the nose wings running to the corners of the mouth, above and below the eyes, the corners of the eyes, and the bridge of the nose. Figure 11-4 shows a face with lines indicating where extra curves should be modeled. Each dark line suggests where you should have three or four extra curves running parallel to each other. For example, if you have three parallel lines for one crease, you would move the middle line in to make a depression in the skin. The lines do not have to be visible when the face is in a normal, relaxed mode. When it is time to model a certain expression that causes wrinkling in those areas, you can move the points on the lines.

When you model the various facial expressions, be sure to only change one part of the expression while keeping the rest neutral. For example, as you model a smile, do not move points on the cheeks, nose, and eyelids. Later, when you animate a smile, you will combine the three separate morph targets, such as the mouth smile, cheeks moving up and out, and eyelids closing.

If your software has the capability of copying morph targets, use it to make other expressions that are similar. An example of this can be seen in Figures 11-21 and 11-22. The mouth shape for the "d" and "th" sounds and the one for the "e" sound are almost identical. After shaping one, copy it and turn it into the other one. The only thing that has to be changed is the position of the tongue.

Expressions that have identical shapes on both sides can be modeled more easily with symmetry on. This will reproduce any changes on a symmetrical face by altering both sides identically.

When you have to model two separate but identical expressions, such as a left- and a right-sided smile, try utilizing a 3D template. Model one side and save the morph target. Freeze or save the deformed mesh as a separate model. Mirror it and place it in a background layer. This will show where you will need to move points to make the reverse side expression. In the foreground layer, select a group of points that will be moved to match the points on the background layer mesh. Make the background layer active. With both foreground and background layer active, use a snap tool to snap the selected points to the corresponding ones in the background layer. This may seem to be mindless work, but it will insure that both morph targets are identical but appear on opposite sides of the face. You may even find that it is not such a bad thing to give the mind a rest once in a while.

The Brows

The following list describes basic brow movements:

Brows depressed and contracted (Figure 11-5): Lowering the eyebrows creates a slight fold over the eyes and a wrinkling at the nose. Compressing the eyebrows moves them toward the center, forming a puckering in the middle of the forehead.

Inner brows raised (Figure 11-6): Raising the inner ends causes a puckering in the middle of the

Fig. 11-5 Brows Down. The brows are depressed and brought in, causing a horizontal wrinkling at the root of the nose.

Fig. 11-6 Inner End Brows Up. Inner brows are raised for looks of grief or surprise.

Fig. 11-7 Left and Right Brows Raised Separately. Raising the eyebrows brightens the eyes and wrinkles the forehead.

forehead.

Brows raised (Figure 11-7): The left and the right eyebrows are modeled separately in a raised position. This results in transverse folds along the forehead.

The Eyes

The following list describes basic eye movements:

Upper eyelids closed (Figure 11-8): Both upper eyelids rotate down for the blink.

Eyes look down (Figure 11-9): Both eyes look down.

Eyes look up (Figure 11-10): Both eyes look up.

Eyes look left (Figure 11-11): Both eyes look left.

Eyes look right (Figure 11-12): Both eyes look right.

Upper and lower lids close (Figure 11-13): Both the lower and upper eyelids meet in the center for the wink. The right and left eyelids are modeled separately.

Eyelids raised (Figure 11-14): The upper eyelids are raised. Both are modeled separately.

The Nose

Simplifying the nose movements to a couple of morph targets should take care of most animators' needs.

The right and left nostrils spread outward (Figure 11-15).

The wings move up, resulting in a crease at the top of the nose (Figure 11-16). Each side is modeled as a separate morph target.

The Mouth

Of all the parts, the mouth has the most flexibility. This means that many mouth positions can be modeled. The following are the most basic ones:

Fig. 11-8 Left and Right Upper Eyelids Lowered Separately. A blink lowers only the upper eyelids.

Fig. 11-9 Eyes Look Down. The basic eye movements can be modeled separately.

Fig. 11-10 Eyes Look Up. By combining the four basic eye movements during animation, you can rotate the eyes into almost any position.

Fig. 11-11 Eyes Look Left. Normally, the eyes move in tandem.

Fig. 11-12 Eyes Look Right. Eye movements make the animation look livelier.

Fig. 11-13 Right and Left Eyes Wink Separately. The eye wink moves both the upper and lower eyelids together.

Fig. 11-14 Left and Right Eyelids Raised Separately.

Fig. 11-15 Right and Left Nostrils Flare Out.

Fig. 11-16 Right and Left Nose Wings Move Up Separately. The wings of the nose are moved up and out. Each side is modeled separately.

Bite down on the lower lip (Figure 11-17): The lower lip is sucked in and up under the upper teeth.

The mouth is shaped for pronouncing "c," "g," "h," "k," "n," "r," "s," "t," "y," and "z" sounds (Figure 11-18).

Closed mouth (Figure 11-19): Modeling the face with the mouth slightly open makes it easier to select the lower or upper lip points. Closing the mouth in a relaxed attitude can be used in place of the original slack-jawed model.

The corners of the mouth are brought down for expressions of sadness, discontent, disapproval, and so on (Figure 11-20).

The mouth is formed to make "d" and "th" sounds (Figure 11-21).

A similar shape to the "d" and "th" mouth is used for the "e" sound (Figure 11-22). The shape and placement of the tongue varies the most.

Open mouth (Figure 11-23): The mouth opens in the shape of a heart.

The tongue touches the roof of the mouth while the lips are parted. This pronounces the "l" sound (Figure 11-24).

The right and left sides of the mouth are modeled separately for the smile (Figure 11-25): The lips form a closed smile when the corners of the mouth are brought up.

The corners of the mouth are retracted as separate morph targets (Figure 11-26). The lips are thin.

The lips are made thinner (Figure 11-27). Moving the jaw up depresses the lips.

Both sides of the mouth are modeled separately to form the right and left orbs (Figure 11-28). This mouth pose appears more often than it would seem.

Extending the lower lip forms a pouting expression (Figure 11-29).

A big grin is made when the jaw drops, and the

Fig. 11-17 Bite Down on Lower Lip. The jaw is moved up and the lower lip in so that the upper teeth bite down on the lower lip.

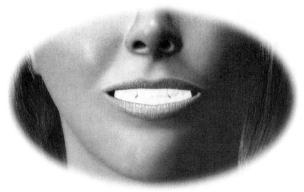

Fig. 11-18 Mouth Pronounces the "c," "g," "h," "k," "n," "r," "s," "t," "y," and "z" sounds.

Fig. 11-19 Mouth Closed. The lips are brought together to close the mouth.

Fig. 11-20 Mouth Corners Turn Down. The left and right corners of the mouth droop down.

Fig. 11-21 Mouth Pronounces "D" and "Th" Sounds. The tongue is inserted between the teeth with the lips parted.

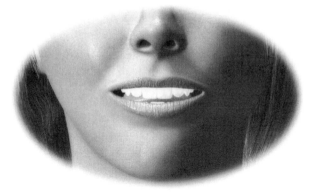

Fig. 11-22 Mouth Pronounces the "E" Sound.

Fig. 11-23 Mouth Forms a Heart Shape. The mouth opens in a heart shape for speech, breathing, astonishment, yawning, and so on.

Fig. 11-24 Mouth Pronounces the "L" Sound. The tongue curls up to touch the roof of the mouth.

Fig. 11-25 Separate Left and Right Closed Smile.

corners of the mouth move back and up (Figure 11-30).

An inward pucker of lips is attained when the lips are brought together to form a small "o" shape (Figure 11-31).

The lips push forward and out for the outward pucker (Figure 11-32).

A closed smile forms when the lips are closed, and both corners are pulled back and up (Figure 11-33).

A sneering expression is achieved when the upper lip curls up to display the canine tooth (Figure 11-34). Both sides are modeled separately.

The lower jaw drops down (Figure 11-35). Only the jaw moves down, while the upper lip stretches.

The cheeks expand to show the effects of blowing out. (Figure 11-36). Exhale through the mouth while keeping the lips together. Each side is a separate morph target.

The cheeks are moved up and out (Figure 11-37).

Blending Expressions

After you finish creating all the basic facial expressions, it is time to test them. Blended shapes are created by combining mouth, nose, eyes, eyebrows, and other expressions. By altering the percentage of each, you can achieve countless facial expressions of varying subtlety.

Figures 11-38 to 11-44 illustrate some of the expressions you can attain by blending the base objects. The examples are only meant as a rough guide.

Direction of the Muscular Pull

A muscle is composed of a bundle of fibers that

Fig. 11-26 Left and Right Mouth Corners Retract Separately.

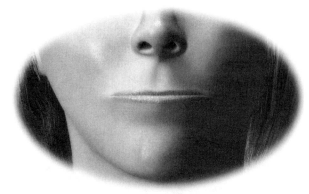

Fig. 11-27 Lips Compressed.

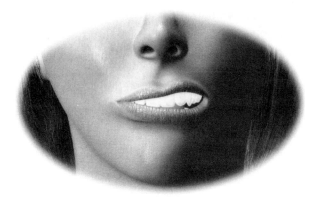

Fig. 11-28 Left and Right Mouth Form Orb Separately. The mouth corners form an orb. This can be very useful for punctuating speech.

Fig. 11-29 Lower Lip Bulges Out. The lower lip is pushed up and out to form a pout.

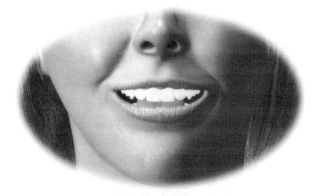

Fig. 11-30 Open Smile. The corners of the mouth are retracted up and out, while the jaw drops to form a big grin.

Fig. 11-31 Lips Pucker In. The lips pucker inward.

Fig. 11-32 Lips Pucker Out. The lips pucker outward.

Fig. 11-33 Smile Closed. A smile is formed when the corners of the mouth are retracted up and back.

Fig. 11-34 Separate Left and Right Side Sneer. A sneer is formed by curling the corner of the upper lip.

Fig. 11-35 Wide Open Mouth. The jaw drops to open the mouth.

Fig. 11-36 Left and Right Cheeks Blow Out Separately. Expelling the breath produces bulging cheeks.

Fig. 11-37 Left and Right Cheeks Move Up and Out Separately. Raising the cheeks crinkles the skin under and at the corners of the eyes.

work in mutual association to perform common duties. Muscles never act alone. When one muscle or a set of muscles contracts, other, opposing muscles become active and regulate or change the behavior of the contracting ones. It is this combination of movements that results in the complicated harmony of the facial muscles. Figure 11-45 illustrates the directional pull of the various muscle groups to achieve specific expressions.

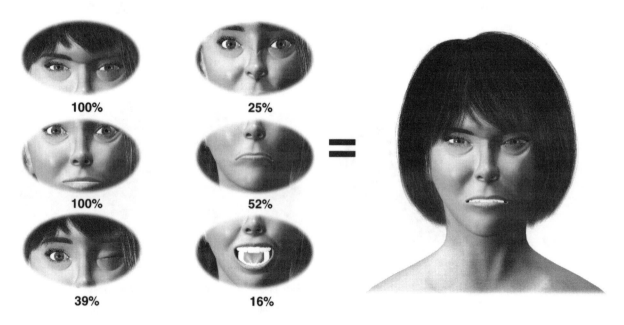

100%   25%

100%   52%   =

39%   16%

Fig. 11-38 A look of anger or disgust results from blending various percentages of the above expressions.

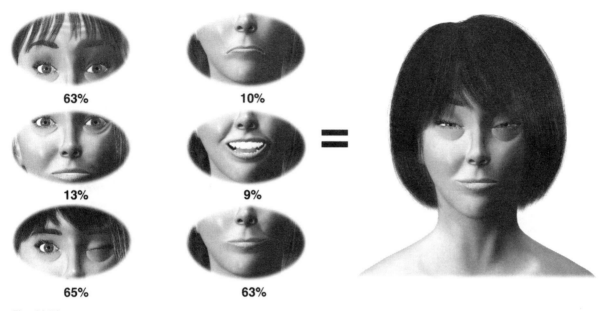

Fig. 11-39 The original shapes are blended to form a daydreaming look.

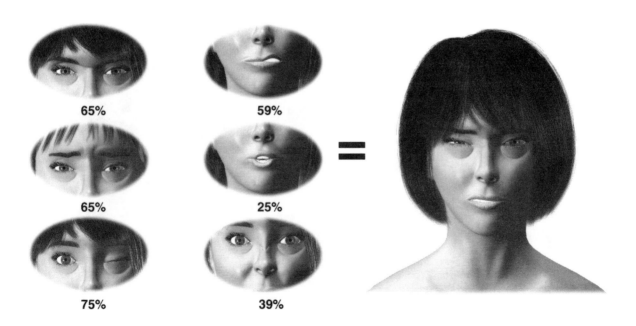

Fig. 11-40 A look of distrust is the result of blending varying percentages of the above base expressions.

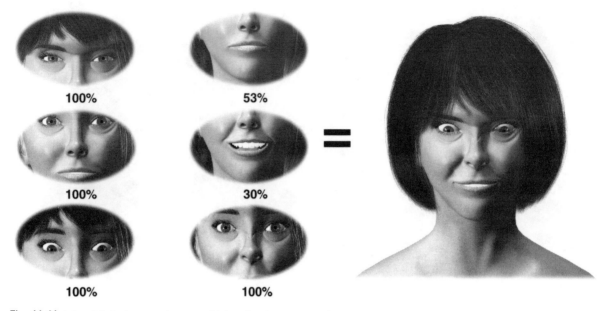

Fig. 11-41 A fiendish look comes from combining the above target shapes.

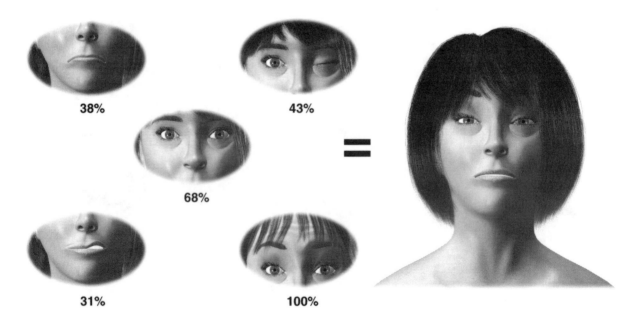

Fig. 11-42 A haughty expression is achieved by combining the above base objects.

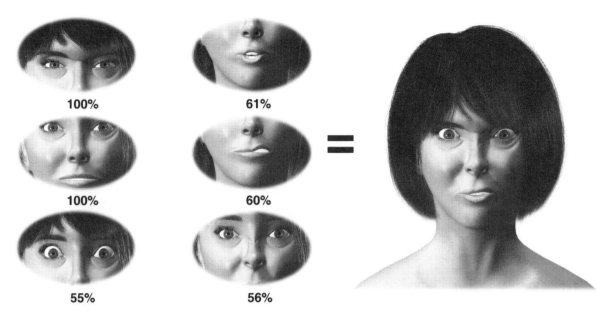

Fig. 11-43 Sometimes, unexpected expressions can be formed by the most unlikely combinations. In this case, a disapproving look is the result of the implausible shapes shown above.

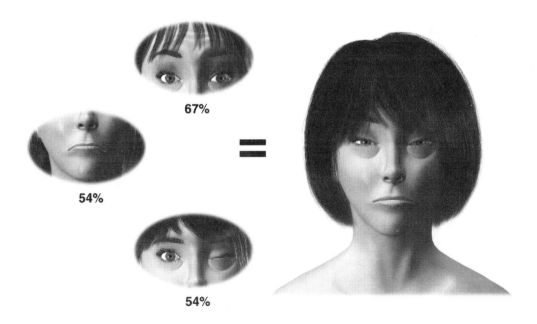

Fig. 11-44 A few target shapes can create an expressive look, like this one of sadness.

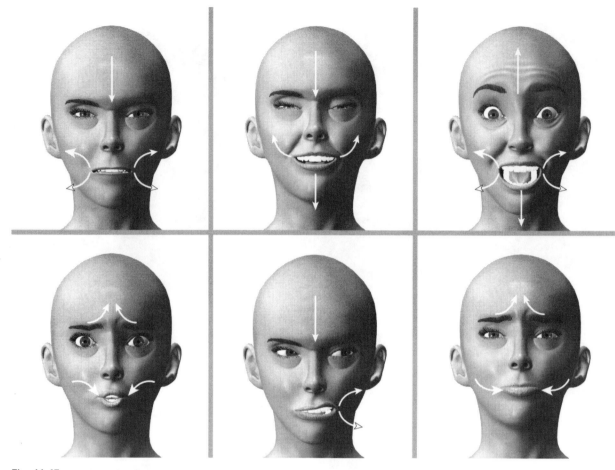

Fig. 11-45 The muscles combine to create aspects of anger, hysteria, surprise, worry, suspicion, and grief.

CHAPTER 12

The Principles of Animation: Elements of Action

Animation often involves the production of basic, everyday actions such as walking, running, blinking, and breathing. There are many tools available to computer animators for simplifying the daunting task of convincingly animating such movements. Some of these include extracting parts of previously animated actions and applying them to other characters, importing video as a template for animation, applying motion plug-ins such as two-legged walk cycles, using motion capture, and so on. Although these devices can sometimes be useful, there is nothing better than relying on your own experiences and creativity. Experience helps you determine the correct timing for specific motions, while creativity applies the right amount of exaggeration to make the movements more noticeable, interesting, and dramatic.

Included with this book are short movies illustrating the various principles of animation and other concepts discussed throughout this chapter. These can be found in the chapter 12 folder of the enclosed CD-ROM.

The Importance of Timing

In addition to having an outstanding computer and software, the animator often relies on two sim-

Fig. 12-1 Besides a powerful computer and software, a stopwatch and mirror are indispensable tools for the animator.

ple tools: a stopwatch and a mirror (Figure 12-1). It is a well-known fact that timing is the most crucial element in animation. Usually, beginning animators rely very heavily on a stopwatch for measuring the cycles of movements. After becoming more familiar with these cycles, the seasoned animator develops an intuitive sense for the correct temporal order of things.

Good animators should also be good actors. They are often called upon to play-act for each other. However, more often, they have to role-play for themselves. It is not uncommon to see them

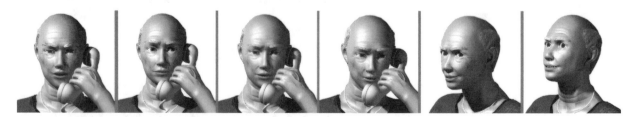

Fig. 12-2 Animating eye movements is an important part of making a character lifelike.

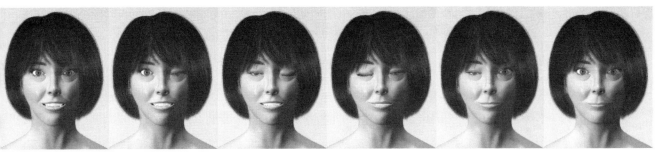

Fig. 12-3 A typical eye blink occurs about every two seconds and lasts for six frames from open eyes to half-closed, then fully closed, back to half-closed, and finally, fully open again. Note that one eyelid lags behind the other by one frame.

stand up for no apparent reason, perform an imaginary action, and then sit back down to continue their work. Thus, a mirror is the other indispensable tool. This is especially true when doing facial animation. Animation students should practice making faces in a mirror and pantomiming without feeling self-conscious if others are watching. Your digital puppets are a reflection of your own acting abilities.

Before considering animating a character's gestures, you should be aware of several basic movements that occur throughout an animation. They are: eye movements, blinking, and breathing. Without these, your digital actors will often appear lifeless. Be sure to apply them for the duration of the entire animation.

Eye motions are constant. The individual that you are animating has eye movements according to its thought patterns and in response to what is occurring around it. A simple back-and-forth eye motion takes about one-third of a second, or ten frames at thirty frames per second. Tracking the movement of something can vary according to the speed of the object. There are no set rules that apply to eye movements. Figure 12-2 shows a few frames from an animation in which eye movements indicate the thoughts running through the character's head.

Blinking is an important part of an animation that should not be ignored. Unlike the squint, only the upper eyelids are rotated down. Normally, a person blinks about every two seconds (every sixty frames). Typically, the blink will run over the course of six frames. Creating an asymmetrical blink makes it more interesting. For example, at frame 58, both eyes are fully open. Frame 59 starts the blink with the right eye half-closed. Frame 60 shows the right eyelid closed while the left one is half-closed. The next frame, 61, has the right eye half-open while the left one is fully closed. Frame 62 returns the right eye to the open position again and the left one to half-open. At frame 63, both eyes are fully open. Figure 12-3 shows the six-frame sequence for blinking. For rapid blinking, skip the half-closed eye frames so that the eyelids go from wide open to closed and back again to wide open. For slow blinks, like someone falling asleep and then waking up suddenly, try closing the upper eyelids over a longer time, like three frames instead of one. The eyelids can remain closed for three or more frames. The speed at which they open depends on how fast you want the subject to wake up.

Breathing is also an important part of animation that should not be ignored. If your characters exhibit breathing throughout the animation, it

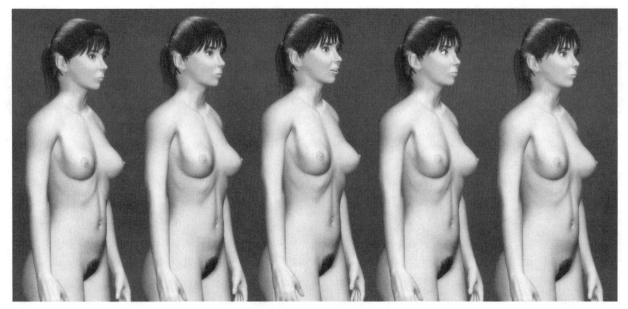

Fig. 12-4 Excerpts from the breathing animation. Frames 1, 15, 30, 45, and 60 show what happens to the stomach, chest, and shoulders during inhaling and exhaling. Note that the body also rises up on the inhalation.

will give them an incredible amount of life. The "breath of life" is a saying that applies very strongly here.

A short animation of a woman breathing can be seen on the CD-ROM (Chapter 12 > Movies > Breathing.mov). When she inhales, notice how the stomach draws in between frames 1 and 30. The chest does just the opposite. It expands between frames 1 and 30. The shoulders rise up over the first thirty frames, while the head is raised slightly. Between frames 30 and 60, the opposite occurs. The stomach area returns to its normal relaxed state, while the chest settles back down upon the exhalation. The shoulders also drop. Figure 12-4 contains frames 1, 15, 30, 45, and 60 from this animation.

Stomach and chest bones can be moved to simulate breathing. The stomach bone is sized smaller, while two chest bones are enlarged and rotated upward. The shoulder bones are moved up. Most

of the time, you can repeat the same motions with these bones. Sometimes, depending on the action in the scene, you may have to vary the breathing time. This can usually be done in your software's motion graph. An alternative to using bones is to set morph targets for breathing motions. The stomach can be modeled in and out, while the chest is made to rise and expand. In either case, you should be able to use the graph editor to repeat the motions of the morph targets, bones, and nulls (IK controllers). Just make sure that the settings at frames 0 and 60 are identical for any object that changes over time.

Besides eye movements, blinking, and breathing, weight transfer is another factor that needs to be considered. A person never stays immobile, but will often shift weight from one foot to the other. This means that the center of gravity moves.

Rendering in Movie or Image Format

Before rendering an animation, consider the two forms that you might want as the outcome. Most software gives you the option of rendering as a movie file (QuickTime, .avi, and others), or as a set of individual images (.bmp, .pct, .psd, .tif, and others).

If you are doing test renderings, you might use a movie format with a video compression of thousands of colors. These are easy to play back without having to go through a conversion procedure. The disadvantage of generating movie formats is that extended rendering times can jeopardize your final animation. If there is a power interruption during the rendering process, you will most likely lose the entire animation, thus wasting valuable time.

Many studios prefer to output files as individual images. It is a safer process. Should the operation be interrupted, you still have the images that were completed before you stopped rendering. Then it is a matter of starting the rendering at the frame where you left off.

Using a video editing program, the image sequences can be converted into a movie format. To view the movie in real time on your computer, make a movie out of all the images. In order for the movie to play in real time, be sure to set the still image duration to one frame, not thirty. Use any compression that you want and set the frame rate at thirty frames per second. If you set your color depth to a thousand or less, your computer should have an easier time playing the movie back. Make the movie and view the animation running in real time.

Postproduction

Computer renderings are like raw data. They often require the application of some postproduction effect(s). Without postproduction, the computer images often appear to be very austere and cold. They lack the warmth and vitality found in other media such as painting, photography, movies, and so on. The postproduction process is a way to treat images with the purpose of improving their appearance. The following technique can be used to infuse your rendering with a warmer and softer quality. You may decide to alter it according to your own tastes.

Step 1. Using an image editor such as Photoshop, duplicate the layer containing the image.

Step 2. Increase the contrast of the duplicate layer to about +50.

Step 3. Apply Gaussian blur to the duplicate layer. Use about a 4-pixel blur.

Step 4. Apply the artistic film grain filter to the duplicate layer. Use a grain of 1, and 0 for all the other settings.

Step 5. Set the duplicate layer opacity anywhere from 15 percent to 50 percent.

Step 6. Flatten both layers and save the image.

You can also record these steps to make an action out of them. The effect can then be applied to image sequences that have either been rendered or converted from a movie file. Batch processing all the images will simplify the postproduction effects.

The Twelve Principles of Animation

It does not matter whether one is learning traditional cel or 3D computer animation. The twelve

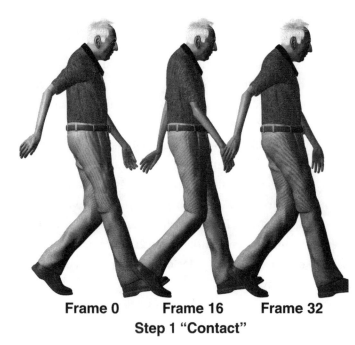

Frame 0   **Frame 16**   **Frame 32**

Step 1 "Contact"

Fig. 12-5 Step 1. Posing the figure for the "contact" position at frames 0, 16, and 32.

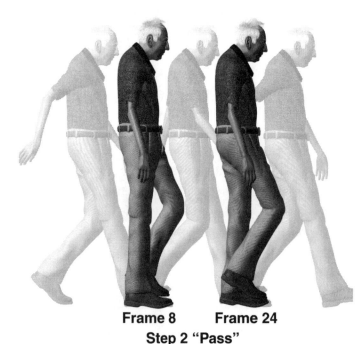

Frame 8   **Frame 24**

Step 2 "Pass"

principles of animation as formulated by Walt Disney animators in the early and mid-1930s should be understood as the foundation of all animation.

The Disney animators did not invent these principles, but discovered them when studying the actions of theater, vaudeville, and movie actors. For example, Charlie Chaplin said that actors should tell the audience what they are going to do, then they should do it, and finally, they should tell the audience that they did it. Out of this simple rule, animators formulated the principle of Anticipation.

The Twelve Principles of Animation are:

1. Squash and Stretch
2. Anticipation
3. Staging
4. Straight-Ahead vs. Pose-to-Pose Action
5. Follow-Through and Overlapping Action
6. Slow In and Slow Out
7. Arcs
8. Secondary Actions
9. Timing
10. Exaggeration
11. Solid Drawing
12. Appeal

Squash and Stretch

Considered by many to be the most impor-

Fig. 12-6 Step 2. The figure is posed in the "pass" position in between the "contact" postures at frames 8 and 24.

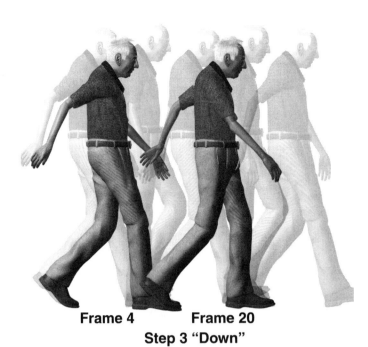

Frame 4   Frame 20

Step 3 "Down"

Fig. 12-7 Step 3. Placing the figure in the "down" pose at frames 4 and 20. This is when squash is applied to the character.

tant principle, Squash and Stretch was utilized more often than any other principle by Disney animators. It basically says that any living thing shows change in its shape as it progresses through an action. Squash and Stretch is what conveys weight and gravity (Chapter 12 > Movie > Weight & Gravity.mov). Without it, characters appear insubstantial and lifeless.

One of the best ways to illustrate Squash and Stretch is during a walk cycle. When the foot lands on the ground, the body compresses. Its mass is pushed together. When the foot lifts up, the body expands and becomes longer.

Creating a Walk

Walking is usually one the first actions that an

animator learns. It is also one of the hardest to master. Walks are considered cycling actions. In contrast to other activities, they are mechanical, repeated movements. Their even pace can be compared to the ticking of a metronome.

During a walk, the moment that a foot hits the ground, it should lock until it is time to lift it again. The forward motion of the body makes the locked foot roll on the ground. Due to its anchor at the toes, the heel comes up while the toes remain in the same spot until it is time to lift the foot off the ground. Since a number of software packages use nulls to manipulate IK chains, the following technique for creating a walking sequence refers to the IK manipulators or goal objects as nulls. As you work through the walking sequence, you can use the 3D poses on the CD-ROM as a general guide (Chapter 12 > 3D walk Templates).

This exercise is for a thirty-two-frame walking cycle, which means that it will take a little over one second to complete all the body motions. Everything begins to repeat at frame 32. In fact, the pose at frame 32 is identical to the one at frame 0. When a walk is set up correctly in the first 32 frames, it is unnecessary to assemble the subsequent keyframes by hand. Using the graph editor, one can simply turn on repeat and offset repeat for the post behavior of specific goal objects, bones, and the character itself. Of course, this means that the walk will go on endlessly without any change in rhythm, speed, or character. However, you can slow down or speed up the walk by shifting or scaling keys.

Some software packages and plug-ins can create automatic walking sequences. Since they generate

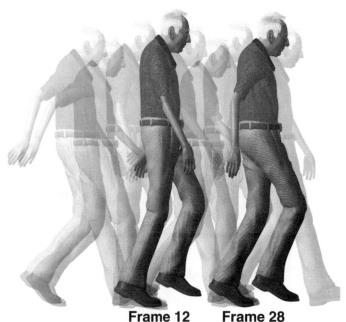

Frame 12   Frame 28
Step 4 "Up"

Fig. 12-8 Step 4. The figure is placed in the "up" pose at frames 12 and 28. This is when stretch is applied to the character.

the same movements for every user, they have earned a reputation for giving a certain look to their animations. If you rely on automated motions, it is important to add small nuances to make the character more individual.

The following steps use classic animation poses to make a basic walk. Once you have everything working the way it should, try adding some refinements to make it more unique.

If you are using the IK setup from chapter 3, parent the toe nulls to the body. The post behavior for all moving and rotating parts can then be set to repeat (except for the body, which will have offset repeat for its post behavior).

Step 1 (Figure 12-5). This is referred to as the "contact" position. Both feet are on the ground and the weight distribution is fairly equal. Pose the figure in the contact position at frames 0, 16, and 32. At frame 16, the body is in the identical but opposite pose to the ones at frames 0 and 32. Assuming the figure is walking along the z-axis, make sure that the position of the nulls (goal objects) and the body at frame 32 are identical to the ones at frame 0. The only difference will be their location of the body on the z-axis. The rotation of bones should also be the same for both frames 0 and 32.

Use nulls to position the extremities. Rotate the wrist, foot, and toe bones to

Fig. 12-9 All the keyframes for a thirty-two-frame walk cycle. Note the wavy up and down line of direction when following the position of the head. The feet should not slide.

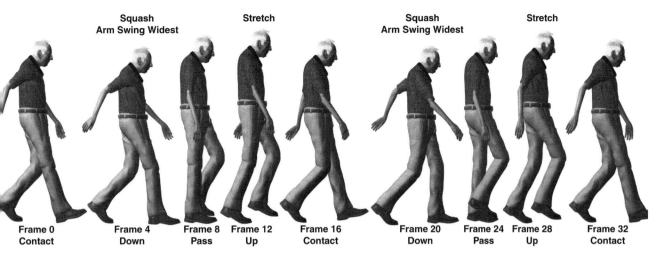

Fig. 12-10 The walk cycle positions, spread apart.

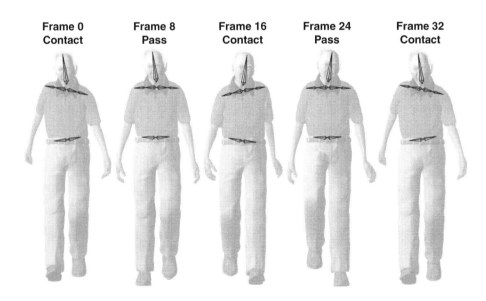

Fig. 12-11 Tilting the head, shoulders, and hips. The shoulder and hip bones rotate in opposite directions. The head tilts toward the shoulder that is up. The bone rotation is delayed at frames 8 and 24, the "passing" position.

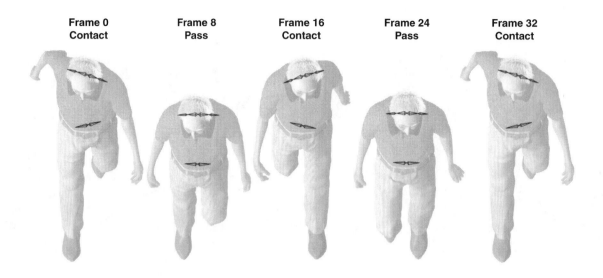

Frame 0	Frame 8	Frame 16	Frame 24	Frame 32
Contact	Pass	Contact	Pass	Contact

Fig. 12-12 The top view shows how the shoulders and hips rotate forwards and back. Except for frames 8 and 24, where they are in a neutral position, they rotate in opposite directions.

Keyframe Positions at Frames 0 and 32 (the body moves along the z axis)			
X	Y	Z	
Same	Same	**Different**	Human
Same	Same	Same	R. Wrist Null (Goal Object)
Same	Same	Same	R. Elbow Null
Same	Same	Same	L. Wrist Null
Same	Same	Same	L. Elbow Null
Same	Same	Same	R. Knee Null
Same	Same	Same	L. Knee Null
Same	Same	Same	R. Toe Null
Same	Same	Same	R. Ankle Null
Same	Same	Same	L. Toe Null
Same	Same	Same	L. Ankle Null

Fig. 12-13 The chart shows which objects' positions differ at frames 0 and 32.

place the hands and feet in the right poses.

Step 2 (Figure 12-6). Place the figure between frames 0 and 16 and between 16 and 32. Keyframe it at frames 8 and 24. This is called the "passing" position. The body is slightly higher because one

of the legs is vertically straight. Note that the same but inverse pose is used for the two frames.

Step 3 (Figure 12-7). Pose your character in the "down" position at frames 4 and 20. Apply squash to the figure to make it shorter. Scaling it down slightly on the y-axis works well. The arms are spread apart the farthest in this pose. The body is arranged identically, except in opposite stances, for these two frames.

Step 4 (Figure 12-8). Position the figure in the "up" pose at frames 12 and 28. Use stretch to elongate the character. You can scale it up slightly on the y-axis. The figure is at its highest point because the back foot is pushing it off to lift it up.

Figure 12-9 illustrates all the key positions that make up the thirty-two-frame walk cycle. The various body sizes may look strange as still images, but during the animation, they make sense.

So far, the illustrations have shown the exact foot placement for each pose. Spreading the figure apart sometimes makes it easier to discern the

Keyframe Rotations at Frames 0 and 32			
Heading (Y axis)	**Pitch** (X axis)	**Bank** (Z axis)	
Same	Same	Same	Head bone
Same	Same	Same	R. & L. Shoulder bones
Same	Same	Same	R. & L. Hip bones
Same	Same	Same	R. & L. Wrist bones
Same	Same	Same	R. & L. Foot bones
Same	Same	Same	R. & L. Toe bones

Fig. 12-14 The bones that are rotated with forward kinematics have the same values at frames 0 and 32.

Graph Editor Post Behavior for Walk Cycle (the body moves on the Z axis)					
Heading (Y) **Pitch** (X) **Bank** (Z)	**X Position**	**Y Position**	**Z Position**	**Scale on Y**	
Repeat					Head bone
Repeat					R. & L. Shoulder bones
Repeat					R. & L. Hip bones
Repeat					R. & L. Wrist bones
Repeat					R. & L. Foot bones
Repeat					R. & L. Toe bones
	Repeat	Repeat	**Offset Repeat**	Repeat	Human
	Repeat	Repeat	Repeat		R. & L. Wrist Nulls
	Repeat	Repeat	Repeat		R. & L. Elbow Nulls
	Repeat	Repeat	Repeat		R. & L. Knee Nulls
	Repeat	Repeat	Repeat		R. & L. Toe Nulls
	Repeat	Repeat	Repeat		R. & L. Ankle Nulls

Fig. 12-15 The graph editor settings for post behavior. Offset repeat only needs to be set for the human and for the right and left toe nulls on the z-axis.

Matching Keyframes for a 32 Frame Walk Cycle								
	Squash		Stretch		Squash		Stretch	
0	4	8	12	16	20	24	28	32
32	36	40	44	48	52	56	60	64
64	68	72	76	80	84	88	92	96

Fig. 12-16 Reading the chart vertically, one can see which keyframes are the same for the repeating walk.

various positions over the course of thirty-two frames. Figure 12-10 shows the person at various stages of the walk.

Head, hip, and shoulder movements are now added by rotating bones. If your IK setup is similar to the one discussed in chapter 3, you will have moved the body and its nulls (goal objects). The wrist, foot, toe, hip, head, and shoulder bones are not affected by IK and thus are rotated with keyframes. The hand is turned with the wrist bone, while the placement of the feet is adjusted with the foot and toe bones.

Figure 12-11 illustrates the rotation of the head, shoulder, and hip bones at frames 0, 8, 16, 24, and 32. Frames 0 and 32 have the exact same heading (y-axis rotation), pitch (x-axis rotation), and bank (z-axis rotation). The turn of the head is keyframed the same at 0 and 8 in order to delay its movement. At frames 16 and 24, the bone is also keyframed the same to make another delay before turning again.

The hips tilt down on the side of the leg that is in the forward position. The shoulders tilt down on the side of the arm that is in the forward position. Therefore, except at frames 8 and 24, where the hips and shoulders are square, they should always tilt in opposite directions. During a walk, the arms and legs always swing in opposite directions for balance.

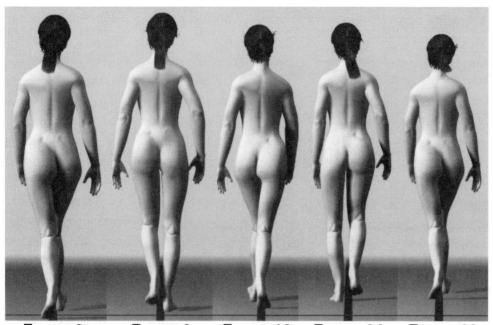

Frame 0 | **Frame 8** | **Frame 16** | **Frame 24** | **Frame 32**
Contact | **Pass** | **Contact** | **Pass** | **Contact**

Fig. 12-17 The hips swing in the direction of the forward leg. The motion can be exaggerated for a more seductive effect.

Frame 0 Contact | Frame 4 Down | Frame 8 Pass | Frame 12 Up | Frame 16 Contact | Frame 20 Down | Frame 24 Pass | Frame 28 Up | Frame 32 Contact

Fig. 12-18 Due to a wider pelvis, the female legs angle inward, more causing the female to walk on a straight line. During a walk, the legs often appear to cross over. This effect can be exaggerated when showing fashion models walking.

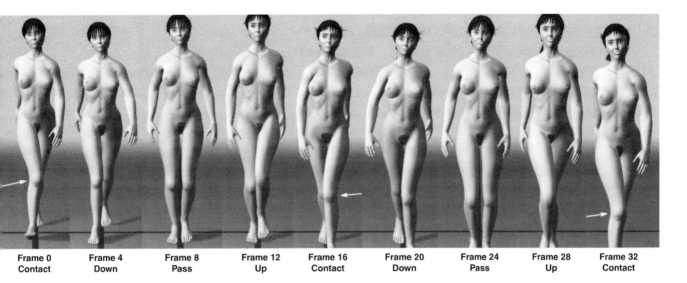

| Frame 0 | Frame 4 | Frame 8 | Frame 12 | Frame 16 | Frame 20 | Frame 24 | Frame 28 | Frame 32 |
| Contact | Down | Pass | Up | Contact | Down | Pass | Up | Contact |

Fig. 12-19 A classical animation device is to break the joint at the knee or elbow by bending it the wrong way.

When the hips and shoulders rotate up and down, they should also rotate forward and back (Figure 12-12). On the contact positions at frames 0, 16, and 32, the hips rotate forward, toward the front leg. The shoulders revolve in the opposite direction, toward the front arm. In the passing position, the hips and shoulders remain square. Make sure the rotation values for the shoulders and hips are identical at frames 0 and 32.

Figure 12-13 explains where the nulls (IK controllers) and the human model remain the same for frames 0 and 32. In this example, the person is walking along the z-axis. Therefore, the character's position will vary between the two beginning and ending frames. Since the wrist nulls are parented to the body and the elbow nulls are parented to the wrist nulls, they will follow the body's movement along the z-axis. So, their placement does not have to be altered on the z-axis. The same holds true for the knee nulls, since they are also parented to the body. The ankle nulls are parented to the toe nulls, which in turn are parented to the

body.

The chart shown in Figure 12-14 illustrates which bones have the same rotational settings at frames 0 and 32. When you keyframe the bones at frame 0, just keyframe them again and specify frame 32.

If you followed the examples shown in the charts, you should have the right settings for the body and its nulls. The two poses at frames 0 and 32 will be identical, except that the body at 32 will be positioned further along in space. Make sure the feet do not slide during the thirty-two-frame walk cycle. To get the body moving past frame 32 without having to pose it manually, simply go into the graph editor and set the post behavior for all the moving parts to repeat. Only the body's post behavior on the z-axis is set to offset repeat. You can refer to Figure 12-15 for the right settings. Note that offset repeat takes into consideration the movement of an object in space, while repeat recapitulates the position in one place. Repeat should also be turned on for the body's scale on the y-axis,

271

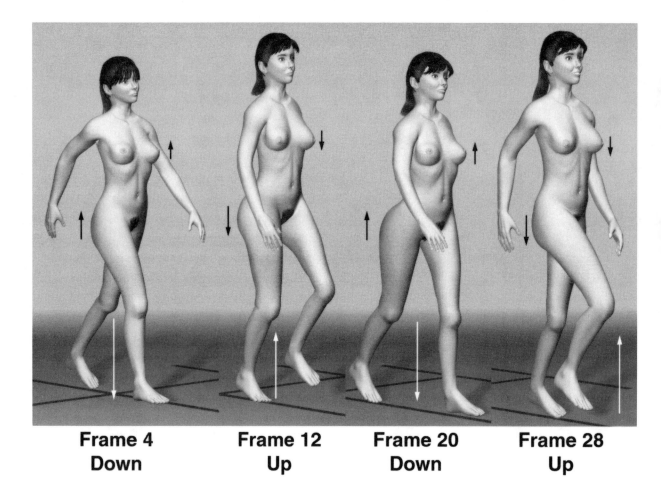

| Frame 4 | Frame 12 | Frame 20 | Frame 28 |
| Down | Up | Down | Up |

Fig. 12-20 When the body goes down, the buttocks and breasts tilt up. When the body moves up, the buttocks and breasts go in the opposite direction and angle down.

so that Squash and Stretch continue past frame 32.

Your person should now walk along a straight line for as long as you want. If any of your settings differ slightly, you will notice the errors as they compound exponentially.

You can use the chart in Figure 12-16 to determine which keyframes are indistinguishable from one another. For example, the body is posed identically at frames 8, 40, and 72.

When animating a female walk, it becomes important to consider the physical differences between females and males and how they affect movement. The female pelvis is shorter, wider, and deeper. It also inclines forward. Since the pelvis is wider, the femur, or thighbone, has a greater separation at the pelvic socket. This causes the thighs to take a more inclined direction toward the knees.

It also affects locomotion. Figure 12-17 illustrates the greater swing of the wider female hips. For a more sexy walk, you can exaggerate the amount of pelvic sway. Some even prefer to delay the swing to the other side by keyframing the hip

Fig. 12-21 Expectation, followed by action, and finally, the result are seen in this cartoon character's preliminary windup before running. It can be compared to tightening the spring of a windup toy before setting it loose. The result is a puff of smoke left behind.

bones the same at frame 8 as at frame 0. The angle of the hip bones would also stay the same at frame 24 as at frame 16. Normally, they would be square at frames 8 and 24.

The pelvic width and angle of the female legs result in a walk that follows a straight line. One foot appears to cross over the other (Figure 12-18). The crossover walk of fashion models on a runway is even more exaggerated.

An interesting trick used by classically trained cel animators is called breaking the joint (Figure 12-19). Breaking the joint at the elbow and knee so

that they bend the wrong way helps to exaggerate movement and makes it more exciting. For example, during the walk cycle, you could break the knee joint by moving the knee goal objects inward at frames 0, 16, and 32 ("contact"). It may seem strange to do this, but in the animation it looks fine.

To give your walk more style, consider swinging the arms in front of the body rather than just along the sides. Since the feet and hands move along parallel lines, try twisting them to the sides more so that they do not always look in profile when seen

Fig. 12-22 Images from the staging and dialogue animation. The character as storyteller is staged at a campfire, narrating an event. The environment, the type of character used, his actions, and the nighttime period make it clear what this animation is about.

from the sides. Other variation might include lifting the arms on the up or down positions, twisting the upper and lower body in opposite directions, swinging the arms with the elbows leading, twisting the foot that is in the air while swiveling the one on the ground, letting the feet fall loosely on the ground, or moving the knees in or out in a relaxed manner. The possibilities are endless, and hopefully you will be motivated to experiment with some of them.

The female figure also has greater fatty deposits compared to a normally proportioned male. Therefore, the breast and buttock movements have to be taken into account (Figure 12-20). When the body comes down, the breasts and buttocks go in the opposite direction—up. The breasts and buttocks come down when the body goes up. In a thirty-two-frame walk cycle, the body comes down at frames 4 and 20, while the breasts and buttocks move up. At frames 12 and 28, when the body moves up, the breasts and buttocks go down. The breast bones can be rotated at those frames and the post behavior set to repeat.

Anticipation

Anticipation forms a mental picture about the future. It carries a feeling that something is about to happen. In animation, it is a powerful method for setting up an event or series of activities. Figure 13-21 shows a few frames from an animation that can be viewed on the CD-ROM (Anticipation .mov). It depicts a cartoon character winding up like a coil, before running off-screen and leaving a puff of smoke behind. A version of the animation without anticipation or the result of the action can also be found on the CD ("Noanticipation.mov"). Notice that this animation without anticipation

and resolution lacks interest and is more difficult to comprehend.

The first part of a motion prepares the viewer for what is to follow. It adds drama to the animation. Other examples of this are crouching before jumping, stretching before crouching, pulling an arm back before punching, and so on.

The "go" part of the animation (action) can take any number of forms, but it is usually the fastest component of the animation. If your character makes contact with something during this stage, try skipping the actual moment of contact. Since it happens within a split second, it does not have to be seen and will make the action appear more concise and less awkward.

The follow-through, or reaction that comes after an action, brings about resolution. It tells the viewer the effect of a specific cause. In the case of the sample animation, a smoke cloud in the shape of the character is left behind and gradually dissipates. Other responses to actions can involve weight and recoil after a character crashes into a wall, a return to a relaxed position, a throbbing fist after a punch, and so on.

Most of the time, it is a good idea to let the viewer know what is about to occur, then show what takes place, and finally, show what has happened. Physically, characters require a kind of preparation before doing something. This could be in the form of shifting weight before running or walking, taking a deep breath before shouting, moving the eyes before turning the head, or winding up before pitching a ball.

Staging

This is one of the more comprehensive principles because it incorporates many others. When a direc-

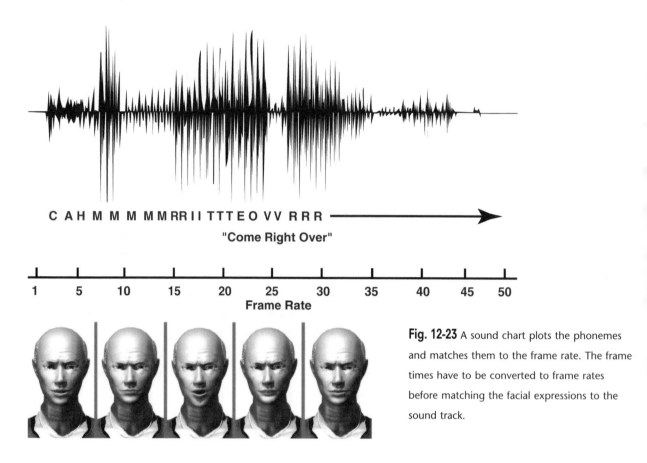

C A H M M M M M R R I I T T T E O V V R R R ⟶

"Come Right Over"

1   5   10   15   20   25   30   35   40   45   50

Frame Rate

Fig. 12-23 A sound chart plots the phonemes and matches them to the frame rate. The frame times have to be converted to frame rates before matching the facial expressions to the sound track.

tor sets up a scene in a movie, the action has to be made as clear as possible. Lighting, camera angles, and the activities of the actors all have to contribute to a certain mood. The director tries to convey certain feelings and ideas to the audience; he or she does this with staging.

The animator has a story to tell and needs to find a way to promote it. The example animation on the CD-ROM (Figure 12-22) stages an old storyteller sitting at a campfire (Chapter 12 > Movies > Staging & Dialogue.mov). The scene recalls memories of sitting around a campfire and telling stories. The environment in the animation reinforces this concept.

When staging an animation, it is important to show only one action at a time. Too many activi-

ties in a scene obscure the meaning and can lead to confusion. A close-up shot has the advantage of bringing the viewer's attention directly to the character and what he or she is saying or expressing.

At the beginning of a scene, movie, or episode, the audience is often shown a full or long shot. This might depict the body of the performer, as well as his or her environment. Its purpose is to identify the person and the environment that he or she is operating in. In filmmaking, this is termed an establishing shot. Subsequent images become less general and focus on specific details.

The initial frames of the sample animation show the body of the actor and his environment (establishing shot). The action then cuts to a close-up of the performer's face, thus eliminating the less important details. Sometimes close-ups do not tell enough of the story. The body may need to be seen, especially when you have arm and hand movements emphasizing certain points the actor is trying to get across.

Traditional animators learned from Charlie Chaplin, who said that emotions had to be clear enough that they could be understood even when seen in silhouette. They would often test the pose of the body by filling it with black. If the performer's attitude was still clear in silhouette, the pose was used.

When describing staging, it is difficult to separate it from dialogue. The manner in which the body expresses emotions and ideas supports the meaning of the words.

Matching facial expressions to your soundtrack might seem at first to be an impossible task. If you can plan ahead by making a graph of your sound and labeling it with the words and frame numbers below, you should be able to do a fairly good job of pairing the two.

Figure 12-23 has a sound graph coupled with the individual phonemes identifying the portion of the graph in which the various vowels and consonants occur. The frame numbers at the bottom are the most important part of keying the location of each phoneme. A sound editing program is used to chart the location of phonemes and frame numbers. Depending on your software, you may have to label these by hand after playing through each part of the sound several times.

Once you have a sound chart plotted with the frame rate, open your shape-shifting software. Set your facial blend shapes to correspond with the labeled frame numbers on the sound chart. Be sure to use a mirror to mimic the mouth forms. The facial expressions that you modeled in the previ-

ous chapter should work fine for dialogue.

Another method for animating dialogue is to import the sound file directly into your animation program. If you watch the video of the performer while listening to the soundtrack, you have the added advantage of being able to observe the actor's phrasings. You can then follow those expressions—especially the mouth movements—while animating your character. If you limit yourself to animating only twenty or so frames at a time, the task becomes much easier. For example, follow and animate only the actor's mouth movements for the first twenty frames. Set your beginning frame to 0 and the ending frame to 20. Make a preview of your animation with the sound, and watch your performer's mouth movements. If everything looks fine, set your beginning frame to 20 and the ending frame to 40. Animate the mouth movements for those frames. Continue animating only the mouth for about twenty frames at a time, and making previews. Try to generalize the mouth motions. Do not try to animate every single lip movement that you see in the video. When you finish making the mouth movements, work on the eyes, then the brows, cheeks, and nose. Animate the body movements—such as the head, arms, hands, fingers, and so on—last.

Some important considerations when animating dialogue are:

1. **Do not exaggerate facial expressions.** Overstated movements by the mouth and other features during dialogue look phony. Your character will appear to be overacting.

2. **Abbreviate mouth movements.** Too many lip and other facial movements will make your performer look really strange and unnatural. For example, when saying the word "abusive," do not close the mouth at the "b."

3. **Use secondary actions to reinforce specific parts of the dialogue.** The head might pull back, a hand may chop through the air, the shoulders might shrug, the body could rise up, and so on.

4. **Keep tongue movements to a minimum.** This also means never in-between the tongue when it rotates up or down.

5. **Do not make sudden changes between facial expressions.** Give them time to switch more gradually. This often means glossing over certain ones. Give your character at least four frames to change an expression.

6. **Concentrate on one or two parts at a time.** For example, you might animate all the mouth positions first. All the eye movements could be animated next, followed by the brows, cheeks, and nose. The body would then be animated last, and you might want to break that up into different parts also. Remember, people watch the mouth and eyes when listening to dialogue. Matching the mouth movements to the dialogue is the most important part.

7. **Eye movements and blinking.** Move the eyes and have them blink at least every sixty frames. Some emotional states, such as anger, slow down blinking, while others, like nervousness, increase it.

8. **Emotional states.** Think about what is motivating your actor to say certain things. Make them appear to be thinking about what they are saying. This means conveying emotions such as anger, sadness, fear, joy, surprise, and disgust.

9. **Put life in your character.** During dialogue, the head and body should not be rigid like a statue. The body weight should shift, the head lowers or turns, the shoulders move, and so on.

10. **Use holds and delays.** Know when to hold a certain expression and when to let it go. Often a hold occurs just before some expansive dramatic gesture. The face, including the mouth movements, should not be constantly changing.

Straight-Ahead vs. Pose-to-Pose Action

Straight-Ahead action is a spontaneous method of animating one move after another. It is recommended for experienced animators who are familiar with proper timing. Straight-Ahead animation means that actions are acted out during the process, and that they are based on a set of loosely drawn storyboards. Every activity is an outgrowth of prior ones. This can lead to unplanned and innovative effects. The animation is frequently an unplanned performance.

Pose-to-Pose action is sometimes referred to as pose planning or pose extremes animation. A sequence of photographs, sketches, or video serves as a template to assist the animator in planning each pose for the duration of the action. Cycling actions, such as walks and runs, are excellent examples of Pose-to-Pose actions. The poses are planned according to sketches or photographs, such as Eadweard Muybridge's stop-motion images. Beginning animators should find Pose-to-Pose planning easier to use than Straight-Ahead animation, which is more improvisational. Pose planning means that you plan ahead by creating a kind of blueprint.

When you have scenes of extreme drama in which you want your digital actors to strike key poses, try using Pose-to-Pose animation. If you want your character to end in a certain position at a specific time, and the first and last frame poses are extreme, pose them that way at the beginning and at the end. Select a few keyframes between the beginning and ending positions. Place your models at those keyframes in the attitudes you think they should be in. Play back a test animation to see

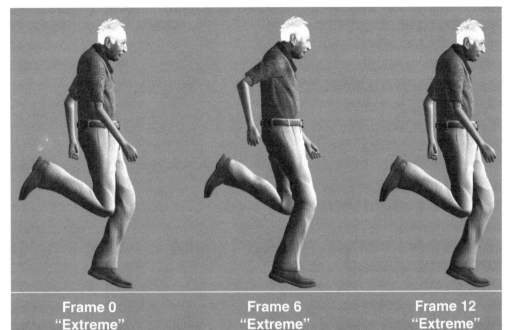

Frame 0
"Extreme"

Frame 6
"Extreme"

Frame 12
"Extreme"

Fig. 12-24 Step 1
Run. At the "extreme" pose, the front foot almost touches the ground. All three poses are identical, except that the one at frame 6 is opposite the other two.

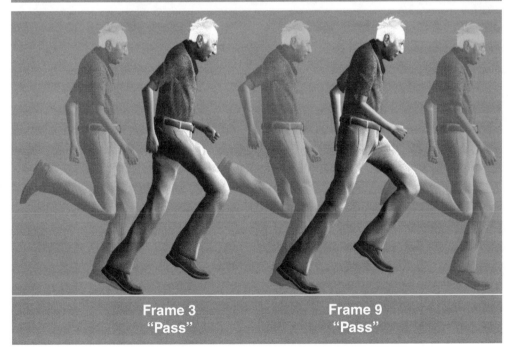

Frame 3
"Pass"

Frame 9
"Pass"

Fig. 12-25 Step 2
Run. The "pass" position stretches the body and pushes off before both legs leave the ground. The body is placed in the middle location of the poses that were previously positioned at frames 0 and 6. The body should also be rotated so it leans forward.

how the software interprets these key poses. Make your adjustments accordingly. For example, if you want your character to sit in a chair, you could pose it standing in the first frame. Once you decide the length of time it takes to have the character sit down, place him in a sitting position at the final frame. Now create some of the keyframes between the first and last frames by posing the character in

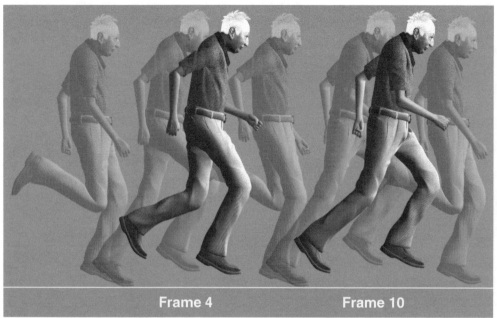

Fig. 12-26 Step 3 Run. The "up" position places the body at the highest point. It should not be raised more than half a head.

Frame 4   Frame 10

Fig. 12-27 Step 4 Run. Adjusting the in-between poses. All twelve positions are shown here according to their exact placement.

the act of sitting down.

A word of caution about pose planning. If you position parts of your character at keyframes that are very close together, you could end up with jerky movements. For more fluid motions, space the keyframes apart. This is especially true with

secondary or overlapping actions. Another common mistake is for animators to keyframe all the parts at the same time (say, every fifth frame). Overlapping actions should occur at different times than the main motions. When the arm swings forward at frame 5, the head might turn a

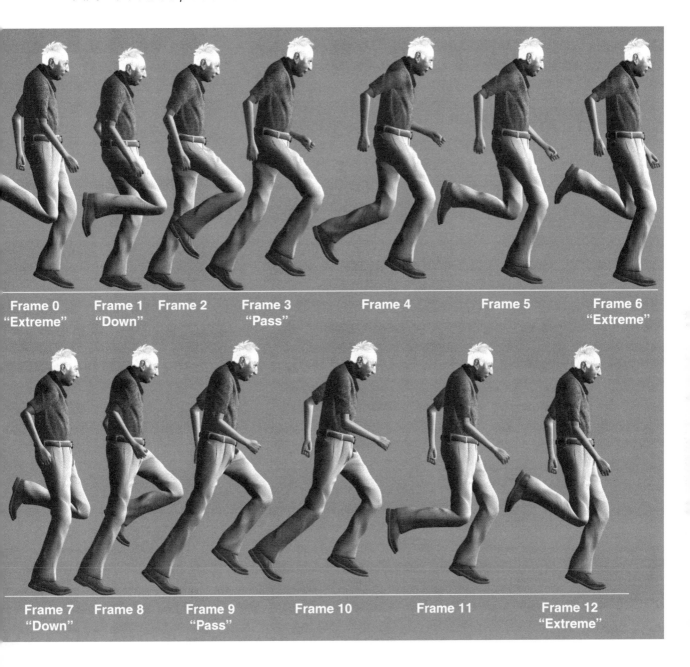

Fig. 12-28 The twelve-frame run poses spread apart. Note the "down" position at frames 1 and 7. The body is squashed at those frames.

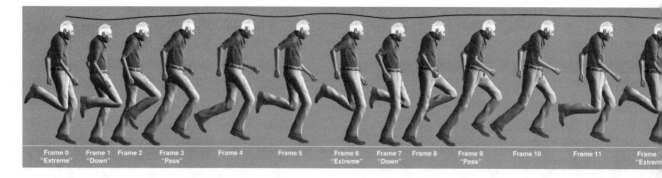

| Frame 0 | Frame 1 | Frame 2 | Frame 3 | Frame 4 | Frame 5 | Frame 6 | Frame 7 | Frame 8 | Frame 9 | Frame 10 | Frame 11 | Frame |
| "Extreme" | "Down" | | "Pass" | | | "Extreme" | "Down" | | "Pass" | | | "Extrem |

Fig. 12-29 The twelve-frame run path of action.

little and end its motion at frame 8.

While the animation is running, movements should never appear to come to a dead stop. Except for when they die, it is not natural for biological entities to become immobile. You can avoid this problem by setting the same keyframes twice, spaced anywhere from three to twenty or more frames. This gives limbs and other parts a little extra bounce. Bending the curve on the motion graph between the two identical frames controls the amount of bounce.

Animating a Two-Legged Running Sequence

As mentioned before, a run animation is an excellent example of Pose-to-Pose Action. It teaches some important lessons. One of them is repeating animation: When one cycle is complete, it can be duplicated with motion graphs. The other important lesson involves weight and recoil: When the foot comes down, it acts like a spring to propel the body up and forward. The character's size determines how much distortion (Squash and Stretch), if any, occurs during the landing and lifting-off interval.

The following steps demonstrate how to create a twelve-frame running animation. After setting it up, you can alter the speed by scaling key times for all items. In order to get the cycling motion without having the feet drag behind, select the toe nulls (goal objects or IK handles) and parent them to the body. If you are using the IK setup discussed in chapter 3, the rest of the nulls will move along with the body.

Step 1 (Figure 12-24). Pose your character like the one in Figure 12-24. This is called the "extreme" position, and the front foot is just about to touch down. The further you space the person apart, the longer the strides will appear. So that the repeating cycle works correctly, be sure to position all parts exactly the same at frames 0 and 12. Frame 6 is identical to the first and last frames, but as the mirror opposite. You can copy and paste values from the opposite goal objects, or create a transformed object of the character at 0 and mirror it as a template for frame 6.

Step 2 (Figure 12-25). This is the "pass" position, and the body is stretched a little as it pushes off from the ground. At frames 3 and 9, place the body in the same postures as the ones in the illustration. Note that these two poses are identical but opposite. The back foot for frames 3 and 9 is in almost the same location as the front one is at frames 0 and 6. Be sure to angle the body forward at frames 3 and 9.

Step 3 (Figure 12-26). This is the "up" position; the body is now off the ground in the highest spot of the entire run. Unless you are animating a deer or a rabbit, you should only raise the body half a head at the most. Note that frames 4 and 10 are identical but opposite.

Step 4 (Figure 12-27). After you finish the extreme poses of steps 1-3, it is time to make adjustments to the in-betweens. Figure 12-27 illustrates the correct placement and overlap of the body, while figure 12-28 shows the same poses spread apart for more distinctness.

Two of the in-between poses that should be adjusted are at frames 1 and 7. They are identical but opposite. The body is squashed at these two "down" positions. The squash varies according to the weight of your character. At the "extreme" frames of 0, 6, and 12, the body is no longer squashed or stretched, nor is it angled.

The head bone should be rotated to one side at frames 0 and 12 (identical rotational axes). At frame 6, it turns to the other side.

The following summarizes which poses are identical:

Frames 0 and 12 = identical.
Frames 1 and 7 = identical but opposite.
Frames 2 and 8 = identical but opposite.
Frames 3 and 9 = identical but opposite.
Frames 4 and 10 = identical but opposite.
Frames 5 and 11 = identical but opposite.
Frame 6 = identical but opposite of 0 and 12.

Paths of action show the overall directions that an animation takes. Figure 12-29 depicts the wavy path that a run creates.

Finally, complete the run in your graph editor by turning on repeat for the post behavior of all nulls (goal objects or IK handles) and bones.

Depending on which axis the body moves, turn on offset repeat for that particular axis position. Turn on repeat for the other axes. For example, if the body moves along the z-axis, turn on offset repeat for the post behavior of the z-axis position. Turn on repeat for the remaining x- and y-axes.

Animating a Four-Legged Running Sequence

Figure 12-30 illustrates the four-legged movement of a puppy running. The animation can be viewed on the CD-ROM. The puppy's movements are similar to the gallop of other four-legged creatures. As might be expected, there are some differences. The puppy's legs are stubby, thus impeding much of his drive.

Overlapping action can be seen in the flapping of the ears and the wagging of the tail. The entire running cycle continues for eighteen frames. The last frame repeats the motions of the first. The bones responsible for most of the movements are listed in Figure 12-31.

The parent bone is responsible for the upward and downward mobility of the body. This makes it easier to move the body from one point to another without worrying about having it go up and down at certain points.

Except for a few instances, rotations for opposite limbs, like the left and right upper back legs, occur at the same frames with reverse values. For repeating movements to work, be sure to study the photographs of Eadweard Muybridge and jot down notes for the rotational values. One other benefit found in the third volume of **Human and Animal Locomotion** is Muybridge's timing charts. These are the travel records of each photographed subject. You can match the time to the specific plate and know how fast the person or animal was moving. Once you have located the time, use the for-

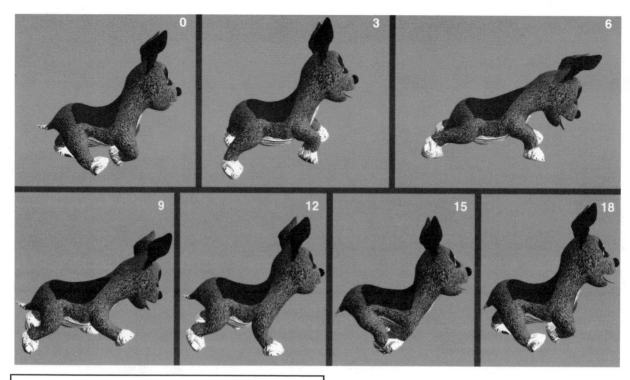

Repeating Rotation or Movement of the Bones							
Parent	✓	✓	✓	✓	✓	Same as 0	
R. & L. Upr. Back Leg	✓	✓	✓	✓	✓	✓	Same as 0
R. & L. Midl. Back Leg	✓		✓	✓	✓	✓	Same as 0
R. & L. Back Paw	✓		✓		✓		Same as 0
R. & L. Frnt. Upr. Leg	✓	✓	✓	✓	Same as 0		
R. & L. Frnt. Lwr. Leg	✓	✓	✓	✓	✓	Same as 0	
R. & L. Frnt. Paw	✓						Same as 0
Frame Number	0	3	6	9	12	15	18

Fig. 12-30 A four-legged running cycle. Frame 18 repeats the motions of the first frame.

Fig. 12-31 This chart outlines the rotations of the bones responsible for most of the motions. The first and last frames have the same values.

mula in chapter 4 (Figure 4-8) to calculate the frame rate for each image.

The following is an example of implementing this formula. Plate 709 of Eadweard Muybridge's Human and Animal Locomotion shows twelve frames of a galloping dog. The chart in the back of Volume Three records the number 41 for the time. Utilizing our formula, you divide 41 by 1,000 to get .041. The number .041 is multiplied by 30, giv-

ing us a frame rate of 1.23. This means that each of the twelve photos is spaced 1.23 frames apart. Applying this to an animation means that the second frame is keyframed at 1.23. The third pose is keyframed at 2.46, and so on. Most people round off the keyframe rate. In this case, if you want your dog to run faster, space each frame by one. If you want it to go slower, use two.

Fig. 12-32 Straight-Ahead animation means that a great deal of the performance is unplanned. This leaves a lot of room for impromptu actions.

Fig. 12-33 Usually a rough storyboard and the playacting of the animator is all that is used for Straight-Ahead animation.

When to Use Straight-Ahead and Pose-to-Pose Action

In Straight-Ahead animation, the animator works straight ahead from the first frame to the last. The artist has an idea in mind, then allows it to develop into any direction that feels right. The results are often unexpected and zany.

Many professional animators who create Straight-Ahead animations pantomime some of the movements before keyframing them. This gives them an idea of the timing and direction of their characters. Facial animation is often practiced this way in a mirror, then animated.

Figure 12-32 shows an example of a Straight-Ahead animation found on the CD-ROM (Chapter 12 > Movies > Straight Ahead.mov). It is based on a loosely drawn storyboard, as depicted in Figure 12-33. This is a sketchy plan of action, which is given more substance and detail during the animation process.

Pose-to-Pose and Straight-Ahead animation can be combined. You can set up key poses in the shot, then animate toward each one in a straight-ahead manner. When animating toward the first pose, you may decide to alter it according to the

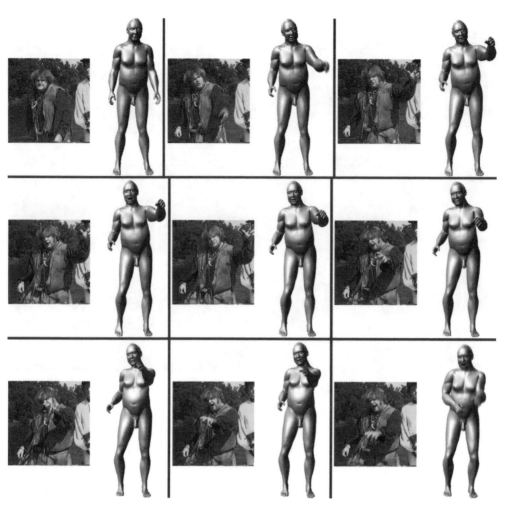

Fig. 12-34

Rotoscoping in animation means having your character follow the motions of an actor or cartoon.

direction you find yourself moving.

No matter which animation method or combination that you decide to use, it is important to utilize the following animation techniques. Without them, the performance will become tedious and unoriginal.

1. **Apply Moving Holds.** During certain parts of the action when you want to emphasize or accentuate a pose, hold it for about eight to sixteen frames. This will not only alter the tempo, but also clarify the activity. During the hold, do not keep every part immobile, but hold the main pose of the character while still keeping some parts mov-

ing, such as the facial expression, hands, and so on. You hit the pose and then gradually change into a stronger version of the same pose. The manner in which you enter and exit a hold is also an important consideration. Does it come suddenly, or does the character settle into it gradually? You can also let follow-through objects—such as hair and clothing—continue moving, as they are affected by soft body dynamics.

2. **Add accents and surprises.** When you want to break up the even pace of an animation, overstate some movements to accentuate them. Disrupting the animation with unexpected actions

will also make it more dynamic.

3. **Use contrasting actions.** When the pace is proceeding smoothly, contrast it with short, abrupt moves. Changing the timing throughout the performance will make it a great deal more enjoyable to watch.

Rotoscoping in 3D Animation

Rotoscoping is a method of importing a movie, image sequence, or animation, then having a digital character follow the movements in an imported file. Figure 12-18 shows an example of a computer graphics actor imitating the moves of a real actor. The rotoscope animation can be viewed on the CD-ROM (Chapter 12 > Movies > Rotoscope.mov).

For some people, rotoscoping is an invaluable guide for realistic movements. Many gaming companies use motion capture for lifelike action moves, while others use rotoscoping. Most beginning animators have problems with correct timing. Rotoscoping helps them to overcome this difficulty. It gives them a guide that has correct timing built into it. All they have to do is follow the actions of the videotaped person, animal, insect, or other character.

Once students becomes more comfortable with the animation process, they may find it unnecessary to always follow filmed action. Their sense of timing will have developed to the point where they can act out certain movements. Although they may become experts in human movement, they will most likely still depend on observing the motions of other creatures, like whales, ostriches, and other animals. Some major animation studios have developed libraries of different creature movements. Their animators can use these video-

tapes for rotoscoping or studying specific actions. If you decide to use rotoscoping, try to keep the following in mind:

1. **Step back to get some perspective on the action.** Try to pick out the key poses (pose extremes) rather than following every little movement. When you scrub through the keyframes, each movement shows up in very minute detail. This may reveal subtle motions, but one can easily miss the overall action. By looking for key poses in the video and having your character strike more dramatic representations of these, you will suffuse the action with strength and emotionalism.

2. **Try not to match each movement to every frame of the video.** This would result in too many keyframes, making the action look choppy at times. For example, if the videotaped actor's arm moves down over a period of thirty frames, you might keyframe your character's arm at frames 0, 15, and 30. You would not keyframe it every step of the way down. When a motion stops, be sure to add a little bounce by keyframing it twice at the end and spacing the two keyframes anywhere from three to twenty or more frames apart.

3. **Eliminate irrelevant actions.** Copying each action slavishly can result in a bland performance. It is better to extract key movements while finding ways to improve upon them. If an action fails to add anything interesting to your animation, do not use it.

4. **Emphasize and exaggerate the motions.** When rotoscoping, it is easy to overlook this important principle of animation. The result is often movements that are too soft. Use rotoscoping as a general guide, but be sure to punctuate motions with distinct mannerisms. Magnifying specific actions makes your animations less mundane and even adds some personality to your char-

acters. Another approach to this is to videotape yourself or others performing in an exaggerated manner.

5. **Add motion holds.** Even if you do not see actions such as motion holds in the video, be sure to put them into your animation. Know when to hold an action to build up tension and when to release it either suddenly or gradually.

6. **Fit the videotaped performer to the digital one.** Unless you are a great actor or actress, it is very difficult to perform actions of a character that does not match your body type or sex. For example, if your digital actor is a powerful bodybuilder on steroids and your videotaped actor is a ninety-pound weakling, the movements and timing will require a lot of adjustment.

CHAPTER 13

More Principles of Animation: Movements of the Figure

During the 1930s, the Disney animators found specific techniques that made their animations more successful. They talked about these, studied them, and improved them. New artists who joined the staff were taught these methods, which became known as the Fundamental Principles of Animation. The previous chapter discussed the first four:

1. Squash and Stretch
2. Anticipation
3. Staging
4. Straight-Ahead Action and Pose-to-Pose

This chapter examines the remaining principles, which are:

5. Follow-Through and Overlapping Action
6. Slow In and Slow Out
7. Arcs
8. Secondary Actions
9. Timing
10. Exaggeration
11. Solid Drawing
12. Appeal

Follow-Through and Overlapping Action

Simple animation involves the movement of one object (for example, a ball). Complex animation consists of various objects and their parts moving at various speeds, times, and directions. Needless to say, the majority of character animations involves complex actions. Characters with multiple joints have primary and secondary movements.

Figure 13-1 shows images from an animation in the chapter 13 folder on the CD-ROM (Follow Through (Soft Body Dynamics).mov) in which the primary movement consists of the character dancing and spinning. Her body carries the action forward. The secondary movements are found in the cloth, hair, legs, feet, arms, hands, breasts, and head. Since their motions do not occur independently of the body, nor of each other, they are called overlapping actions. Facial expressions can also be considered secondary actions. They are just as important as the movements of the limbs. Facial animation tells the viewer what the character is thinking and makes the performance more emotional.

Overlapping actions can precede as well as follow the main action. These lesser motions relate to or are the result of the main action. Overlapping action enhances the animation. As one movement ends, another begins.

Follow-through is another kind of overlapping action. It is usually associated with elastic objects, which adjust readily to different conditions. These are prescribed by the primary object to which they are attached. In Figure 13-1 and on the CD-ROM animation, you can observe the movements of the cloth that the character is holding, which follows the actions of the character it is connected to.

Follow-through indicates the completion of a motion. In the animation, the cloth is the last object to move as it flutters up and settles. It is propelled by soft body dynamics, which try to follow the laws of physics. If the woman were to stop all her movements, the cloth would be the last to complete its motions before settling down.

Other common objects that have a certain amount of give, and thus exhibit follow-through, are hair, tails, floppy ears, loose-fitting clothes like a skirt, and so on. If at all possible, 3D animators should apply soft body dynamics to these for more realistic states of change.

If your software has limitations, such as the lack of soft body dynamics, consider moving objects like capes by manually placing bones inside them. The skeleton can have goal objects or IK handles

Fig. 13-1 Objects that are flexible, like the cloth, behave in accordance to modifications in the primary entity they are attached to. These loosely waving artifacts change a split second after the action of the primary object. In animation, this is referred to as follow-through.

on certain parts to make their manipulation easier. In a case like this, it is usually a good idea to parent all the handles or goal objects to one cluster handle or goal object (null). This makes it easier to move or rotate the entire object, as well as to manipulate parts of it. The CD-ROM has an animation that shows a cape being manipulated manually with a skeleton (Chapter 13 > Movies > Follow Through (Manual Bones).mov).

Overlapping Action and Follow-Through illustrate an important principle of animation: Not all parts of a character arrive at the same time. If every action ended at the same frame, the character's movements would look too mechanical. The skeletal hierarchy can be compared to a chain. Force and drag cause each part of a limb to move and stop with slight time lags. When one part is beginning to end its motion, a second attached object might be in its beginning movement stage. This works its way up or down the hierarchy in a whip-like action. For example, when a character turns toward someone, the head might revolve to look at the person first. This would be followed by the turn of the shoulders, then by the body and hips, and finally, by the arms. The motion can continue down to the fingertips. An IK chain with several handles or nulls as goal objects gives you more control to simulate this kind of action.

As mentioned previously, whenever a limb comes to a complete stop before changing its direction, be sure to keyframe it twice. The two identical keyframes can be spaced anywhere between three and twenty or so frames apart. The motion graph's natural curve between these two frames makes the limb appear to have a slight adjustment or settling-down movement at the end.

As you animate the character, think in terms of striking interesting key poses. Be sure to apply motion holds or delays to different components. If the body is held in position for a certain number of frames, the arms or other parts can still continue their motions.

One of the most challenging tasks that the computer animation artist faces is conveying mass or weight. Working in a virtual environment, where the rules of physics do not apply, the animator has to be resourceful in convincing viewers that his characters and the objects they interact with have weight. His creatures and the things that they manipulate have to exhibit the ability to rebound in response to specific actions.

Slow In and Slow Out

Objects, when acted upon by another force, tend

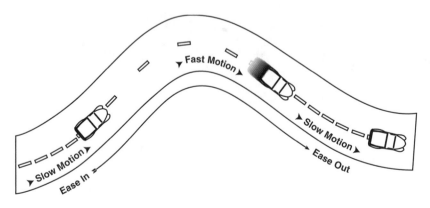

Fig. 13-2 Slow in, slow out means that an object starts slowly, gradually overcomes inertia to speed up, and then slows down again. Using a line-painting truck analogy, one can see that during the acceleration stage, keyframes are spaced out further, since more distance is covered. There are more keyframes closely packed together during the slow stage.

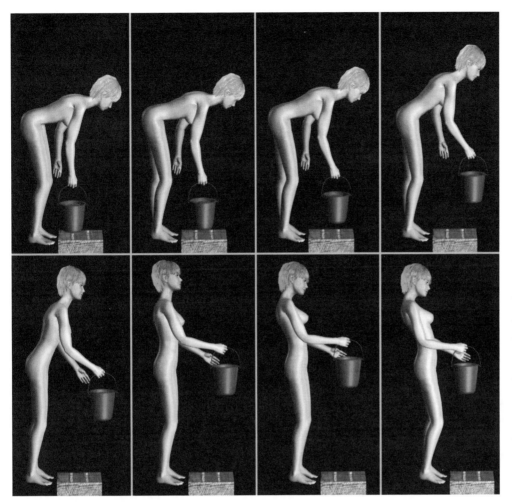

Fig. 13-3 Some scenes from the slow in, slow out animation. At first, the woman has to overcome the inertia of the heavy bucket. After picking it up slowly, her motions become faster. In the end, she slows down to stabilize her movements.

to speed up and then slow down. The larger the mass of the body, the longer it takes to accelerate. In animation, most movements start gradually, speed up, and then come to rest. This is referred to as Slow In and Slow Out.

Whenever a muscle or set of muscles contracts to pull a limb, other, opposing muscles become active to oppose and slow down the contracting muscles. This works to regulate and fine-tune the body's actions. In addition, all bodies have to overcome the attraction of the earth's mass. When applied to animation, characters that appear to move according to the actions of the muscles and

the influence of gravity have more convincing motions.

Figure 13-2 depicts the analogy of a line-painting truck as it relates to slow in, slow out. Closely spaced frames shown as stripes painted near each other are the result of the initial slow motion. The slow movement covers less distance; therefore, the beginning actions are packed closely to each other. As the truck accelerates and passes over more area, the space between actions (stripes) becomes wider. Slow out can be seen in the truck slowing down and the space between frames becoming tighter again.

An animation of Slow In, Slow Out can be seen on the CD-ROM (Slow In Slow Out.mov). Figure 13-3 illustrates some of the image sequences from the CD-ROM animation in which a woman picks up a heavy bucket. Her movements are slow at first, as she overcomes the weight of the bucket's contents. Approximately halfway through the animation, her movements pick up tempo; at the end, they slow down again as she struggles to hold up her burden. Slow in and slow out play an important role in communicating weight.

A graphic depiction of the movements involved in picking up a bucket can be seen in Figure 13-4. When bending over, the frames are spaced evenly apart. As the character begins to pick up the bucket, the struggle to overcome its heaviness slows down her movements. The pattern of her actions at this point is closely spaced. Once inertia has been overcome, the spacing is wider between motions as she speeds up. At the end, she slows down, creating a tightly packed pattern.

Slow in, slow out does not always mean slow. It can mean medium speed that picks up tempo gradually and then returns to a slower rate. Sometimes,

the opposite happens when a character is caught in the middle of an action going at full speed, slows down, and again speeds up. This is generally referred to as fast in, fast out.

Arcs

Arcs, or the curving direction of movements, are the normal result of anatomical construction. Figure 13-5 shows some of the curving motions in the female character's actions.

The previous slow in, slow out animation can also be viewed as an example of arcs, or curving movements. The spinal cord, ball and socket, and hinge joints are the determining factors for pivotal motion. The woman in the animation bends back when the joints or bones in the skeleton's spinal column are turned. When these motions are combined with the entire body's rotation, they create a 45-degree arc moving in a counterclockwise revolution. The secondary movement of the lower arm holding the bucket also follows a curving path. The other overlapping action, of the head trying to stabilize the body, makes a small arc at

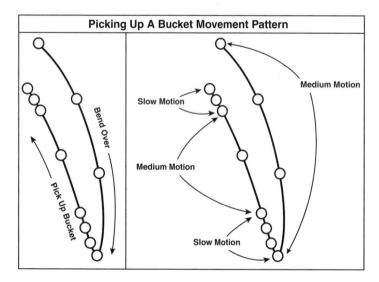

Fig. 13-4 A graphic depiction of the slow in, slow out motion during the picking-up-a-bucket action. The circles show how movements are spaced further apart during faster movements and closer together during slow movements.

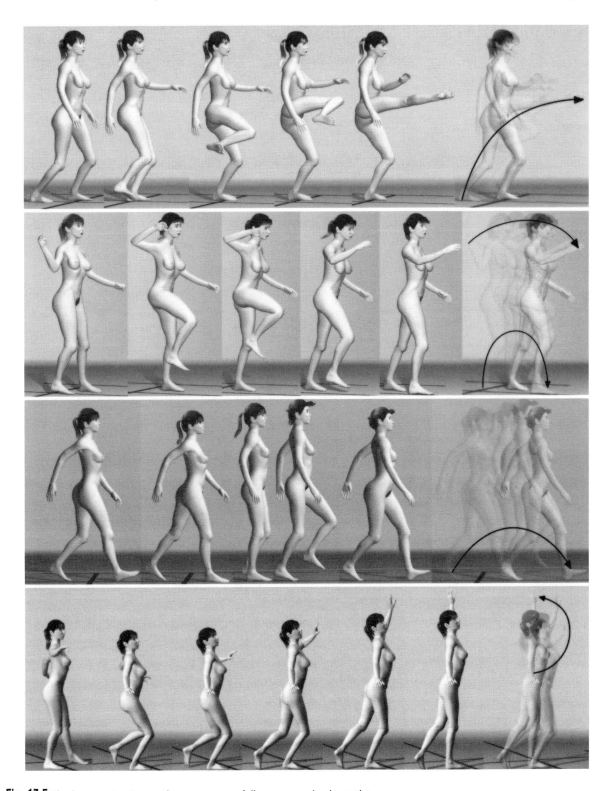

Fig. 13-5 The human structure makes movements follow arcs or circular paths.

the end in the opposite direction. One thing to remember is that, except in the mineral world, straight lines do not exist in nature.

Secondary Action

When supportive actions occur during and after a primary movement, they are referred to as secondary actions. A runner's head bobs up and down as a result of the body's movements. A person shows surprise on his face while jumping back. A dancer lifts her arms while spinning around. These are all examples of secondary actions that reinforce and support the main movements of the body.

Figure 13-6 depicts some images from the secondary action animation found on the CD-ROM (Secondary Action.mov). The primary action takes place within the body motions. As the performer anticipates the throw of the football, he positions himself, then reacts to the violent impact by bending over, and finally straightens himself up. Other secondary motions support his body language. The arms and hands move in anticipation of catching the ball. The head responds to the impact. The facial expressions change in reaction to the circumstances.

One way to communicate weight is through delayed secondary action. When a character lands on a surface, a chain reaction takes place. The impact starts at the point of contact and travels upward through the body, causing certain limbs to move in a time lag. A good follow-through is achieved when various parts arrive at a certain point at different times. Other methods for achieving weight are Squash and Stretch, timing, slow in and slow out, arcs, anticipation, exaggeration, staging, follow-through, and overlapping action.

Timing

Characters move according to the space between keyframes. A fast walk means that the arms and legs move back and forth within a shorter span of frames. These motions can be timed according to a certain beat. It is similar to the ticks of a metronome helping a beginner play the piano at a certain pace. Intuition and experience are the determining factors for knowing how quickly or slowly to move a character.

Figure 13-7 illustrates some scenes from a CD-ROM animation in which an old man raises his hands to his head (Chapter 13 > Movies > Timing.mov). When the man moves quickly, he seems to be in shock about something. When his actions are at a medium pace, he appears to be fixing his hair. Slowing down the movements even more makes it seem that he is stretching. Greater spacing between keyframes changes the intent of the animation. The section about scaling keys in chapter 4 tells how to alter the overall speed of an animation.

A clock's ticks are evenly spaced. Walking and running movements are evenly spaced. Figure 13-8 depicts a highway line-painting truck. It serves as an analogy to a character's movements and how far apart they are spaced. The spray mechanism on the truck paints stripes on the road at the same even pace. When the truck moves slower, covering less distance, the lines are spaced closer together. As it speeds up to cover more distance, the stripes become more separated.

Let us assume that each stripe represents a character's keyframed movement and that the rate of spray is similar to the even rate at which its limbs move. When the duration of the animation is set too quickly (refer to the fast animation on the CD-

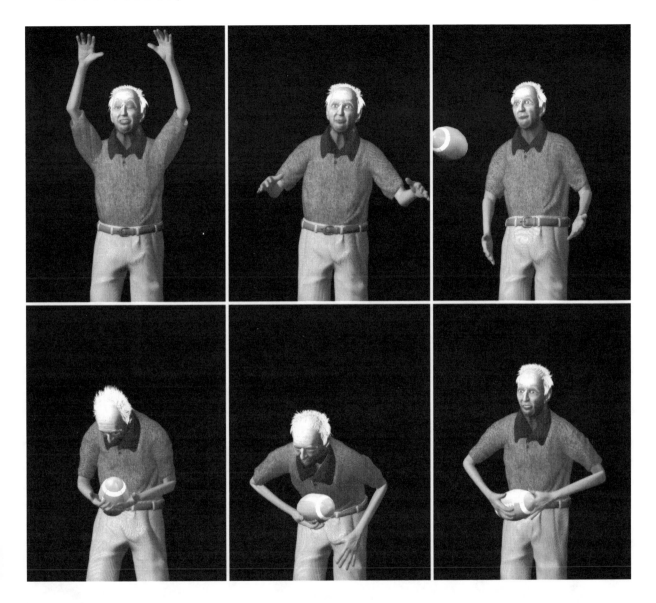

Fig. 13-6 Images from the secondary action animation. The arms, hands, head, and facial expressions support the main body movements.

ROM), each body part's motion is spaced too closely to the next. This can result in jerky movements that are often difficult to discern, just as stripes that are too close together appear to almost blend into one long strip. If the overall animation is spaced out for a longer period of time, as seen on the CD-ROM, each body movement—which is still the same degree as before—is now spaced further apart and appears smoother and more distinct. This is similar to the truck covering more distance on the road so that the painted stripes become separated from each other and much more

Timing Fast (person appears to be in shock)

Timing Medium (person appears to be fixing his hair)

Timing Slow (person appears to be stretching)

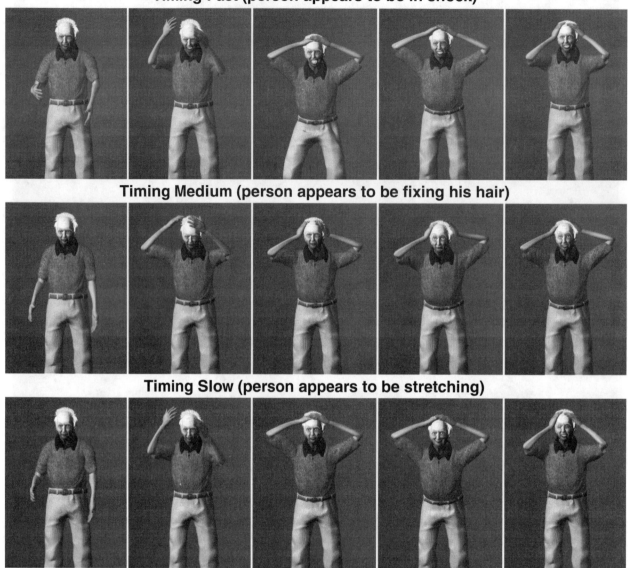

Fig. 13-7 Timing and spacing are based on content. The intent of an action defines its duration. In the example above, similar motions carried out at different speeds change the meaning of the animation.

distinct.

Oftentimes, characters' movements appear to have a light or buoyant feeling. This can happen when the space between movements is too far apart or the motion graph for a moving part curves up too much. Imagine a deer jumping and landing. If the keyframes for the creature are too close together, it appears to land hard and take off quickly. When they are spaced further apart, it seems to almost float and land lightly on the

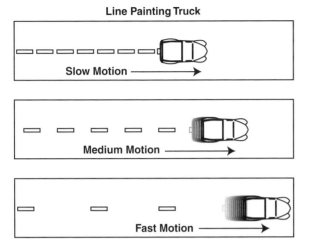

Line Painting Truck

Slow Motion ⟶

Medium Motion ⟶

Fast Motion ⟶

Fig. 13-8 Timing can be seen in the above analogy of a paint truck painting white stripes on a road. Each paint stripe represents a keyframed motion. The truck sprays paint at the same rate no matter how fast it goes. Similarly, a character might have a specific set of movements that it performs during a run cycle. If the character runs slowly, each of its leg and arm motions are keyframed closely together. The further it runs, the more ground is covered; the keyframes for its other motions, which are still going at the same rate, are spaced further apart and thus appear smoother.

ground. A situation like this needs more uneven spacing of frames. When the deer is in the air, more keyframes are set than when it lands on the ground. This puts the accent on the upward motion of the creature and less emphasis on the landing. A heavy character such as an elephant would need the opposite, with more keyframes as it lands on the ground, because it spends more time trying to overcome mass and gravity. Proper timing requires a balance between movements that are snappy (spaced closely together) and floaty (spaced far apart).

Exaggeration

For viewers to register certain actions, animators will resort to amplifying their characters' motions. Sometimes, this can take the form of anticipation and the take. A fat man spots a delicious-looking cake. His eyes pop out in anticipation of a feast, followed by the take in which he flies up, smacks his lips, claps his hands together, and then lunges toward the cake.

When you use exaggeration, it has to make

sense. Whatever takes place should have a meaning or reason behind it. Once you have decided on the objective of a scene, figure out which motions are to be amplified to reinforce meaning.

Emotion plays an important role here. It helps to get inside a character and act out a scene first before trying to animate. Ask yourself what would you be thinking and feeling in this circumstance. Even though you may think that the movements are overblown, you should notice that the animation becomes more fun to watch and often more realistic.

Figures 13-9 and 13-10 contain some excerpts from an animation found on the CD-ROM (Chapter 13 > Movies > Exaggeration 1.mov). The animation shows the artist's character having a daydream about Botticelli's *Birth of Venus*. As he approaches, his steps are exaggerated. You can see this in the deliberate manner in which he shifts his weight each time one of his feet touches the ground. He is a little self-conscious in Venus's presence, so his movements are somewhat stiff. Her movements, on the other hand, are languid and slow.

Fig. 13-9 The first set of frames from the animation showing exaggeration. The walking motions are very measured and display the overstated shifting of weight. When the tentacle appears, there is a brief anticipation, followed by a subtle take.

The highlight takes place when this pastoral scene is suddenly disrupted by the appearance of a giant tentacle that bashes the artist on the side of the face. He freezes for a brief moment before collapsing. This is referred to as a motion hold. It occurs when a character interrupts a motion by pausing for an instant before resuming the rest of the action. It gives the audience a little time to comprehend what has happened and also indicates that a new action is about to begin. Usually, motion holds have a few minor movements, like the twitching of a limb or blinking of the eyes.

The struck character is an example of action followed by reaction. Anticipation and the take become more noticeable when the tentacle appears. The tentacle is also given a personality, which becomes more apparent when it pauses briefly to observe the artist collapsing, just before disappearing underwater. In cartoon animation, inanimate objects as well as creature parts can be given a life of their own. It is another example of exaggeration.

Exaggeration is an important element in animation that should not be ignored. Whether you are using motion capture, rotoscoping, Pose-to-Pose, or Straight-Ahead animation, be sure to add those important accents at key times.

Fig. 13-10 The action becomes more amplified when the tentacle strikes the character, who then reacts with an overdone take, showing him frozen for ten frames before collapsing.

Solid Drawing

Although Disney animators referred to solid drawing as the ability to draw well, this principle still applies today to 3D art. Good 3D modeling skills are necessary if one hopes to create good animations. The artist should have a sound understanding of anatomy and proportion, and the skills to translate what he or she sees into his or her models (Figure 13-11).

Besides having good artistic skills, it is also important to have good judgment and aesthetic sensibilities. A model has to be constructed in such a way that it will not only look good, but will also deform well during animation.

Figure drawing is an important part of an artist's training. Even though 3D modelers end up using only the computer, the skills they have learned in their traditional drawing classes translate directly into their 3D work. Learning to sculpt in a representational manner is also a useful skill that will carry over into computer modeling.

Appeal

The 3D modeler and the animator are forced to overcome the mechanical nature of computer graphics. Hardware and software place a barrier between the artist and the creative process.

301

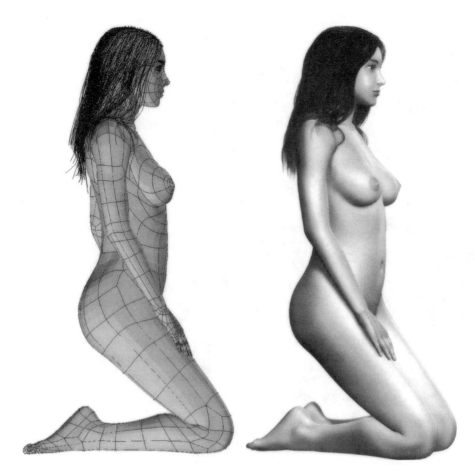

Fig. 13-11 Disney animators referred to solid drawing as the ability to draw characters that have weight, balance, and depth. Today, this principle is still relevant to 3D computer modeling.

Traditional tools like a pencil and paper offer less resistance and a more direct approach to making art. If computer artists can make characters appear to be full of life, they have achieved a great deal.

Appeal in animation does not mean cute and cuddly characters. Instead, it refers to a performer who has a strong stage presence. An evil and despicable character can have appeal.

A vital character conveys appeal. It communicates a personality, which the audience responds to in a positive or negative way, but not in an apathetic way. Charisma is that elusive trait which draws interest to a character. It has been said that the best compliment you can give an animation is to say that it makes you feel something about a character.

Figure 13-12 illustrates some images from an animation found on the CD-ROM (Chapter 13 > Movies > Appeal.mov). It serves as an example of a female who expresses temperamental characteristics. The female's behavior distinguishes her from the other characters that appear later in the animation.

When working on a script and drawing storyboards, think about each character's identity: How will each of them communicate on both emotional and mental levels?

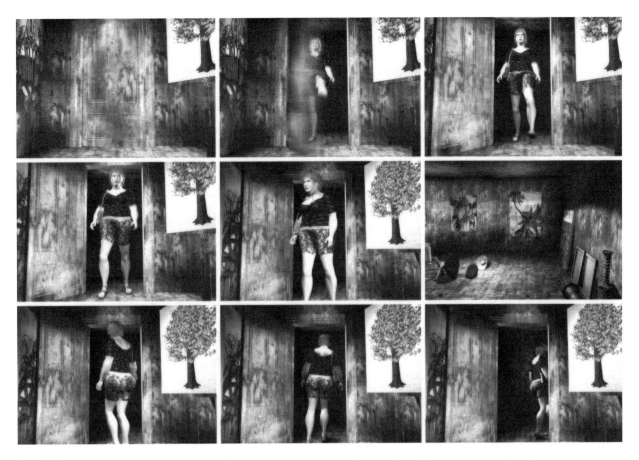

Fig. 13-12 Images from an animation of a lively character with appeal. The female exhibits certain characteristics unique to her personality.

Other Considerations

Although this chapter and the previous one covered all the principles of animation, there are a few fundamentals beginning animators should be aware of. These can be classified under the various principle headings, but are sometimes overlooked due to their specific characteristics.

Pacing and Impact

Just like music, animations are time-based. Music has a certain tempo or beat. This holds true for animation. Animators regulate the pace of animation. They develop an instinct for acting at the right moment to change the pace or speed of their characters and the entire flow of events. Dramatic impact is measured by the right timing. Every circumstance should have a meaning. Even occurrences that appear random have a purpose behind them. Timing is the arrangement of temporal events. It is usually the first skill an animator develops. The audience needs a certain period of time to comprehend each circumstance. If a character picks something up, the action should be performed at a rate that gives people a chance to see what was lifted up.

The pattern of actions can be planned before

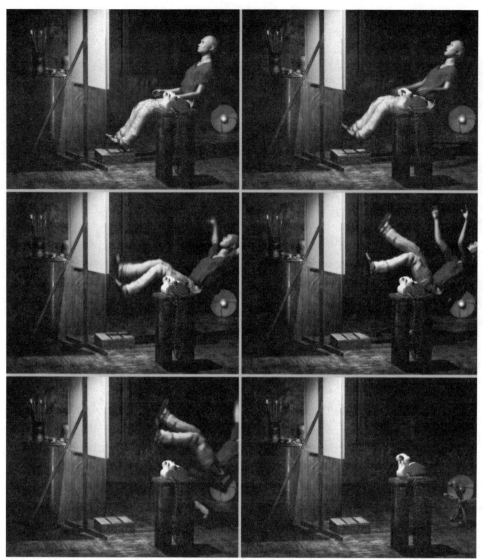

Fig. 13-13 Equilibrium and disequilibrium in an animation indicate the presence of physical forces.

beginning the animation. However, the animator develops the structure intuitively during the animation. At first it may appear awkward to interpret seconds as numbered frames, but after a while, you develop a second sense for patterns of spacing. A thirty-frame animation lasts one second. The viewer normally does not registered one frame consciously. At least three to five frames are needed to read a scene. A quick gesture requires between eight and fourteen frames.

Equilibrium

Balance, or equilibrium, refers to a situation in which the masses of the body work to create a stable condition. Usually, the body's base of support is in the feet. Thus, the center of gravity moves toward the ground and rests between the feet. Whether a figure is stationary or in motion, the muscles work to maintain equilibrium. The animator is often faced with the challenge of making the characters appear to be influenced by gravita-

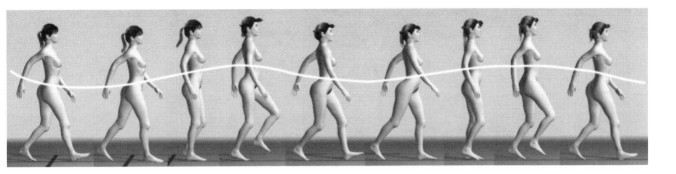

Fig. 13-14 The walking female illustrates the path of action that her movements create. This wave motion varies according to the weight of the character. In order to distinguish the poses, the frames were spread apart.

tional forces. By depicting elements in the body striving to maintain equilibrium, the artist shows tension generated by opposing fields of energy.

Balance can be either symmetrical or asymmetrical. A symmetrical pose means an equal distribution of body mass. The figure appears stable and the center of gravity falls between the feet.

Asymmetrical balance is a result of the unequal distribution of body weight. The center of gravity is no longer between the feet, but now rests somewhere else. The arms and head attempt to uphold equilibrium by assuming new positions. These secondary movements of the limbs have to occur almost simultaneous and appear spontaneous. When a person stands and shifts body weight from one foot to the other, the center of gravity moves. It may start out centered between the two feet, but switches to one foot during the weight transfer.

A very effective method for learning how to depict gravitational forces is to create an animation in which the body starts out in a stable posture, begins to lose equilibrium, tries to regain it, and either fails or succeeds. Figure 13-13 shows an example of this type of animation. The animation itself can be viewed on the accompanying CD-ROM (Chapter 13 > Movies > Equilibrium.mov).

Figure 13-13 shows an opening shot with an artist sitting in a chair, contemplating his next painting. At this point, his position is fairly stable. When the phone rings, he suddenly jumps out of his half-awake state. Animations that are more cartoon-like give life to objects that are normally inanimate. In this case, the phone becomes the obnoxious intruder.

His startled reflex triggers a state of instability, making him and the chair fall backward. Compared to the opening shot, we now see a dramatic shift in weight distribution. The only stable point left is on one or two of the wheels on the chair.

An important part of this animation occurs when the character tries to gain stability. This must look like a reflex action, without any conscious effort by the digital actor. It occurs over the course of approximately fifteen frames.

In the animation, we see that any effort to counteract the effects of force and gravity are futile, and the artist continues to fall. Sometimes, it is better to let the audience imagine the result of an action. Therefore, rather than letting it see the artist fall, the camera remains stationary and the figure lands outside of the shot. It also makes the animator's job easier. Remember, one of the most important rules of animation and moviemaking is

Fig. 13-15 Lines of action are illustrated for the body, and secondary motions for the arms and legs.

to show viewers only what you want them to see. If it gets the point across, there is no need for anything else. The parting shot shows an empty scene, with the phone showing the only sign of life.

Paths of Action

Most characters move in paths of action that curve. When keyframing, be sure that each action follows an established path or moves sequentially toward a specific goal. Any keyframes that do not follow that route can appear out of place. The action might look unsteady, unreal, or jittery.

Most of the time, it is difficult to spot out-of-place actions until a preview is made of the entire sequence. If you find any movements that seem inappropriate to the entire arrangement, try deleting that keyframe. This should smooth out the angle of the curve in the motion graph, resulting

in a more fluid action. If the motion appears to be too soft and floating, change the motion graph's curve. Try making the angle sharper, or insert another keyframe in place of the deleted one. This time, the frame's settings might be closer to the previous and following frames. Another solution is to place the keyframe closer to either the previous or following frame, rather than in the middle of the two.

Figure 13-14 shows the path of action that a figure creates when walking. You can see how it curves up and down like a wave. Squash and Stretch are usually the determining factors for the angle of this motion curve. A lighter character will create a higher curve, while a heavier character's motion curve will be lower.

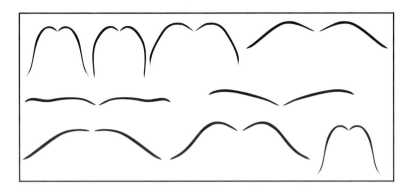

Fig. 13-16 Some basic lines of action illustrating rhythmic motion. The top set shows the steady beating of a bird's wings. The bottom group depicts the tempestuous opposing lines of a bucking bronco.

Lines of Action

Experienced animators can see beyond the visible form to observe the movements of the lines of action. They can usually spot clumsy and ill-timed motions. Therefore, it is important to visualize an imaginary line that extends through the main action of a figure. Secondary movements, like those in the arms and legs, can also be visualized as lines of motion.

Figure 13-15 depicts images from a simple animation of a man throwing a rock. The primary force is seen in the lines of action illustrated against the silhouette. The thirty-six-frame animation can be found on the CD-ROM (Chapter 13 > Movies > Lines Of Action.mov).

Lines of action usually have one primary line—the thrust of the body. Secondary movements, such as those of the arms, hands, head, legs, feet

and so on, form the basis for other lines of action. When planning an animation, it is often advantageous to sketch the main lines of action first. Drawing your figures comes after this. Details are meant to accentuate the line of action.

Animations created without a conscious effort to delineate a line of action often appear to be drifting aimlessly. They lack the dynamic quality, rhythm, simplicity, and directness found in great animation. When viewing the actions of your characters, try to see beyond the forms, to the actual motions of the splines.

Rhythm

Repetition of similar characteristics of any kind produces rhythm. Lines of action that form a pattern have a certain tempo. These can be discerned among unlike elements. Contrasting lines of action can make an animation appear more dynamic and interesting. It is similar to contrapuntal music, where two or more independent but harmonically related melodic parts work together.

Action that has a specific direction can be perceived as having a beat. Rhythm becomes stronger when it is reinforced more frequently. Overlapping actions form an integral part of rhythm. The rhythmic accents in lines overlap each other. Normally, the lines form curves that wave back and forth.

Walking and running cycles are examples of rhythm. A dancing character is another representative of rhythm.

In their most basic forms, lines of rhythm wave back and forth and up and down like a whip. Figure 13-16 depicts a few of these. The top illustration shows the rhythmic lines of a bird's wings, while the bottom set shows the curving actions of a bucking bronco. The bird's wings have a steady rhythm, while the horse illustrates opposing lines full of accents.

Conclusion

As you become more experienced in animation, you may start to perceive how all the underlying principles overlap each other. It is difficult to concentrate on one aspect without making use of others. All of them play an important role in the overall animation.

A conscious awareness of the basic ideas of animation is the first step. Experience moves this awareness to a subconscious level, where it becomes instinct and no longer subject to argument and reasoning. The subconscious mind acts. It accepts the conclusions of the conscious mind as final. This is the reason great art, music, and liter-

ature appear to have been created effortlessly. Through experience, these artists radiated courage, confidence, and power in their work.

CHAPTER 14

Composition and Cinematography

The arrangement of a character's environment entails knowing what makes a good composition. All the objects seen through the camera should relate to each other and to the whole in a cohesive manner. Since animation is not a static art form, a basic understanding of cinematography is another element in the process that should not be ignored. A discussion of some basic techniques for composition or design of a scene and an overview of digital cinematography should assist you in establishing the proper staging.

Composition

An animator's goal is to keep the work fresh and spontaneous. This can sometimes be difficult when screen redraws and previews have a sluggish response time. The entire workflow becomes disjointed when you have to wait several seconds or minutes for an outcome after each action.

Blocking

To speed up screen redraws, block in most of your objects, and substitute them with the actual high-quality versions later. One way to do this is to have a set of low-polygon substitute objects. When animating, use these low-resolution characters and their basic surroundings. This should help your work appear more natural because you will get faster feedback after each move. When you are ready to do a final rendering, substitute each low-resolution object with its equivalent in high-resolution.

Spatial Arrangement

Composition is the ordering of forms, colors, lines, values, and textures in a picture. Expression is the emotive effect of these conditions as they occur in an image. A good design is one in which all the relational parts form a balanced unity. A 3D image or animation shares many of the abstract principles of design. Different parts exist to tell a story or express a dramatic mood. There are several considerations when examining composition. These are the arrangement of forms, balance, direction, and rhythm. Even though this discussion treats them as separate entities, in reality, they influence each other to the degree that none could exist without the others.

The way in which forms are arranged is the foundation of a scene. Some of the more commonly known arrangements are oval, vertical, horizontal, diagonal, triangle, and their combinations. An effective use of these organizing principles can bring forth specific feelings in a viewer. This type of focus makes the work very powerful. Many artists learn about composition in school and then forget about it. Their design judgment becomes an intuitive function. They no longer rely on reasoning and deduction. Their instincts tell them what works and what does not.

Oval Composition

Composition based on the oval can be seen in Figure 14-1. The direction of the arms, the two heads, and the child's back form a kind of egg shape. Oval structures tend to be unified and harmonious. They often convey a sense of well-being.

Vertical Composition

Vertical design (Figure 14-2) implies strength, stability, and sometimes, spirituality. Early religious paintings employed vertical design to show a holy person reaching upward. The person or groups of people appeared to be in this world but

Fig. 14-1 Composition based on the oval.

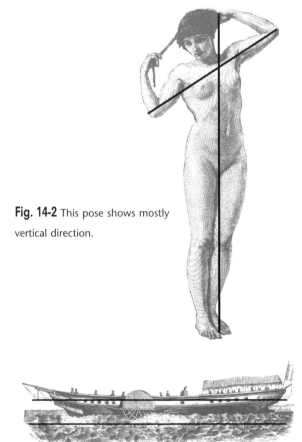

Fig. 14-2 This pose shows mostly vertical direction.

not of it. Even though the pose in Figure 14-2 shows mostly vertical direction, it is broken up by the diagonal line of the arms. This makes the image much more interesting than if the character had her arms down at her sides.

Horizontal Composition

Horizontal composition (Figure 14-3) usually denotes calm and steadiness. Landscape art is often composed of strong horizontal lines. Nature appears constant, with its continually recurring seasons. Compositions based on the horizontal line appear grounded and secure. They can also convey a sense of speed, as evidenced by the ship in Figure 14-3.

Diagonal Composition

Diagonal designs (Figure 14-4) often show a state of instability, with dynamic forces at work. The direction of the line leads the viewer immediately into the picture. Crossed diagonal lines are a very effective method for portraying action in a scene (Figure 14-5). The patterns formed create tension and disorder. The angles of arms, legs, a tail, spears, and so on express feelings through gesture.

Fig. 14-3 Composition based on horizontal lines.

Fig. 14-4 Diagonal design.

It is no wonder that crossing lines are often found in battle scenes.

Triangular Composition

The triangular composition (Figure 14-6) can be thought of as a symbol of unity. Based on a firm foundation, it forms a harmonious relationship that is always striving upward. In the Christian faith, it symbolizes the Trinity. Renaissance artists often painted the Madonna and Child in a triangular composition.

If you are so inclined, you can find other composition forms, such as the rectangle, spiral, radial, and so on. Most designs utilize a combination of the various line arrangements.

Balance

Balance is the equilibrium of visual weight, in seesaw fashion, on either side of an imaginary fulcrum and lever. When matching weights are placed equidistant from the center, we have symmetrical balance (Figure 14-7). Asymmetrical balance in a composition entails elements of varying weights distributed unevenly from the center fulcrum. Equilibrium is achieved when all the elements counterbalance each other to attain a unified whole. Figure 14-8 depicts asymmetrical balance. The woman is offset, throwing the weight some-

Fig. 14-5 Crossed diagonal lines can make an image more dynamic.

Fig. 14-6 The triangle conveys unity and stability with an upward striving to reach a lofty goal.

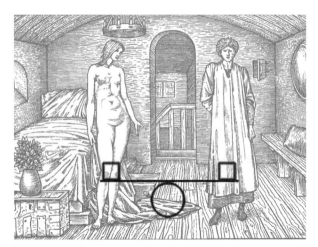

Fig. 14-7 Symmetrical balance means that visual elements even out identically on both sides of a central axis.

Fig. 14-8 Asymmetrical balance achieves equilibrium through the unequal distribution of visual weight.

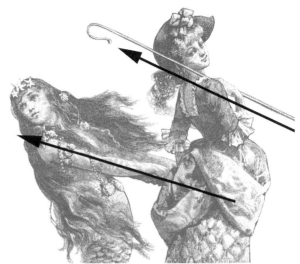

Fig. 14-9 Direction means that a picture's components can be arranged to guide your attention toward specific areas of a scene.

Fig. 14-10 Rhythm is the repetition of a picture's elements directed in a pattern of movement.

what to the right of center. Even though the hand and flower are smaller than the rest of her, their positions on the extreme left balance the image. While symmetrical balance conveys stability and serenity, asymmetrical balance can express tension and restlessness.

Direction

Direction is the orientation of various elements with the express purpose of guiding the viewer's observation to specific points in the picture. Abstract parts of an image line up to point toward a center or lead the viewer's gaze around the entire scene. Figure 14-9 shows two bodies posed in a way that pulls toward the upper left of the composition. The staff's orientation in the woman's hand substantiates the direction toward which the main elements point. In animation, you can also have

objects or their parts move toward certain areas of a scene. The use of motion blur indicates faster movement.

Rhythm

Rhythm is produced from elements placed in a

way that establishes a pulsation. When colors, shapes, lines, values, textures, and forms are placed in a recurring fashion, or in a discernable pattern, a certain beat is established. Movement becomes more pronounced when the rhythm of a piece is reinforced. Figure 14-10 shows a pattern that is established by similarly posed figures.

Camera Techniques

The placement and movement of the camera takes on an important role in determining the composition of a scene. In essence, the animator can think of the camera as the spectator's eyes. Novice animators are often guilty of improper or exuberant use of the camera. Lacking the skills of motion picture photography, they will move and rotate the camera excessively. The result is a bewildering array of images that can baffle viewers or even make them dizzy and nauseous. The first thing beginners might want to learn is to exercise some restraint. The audience should not even be aware of the presence of a camera.

Movies often create the illusion that there is no camera between the scene and the viewer. Aspiring animators may find it beneficial to study the cine-

Fig. 14-12 An image from the animation, shot through a 15mm wide lens.

matography employed in the best movies. Over the years, filmmakers have developed certain techniques that are applicable to animation. Unlike traditional moviemaking, 3D cinematography is not restrained by physical limitations. Therefore, animators often achieve a greater degree of control and creativity with the camera.

Field of View

The field of view on a computer graphics camera mimics the lenses in a real camera. A long lens means that the camera has a narrow field of view (Figure 14-11). A wide-angle or wide lens has a large field of view. Figures 14-12, 14-13, and 14-14 illustrate images from an animation. The first part was shot through a 15 mm wide-angle lens, the second one was filmed with a 50 mm medium lens, and the third with an 85 mm lens. This animation can be found on the CD-ROM (15 50 85 mm Lenses.mov).

When you compare the three parts of the animation, notice how the shot gives the impression that the man is covering more ground in the 15

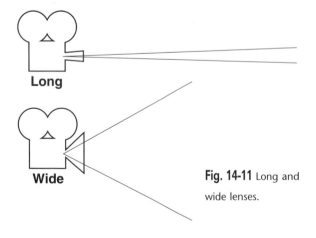

Fig. 14-11 Long and wide lenses.

Fig. 14-13 The same scene shot through a medium 50mm lens.

Fig. 14-14 This animation was filmed with an 85mm long lens.

mm, wide-angle lens version and the least amount in the 85 mm lens animation. The long lens animation shows less of the background and thus makes it seem as if the man is walking over less territory. Each part of the animation is the same length, 113 frames.

As you can see, an effective use of long lenses is

having the camera appear to linger longer over a scene of characters moving across the screen. Another application of the long lens might be to show a person walking or running and seemingly going nowhere. If you want the shot to appear more frenzied, consider utilizing a wide lens.

The way objects appear in scenes shot with

Fig. 14-15 This scene was shot through a 100mm long lens. Objects appear to be flattened and less distorted, and the background seems to be closer to the camera.

Fig. 14-16 The exact same scene when shot through a 15mm wide lens. This time, the foreground objects appear to be distorted and the background seems farther away.

wide and long lenses can be radically different. Figure 14-15 illustrates a scene rendered with a 100mm long lens. All the elements appear to be brought closer together. Depth seems shallower, and there is less distortion. The field of view is compressed. Characters that are distant from each other can be brought closer together with the long lens. When you are shooting a scene that is very large, a long lens will work fine. Wildlife pictures are often shot with long lenses so that the photographers can remain far away from their subjects.

On the other hand, when you are in an enclosed space and do not have the luxury of moving the camera far away from the subject, a wide-angle lens can be used. Indoor pictures are often shot with a wider lens so that the photographer can take in more of the scene. Figure 14-16 shows the exact same scene as the previous illustration. This time, the field of view has more depth, and the background objects appear to be farther away. The space between objects expands, and the wider field of view amplifies perspective. The foreground objects are more distorted. The lens seems to make a figure more rounded, as if seen through a magnifying glass. This may be useful for having a scene look more three-dimensional, but it is at the expense of accuracy. Wide lenses can make characters close to each other appear to be distant. If you move a wide-angle lens through a scene, you should notice a distortion at the edges, as if space were bending around the camera.

Most people are used to the 50mm standard lens when viewing movies and photographs. Realistic scenes are usually shot with a 40, 50, or 60mm lens. For more variety, you may want to consider switching between lenses. An animation might be filmed mostly with a standard lens and

switching to a wide or long lens could emphasize certain parts. For example, an evil character could be shot with a wide lens and the good guy with a standard lens. Objects that are usually filmed from far away, such as sporting events, wildlife, airplanes, and so on, can be shot with a long lens. Since people are used to seeing these activities filmed with long lenses, they may find your animation more credible. If you want a shot to appear somewhat strange, try using a wide-angle lens.

Depth of Field

Depth of field measures the amount of area that falls within the range of focus. Lenses have a point of focus that is usually set on the subject. Other parts of the image that fall outside of the focal range are blurred. Figure 14-17 depict the same scene and subject matter as the previous two illustrations, except that this time, a standard 60mm lens and depth of field were used. The f-stop was fixed at 8. A lens's f-stop determines the amount of light that is allowed into the camera. Higher set-

Fig. 14-17 Depth of field blurs the objects that are outside of the camera's focal point. This time, the scene was shot with a standard 60mm lens.

tings represent smaller lens openings; therefore, less light enters the camera. Lens f-stops at higher numbers also widen the depth of field and ensure that more elements are in focus.

In computer graphics, everything in a scene can be in focus. Even though software does not have the limitations of a physical camera, many artists utilize depth of field to draw attention to the main subject. In addition, people are used to seeing depth of field in photographs and movies. Depth of field becomes important when animation companies have to match computer graphics to actual filmed footage.

Because computer artists do not operate under the same constraints as cinematographers, the option to use depth of field becomes an aesthetic one. The two main concerns are the area you focus on and the depth of your area of focus. When animating several characters, you might want to switch depth of field among them. Whoever is talking or doing something can be the focal point.

Using depth of field can increase rendering time significantly. If the camera in a shot is not moved, consider rendering the background as one image with depth of field. The characters and any objects in front of them can be shot without depth of field separately, using alpha channels. The blurred background and foreground images can be composited in a movie editing program. This method also works when the camera moves. Shoot the background separately from the foreground. Instead of using depth of field, you can blur the background images in the movie editing program.

Dolly, Truck, and Boom

In cinematography, cameras are often moved about on traveling platforms. Specific mechanical rigs are designed to create smoother camera move-

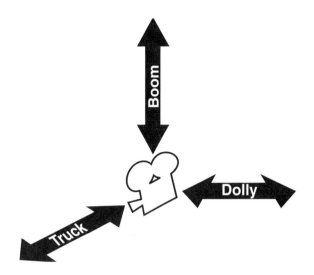

Fig. 14-18 Camera movements along the x-, y-, and z-axes.

ments. A wheeled cart that propels the camera along a track is referred to as a dolly. Many cinematography terms stem from the devices used to manipulate the camera.

Dollying the camera refers to its movement along the x-axis (Figure 14-18). For example, the camera may keep pace with someone walking. Truck-in and truck-out means that the camera moves along the z-axis. Truck-in refers to the camera moving in closer to the subject and truck-out means moving away from it. Sometimes, truck-out is called a reveal. Boom denotes the up-and-down movement of the camera on the y-axis.

Figure 14-19 illustrates some images from an animation on the CD-ROM in which the camera moves closer to the subject (Chapter 14 > Movies > Truck In.mov). This truck-in action is a very common method for drawing near the point of focus. The field of view remains the same while the distance between the camera and subject narrows.

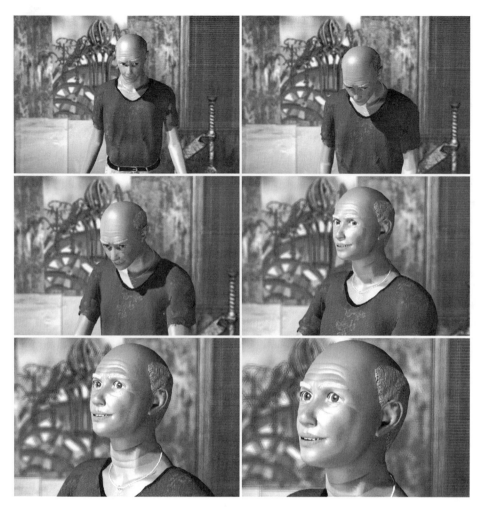

Fig. 14-19 A truck-in movement of the camera.

Zoom

Zooming the camera means changing the camera's focal length. The result is a shot in which the field of view expands or contracts. Figure 14-20 shows some scenes from an animation found on the CD-ROM (Chapter 14 > Movies > Zoom.mov). The character and background are identical to the previous animation that used a truck-in action. This time, the camera does not move; instead, the focal length of the lens becomes narrower. It changes from a 60mm standard lens to a 160mm long lens. The result is that the scene compresses to bring the subject closer to the viewer. When you compare the two animations, notice how the background expands with the zoom. This distortion is one of the reasons why movies do not use zooming as often as moving the camera. The shot tends to look somewhat flat. Because television shows are often filmed from fixed-camera positions, they utilize zooming. The choice of whether to use camera movements or zooming depends on the effect that you are after. If you want to emulate the fluid and coherent camera movements of films, move the camera. On the other hand, if your animation is done in the style of low-budget movies, documentaries, nature films, or TV shows, you might as

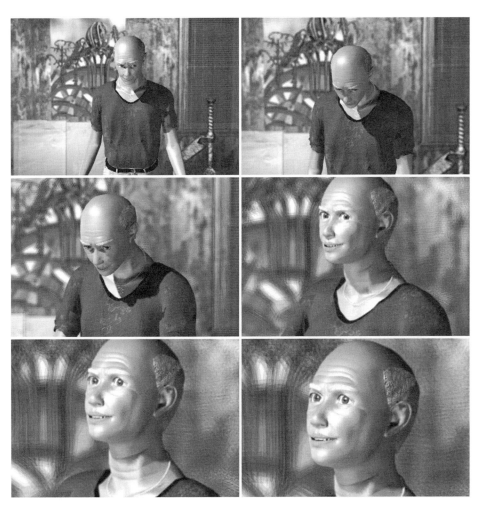

Fig. 14-20 A zoom-in lens change. Notice the difference in the background from the previous illustration. The field of view flattens out as the lens changes from a standard 60mm to a 160mm long lens.

well use zooming.

Pan, Tilt, and Roll

Pan, tilt, and roll are all methods for rotating the camera around a specific axis. Figure 14-21 illustrates the manner in which the camera revolves around the x-, y-, and z-axes. Panning is a commonly used method for scanning a scene from side to side or following an action. The camera rotates around the y-axis while remaining in one place. It can be compared to the direction that an airplane flies in—its heading. Pan is sometimes identified as yaw. The top, front, or camera views

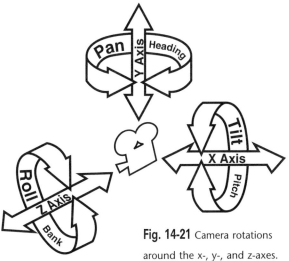

Fig. 14-21 Camera rotations around the x-, y-, and z-axes.

Fig. 14-22 Truck-in combined with zoom-out creates a disconcerting effect. The subject appears to remain the same distance from the camera, but the background seems to move away. When the lens becomes wider, a greater amount of the background appears.

are the windows used for this action.

Tilt means the camera is turned on the x-axis. Continuing with the analogy of an airplane, when it takes off or turns its nose down to land, the action is referred to as pitch. It can also be called a pivot. A common use of tilt is having the camera scan someone up and down. Tilting works best in the side or camera views.

Roll is the rotation of the camera around the z-axis. Using the airplane analogy, when its wings are tilted up and down, this action is called a bank. Rolls can be seen in fly-through animations. The front and camera views are the most commonly utilized windows for executing a roll.

Pan, tilt, and roll are more easily associated with the way people look at things. When they are watching something, they do not usually get up and follow it. More likely, their heads will turn, lean to the side, or tilt up and down. This is one reason for using camera rotations. Since they mimic our behavior, they feel normal to people. A common use of camera rotations occurs in movies or TV shows where the camera is used to introduce us to a cast of characters and the environment they live in. It may start by panning across a scene as it follows one person. When the person crosses paths

Fig. 14-23 Truck-out combined with zoom-in creates another disconcerting effect. The subject appears to remain the same distance from the camera, but the background seems to move forward. When the lens is made long, less background is visible.

with someone else, the camera shifts to follow this new character. When the person stops to kick a ball, the camera follows the ball to the youngster it belongs to. Of course, this can continue for a long time.

Truck-in Combined with Zoom-out or Truck-out Combined with Zoom-in

A combination of the truck and zoom can bring about some unsettling effects. The camera is moved closer to the subject in a truck-in, while the lens is made wide with a zoom-out. The result is that the subject appears to remain the same con-sistent distance from the camera, but the space around the person warps. Figure 14-22 illustrates some images from the truck-in/zoom-out animation found on the CD-ROM (Truck In Zoom Out.mov). Notice how the space enlarges due to the widening of the lens. Normally, making the lens wide would create greater distance between the camera and subject. To compensate for this, the camera is moved closer to the person.

Truck-out with zoom-in reverses the process. While the camera moves away from the subject, the lens is made narrow to keep the person at a constant distance from the camera. Figure 14-23

Fig. 14-24 The crane or boom shot moves the camera up or down. In these images from the animation, this type of shot is used to open the first scene and to reveal the main character.

shows some images from the CD-ROM animation (Truck Out Zoom In.mov). You can see that the background appears to move closer to the camera. Unlike the previous truck-in/zoom-out animation, the space compresses.

Truck combined with zoom is sometimes referred to as a rack focus or the Vertigo shot. Used correctly, it can convey a disorienting effect. It is commonly used to show a character's state of mind. Often, it is used to indicate changing circumstances. Since this is a very dramatic move, one has to be careful before deciding to use it. If there is no meaning behind this action, the audience will only be confused by it.

Crane or Boom

This shot derives its name from a camera attached to a moveable crane or pivoted boom. It is used when the camera needs to be moved up or down. Rarely is the camera moved only on the y-axis. The crane or boom is usually combined with a dolly or truck shot. Figure 14-24 shows some images from an animation on the CD-ROM using the crane or boom with a truck shot (Crane.mov). Its purpose is to reveal the scene and swoop down on the main character.

The crane or boom shot can be very useful at the beginning of an animation when you want to display an overview of the environment or the characters. It can also be used to communicate dis-

tance between your characters and the viewer. For example, a person who has lost his family and friends is seen as a lonely person in an alien environment. When the camera pulls up and away, the person appears as a small speck in his surroundings.

Hand-held Camera

Movies that show ordinary people engaged in real or mocked-up activities sometimes have a bold look to them. These are usually shot on a low budget with hand-held cameras. Often, they are not even controlled by a director.

In computer graphics, you can imitate the hand-held camera style by having it shake, tilt, and roll while following the action. Figure 14-25 displays some frames from an animation on the CD-ROM in which the camera acts as if it were hand-held (Hand Held Camera.mov). There is no effort to hide the presence of the camera. Mistakes are visible as when the camera loses track of the subject or is jolted. The idea is to make it look as if an amateur is running the camera and that the animation was not planned.

Transitions

Transitions are a way to blend or skip from one image to another. They can be simple or complex. Some can be performed during the action, while

Fig. 14-25 Images from the hand-held camera animation.

Fig. 14-26 Fade-to-black images from the animation.

others require video editing software. Transitions can be used to add variety to an animation, depict the passage of time, anticipate upcoming events, slow down a scene, and so on. They are mostly used to define time and space between shots. The most common transitions are the fade, dissolve, cut, and wipe.

Fade

A fade occurs when a shot disappears gradually. If the shot fades to a still frame of a solid color, it is referred to as a fade-out. A more common transition is the fade-to-black. Figure 14-26 shows a few clips from a short fade-to-black animation (Chapter 14 > Movies > #2 Fade Blk.mov). Instead of creating the fade in a post-processing program, it was performed directly during the animation.

Figure 14-27 illustrates a method for creating the fade-to-black. The camera is placed inside a black box. The box has a dissolve envelope, making it 100 percent transparent for the first thirty frames. Between frames 30 and 60, the dissolve envelope changes the opacity of the box until it is 100 percent opaque (0 percent dissolve). During the fade-to-black sequence, the dissolve envelope gradually enshrouds the camera with the black box. This method also works for fading to white (or any color) simply by making the box that color.

The process can also be reversed. The box can

start with a 0 percent dissolve, which changes over time to a 100 percent dissolve. This is called a fade-in transition. A still black, white, or color frame starts the sequence and gradually disappears to reveal the scene.

Dissolve

A dissolve or cross-dissolve is a transition effect where one shot blends into another. The first shot

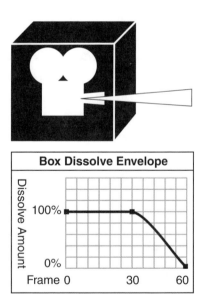

Fig. 14-27 A camera inside a black box can make a fade-to-black transition. A dissolve envelope on the box sets the interval for making the box opaque.

Fig. 14-28 Images from the cross-dissolve animation.

disappears, revealing 100 percent of the second shot. Figure 14-28 illustrates this type of transition. The animation can be found on the CD-ROM (#1CrossDisslove.mov). Midway into the dissolve, both images appear at 50 percent opacity.

Dissolves are an effective way of linking two separate scenes. They work very well when two subjects from different scenes are similar in some way. They can be alike in physical terms like shape or pose, or similar in mental or spiritual outlook. An example of psychological and physical similarities is having a person become a werewolf in one scene. The camera can then move in close to show the change in the person's eye. The cross-dissolve gradually turns the eye into an image of the full moon.

Other uses for dissolves are to give the audience time to ponder an event that occurred, to show a flashback, to depict a future event, or simply to

state what is in a character's mind. Dream sequences can be made up of a series of cross-dissolves layered on top of each other. Short dissolves are called soft cuts. Longer ones can be used to slow the pace of the action.

Cut

A cut is an immediate change from one shot to another. The transition occurs so rapidly that it is usually not noticed. Commercials and music videos use cuts extensively to set up a rapid pace and build up some excitement in the viewer's mind. The cut derives its name from movies in which two separate strips of film were cut and spliced together.

In computer animation, you can create a cut by moving the camera from one view to another over the course of only two frames. For example, the first shot can show the interior of a house until frame 60. At frame 61, the camera is moved outdoors to show the outside of the house. The one-frame interval occurs so quickly that the viewer does not perceive the motion of the camera. Another purpose for the cut is to simply start a new scene. When two separate sequences are put together in a final animation, it is seen as a cut.

Wipe

Wipes occur when a second shot slides over the first one and replaces it. The transition can take on a variety of configurations and can come from any direction. Some of the more common forms of wipes are the page turn and the page peel, where the corner of an image curls to unveil the next shot underneath. The curtain has one image draw back to display the second. The flip over has the first image turn over to reveal the second one underneath. The cube spin shows the first image spinning around to show the second one. The pinwheel has multiple wipes from the center of an image to uncover the second one underneath it. If you use a video editing program, you are probably already aware of the numerous wipe transitions available.

Conclusion

As you can see, the art of 3D animation is a complex but highly interesting field of study. You have to invest many years of hard work to bring modeling, surfacing, lighting, and animation skills to perfection. New technologies and discoveries by other artists continually challenge the most experienced animators. The adage, "Roads were made for traveling, not destinations," is applicable here. No matter how much you think you know, there is always something to make you take the next step.

Since this is a book about computer graphics, it might be of benefit to discuss the parallels between a computer and the mind. Some minds are more powerful than others. They may have more memory or be better equipped. A certain number of them are more flexible and find it easy to interface with others. No matter what aptitude the mind displays, it has the basic capability to grasp what the senses tell it, to comprehend the information, and then to act on it.

The diagram in Figure 14-29 illustrates the four faculties of the mind. The aesthetic part recognizes beauty, harmony, form, color, rhythm, and perspective. It is limited by its likes and dislikes. People who do not know this can mistake reality for what is actually their narrow state of awareness.

The sensory faculty of the mind absorbs impressions through smell, taste, hearing, and feeling. Its judgment is also colored by what it likes and dislikes. Thus, the two sensory parts of the mind can cloud your judgment. A person may think he or she is unique, but often, this is based on selective limitations.

Reasoning and intellect form another part of the mind. This is a higher level that receives information from the sensory abilities. It assesses the opinions of the first two mental faculties, makes its decisions, and passes its judgment on to the final evaluator, which is the ego.

The ego is the executor of the mind. Based on the opinions of other parts of the mind, it carries out the judgment of the reasoning and intellect faculty. The ego is the part of the mind that asserts itself. It differentiates itself from others and recognizes what is in its self-interest. Its chief concern is

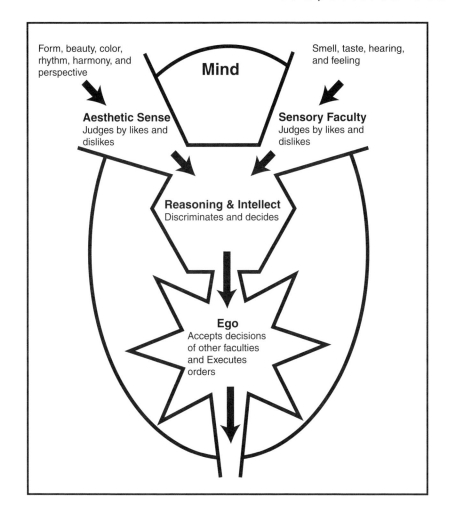

Form, beauty, color, rhythm, harmony, and perspective

Smell, taste, hearing, and feeling

Mind

Aesthetic Sense
Judges by likes and dislikes

Sensory Faculty
Judges by likes and dislikes

Reasoning & Intellect
Discriminates and decides

Ego
Accepts decisions of other faculties and Executes orders

Fig. 14-29 The four parts of the mind.

self-preservation. Conceit is the result of an overblown ego. A person with strong likes and dislikes can easily become self-righteous and inflexible.

Artists may find it more desirable to develop a sense of randomness. Rather than being incapable of adapting or changing to meet new circumstances, you might think of becoming more flexible. Creating with computers may be a boon, but it can also train us to work under fixed conditions. A possible future could be that the more we work with machines, the greater the chances that we

will become a part of them.

Even though computer animation is created mostly for commercial reasons, its roots are in the fine arts. There is no reason computer graphic artists, who now possess the most remarkable tools a creative person could ask for, cannot produce work as great as that made with traditional tools. Perhaps, with some, their first step is to become aware of the creative force within.

Glossary

Absolute value: A value or a change in the value of a property that is made with respect to the original value.

Alpha channel: The information that is embedded in an image that describes empty space around rendered pixels. It is used for compositing or transparency mapping.

Ambient light: The overall light that saturates an entire scene. Unlike radiosity rendering which calculates the effect of light bouncing off objects, ambient light only simulates this process.

Anti-aliasing: The process of smoothing edges of forms in a rendering by blending pixels with background colors and values. It removes the stair-casing effect that is often referred to as jaggies. Sometimes, textures can have the option of being rendered with anti-aliasing to prevent flickering and moiré patterns from occurring during an animation.

Area light: An array of lights that illuminate in all directions and whose size can usually be scaled.

Axis: The coordinate system of 3D space. *X*-axis means side to side or movement along the horizontal plane. *Y*-axis refers to top and bottom or vertical movement. *Z*-axis is front to back or in and out movement.

Back-facing polygons: Polygons whose normals face away from the viewer or camera.

Bevel: Extruding an object to produce an angled or shaped cut. It can produce the kind of shape found on the edge of ledges, computers, moldings, and so on.

Bezier curve: A curve that contains all its control points on the line itself.

B-spline: A spline that rarely goes through the points that created it. The curve tries to find a way between the points in a smooth manner.

Bitmap: An image that is composed of pixels.

Booleans: Refers to the joining or removing of one object from another.

Boom: The up and down movement of a camera on the y-axis. Its name originates from a moveable crane or pivoted boom that carries a camera.

Bounce lights: Colored lights that are placed next to objects in a scene to simulate radiosity.

Bump map: A procedural or bitmap image that is used to perturb the surface normals to create the illusion of bumps on a surface. The values of the image are treated like a height field.

Cardinal spline: A curve that passes through the points that created it.

Contact shadows: A technique for creating shadows through the use of negative and positive lights. Two lights of the same intensity values, except that one is positive and the other negative, are placed in the same space and directed at a subject. The result is that the object casts a shadow, but whose surface illumination remains the same.

Cubic mapping: A method of placing a texture map on an object so that the map is duplicated six times. Cubic mapping does not distort the bitmap but seams can often be seen on the object.

Cut: An immediate change from one shot to another.

Cylindrical mapping: A method of placing a texture by wrapping it into a cylindrical shape around the object.

Diffuse: The manner in which light is scattered across a surface. The surface appearance is governed by its shape and the location and angle of the light source(s).

Dissolve: A transition effect in which one shot blends into another.

Distant light: Sometimes referred to as directional light, this is light whose effects do not diminish over distance. This type of light is often used to simulate the phenomenon of sunlight.

Dolly: Camera movement along the x-axis. Its original name stems from a wheeled vehicle called a dolly, which carries a camera along a track.

Ease-in/Ease-out: The manner in which an animation is interpolated between keyframes. Ease-in gradually accelerates the animation from zero velocity. Ease-out gradually decelerates the animation to zero velocity.

Extrude: Creating a surface by extending it in space.

Fade: A transition in which a shot disappears gradually.

Fall off: The point at which a light's illumination degrades with distance.

Fillet/Blend: Builds a surface by forming a blend between two boundaries defined by a set of curves.

Frame: An individual image contained in an animation.

Front-facing polygons: Polygons whose surface normals face toward the viewer or camera.

Front projection image map: A method of projecting the image seen through the camera and applying it to a surface.

Gimbal lock: A situation in which an object no longer rotates correctly around one or more of its axes. With some software packages, gimbal lock can occur when the object is rotated past 90 degrees.

Interpolate: The calculation performed by the software to determine the values between two keyframes.

Isoparm: Flow lines or constant U or V parameter curves on a surface.

Keyframe: The specific property along a timeline that is set by the animator.

Layer: The manner in which objects are organized in certain programs so that they can be hidden or shown in specific groups. Layering can also refer to placing multiple textures on objects.

Lathe: A method for creating a surface by rotating a profile around an axis.

Linear light: Similar to a row of lights, these lights can usually be scaled in size.

Linear spline: A straight spline that passes through

all its connecting points.

Loft: Often referred to as skinning, this is a method of stretching a surface over a series of profiles composed of splines or polygons.

Luminosity: The brightness or value of a surface. The total amount of light emitted by the object's surface.

Model: An object that is created with 3D tools.

Negative light: A light with an intensity less than 0.

Normal: The direction that indicates which way a polygon is facing. It tells the viewer which is the front side and which is the back.

NURBS curves: The most complex and flexible of curve types. The points can be weighted unequally so that some portions of the curve can bend more than others—hence the name Non-Uniform, Rational B-Spline (NURBS).

Object: Any 2D or 3D surface that can be manipulated in 3D space.

Pan: Rotating the camera on the y-axis so that it scans a scene from side to side.

Penumbra: A fringe region of partial shadow around an umbra.

Pitch: Rotation around the *x*-axis.

Pivot point: Sometimes referred to as the center point or rotation point, this is the coordinate around which an object rotates. The pivot point can be moved, and its location determines how an object will be linked to another.

Pixel: One of the small dots or squares that constitutes a computer image.

Planar mapping: A method for texturing a surface by projecting an image on the object similarly to a slide projector.

Point light: Illuminating equally in every direction from a central source, this can be compared to an incandescent light bulb.

Polygon: A plane that is defined by points connected with straight edges.

Procedural textures: Sometimes referred to as shaders, they are image maps based on mathematical functions or short programs that create abstract patterns.

Radiosity: A renderer that calculates the amount of light that is transmitted from one surface to another. The renderer continues to follow the light until it is fully absorbed by all the surfaces or dissipates in space.

Ray tracing: A method of rendering that creates a ray for each pixel in a scene and traces each ray's path, one at a time, all the way back to the light source. The value for each ray is calculated as it travels through and bounces off various surfaces.

Reflection: The phenomenon of a propagating wave (light) being thrown back from a surface.

Refraction: The manner in which light is bent as it passes through a surface of varying density.

Render: Producing an image or series of images from a 3D scene.

Roll: Rotating the camera around the z-axis. Often used in fly-through animations, this technique sometimes involves the camera banking from side to side.

Roughness: The material attribute that determines the amount and quality of specular reflection from a surface.

Saturation: The degree of intensity in a color.

Scale: Making an object larger or smaller in any of the three *x*, *y*, and *z* directions.

Scene: The 3D world that can contain models, lights, cameras, and materials.

Shaders: Sometimes referred to as procedural textures, they are image maps based on mathematical functions or short programs that create abstract patterns.

Shadow maps: Shadows that are calculated by how far they are from the light(s) that are casting them. The renderer uses this information and the position of the light source to determine which items produce shadows. Shadow maps are sometimes called depth-map shadows.

Skin: Often referred to as lofting, this is a method of stretching a surface over a series of profiles composed of splines or polygons.

Specular: The manner in which light is reflected off a surface. The angle and location of a light(s) creates highlights on the surface.

Spherical mapping: A technique for wrapping a texture around an object and pinching it closed at the two ends.

Spline: A curve that is defined by points or vertices.

Spotlight: A light whose beam is emitted as a cone of light in varying degrees.

Sweep: A modeling procedure that creates surfaces by pulling a profile along a specified path.

Tangent line: A line that passes through the control vertices of a spline but does not touch the curve itself. A tangent line is used to adjust the angle of the curve.

Tessellations: A series of joined polygons forming a tiling pattern. Semi-regular tessellations are tiling patterns composed of a combination of regular and semi-regular polygons.

Texture map: An image that is applied to a surface. The size aspect ratio of the image is matched to the object's surface coordinates by various methods such as planar, cylindrical, spherical, cubic, front projection, or UV mapping.

Tilt: Turning the camera on the x-axis so that scans the subject up and down. Its action is sometimes referred to as pitch.

Timeline: The time continuum of an animation, as calculated by frames-per-second values.

Translucent: Almost transparent; allowing light to pass through diffusely so that objects cannot be seen clearly on the other side of it. Frosted glass has translucent surfaces.

Truck: The movement of a camera along the z-axis. Truck-in moves the camera closer to the subject, while truck-out moves it away.

Trim curves: A curve drawn on an object's surface after a profile has been projected onto it or another object has intersected it. Trim curves allow one to trim away parts of a surface.

Umbra: A region of complete shadow resulting from total obstruction of light.

UV coordinate mapping: A precise method for mapping textures on curved surfaces. Unlike other mapping features, which treat all objects as if they were simple shapes, UV coordinate mapping allows one to match a texture to the structure of the geometry.

Vertex: A point along a spline, mesh, or polygon defined by x, y, and z coordinates. A series of points are called vertices. Control vertices are found on tangent lines.

Wipe: When a second shot slides over the first one to replace it.

Yaw: Rotation around the y-axis. This type of motion can also be defined as heading or pan.

Z-buffer: Depth information that is stored in a buffer and made available during the rendering process. The distance of each pixel from the camera plane (z-distance) is calculated in the order of proximity to the camera. Pixels closest to the camera are rendered last.

Zoom: Changing the focal length of a camera so that the subject appears closer or further away.

Schedules

Fall or Spring Semester

Animation 1 Calendar 2.5-hour class

1   Introduction to class. Buy *Mastering 3D Animation, Second Edition* book.

2   Homework: read pp. 4–6 in book. Model a bookshelf; due next week (chap. 8, Fig. 8-29). In class, model a simple object such as a lamp (chap. 8, Fig. 8-33).

3   <u>Lamp model due.</u> Homework: continue modeling the bookshelf. In class, model a TV stand (chap. 8, Fig. 8-16).

4   <u>Bookshelf model due.</u> Homework: pick a project from chap. 8 to model; due next week. In class, model a cartoon character; refer to chaps. 1 or 2.

5   Homework: continue modeling from chap. 8. In class, continue cartoon. Take photos for self-portrait.

6   <u>Model from chap. 8 due.</u> Label portrait photos. Continue cartoon character. Homework: pick another object to model from chap. 8; due next week.

7   Homework: continue chap. 8 model; due next class. In class, finish cartoon character and hand it in.

8   <u>Model from chap. 8 due.</u> Homework: model a room with windows; see chap. 8. In class, begin modeling a human head (chap. 1 or 6).

9   In class continue human head model. Homework: continue room; due next class.

10   <u>Room model due.</u> In class and for homework, continue modeling the head.

11   In class, finish the head. Homework: refine the head to hand in next class.

12   <u>Finished head due.</u> Use body templates to begin modeling the torso (see chaps. 2 or 6).

13   Finish torso. Homework model teeth, gums, tongue, and eyeballs (chap. 7; due in two weeks).

14   <u>Self-portrait model with torso due.</u> Complete arm but not the hand. Homework: continue work on refining the arm and torso.

15   In class, work on hand. Homework: continue the hand and teeth, gums, tongue, and eyeballs.

16   In class, finish hand. Turn in the figure with the head, torso, arms, and hands. Homework: refine the figure. Start legs.

17   Work on legs. Homework: teeth, gums, tongue, and eyeballs; due next class.

18   <u>Eyeballs, teeth, gums, & tongue due.</u> In class, continue the legs and shoes. Homework: complete the legs.

19   Work on shoes. In class, make and finish skeleton (see chap. 3). Homework: finish shoes.

20   <u>Shoes due.</u> In class, make weight maps (see chap. 3). Homework: finish weight maps.

21   Set up IK-rig character. Homework: complete rigging.

22   <u>Entire human model with skeleton and weight maps due.</u> Test IK setup. Start animating; use Pose-to-Pose handouts from chap. 4 folder of Muybridge on CD-ROM.

23   In class, work on animation. Animation movie due in two weeks. Learn about Squash and Stretch (chap.12, Fig. 12-7).

24   Start UV mapping of face (see chap. 7, Fig. 7-23–7-27). Homework: continue Pose-to-Pose animation.

25   Continue UV face. Homework: continue Pose-to-Pose animation; due next class.

26   <u>Animation due.</u> Complete UV face; hand in model. Check rough movie preview of animations. Homework: render final animation with textured character; due next class.

27   <u>Final animation due.</u> Start second animation; choice of Pose-to-Pose handouts. Animation movie due last day of class.

28   Continue final animation; due next class.

29   **Last day of class. Final model & animation movie due.**

Fall or Spring Semester

Animation 2 Calendar 2.5–hour class

1 Introduction to class. Hand out syllabus. Assignment: Purchase textbook, *Mastering 3D Animation, 2nd Edition.*

2 Make hair guides or helmet hair for the human model; finished hair due next week. See chap. 7, Fig. 7-18–7-50.

3 In class, continue hair guides; due next class. Learn about animating in stages (chap. 4, Fig. 4-10–4-14).

4 Hair guides due. In class, work on naming surfaces and parts for hair and soft body dynamics. Homework: Pick Pose-to-Pose copy from Muybridge photos (chap. 4 CD-ROM) and start Follow-Through animation (chap. 13, Fig. 13-1).

5 In class, learn about pixel shader hair and soft body dynamics. Apply these to the Follow Through animation. Homework: Follow Through animation due next class.

6 Follow through animation due. In class, begin modeling 44 morph facial expressions; see chap. 11. Due in three weeks.

7 Continue modeling facial morphs. In class, learn about the graph editor (chap. 4, Fig. 4-15–4-35).

8 Continue modeling facial morphs. In class, learn more about the graph editor.

9 Continue modeling facial morphs. In class, learn more about the graph editor.

10 Continue modeling facial morphs. In class, learn about lighting and surfacing; see chaps. 9 and 10 of book.

11 Continue modeling facial morphs. In class, learn more about lighting and surfacing. Forty-four facial morphs due next class.

12 All 44 facial morphs due today. Learn how to do a dialogue animation; hand out movies for rotoscoping. See chap. 12, Fig. 12-23.

13 Continue dialogue animation; due next week. Study camera techniques (chap. 14).

14 Continue dialogue animation; due next class. Continue study of camera techniques.

15 Dialogue animation due. Put dialogue animation and sound file together in a movie editing program. Begin work on walk cycle. See chap. 12, Fig. 12-5–12-20.

16 Continue walk cycle animation; 32 frames due next time.

17 Thirty-two-frame walk cycle due today. Repeating final walk cycle due next class.

18 Final repeating walk cycle due. Begin running animation. See chap. 12, Fig. 12-24–12-31. Due in 1 1/2 weeks.

19 Continue running animation.

20 Continue running animation; due next class.

21 Running animation due. Record video for rotoscoping. You can work in pairs or by yourself. Animate from video. Due in two weeks.

22 Continue rotoscope animation. See chap. 12, Fig. 12-34.

23 Continue rotoscope animation.

24 Continue rotoscope animation. Due next class.

25 Rotoscope animation due. Begin work on Straight-Ahead animation. See chap. 12, Fig. 12-32–12-33. Final animation due last day of class.

26 Continue Straight-Ahead animation.

27 Continue Straight-Ahead animation.

28 Continue Straight-Ahead animation; due next class.

29 **Last day of class. Straight-Ahead animation due.**

Fall or Spring Semester

Animation 3 Calendar 2.5–hour class

1   Introduction to class. Hand out syllabus. Assignment: Purchase textbook, *Mastering 3D Animation, 2nd Edition.*

2   Study and work on **Anticipation** animation, chap. 12, Fig. 12-21. Due in 1 1/2 weeks.

3   Continue the Anticipation animation.

4   Continue the anticipation Anticipation animation; due next class.

5   <u>Anticipation animation due.</u> Create a **Staging** animation with dialogue (chap. 12, Fig. 12-22). Due in 1 1/2 weeks.

6   Continue Staging animation.

7   Continue Staging animation; due next class.

8   <u>Staging animation due.</u> Study **Slow In** and **Slow Out** (chap. 13, Fig. 13-2–13-3). Create an animation illustrating this principle. Due in 1 1/2 weeks.

9   Continue Slow In and Slow Out animation.

10   Continue Slow In and Slow Out animation; due next class.

11   <u>Slow In and Slow Out animation due.</u> Study **Arcs** and **Secondary Actions** (chap. 13, Fig. 13-4–13-6). Assignment: create an animation illustrating these. Due in 1 1/2 weeks.

12   Continue Arcs and Secondary Actions animation.

13   Continue Arcs and Secondary Actions animation; due next class.

14   <u>Arcs and Secondary Actions animation due.</u> Study the principle of **Timing** (chap. 13, Fig. 13-7 & 13-8). Create three versions of the same animation showing how timing changes the meaning. The speeds should be slow, medium, and fast. Due in two weeks.

15   Continue the three Timing animations.

16   Continue the three Timing animations.

17   Continue the three Timing animations; due next class.

18   Continue the Exaggeration animation; due next class.

19   <u>Exaggeration animation due.</u> Study Solid Drawing and Appeal (chap.13, Fig. 13-11 & 13-

12). Appeal due in 1 1/2 weeks.

20   Continue the Appeal animation.

21   Continue the Appeal animation; due next class.

22   <u>Appeal animation due.</u> Learn about **Equilibrium** (chap. 13, Fig. 13-13). Create an animation showing a figure going from equilibrium to disequilibrium. Due in 1 1/2 weeks.

23   Continue Equilibrium/Disequilibrium animation.

24   Continue Equilibrium/Disequilibrium animation; due next class.

25   <u>Equilibrium/Disequilibrium animation due.</u> Begin animation showing **Rhythm.** See chap. 13, Fig. 13-16. Due last day of class.

26   Continue Rhythm animation.

27   Continue Rhythm animation.

28   Continue Rhythm animation; due next class.

29   **Last day of class. Rhythm animation due.**

Fall or Spring Semester

Special FX Calendar 2.5–hour class

1   Introduction to class. Buy the textbook, *Mastering 3D Animation, 2nd Edition.*

2   Create an explosion; see chap. 5, Fig. 5-1–5-3. Explosion animation due next week.

3   Continue explosion; due next class.

4   <u>Explosion due.</u> Start particle effects. Show them bouncing off an object(s). See chap. 5, Fig. 5-5–5-16. Explosion with particles due next week.

5   Continue work on particle explosion; due next class.

6   <u>Particle explosion due.</u> Begin work on fragment explosion, smoke, fire, fragments, particles, and lens flare explosion. See chap. 5, Fig. 5-28–5-32. Due next week.

7   Continue fragment, smoke, fire, particles, and lens flare explosion animation; due next class.

8   <u>Smoke, fire, fragments, particles, and lens flare explosion due.</u> Start water drop animation. See chap. 5, Fig. 5-33–5-35. Due next week.

9   Continue water drop animation; due next class.

10   <u>Water drop animation due.</u> Create running water with particles and voxels. See chap. 5, Fig. 5-36–5-37. Due next week.

11   Continue running water animation; due next class.

12   <u>Running water animation due.</u> Begin work on sludge animation. See chap. 5, Fig. 5-38–5-39. Due next week.

13   Continue sludge animation; due next class.

14   <u>Sludge animation due.</u> Steam animation. See chap. 5, Fig. 5-40–5-44. Due next week.

15   Continue steam animation; due next class.

16   <u>Steam animation due.</u> Begin work on sprite, volumetric or hyper voxel fire. See Chap. 5, Fig. 5-5 and 5-45–5-49. Due in two weeks.

17   Continue work on Fire.

18   Continue work on Fire.

19   Continue work on Fire; due next class.

20   <u>Fire due.</u> Start work on Electrical Effects. See chap. 5, Fig. 5-50–5-54. Due next week.

21   Continue electrical effects animation. Due next class.

22   <u>Electrical effects animation due.</u> Begin displacement mapping to make a body of water (chap. 5, Fig 5-55–5-56)

23   Continue body of water animation; due next class.

24   <u>Displacement water animation due</u> today. Start pinhead displacement animation. See chap. 10, Fig. 10-27–10-34. Due next week.

25   Continue pinhead displacement animation; due next class.

26   <u>Pinhead displacement map animation due.</u> Begin work on transparency and clip mapping. See chap. 10, Fig. 10-16–10-25. Landscape with trees due next week.

27   Continue transparency and clip mapping animation.

28   Continue transparency and clip mapping animation; due next class.

29   **Last day of class. Transparency and clip mapping animation due.**

Biography

Peter Ratner is the founder and head of the computer animation program at James Madison University. As a professor of 3D animation, he has taught thousands of students. Many of them have attained successful careers in the video game, movie, television, multimedia, and Web design industries. His paintings, animations, and computer graphics have been displayed in numerous national and international juried exhibitions. *Mastering 3-D Animation, 2nd Edition* is his fourth book about 3D modeling and animation. He is also the author of the first and second editions of *3-D Human Modeling and Animation*.

International Gallery of Images

Jamie Lee by Sven Moll, Spain

Aida by Steven Stahlberg, Malaysia

Couple by Kei Nakamura, Japan

Klaus by Loic Zimmermann, France

Mech by Syunichi Shirai, Japan

Woman by Allessandro Vannini, Italy

Ilana by Alceau Baptistao, Brazil

Index

Books from Allworth Press

Allworth Press is an imprint of Allworth Communications, Inc. Selected titles are listed below.

Animation: The Whole Story, Revised Edition
by Howard Beckerman (paperback, 6 7/8 x 9 ¾, 336 pages, $24.95)

Makin' Toons: Inside the Most Popular Animated TV Shows and Movies
by Allan Neuwirth (paperback, 6 x 9, 288 pages, $21.95)

The Education of an Illustrator
edited by Steven Heller and Marshall Arisman (paperback, 6 3/4 x 9 7/8, 288 pages, $19.95)

Business and Legal Forms for Illustrators, Third Edition
by Tad Crawford (8 1/2 x 11, 160 pages, includes CD-ROM, $29.95)

Legal Guide for the Visual Artist, Fourth Edition
by Tad Crawford (paperback, 8 1/2 x 11, 272 pages, $19.95)

The Fine Artist's Guide to Marketing and Self-Promotion, Revised Edition
by Julius Vitali (paperback, 6 x 9, 256 pages, $19.95) .

Licensing Art and Design, Revised Edition
by Caryn R. Leland (paperback, 6 x 9, 128 pages, $16.95)

The Business of Being an Artist, Third Edition
by Daniel Grant (paperback, 6 x 9, 352 pages, $19.95)

How to Grow as an Artist
by Daniel Grant (paperback, 6 x 9, 240 pages, $19.95)

The Fine Artist's Career Guide, Second Edition
by Daniel Grant (paperback, 6 x 9, 320 pages, $19.95)

Business and Legal Forms for Artists, Revised Edition
by Tad Crawford (paperback, 8 ½ x 11, 160 pages, includes CD-ROM, $19.95)

The Artist's Complete Health and Safety Guide, Third Edition
by Monona Rossol (paperback, 6 x 9, 416 pages, $24.95)

Business and Legal Forms for Graphic Designers, Third Edition
by Tad Crawford and Eva Doman Bruck (paperback, 8 1/2 x 11, 160 pages, includes CD-ROM, $29.95)

Please write to request our free catalog. To order by credit card, call 1-800-491-2808 or send a check or money order to Allworth Press, 10 East 23rd Street, Suite 510, New York, NY 10010. Include $5 for shipping and handling for the first book ordered and $1 for each additional book. Ten dollars plus $1 for each additional book if ordering from Canada. New York State residents must add sales tax.

To see our complete catalog on the World Wide Web, or to order online, you can find us at *www.allworth.com.*